B
WAG

D0287025

10/14

Sitting on
Top of the World

Steven L. Richards

Copyright © 2014 Steven L. Richards
All rights reserved.

ISBN: 1494925419
ISBN-13: 9781494925413
Library of Congress Control Number: 2014900441
CreateSpace Independent Publishing Platform
North Charleston, South Carolina

Sitting on Top of the World is dedicated to brothers,
Kurt and Heinz

ACKNOWLEDGMENTS

Throughout the researching for Sitting on Top of the World, Kurt Wagner and I discussed how his story might be written. Would the book be better suited as a biography or a novel? Should I become the narrator who explains the discovered truths of Kurt's life? We quickly dismissed these options. We wanted the reader to feel the emotions of the real people portrayed in Sitting on Top of the World.

When the research was completed there remained only a few unanswered questions. Deaths, failed memories, and the loss of important historical documents and personal papers made this an unfortunate reality. But it gnawed at me. What were the exact words that were said by the people in Sitting on Top of the World? How or why did a certain event happen? Again we asked, how do we tell a true story in a way that would allow the reader to hear words spoken decades ago by Kurt's grandfather or listen to the private thoughts of his mother?

The writing style of Sitting on Top of the World is narrative nonfiction. The book reads like a novel, but the underlying story is true. It has been described as a marriage of the arts of storytelling and journalism. In order to validate the dialogue and events in Sitting on Top of the World, I examined both the oral and written history available to me in the United States, France and Germany.

The completion of this book and therefore, the marriage of storytelling and journalism resulted in part from the following:

The interviews of Kurt Wagner, Hugo Schiller, Renee Krauss, Frederick Raymes (Manfred Mayer), Richard Weilheimer, Edith Mann Cohen, Jolene Kastel Shapiro, Studs Terkel, Rolf Weil, Gerhardt Schmalz, Lynne Galvin, Irene Walker, Ben Walker, Mariann Walker, Jenny Walker, Karen Hardaway, Harold Lukatsky, Marilyn Wagner, Stuart Wagner, Irvin Wagner, and Andre Laufer; the review of original documents from the Chicago Board of Education, Francis Parker School, the Jewish Children's Bureau of Chicago, Jewish European Children's Aid, Judge Kasper Jarecki, the former Nazi government of Germany and Anshe Emet Synagogue; letters from and to Alice Resch Synnestvedt & Kurt Wagner, from and to I.J. Wagner, Belle Wagner and Kurt Wagner, from and to Ilse Walker and Kurt Wagner and from and to Julius Walker to Heinz Walker; photographs from the Walker family, scores of video tapes from the Shoa Foundation, audiotaped interview of Hannah Moses from 1993, mini-biography written by Belle Wagner, biography written by Rolf Weil, ship manifest for the Nyassa, Kurt Wagner's adoption file, visits to the cities of Gurs, Aspet and Drancy in France and Karlsruhe, Germany, the resources of the Illinois Holocaust Museum, Yad Vashem, Jewish Museum Berlin, National World War I Museum, Stadtmuseum Baden-Baden, United States Holocaust Museum, University at Buffalo, The Association of Camp de Gurs and innumerable books, newspaper articles and documentaries.

When the research for Sitting on Top of the World began, I had no idea whether my expected personal journey of a few months would result in anything other than the accumulation of some records. Almost seven years later, I have reflected on the selfless sacrifices my wife and three children have made in allowing me to undertake something that literally took over all of our lives. A simple thank you seems so in adequate. Nevertheless, to Mary, Jacob, Matthew and Sarah, I give you my love and my thanks.

FOREWORD

As an author, I'm often approached by people who tell me they are going to write a book. I don't think it is an exaggeration to say that I have heard it hundreds of times. I met Steve Richards in 2007 because of the interest he had in my book, Playing with the Enemy. We immediately had a connection and eventually he told me of a story he wanted to tell. Of all the people who claimed they will write a book, I only know of one who delivered. I feel very privileged to know Steve Richards and to write his Foreword.

Any attempt I make to summarize this remarkable story would fall short, so I'll leave the telling to Steve. I experienced his pain and anxiety, as well as his enthusiasm, as he undertook this journey of love and passion. Steve is a good man. He has taken on this massive task because of his friendship and respect for the man he lovingly calls "Mr. Wagner." Even though this is an important story, I believe Steve took on this project, worked thousands of hours and travelled across the ocean for no other reason than his sincere desire to honor his friend by capturing, telling and preserving his story. With compassion and bare brutality, this story leaps off the pages in a way that captivates the reader. It is a story that both warms the heart and brutalizes the mind. I had to keep reminding myself that this is not a cleverly devised work of fiction inspired by true life events, but a deeply moving story of the lives of real people. Sitting on Top of the World really happened.

Congratulations Steve for a job well-done. I know you well enough to imagine you rolling your eyes when you read this, but I think you have performed a wonderful act and given the world a beautiful gift.

Gary W. Moore
www.garywmoore.com

INTRODUCTION

The story took only a minute or two to tell. He was born Kurt Rudolf Walker in Karlsruhe, Germany, on May 17, 1931, to a Jewish mother, Ilse Ettlinger, and a Protestant father, Julius Walker. His parents separated before his birth and eventually divorced in 1934. Kurt's older brother, Heinz, would live with his father's parents and be raised as a Christian, and Kurt would live with his mother's parents and be raised as a Jew. Years later, in October 1940, Kurt and his mother's family were given thirty minutes' notice before they were taken to the town's train station. At that same moment, thousands of Jews from surrounding towns were also removed from their homes and, like Kurt, were taken to a concentration camp in the small town of Gurs in southwest France where they were ravaged by disease and malnutrition. Relief organizations did their best to come to their aid, but for so many, especially the elderly, it was too late. For a few such as Kurt, a brief window of opportunity was realized at the end of February 1941, when his mother made the tortured decision to say yes, so that Kurt could leave Gurs.

Over the next eighteen months, Kurt lived in a former tuberculosis sanitarium in the Pyrenees Mountains, until he was taken to a shack on the outskirts of Marseille, France. After days of uncertainty, he boarded the first of two ships that took him to Casablanca, Bermuda, and finally, on July 30, 1942, Baltimore, Maryland. In the early years that followed he "moved on" with his new life in Chicago, and when innocent inquiries were made of him, he would refuse to talk about Ilse and Julius. There would also be no mention of his brother, Heinz, and the unspoken truth that both bound and burdened them: their father was a Nazi Brownshirt. Decades later when Kurt was again asked about his past, an adult Kurt Wagner would say unflinchingly about his life's journey, "I have nothing to be guilty about. I did nothing wrong."

After I first heard these few facts, there was nothing to suggest that I would or even could write a book about my friend's father's experiences in Nazi Germany. Nonetheless, I found myself repeating Kurt's story to friends and family. There were always the same moving questions: How could a mother give up her children? What was Kurt's brother told? Did Heinz and Kurt ever learn the truth about what really happened to each other? Was the family ever united? But most importantly, they all asked, why did this happen? Of course there must have been answers to those questions and the many others that were asked, but they were unknown to me.

It would take four years of growing curiosity before Kurt and I finally met on August 13, 2007. We did not know each other, but there I sat in the kitchen of his modest suburban Chicago home attempting to question him about the missing pieces to the middle of the story. To my dismay, it became readily apparent that Kurt did not appear to know many things about his early life. The few additional things I did learn in that guarded meeting caused me to wonder how I would have fared if I had lived those early years of Kurt's life. Could I have been so strong, so resilient? Could I have met the challenges of the choices made by his mother, his father, and his country? The answer was clearly no. By the end of the meeting, it was also obvious that the selfish curiosity that had been the impetus to find the lost middle of the story was replaced with a respect for the man who had been the boy that had lived this improbable story.

Over the months that passed in which we talked and the research progressed, I gained his confidence and he gave me a great gift: he confided in me the recollections of his early life that had remained dormant for many decades. However, it was not until my visits to the small towns of Drancy, Aspet, and Gurs, France, and a final **poignant** and unsettling meeting on August 21, 2008, when I sat in the kitchen of a modest home in Karlsruhe, Germany, that the final questions were tearfully answered. And it is with the gift of those answers, eighty-three years after the birth of a little boy named Heinz Christian Walker, and eighty-two years after the birth of a little boy named Kurt Rudolf Walker, that the beginning, end, and elusive middle of their story can be told.

"...I must confess that few letters from survivors have disturbed me as much as this one..."

December 17, 1946, letter from Lotte Marcuse of the German Jewish Children's Aid to Mary Lawrence of the Jewish Children's Bureau. The referenced letter written by Heinz Walker to Kurt Walker was intentionally withheld from Kurt. He did not see it until 2008.

PART I
GERMANY

I'M HOME

When Isack Ettlinger sat on the unforgiving wooden bench of the train, he was thankful that he was finally on his way home. He tugged on his long, thick brown beard as the seemingly endless line of soldiers collapsed around him. Isack and the few other obvious Jews rocked back and forth in silent prayer before the violent movement of the forty-car train brought cheers from all. Shortly, the raucous shouts gave way to a restless sleep that left Isack staring out a fogged window that blurred the eerie visions of a German countryside scarred by British 18 and 60 pounders, French 75 mm cannons, and centuries-old buildings disfigured by war.

When Isack awoke on the last Friday of November 1918, he hurried past the other newly retired soldiers until he reached the Bahnhofplatz in front of the pristine five-year-old train station. When the massive clock on the gray façade of the art nouveau building struck 11:00 a.m., Isack's shaking hand pulled out his watch and corrected the time. Moments later, after accepting a ride on a horse-drawn wagon carrying the local Moninger beer, he stood in the undamaged Marktplatz. Isack touched the out-of-place pyramid and watched the golden boy weather vane move with each gentle gust of wind. "Yes," he thought, "everything will be fine."

During his unsure walk home, a pragmatic Isack became consumed with both the reality of a family he no longer knew and employment. He had been a salesman before the war and was confident that in these bad economic times, one of the many Jewish businesses of Karlsruhe, Germany, would hire a Jewish veteran, even a forty-four-year-old one. And for his broken family, he prayed for better times.

ISACK ETTLINGER, OPA AND VATER

In any year in history there will always be certain events that define those 365 days. In 1906, Americans witnessed San Francisco's destruction by an earthquake. Italy and Switzerland were connected through the Alps by the Simplon, the longest railroad tunnel in the world. Finland became the first European nation to give women the vote. In that same year in Rastatt, Germany, Ilse Ettlinger, the second child of Isack Ettlinger, was born. Her birth neither defined the year 1906 nor did it become synonymous with some momentous accomplishment. She was objectively no more important to her family than any other child born into any other family. Ilse was simply a loved daughter and sister, and eventually, like many other little girls, she became a wife and mother. However, for Heinz Walker and Kurt Walker, the two sons she would have years later, Ilse's life would resonate with them in a way that she could have never expected.

Each night in Rastatt an important ritual for Isack Ettlinger began with a simple question to his infant first child and only son, Julius, "Do you want to hear a story?" Four years later when Ilse was born, the nightly stories had been honed to perfection. Using drawings, photographs, documents, and Isack's memories of what had been passed down from prior generations, the stories became an oral history for Julius and then Ilse of what it meant to be an Ettlinger, a German, and a Jew. For Isack, those evenings became a cherished time spent with his

4

children sitting on his lap as they pleaded, "Please, Vater, tell me the story of..."

On Julius's seventh birthday he abruptly announced to his father that he was too old for the stories. The bittersweet moment for Isack quickly dissolved into laughter when Ilse shouted enthusiastically, "Vater, now only I sit on your lap!" On later occasions when Julius tried to reclaim his position on his father's knee, he was met with the screams and fists of his little sister. A wide-eyed Isack was left watching his defeated son trudge away as Ilse yelled, "Go to bed, Julius!"

As the years went by and the nightly rituals between father and daughter were refined, a script of sorts found Isack asking, "Ilse, have you ever seen my library?"

Ilse's "no" belied her Cheshire grin while she took her father's hand and glided to the huge rolltop desk. "This library may look like a desk, but I can assure you that it is not just a desk," whispered Isack. "Each drawer holds the most important documents and papers in the world."

Then, on cue, Ilse looked at her father, who nodded yes. Ilse swept her hands over the library. "What kind of papers does it have, Vater? Treasure maps?"

"No treasure maps. But there are records that trace the Ettlingers back to 1714 in Ettlingen. I also have some other documents—very important documents." Ilse pretended that she was disappointed with Isack's answer until her smiling father corrected himself. "Well, I think there must be at least one treasure map buried under all of my papers." Ilse's face became one huge smile given the exciting news and the mutual promise that no one could know this other than Isack and Ilse.

"Ilse, do you like fairy tales?" asked Isack. But Isack never let his daughter answer. He pulled back the creaking roll top of the desk to expose the numerous cubbyholes and stacks of books. Ilse reacted as she had done in the past and ran to the deep-blue cushioned chair embroidered with flowers. With the final act almost completed, a humming Isack pulled himself away from the library. "Ah yes. Which one will it be tonight, Ilse?"

Ilse bit her lower lip and frantically turned the crisp white pages past Tom Thumb, Red Riding Hood, and Rumpelstiltskin until the Grimm's fairy tale of Hansel and Gretel left her squealing, "This one! Please, Vater!"

Isack pulled his daughter close to him. "Close to a large forest there lived a woodcutter with his wife and two children. The boy was called Hansel and the girl was called…"

Each night when a Grimm's fairy tale began, Ilse pulled on Isack's full beard and drew his mouth close to her ear so that the gift of the story was hers alone. Then, just before sleep overtook her, she begged her father to tell her about himself, a relative, or his birthplace of Eppingen. The loving father pulled Ilse even closer. "The small town of Eppingen…"

Located in southwest Germany, the small town of Eppingen gained notoriety for its beautiful cuckoo clocks and for being the inspirational setting for many of the fairy tale books written by the brothers Grimm. For the nine Jewish families living in Eppingen in 1714, this small village became a place where they could live a life centered on family and faith. Many decades later, when Isack spoke with reverence about those "Good Jews," Isack praised their respect for Halacha, or Jewish law.

Each night he reminded his young daughter that without the observance of shechitah, the ritualistic slaughter of meat, the following of kashrut, dietary laws, the mikveh, or ritual bath and circumcision, the most fundamental Jewish rite, there could be no Jews.

Isack also told Ilse the truth that the same laws that unified the community of Jews also generated mistrust between the Jews and their Christian neighbors. He explained how over centuries the German Jews attempted to reach a compromise in which their religious beliefs merged with German folk practices to forge a more acceptable union between faith and land.

"Ilse, this is why your Opa ate cabbage stuffed with rice on the seventh day of Sukkot and white bean soup on the night before Passover." He closed his eyes. "I can still remember how during Yom Kippur all the men gave each other forty lashes with a pair of suspenders in order to atone for their sins." When his eyes opened, he told Ilse that when a couple married, a special wedding jester sang songs, advised the bride and groom about their responsibilities to each other, announced the wedding gifts, and put on theatrical performances.

Ilse ached for more, but she came to accept that somehow the stories about the Ettlingers ended when her twenty-seven-year-old father married her twenty-two-year-old mother, Sophie Weil, on September 26, 1901. She also came to accept that she would never learn the answer to why the new husband and wife, unlike the other Ettlingers, eventually left Eppingen and moved to the big city of Karlsruhe. Whatever Ilse did learn, she loved, and over time, she became a storyteller and historian who could best her father and correct his infrequent errors.

"No, no, Vater. This is how it goes," said Ilse. "On April 1, 1793, Isaak Loeb Ettlinger, my great-grandfather, was born into one of the sixteen Jewish families of Eppingen, Germany."

This same small town became the place of Isaak Loeb Ettlinger's marriage to eighteen-year-old Karolina Heinsheimer on February 23, 1825. One of ten children, Karolina gave birth to two children before her tragic death four and a half years later on August 20, 1829. Ten months after Karolina's death, thirty-seven-year-old Isaak Loeb Ettlinger married Karolina's eighteen-year-old sister, Sara. "Now if God takes me," Isaak said, "I know that my children will have a mother."

On the day of their marriage, Isaak and Sara stood under a draped prayer shawl waiting for the approaching jester, who rode backward on a chestnut horse. After the jester dismounted, he took his place next to the rabbi, who presented a communal wedding ring in the shape of an elaborate house, which was later replaced with a simple ring. The silent guests encircled the rabbi as he completed the prayers, and the couple sipped wine from a cup that was crashed against a wall. When the shattered pieces of glass fell to the ground, the crowd cheered for the new Jewish couple who would be blessed with twelve children over the next twenty-four years. Three and a half years later, Jakob Ettlinger, Ilse's grandfather, was born. The next day, Mayor Friedrich Hochstetter dutifully recorded the name of the newest addition to the town of 2,500 people.

On May 7, 1863, Ilse's grandfather and twenty-six-year-old Sophia Weinheimer married. Their firstborn and only daughter, Johanna, was followed by Ludwig, Max, and Julius. On October 30, 1874, the last child of Jakob and Sophia, Isack Ettlinger, the future father of Ilse and grandfather of Kurt and Heinz Walker, was born.

Eight days after Isack's birth and in conformance with the Jewish ritual of circumcision, the mohel welcomed Isack into the covenant between the children of Israel and God. The night before, a group of men gathered at Sophia's bedside to pray and study the Torah, the Jewish Bible, in order to ward off the evil spirits, especially the demon Lilith. The next morning, after the mohel completed the incision and bandaged the wound, Isack sucked on a piece of cloth that had been dipped in wine. Isack's sister, Johanna, watched as a Wimpel, a long strip of swaddling cloth embroidered with prayers, was draped around the infant. While Isack slept, his proud father, Jakob, recited the blessing that Isack had now entered into a covenant with "Abraham our Father." The assembled family and friends answered, "May he be brought to study the Torah, to the marriage canopy, and to the practice of good deeds." Cheers filled the air before a meal of sweet challah bread and special foods brought by guests was enjoyed.

The loudest cheers came from ten-year-old Johanna, who came to relish her role as a second mother. While she chewed on a piece of challah, Johanna swung her long brown braids over Isack's face and spoke to him in the local dialect of Eppingerish. "Mutti, Vater," whispered Johanna as she pulled her parents to her new brother. "I do not want the others to hear this, but I already like him the best."

Before the long day ended, there was one last ritual. It signified that Isack had become not just a Jew but a German. Johanna and the other children gathered around Isack and lifted the well-worn cradle into the air three times. While the cradle floated up and down, the children shouted to Hollekreisch, the German pagan goddess who brought children into the world, "What shall the child's name be?" Isack's father placed his hand on his tiny son and proudly declared his Hebrew name. The next day, Mayor Raübmuller recorded Isack's birth in the Eppingen town records. He had become the 147th Jew living in the town of 3,274 people.

Over the next five years Eppingen saw its population increase to four thousand and its Jewish population increase to 215. This growth allowed for a synagogue, the center of Jewish life and Isack's religious home, to be consecrated. The stark exterior of this house of God was in contrast to the simple beauty of the sanctuary, where local craftsmen had transformed pieces of wood into benches with intricate inlays of menorahs and Stars of David. Each time Isack entered the synagogue as a boy and then as a man, he gazed upon the things that meant so much to him.

When he saw the ornate metal gate that protected the ark, the repository for the Torah scrolls, his faith was strengthened. When he saw the ten-by-twenty-foot bimah, or platform, from which the scrolls were read, his faith was strengthened. When he saw the simple balcony for the women, which ensured compliance with the orthodox requirement of the division of the sexes during prayer services, his faith was strengthened. When Isack looked at the small windows placed near the roof line in order to avoid the stone of the occasional anti-Semitic vandal, his faith was strengthened. And when on occasion glass from a window crashed to the ground, it only emboldened a young Isack to enthusiastically direct strangers to his synagogue at Kaiserstrasse 6. "If you are looking for my synagogue," said Isack, "it's across the street from the public school and next to the Lutheran church."

Like the other Jews of Eppingen, Ilse's father's view of the world was framed by not only his orthodox community's accomplishments of building his synagogue, a Jewish school, and a matzoh bakery but by its strict compliance with important rituals. Isack's stories to Ilse spoke of the shochetim, slaughterers who traveled from town to town, where, for their services, they were provided food and a place to sleep. Ilse never liked these stories, but she nonetheless repeated how Isack and the other boys followed the shochetim to the small fenced area just outside the rear of the synagogue. They watched him inspect the blade for imperfections while a chosen animal was hung upside down so its blood could easily drain into a barrel. With the sounds of the last kicks of the animal muted by the continuous prayers of those present, the shochet initiated a series of quick back and forth sawing motions. "By these acts, Ilse, God could clearly see that we Jews are obedient to his word," said a comforting Isack.

For a minority of Jews there were questions of why. But for Isack and then Ilse, there were never any questions. It was understood that to be a good Jew this is what you did, this is how you lived, and this is why you survived. Isack's faith defined how he viewed himself and the reality of how the world viewed him.

Isack also took great pride during his reflective walks up the Jewish Rise, to the Jewish cemetery in Eppingen. Two centuries after the birth of the iron-fenced cemetery, it became the home of a thirteen-foot stone tablet memorializing the names of eight Jews from Eppingen who forfeited their lives for Germany during World War I. With the exception of Isack's cousin Bernhard, who married and died in a place called Sacramento, California, the Jews of Eppingen remained. Like her father, Ilse also appreciated that she was not just a Jew but a German. "I pray and hope," Isack told Ilse, "that my words and actions as a proud German Jew lessened the suspicions from the people that forced the placement of small windows high up the wall in my synagogue."

Unfortunately, his prayers went unanswered when, on November 9, 1938, Eppingen's sixty Jews out of a population of five thousand watched in horror as centuries-old suspicions emerged in a torrent of pure hate. On that date, Isack's synagogue with its inviting windows, four times their original size, became one of the 268 synagogues destroyed in Germany by Adolf Hitler's radical Nazi Brownshirts.

SOPHIE WEIL,
MUTTI AND OMA

K nown as the jewel of the Black Forest, Freiburg is situated in southwestern Germany on the western edge of 4,600 square miles of huge pine and fir trees. Although centuries of wars and plagues tore at this part of the world with devastating consequences, nineteenth-century citizens of Freiburg who walked along the periphery of the vastness of the Black Forest found themselves transported back in time to an ancient Germany. Founded in 1120, Freiburg, considered the warmest, driest, and sunniest part of Germany, became synonymous with its iconic red sandstone gothic cathedral and its 380-foot-high bell tower. Installed in 1258, the oldest and most important of the sixteen tower bells, the massive 3,300-pound Hosanna, rang each Thursday evening to announce the ending services for the devotion of Angelus in memory of the Incarnation. It also rang as a symbolic invitation to come to Freiburg.

In the centuries that followed the Hosanna's installation, instability in the region allowed for the Spanish, Swedish, French, Austrian, and various German confederacies to rule Freiburg. This divergent cultural mix of people seemed a contradiction for a city that had allowed its Jews, except for pregnant women and children, to be burned in a single massacre in 1348. Although Jews were later admitted on occasion into Freiburg from 1411 until 1423, hatred prevailed in 1424 when all of its Jews were finally expelled. The eventual slow process of Freiburg's acceptance of

Jews began in the seventeenth century, when they were allowed into Freiburg for business purposes, but only if they were accompanied by a constable. It took until 1809 for Jews to return on a more permanent basis to a seemingly more tolerant Freiburg.

But by 1846, only twenty Jews were willing to dismiss centuries of hatred and call Freiburg home and still another forty more years before a single synagogue was consecrated. The process of substantial and meaningful changes reached a high point fifty years later, in 1900, when the University of Freiburg became the first German university to admit a woman. At the same time, Freiburg's former hated Jewish population swelled to over one thousand out of a total population of 61,500.

Two decades earlier, on Thursday, June 20, 1878, when Ilse's maternal grandfather pled for his pregnant wife to push, he was ushered out of his home by a group of annoyed women. Over the succeeding decades when he regaled family and friends with the events of that summer night, he proudly proclaimed, "My simple request to push was meant to ensure that when the people of Freiburg heard the Hosanna, it was not because of the devotion to Angelus, but because my Sophie was born."

Even though Sophie Weil, Ilse's mother, was not born until the early morning of Friday the twenty-first, Ilse happily carried the image of the Hosanna ringing while her grandfather begged, "Push! Push! I want to see my baby!"

Sophie's parents were blessed with three more children, Irma, Jenny, and, on December 19, 1886, their only son, Heinrich. Sophie loved her parents and her sisters, but her clear devotion to Heinrich annoyed her jealous sisters, who saw their time with Sophie being stolen away. That jealously often left an inconsolable Heinrich in tears when his sisters screamed, "Your Mutti Sophie has run away forever!" Unable to console her hysterical son, Sophie's mother called, "Sophie, hurry! Your little man Heinrich needs you!" Although still a child herself, she eagerly embraced her role as Mutti Sophie and the closeness that developed with her "little man."

It was that maturity as a young person that allowed Sophie to appreciate how her father's humble beginnings set no limits on what he could accomplish. There would be a move to a larger house on Kirchstrasse, an education for his children, and the many material things that wealth could provide. Like Isack, Sophie respected how her father never retreated from his Orthodox Jewish faith when it was convenient. However, in one defining moment, the tenets of faith and family that defined Sophie destroyed her relationship with her family.

When twenty-three-year-old Sophie opened the door to her parents' impressive home in the fall of 1901, her father was not impressed with the new suitor. The senior Weil's folded arms remained just so when Isack Ettlinger extended his right hand. "Sophie did not do your home honor when she described it, Herr Weil." When the sounds of the hopeful Hosanna rang out, a crushed Sophie watched her father turn his back and mutter, "We have coffee."

Isack followed Sophie past her giggling siblings, who watched the somber couple sit on the small couch before Irma, Jenny, and Heinrich retreated to a nearby room. Sophie's mother squeezed between her daughter and the stranger as she poured cups of coffee, while Sophie's father tightly packed a seemingly endless supply of tobacco into his pipe. His tortured victims sat in an uncomfortable silence that was broken only by the laughs of Irma,

Jenny, and Heinrich. The resulting tension that caused Sophie to excuse herself left Isack's eyes exploding with a sad appeal to not leave. His pleas went unacknowledged by Sophie, who pushed open the nearby door and grabbed at Heinrich and kicked at her sisters. She wiped away her tears. "I never ask you for anything. But please, this one time..." Irma cried as she whispered an apology to the storm of emotions that had become Sophie.

Heinrich pressed his ear against the closed door and listened to each explosion by his father. Heinrich repeated to his terrified sisters the tearful cries from Sophie, "That's not true, Poppa. I do love him." Moments later, the sounds of the front door opening and someone running up the stairs were heard. It was only then that the children bravely ventured to the parlor where their parents sat alone. Words cannot describe what happened in 1901 to Irma, Jenny, and Heinrich, but clearly they were all traumatized by the explicit dismissal of Sophie from their family.

In 1918, seventeen years after Sophie's siblings saw her tears and heard the front door to their home slam shut, Heinrich married Lina Landauer, his fiancée of many years. Sophie's absence and the premature death of the Weil children's mother before the wedding made the otherwise happy occasion bittersweet. Within months of Heinrich's marriage, Irma and Jenny saw less of their brother and Lina, whose private resentment of the spinsters' financial draining of the Weil fortune could no longer be contained. "They only take from the family. How could two old women need a dowry? This is money my Heinrich could use to go to medical school," complained Lina.

To Lina, an unemployed and unmarried Jenny was an unjustifiable beneficiary of gifts and money from a father who was compelled by guilt into assisting his daughter. Although Irma enjoyed a career as a nurse, she too did not escape the constant attacks and criticism that she had benefited from living in their father's large home on Kirchstrasse in Freiburg. "They never paid anything to live there!" attacked Lina. The subsequent friction and strain over money given the "Outsiders" as Lina called them became incomprehensible to the sisters, given Heinrich's subsequent employment with the Singer Sewing Machine Company that brought him both wealth and world travel. For the hurt sisters, they simply withdrew to the house on Kirchstrasse where, thankfully, they had each other.

Sophie, who was no longer a part of the lives of her family after the fall of 1901, married Isack Ettlinger in the only synagogue in Freiburg. After the simple ceremony was completed, Isack wiped away Sophie's tears as the nearby Hosanna sang.

After their wedding, Isack and Sophie moved to nearby Rastatt with Isack's mother, who had been widowed on April 30, 1901, when her sixty seven year old husband, Jakob died. For Isack, the move away from Eppingen was strange and inconsistent with all it meant to be an Ettlinger. Always the salesman, Isack looked for anything positive during this period of transition. He took great satisfaction that his aged mother assisted in the birth on May 6, 1902, of his first child, Julius. After Isack's mother's death and then Ilse's birth on January 14, 1906, Isack took his family to the big city of Karlsruhe. But Ilse heard none of this, even as she begged her father each night to tell her more. They were stories that would have ended with Isack's request at the Weils' home for Sophie's hand in marriage and her father's unknown pointed questions.

KARLSRUHE AND ITS JEWS

S tarting in the last half of the nineteenth century, Karlsruhe's teachers began each school year by reading about the birth of Karlsruhe.

"In the depths of the Hardtwald, the gloomy forest that stretched from Durlach, the seat of the Margraves of Baden, to the impenetrable swamps and unchartered backwaters of the Rhine, woodsmen began felling trees to make a circular clearing. The countless trunks were buried in the ground somewhere; no one knew what to do with them. On another day, the princely court appeared in solemn procession. The sounds of trumpets and drums preceded the Margrave Karl Wilhelm von Baden-Durlach who entered the cleared forest and laid the foundation stone of the new palace. The message had been received, 900 cartloads of wall bricks will be required. The date was June 17, 1715, and it was on that day the history of the city of Carols-Ruhe began...."

The new village grew quickly in response to Karl Wilhelm's invitation, regardless of race or religion, to settle in Karlsruhe. The huge Schloss, or palace, with its two angled structures and central tower became the center of the village. Like ribs on a fan, thirty-two streets radiated from the palace, while tiny red timber homes dotted the roads. This impressive and distinctive design was not lost on a new nation to the west, the United States of America and, more importantly, its French architect, L'Enfant, who modeled its capital city, Washington, on the "Fan City" of the forest.

18

Upon the death of Karl Wilhelm twenty-three years after the foundation stone was first laid, his successor and grandson, Karl Friederich, began the process of transforming this forest village. From two thousand people in 1719, he saw his village grow into a city of almost fifteen thousand people by the time of his death in 1811. The fan-shaped layout and subsequent classic Roman-designed structures by architect Friedrich Weinbrenner, a native of Karlsruhe, led the physical transformation from a village one passed through to a city of destination. Weinbrenner, the first important German architect of the nineteenth century, worked with Karl Friederich to oversee the introduction of the city's lighting, the disposal of water and waste, and the paving of roads. The focus of Weinbrenner's vision came in the form of his 1791 design of the rectangular-shaped, centrally placed Marktplatz, or square, just south of the palace. Framed by a Protestant church and town hall, it became a place to sell goods, conduct business, enjoy festivals, and hear the news of the day. No other structure became more identified with Karlsruhe and the Marktplatz than the unique twenty-one-foot-tall sandstone pyramid, the final resting place for visionary Margrave Karl Wilhelm von Baden-Durlach.

Karlsruhe, the eventual capital of the state of Baden, attracted an eclectic group of people, including such men of the arts as Goethe and Voltaire. But none were more famous than American Buffalo Bill Cody, who arrived in Karlsruhe on April 23, 1891, to lead a procession of two hundred cowboys and Indians, 175 horses, stagecoaches, buffalos, and a diminutive sharpshooter named Annie Oakley down the Kaiserstrasse. Cody's presence alone confirmed forever that this former village near the Black Forest had arrived on the world stage.

Well before Cody's 1891 arrival and Karl Wilhelm's 1715 placement of the foundation stone, the margrave set forth a plan for the growth of Karlsruhe and an offer for a better life. His simple plan began with the change of his official residence from the town of Durlach to this clearing in the woods. Those who answered yes to his pledge for a new life, the Saxons, Poles, Bavarians, Russians, and some locals, were given both land and freedom from taxes for twenty years. The resulting fusion of diverse cultures and languages also gave birth to a new dialect in Karlsruhe, "Brigantendeutsch."

Jews who sought to take advantage of this offer were granted refuge under personal letters of protection and a promise of equal rights. However, by 1733 the growing community of 282 Jews saw the introduction of many laws that ensured their second-class status. All aspects of their lives were regulated, such as the 1752 ordinance prohibiting Jews from leaving Karlsruhe on Sundays and Christian holidays. Then, in 1783, the first signs of moderation toward the Jews occurred. Margrave Karl Friederich decreed that Jews were no longer serfs, could settle where they desired, and were freed from the Todesfall tax, which required a fee for every Jewish burial.

This unsure road of the Jews' acceptance into German culture and society was met with repeated obstacles in the form of legal restrictions, killings, and wholesale riots, such as the Hep Hep riots of 1819. At the time of these riots, Germany consisted of thirty-six independent states and a number of free cities. The status of Jews varied from state to state, and as such, the introduction of new laws in various states did not make the Jews of all these regions equals. Nonetheless, during the riots of 1819 most cities heard the rally cry, "Hep! Hep! Death and destruction to every Jew! If you don't flee, then you are through!" When the threats of death rang out in the streets of Karlsruhe, it became necessary on the third day of rioting for the infantry to be called to action and cannons to be prominently displayed.

The Grand Duke of Baden protested, "Emperors, kings, dukes, beggars, Catholics, and Jews are all human and as such our equals." But it was his slow carriage ride from the sanctuary of his castle to the home of a prominent Jew in Karlsruhe that truly proclaimed his unity with the Jewish victims of the riots and restored peace. Although peace was restored and more favorable laws were eventually adopted, national demonstrations and continuing riots against the Jews of Germany in 1843, 1848, and the 1880s forced the Jews to acknowledge the unshakable distrust by their fellow countrymen.

These mixed messages of hate and acceptance strengthened the Jews' resolve that they too were Germans. Such a message of loyalty to the land and its people was presented on June 6, 1849, by Gabriel Reisser, one of seven Jews and the vice president of the revolutionary General National Assembly, the first freely elected parliament for all of Germany. On that date he rose before the assembly to dispute the argument that the civil rights of the Jews be legislated separately. Self-declared as "an oppressed Jew," he proclaimed to all:

"We are not immigrants—we were born here—and so we cannot claim any other home: either we are Germans or we have no homeland. Whoever disputes my claim to this, my German fatherland, disputes my right to my own thoughts, my feelings, my language—the very air I breathe. Therefore, I must defend myself against him as I would against a murderer."

The passion exhibited by Reisser spearheaded the success of Karlsruhe's Jews, who, after being given absolute legal emancipation in 1862, became leading businessmen in Karlsruhe. The factories of the Seligmanns epitomized this given their employment of eight hundred workers. But the greatest economic success came not from the four floors of merchandise and employment of over forty employees by Gebrüder Ettlinger, but by the fact that his store enjoyed the patronage of Karl Wilhelm's descendant, Grand Duchess Hilda von Baden. Her actions told the German people that Karlsruhe's Jews were Germans.

In addition to the economic successes of Karlsruhe's Jewish community, its Jews won elections as city officials and appointments to the judiciary. Individual successes such as Moritz Ellstätter's appointment as Baden's minister of finance from 1878 to 1893, Dr. Nathan Stern's appointment to the Supreme Court in 1900, and Professor Richard Willstaetter's victory as the 1915 Nobel Prize winner for chemistry were praised by the rabbis in their sermons.

Better times had arrived not only for Karlsruhe's Jews but for the city. Between 1883 and 1912, approximately five thousand industry jobs were created per year in the state of Baden, mostly in the cities of Karlsruhe, Mannheim, and Pforzheim. A new port was opened on the Rhine River, and as of 1902, it handled 280,000 tons of cargo. By the beginning of the twentieth century, the fan shape that had defined Karlsruhe was abandoned as more buildings were constructed and surrounding villages were absorbed. Karlsruhe, the former forest village, had become a modern city. Then with one single act, the assassination of Archduke Franz Ferdinand of Austria on June 28, 1914, the optimistic future for both Karlsruhe and its Jews ended.

WORLD WAR I

When the formal fighting of World War I came to an end, Germany's dead and wounded totaled six million. The politics of this war continued until June 28, 1919, when the final terms of peace were reduced to writing in the Hall of Mirrors of the Palace of Versailles. The terms held in part that the centuries-old disputed territory of Alsace-Lorraine, located on the France–Germany border, was to be returned to the French. Germany's army was to be reduced to 100,000 men with no tanks or air force, a navy restricted in size to no more than six ships and no submarines, a prohibition to unite with Austria, a mandate that war reparations be made in the amount of $39 billion, an amount that would take until approximately 1988 to repay, and an admission in clause 231 that Germany was responsible for World War I.

The eventual signing of the Treaty of Versailles on August 31, 1919, ushered in the new Weimar Republic. Named for the city where, after months of debate, Germany's new constitution was ratified, the charter combined the process of referendum from Switzerland, a cabinet government from England and France, and the strong position of presidency from the United States. It also allowed for a complicated voting process for minority views to be represented in its parliament. The stage had been set for a democracy that was viewed as perfect in concept and flawless in its future implementation. No document in the free world spoke more directly about the rights of its people than this new constitution, which stated in part:

"...Political power emanates from the people...All Germans are equal before the law...Personal liberty is inviolable...Every German has a right to form associations or societies...All inhabitants of the Reich enjoy complete liberty of belief and conscience..."

By the time of the signing of the treaty, the state of Baden, the home state to Karlsruhe, had a population of 2,208,507. At 1 percent of the total population, the Baden Jews read the newspaper headlines about the ratification of the new constitution and understood its implications; they had gone to sleep the night before in the eyes of many as second-class citizens and awoke as legal equals. However, with the Treaty of Versailles in place and the imposition of severe financial and military sanctions, there came a rallying cry of revenge from a zealot minority. Their indictment was directed against the traitors and criminal negotiators such as the "Jewish father of the Weimar Constitution," Hugo Preuss. It was alleged they never fought on the field of battle for Germany, but instead chose to give away Germany's land, subjugate its people, and destroy the future for generations to come. Over the next fourteen years those same detractors called upon a common refrain from the past, the fault for all the ills of Germany fell at the feet of the Jews.

FAMILY

When Isack Ettlinger left for war, his last vision was of his young son, Julius, crying at the very same Bahnhofplatz that later welcomed him home. When Isack saw a sixteen-year-old stranger with thick, curly black hair and the hint of stubble approaching him on the street, he needed to hear, "Vater, it's me, Julius!" before Isack embraced his son. An emotional Julius smiled as he looked enviously at his uniformed father. Isack once again wrapped his arms tightly around his saluting son while he relished a private victory that his son had avoided the war to end all wars.

While father and son walked arm in arm, Isack learned that his son, who now towered a full inch over his own height of five feet six inches, was digging graves and doing maintenance work at two local cemeteries. Sadly, he also learned that Julius had moved into a men's boarding house under the transparent excuse "To give you and Mutti more room."

At the same time, twelve-year-old Ilse sat on the stoop to her family's apartment building. She pulled at her sweaty hands until in the distance she saw her father. Ilse slowly stood up and took her coat off so that her father could see the brightly colored dress that she had made for the special occasion. A trembling smile exposed her perfect teeth. The slight breeze blew her long black hair in front of her brown eyes. It took only seconds more before Isack fell to his knees and stretched out his arms. Ilse, blind to the others on the street, screamed "Vater!" while she raced down the narrow street. Her tearstained face and shouts of happiness announced a common experience in the latter days of the war. Another hero was home.

Neighbors who had lost so much during the war gathered around the returning soldier and showered him with spontaneous gifts of flowers, bread, and wine. Isack was rendered speechless as Ilse pulled her father into the privacy of their apartment. When Julius pushed open the apartment door he yelled, "Mutti, Vater is home." Sophie licked her hands and pushed her graying hair off her face. Husband and wife awkwardly approached each other while Ilse watched the forced embrace between her parents. They spoke over each other uncomfortably. Isack put his hand on Sophie's face, drew her close to him, and whispered something private, until the moment was stolen by the well-intentioned neighbors who had come to wish Isack Ettlinger well.

Even as the small apartment filled with contagious euphoria, Ilse prayed that the reunion between her parents replace her vivid memories of the way it used to be. There had never been screaming between her parents before Isack left for war. To the contrary, her recollections were that they were quiet, respectful, and polite to each other. Ilse loved her parents, and it was clear they loved her, but she was always jealous of her friends' parents who held hands or kissed each other on the cheek in public.

As the years went by, the courteousness that had characterized Ilse's parents' relationship was abandoned. It was a coldness that caused Ilse to search for the family she desperately needed.

On the last Friday before the sun set in November 1918, Isack trimmed his beard before he sat down at the dinner table. When the wonderful kosher meal was completed, Isack put on his black suit that hung unflatteringly from his skinny frame. It made no difference to Isack, who stood in front of a large mirror and smiled approvingly before he made the last of three pulls on each cuff of his stiff white shirt. The new civilian winked at Ilse through the mirror and clapped his hands. "It's time to go."

Ilse clung to her father's arm and scanned the narrow road in hopes of seeing a friend so she could yell, "Look! This is my family!" The moment quickly passed as her father's gaze fixed on the ornate four-story synagogue.

"Slow down, Isack! Remember you have Ilse!" yelled Sophie. When he stopped at the first of five steps, Isack's chest heaved. He stared at the circular windows on the first floor and the rectangular stained glass windows on the second floor of the masonry structure. Although by law no building could be taller than the four stories of the Schloss, Isack had always argued that his synagogue was clearly taller than the Schloss and therefore the most magnificent building in Karlsruhe.

"Yes, I remember," whispered Isack. He pulled the black iron handles of the heavy dark-brown door that led to the huge sanctuary. The smiling rabbi stood at the bimah and waved at an unresponsive Isack, who walked to the water-filled basin where he washed his hands. Isack was back in Eppingen, a child once more. He slowly slid his hands back and forth against the wooden pews and once again whispered, "I remember." After the final rays of the setting sun filtered through the stained glass ceiling onto the balcony where the women sat, Isack and Julius were ushered to a place of honor, the front pew in front of Rabbi Dr. Sinai Schiffer.

When the formal service was over, the sixty-six-year-old mustachioed rabbi, known for his scholarly endeavors and black bowler hat, asked Isack to stand. Spontaneous applause erupted and Isack answered with a clumsy bow while Sophie and Ilse looked down on him from the balcony. After Isack was seated, the rabbi's voice carried throughout the sanctuary with his impromptu concluding sermon.

"Since my appointment on January 1, 1883, I have read and researched about our city's Jews. I also have talked with many of you who have made up that very history. Those times are so much a part of me that when I reflect and pray, it is as if I was there. In 1806, a new synagogue on Kronenstrasse Seventeen was consecrated in Karlsruhe in the presence of Karl Friederich. In 1809, most Jews were granted full civil rights under the law. In 1816, a new Jewish elementary school was opened, and within a few years there were some one hundred children in attendance. In 1825, there were 893 Jews in our city, and by the close of the century there were 2,577 Jews out of a total population of 107,065 who called Karlsruhe home.

A sweeping fire in the evening of May 29, 1871, destroyed the synagogue. I know this because I saw this with God's eyes. We were left with nothing. We held services for the next four years on the top floor of the old Jewish hospital. On May 2, 1875, at a cost of 100,000 guilders, a new synagogue was consecrated in the presence of Princess Wilhelmina, Princess Hohenlohe, and delegations from both civilian and military authorities. I know this because I saw this with God's eyes. We were all so proud, so happy, so unified."

The older men of the congregation, all dressed in the same black suits and hats as Isack, nodded in agreement with the recollections of their rabbi.

"The fight to obtain our new place of worship brought our community together. But unfortunately we grew apart. The reformers came with their new views and installed an organ with a space for a choir, which caused the members of the orthodox community to say enough. I know this because I was there. This I saw with my own eyes! Six years later, there was a division in our community, and as a result, a new orthodox synagogue at Karl-Friedrich-Strasse Sixteen was dedicated. This new synagogue, where we worship today, a truly orthodox synagogue with its own school, a mikva, and space to carry out shechita, unites us as Jews. Our reform friends and their synagogue on the Kaiserstrasse, or should I say a temple, may have many more congregants…"

The rabbi stopped briefly to enjoy the snickering of the congregants, who appreciated his sarcasm about the reformer's use of the word "temple" instead of "synagogue" before he continued.

"But our goal is not to increase our numbers but to honor the word of the Torah. When our friend Isack Ettlinger and the others return back to their homes, families, and synagogues, they do so not just as Jews but as German Jews."

The rabbi could not give exact numbers of Jewish casualties as he continued his sermon of patriotism and sacrifice. In future sermons, he made sure to remind his congregants of the Jewish sacrifice for Germany in World War I. They would hear that out of a population of 550,000 Jews in Germany during World War I, 100,000 served in the military and, like Isack, 78 percent saw frontline duty. Rabbi Schiffer would also remind his congregation that twelve thousand Jews, including fifty-six from Karlsruhe, had made the ultimate sacrifice for their country.

Decades later, Isack recalled Rabbi Schiffer's final words on that November day in 1918.

"Four years ago, the Central Association of German Citizens of Jewish Faith wrote, 'The well-being of the fatherland supersedes everything.' I disagreed then. I told you all as much. Now four years later we see a Germany that has lost a war. The world saw that our German faces were ground in the dirt when we were made to sign an armistice in a converted dining car in Compiègne, France. But with that loss, the Jewish community has shown Germany and the rest of the world that we are patriots, loyal and dedicated."

The rabbi walked to the edge of the bimah and closed his eyes.

"Two years ago, German Jewish philosopher Hermann Cohen, who died in April of this year, said, 'Thus, in these times of epoch-making fatefulness for our people, we, as Jews, are proud to be Germans. For we are conscious of our task to convince all our coreligionists the world over of the religious significance of Germandom, of its influence, of its rightful claim over the Jews of every nationality, in religious developments as in general culture.'"

When his eyes opened, he spoke one last time.

"A pipe organ destroyed our community. We have worked to repair those wounds. It is a process that continues to this day. A war has torn our country apart. We have all lost something, both Christians and Jews. Eventually we will all come to learn that through that common loss, the union of Christians and Jews will grow stronger in the years ahead. For we are not defined by whether we are Christians or Jews or by reform or orthodoxy, but by one thing: we are all Germans."

CHANGES

In the early years after the signing of the Treaty of Versailles, Karlsruhe, like most other German cities, was forced to deal with a growing violence among its people. This included the July and August 1920 protests over the costs of living, which left roving mobs sacking warehouses for food and clothing. Although largely contained over the next decade, the new republic was called upon with greater frequency to quell sporadic pockets of violence containing an ominous common theme of ending the Weimar Republic.

However, by the end of the 1920s, the world had taken notice of Germany's emergence as both an economic and political giant. By 1929 it was producing 10 percent more coal, 100 percent more lignite, and 30 percent more steel than the pre-war period. In 1927, unemployment insurance became law, and upward of 14,000,000 workers operated under collective bargaining agreements. In 1928, unemployment fell below 1,000,000 people to 650,000 for the first time since the war. That same year, retail sales were up 20 percent over those of 1925. In 1929, wages were 10 percent higher than in 1925. The number of patents doubled each year after the war compared to the prewar years. Production of electricity rose 50 percent from 1925 to 1930. In 1930, Germany ranked second only to the United States among the world's exporting countries. By the close of 1925, Baden was home to over 2,400 factories employing more than 250,000 people. In 1928, the port of Karlsruhe, which had handled 280,000 tons of goods in 1902, handled over 2,000,000 tons. The citizens of Karlsruhe proudly saw the construction of resorts like Rappenworth bathing beach, the completion of the Dammerstock housing development, and the French firm Michelin opening a new plant.

While the Weimar Republic rejoiced with its new economic prosperity, the Jewish community in Karlsruhe acquired two senior citizen homes, a school, a hospital, and cemeteries. It proclaimed with pride that the famous Jewish-owned Knopf chain of department stores had chosen Karlsruhe for its headquarters, four banks were owned by Jews, and Jews made up 26 percent of the city's lawyers and 40 percent of its doctors. Remarkably, Jewish Dr. Ludwig Marum became Karlsruhe's representative in the Reichstag from 1928 to 1932.

Isack's good fortunes paralleled the growth of the Jewish community. His continued employment enabled his family to enjoy a middle-class life. There were no excesses, but there was always food, a nice apartment, an occasional meal at the Karpfen, the Reichshof, or at the Germania Hotel and even a movie at the Staatstheater. Most of all, Isack enjoyed the informal get-togethers at one of the many beer gardens on the Marktplatz with his friends. Isack also went to his synagogue every day to fulfill his promise to God that if he returned home from the war, he would be a better Jew.

By 1925, when the Jewish population in Karlsruhe peaked at 3,386 out of a total population of 145,000, differences between the Reform and Orthodox Jews intensified. Eighty-five percent of Jewish children were educated in non-Jewish schools. In 1927, 26 percent of Jewish men and 16 percent of Jewish women married a non-Jew. The children of these unions, Mischlinge, or mongrels, as they came to be known, were usually not raised as Jews. These unions were considered a threat to Judaism. The family, the core of the Jewish community, came under threat as a worsening economy in the early 1930s brought a lower birthrate for Jews and an increased rate of abortions. Isack's orthodox community acknowledged the painful reality that their young people had lost both their moral foundation and Jewish faith.

The catalyst for a different change began years earlier when the future leader of Germany, Adolph Hitler, recovered from temporary blindness as a result of a British gas attack during the waning days of World War I. While Hitler was being treated for his injuries in a military hospital on November 10, 1918, a pastor walked into a large dormitory room filled with injured German soldiers. Through tears, he asked the men to pray with him as he confirmed that on the following day an armistice would be signed, leaving Germany at the mercy of the Allies.

Adolph Hitler recounted, "I could stand it no longer.... Everything went black again before my eyes...threw myself on my bunk, and dug my burning head into my blanket and pillow.... So all had been in vain...in vain for the death of two million who died....Did all this happen only so that a gang of wretched criminals could lay hands on the Fatherland?"

Years later, on Christmas Eve 1924, Adolph Hitler, the former corporal in the German army, was released from prison for his part in the attempted coup of the Weimar Republic. Ironically, Hitler's nine months in Landsberg prison for his Beer Hall Putsch allowed him the time to reduce his disjointed vision of change into his autobiography, *Mein Kampf.* His book, which became his chief source of income, continued to advocate for the overthrow of the Republic of Germany. However, this time he would set aside the bullet in favor of the pen and the vote. This minor national figure continued to peddle the anti-Jewish theme of *Mein Kampf* in hopes that the Aryans, the real Germans, would be inspired just as he had been on that November day in 1918. By 1925, national sales figures for Hitler's manifesto came to 9,473 copies. The 60 million Aryans were not listening.

After Hitler's failed Nazi Putsch, the proactive government of Baden arrested all of the Nazi leaders within its state. By virtue of those arrests, the president, Heinrich Köhler, reaffirmed Baden's loyalty to the new constitution and its Jews. By the end of 1924, the right-wing Nazi Party in Baden was left with 1,500 members. The citizens of Karlsruhe stood at the forefront in rejecting the message of hate by Hitler. Simple but nonetheless dramatic actions, such as the public repudiation by a coalition of Christians and Jews against the local Schremp brewery, long considered a Nazi stronghold, resulted in the brewery dismissing its Nazi employees. The unrelenting public denunciation of the Nazis by the citizens of Karlsruhe culminated with the December 7, 1924, election when the Nazi Party received 1.6 percent of the vote.

Rebuked by the electorate, the Nazis called upon new and old zealots to continue the fight to make the vision of *Mein Kampf* a reality. One such instrument of change would be the future Nazi governor of Baden, Robert Wagner. After his release from prison for his actions in Hitler's putsch, Wagner moved to a tiny apartment in Karlsruhe where he operated the Baden Nazi Party. Wagner conceded his efforts during the 1925 elections in Baden resulted in a total defeat for a Nazi Party that received only 1.2 percent of the vote. Local newspapers confirmed that Hitler was of no further interest. *Der Democrat* noted, "He had disappeared from history." Only the socialist paper of Karlsruhe, the *Volksfreund*, took a contrary position: "The Nazis were becoming a plague again."

By July 1927, a crestfallen Wagner reported to Hitler that four out of ten Nazi Party locals in Baden had abandoned the party. However, with the end of Hitler's speaking ban on April 21, 1927, Wagner began an aggressive campaign to expand the Nazi Party. Nonetheless, his establishment of Baden's weekly Nazi Party paper, *Der Führer*, on November 5, 1927, proved to be another failure given the sale of only 446 copies for its inaugural issue. A few months later, Wagner's almost maniacal persistence began to garner attention for not only the Nazi Party but for himself.

The first serious recognition by Jews and Christians in Karlsruhe that the Jewish struggle for acceptance into the broader German society might not be permanent occurred on Saturday, March 3, 1928. On that date, Adolph Hitler confidently marched onto the stage at the Festhalle at Kanzlerstrasse 12 in front of three thousand Nazi Party members. The mostly trucked in outsiders who responded to the rally cry of help for the upcoming May elections cheered and saluted as their leader took his first steps from behind the maroon curtain. With his black hair parted on the right and swastika armband placed over his left bicep, he stood in silence while the barrel-vaulted ceiling that ran the length of the hall amplified the fanatical cheers and foot stomps out onto the Kanzlerstrasse.

Adolph Hitler, the future chancellor of Germany, dramatically waved his arms to quiet the assembled Nazis before he presented his emotionally charged vision of a new Germany. Germany, Hitler argued, with his hands stiffly planted on his hips, lost its power to grow when the traitors and criminals signed the Versailles treaty. He released his hands from his hips and raised them into the air. Hitler's conductorlike fists pumped like pistons. He proclaimed to the frenzied audience that this power deficiency would be corrected when Germany's population problems were resolved. Hitler's ramblings were dismissed the next day by the local press as "...strange comical theater..."

When Isack and his friends sat reading newspapers in their favorite café on the Marktplatz the next day, they raised their steins and toasted without fear to the certain demise of Adolph Hitler.

In the weeks following Hitler's appearance, members of the SA, also known as Brownshirts, traveled each weekend and holidays to Karlsruhe. They marched throughout the streets passing out Nazi literature and singing propaganda songs in anticipation of the May 20, 1928, national elections. This paramilitary wing of thugs for the Nazi Party saw their efforts rewarded with a mere 3.1 percent of the vote. The fanaticism displayed in March 1928 at the Festhalle in Karlsruhe was clearly not shared by the rest of the country—nor were the sales of *Mein Kampf,* which plummeted 66 percent from 1925 to 1928.

In April 1929, the political enemy of the Nazi Party, the communists, and five hundred local Nazi party and SA members battled in the streets of Karlsruhe in a vicious street fight. Isack was not alone when he happily watched the police easily control this first of many more frequent street battles that erupted over the ensuing months. By the close of the decade, the inflammatory rhetoric of the Nazi Party had fallen on deaf ears at the same time the economic engine of the Weimar Republic pulled both Christians and Jews into relative prosperity.

A new reality took place with the collapse of the US stock market on October 24, 1929. In 1929, unemployment that averaged 71,366 people in Baden had by 1930 increased to 99,813.

Germany's economic prosperity, which had resulted in large part from its loans with the United States and its world trade, fell by one half from 1929 to 1932. From 1928 to 1933, Baden's welfare recipients rose from 55,395 to 120,023 as millions of Germans became unemployed and thousands of small business collapsed. While the Weimar Republic fell into an economic depression, a willing audience began to listen to the Nazis. Social issues relative to family life, education, and sexual mores came under ever-increasing criticism by the Nazis. Increasing numbers said yes to the argument that the Weimar Republic's relaxation of censorship led to lesbian and homosexual publications and literature on all aspects of sex, abortions, male and female prostitution, and sex education in schools.

The Germany of the 1920s that had twice the amount of pre-war cosmetic expenditures, an increase in smoking by women, and an unnatural focus on bicycle races and sexually provocative reported murder trials, was, argued the Nazis, inconsistent with all that was truly German. The arts that were controlled by a few, asserted the Nazis, dismissed German music for jazz and dances such as the tango. Similarly, the heroic age of German cinematography came to an end when the showing of the 1930 American version of *All Quiet on the Western Front* resulted in Nazi-provoked disturbances and its eventual banning in the interest of public safety.

In the month before the worldwide economic collapse, Baden's growing Nazi Party held one hundred rallies in anticipation of state elections. Although the rallies netted a nominal result of only 7 percent of the vote and the election of six of its members to the state legislature, the Nazis became the fourth largest party in the state of Baden. Of the 40 percent increase in the party's vote total, 30 percent came from two cities; one of them was Karlsruhe.

Few Jews in Karlsruhe acknowledged the significance of the election or heeded the warnings of the *CV Zeitung*, the largest German Jewish newspaper. It attacked the Baden Jews for "...`failing to fight the anti-Semitism that represented the growth of the Nazi party in this liberal state.`" The democratic paper *Frankfurter Zeitung* similarly asserted that the Nazis' successes in Baden should cause "...`serious introspection.`" By the close of 1929, *Der Führer*, Baden's Nazi weekly, was profitable. Between January and June 1930, Nazis carried out 150 rallies per month. The forty-eight Nazi Party locals that existed in Baden in May 1928 increased to two hundred by August 1930. From May 1929 to August 1930, the Karlsruhe local doubled to one thousand members. Robert Wagner, the persistent head of Baden's Nazi Party, proudly pointed to these accomplishments and the fact that by the summer of 1930, a financially sound Nazi Party was operating out of a five-room complex.

As the Nazi Party membership increased, the coalitions of Christians and Jews that once almost shuttered the pro-Nazi Schremp brewery began to fracture. In October 1930, employees of Karlsruhe's newspaper the *Badische Observer* ran to the first floor of its building when they heard the sounds of crashing glass. They watched in disbelief as Karlsruhe police who only a short time earlier had arrested party leaders, now looked away as Nazi Brownshirts smashed the building's windows. "Now you have an excuse to say no when we ask to place our literature on your windows," laughed an SA leader.

The Nazis' brutality helped to realize 19 percent of the vote in the September Reichstag election and an increase in the Baden

Nazi Brownshirt membership from 2,400 in mid-1930 to 5,000 by October 1931. At the same time, Karlsruhe's five hundred Brownshirts represented a tenfold increase from 1928. Dramatic increases in those numbers by the spring of 1932 caused the chief of the four thousand-member police department of Baden to plead for help to control the hostile ten thousand Brownshirts in Baden. This plea continued as the outnumbered police saw the Nazis' youthful counterpart, the Hitler Youth corps, increase from 498 members in 1931 to 5,200 by January 1933.

MODERN GERMANY

As Ilse Ettlinger matured into a young woman in the early 1920s, she continued to embrace the stories of Ettlingen, her ancestors, and, most of all, her faith. Her requests to her father for a story and a walk to the Platz, the Schloss, or the zoo under Karlsruhe's constant sunny skies reinforced Ilse's knowledge as her family historian. Isack, the teacher, beamed with pride when Ilse, the student, corrected him on those daily walks. "No, Poppa! It was Bernhard, not Maier who married Sarah in Sacramento, California, United States of America!" And while Ilse's relationship with her father continued to flourish, she watched her parents' courteous and then distant relationship transform into hours, days, and then weeks of silence. Life at home became intolerable as she tried to maneuver between her parents' simmering resentment.

By 1927, when Ilse turned twenty-one, she, like many of the other young women of Karlsruhe, had embraced the new wave of liberal modernity in Germany. Decisions that declared she was in control of her life were never intended to insult her parents or her faith. Nonetheless, her life became a series of well-intentioned lies that hid purchases of cosmetics and cigarettes and unescorted walks in the gardens of the Schloss and the zoo. She enjoyed a sense of boldness by partaking in a public meal alone at the restaurant inside the Festhalle or riding the tram up to the 840-foot-high Turmberg, dancing the tango, and listening to jazz music at the nontraditional cafés and beer gardens with her like-minded friends.

The confrontations with Ilse's parents over the discovered lies left an angry Isack spending more time away from home, while a conflicted Sophie secreted herself away in her bedroom. "But Papa, Mutti—I want to be like the other German girls," cried Ilse. Sadly, she had become in Isack's eyes what he had silently feared, a victim of the Jewish people's acceptance into a broader German society. For Isack there was no apology sufficient to explain Ilse's choices that took preference over her Jewish faith. By the beginning of 1928, the remnants of what had been an ideal and loving relationship between Isack and his daughter barely existed.

A BEER AND PRETZELS,
JANUARY 31, 1933

On the surface, fifty-eight-year-old Isack's life was not substantially different than that of the other Jews of Karlsruhe. The fewer employment opportunities in the years before 1933 forced the Ettlingers to move to an apartment across the street from the seedy Gypsy apartments and brothel. Even with the unsettling move, Isack was thankful he worked two to three times a week and thereby avoided total unemployment, which had risen from two million in 1929 to six million, one-quarter of the working population in Germany.

When Isack opened the café door, his unemployed friends were sitting around a wooden table enjoying their beer and warm pretzels. When he took his seat between brothers Max and Meyer Stern, it was clear that the argument among the Jewish war veterans was edgier than usual. Isack had to look no farther than the beer-stained headline of "January 30, 1933 President von Hindenburg appoints Hitler Chancellor."

So much had happened since the end of the Great War, thought Isack after he covered the headlines with warm pretzels. There had been bad times, good times, and now there were these confusing times. For the older Jews in the café, such as Isack, who vividly remembered the bad times, the Joke, Adolph Hitler, was another short-term annoyance who would fade away. While Isack quietly sipped his beer, his thoughts were interrupted by an angry voice that instantly quieted the jabbering men. "Listen to me," growled Abraham. "He is not even a German, he is Austrian. When they have something to complain about, it's the Jews." Isack put down his beer as the attack continued.

"The truth is, they will always hate us, but hate takes effort. Each year, each decade, and each century that goes by, it becomes too much of an effort." Abraham smiled. "It may take two centuries more, but eventually they just won't care anymore—at least, not enough to do anything about it."

The Jewish Knights of the Round Table, as they called themselves, raised their steins and nodded in agreement with the cynical observation. "Besides," whispered a knight. "He is a vegetarian, and everyone knows you can't trust a vegetarian." Isack smiled as he emptied his stein.

"Yes," followed another laughing whisper. "And they will always have the Gypsies to blame."

Max waved away the approaching waitress, and the giggling men drew their chairs closer to the table. Bent at the waist and shoulders drawn forward, their heads almost touched while they tried to best one another at the expense of Germany's new leader.

"So our friend Adolph is visiting a lunatic asylum," continued Max. "The patients give him the salute." Max bent his elbow at his side. His crooked version of the Nazi greeting drew muffled laughter. "As our führer passes down the line he comes to a man who is not saluting. 'Why aren't you saluting me like the others?' demands our leader.

"'But my führer—I'm the nurse,' declares the man. 'I'm not crazy!'"

The men erupted into laughter while Nathan discreetly stood up and placed his half-filled stein on the table. His exit was disrupted by a chorus of "Nathan, stay for one more beer!"

Nathan's face became flushed. He pushed his way through the tight ring of men and pounded away at the center of the table.

"You fools," said Nathan through gritted teeth. "That bigger fool was just here on November first—right there on Daxlander Strasse. Fifty thousand proud Germans heard him." Nathan paused to regain his composure. "If he is such a joke, and if it will take such an effort from our fellow countrymen to hate us, then why do you sit here whispering like little children?" The Knights sat in silence and watched Nathan walk out and join his family, who in a matter of days became part of the 37,000 Jews to leave Germany over the next six months.

After Hitler's appointment, the efforts of hate did not abate. To the contrary, the knights watched with concern the one-day boycott of all Jewish businesses on April 1, 1933. The boycott was followed by the April 7, 1933, order that non-Aryans be fired from all civil service jobs and lawyers be denied admission to the bar. Then on April 21, 1933, legislation was passed banning kosher slaughtering under the guise of animal rights activism.

On May 9, 1933, Isack stood on the steps of the Karlsruhe police station and witnessed the renaming ceremony of the Marktplatz to the Adolf-Hitler-Platz. Weeks later on September 28, 1933, Isack read in the local newspapers that Jews were formally dismissed from all artistic, film, dramatic, and literary enterprises. The next day, Germany's Jews were banned from owning farmland in one of the more than four hundred anti-Jewish laws instituted from 1933 to 1939.

When Adolph Hitler's first year in office was completed, the chancellor of Germany who had sold only 3,015 copies of *Mein Kampf* in 1928 sold over one million copies. By 1940, the sale of six million copies of *Mein Kampf* made its author a millionaire.

When Nathan and his family emigrated out of Germany, Hitler's new Germany boasted a population of sixty-seven million. Five hundred and five thousand, or less than .75 percent of the overall population, were Jews. By the close of 1939, the Knights of the Round Table who remained in Karlsruhe were part of the 210,000 Jews living in Germany. Six years later when World War II came to an end, fifteen thousand Jews remained in Germany.

WOULD YOU LIKE TO DANCE?

Five years before an introspective Isack had that beer in January 1933, his twenty-two-year-old daughter met twenty-one-year-old Protestant Alfred Julius Walker. It became obvious to Ilse's girlfriends who danced in the smoke-filled beer garden that she was taken with the young man. "It is so loud in here," said the approaching man, "that I'm sure you can't hear a word I'm saying." He raised his voice above the music while Ilse clumsily dropped the makeup mirror she had been using to follow her obvious suitor. "My name is Alfred, but my friends call me Julius."

She puffed on her cigarette and meekly said, "I'm Ilse."

Julius's slender build at five feet seven inches was hidden by his thick, coarse brown sweater and the dark lighting. He looked huge compared to the willowy five-foot-one Ilse, who only sipped her beer. Ilse followed his hands that swatted the air in an effort to make some point over something unimportant while a distracting thatch of brown hair swung over his right eye. Seconds later, Ilse placed her hand over her mouth to conceal the smile brought on by Julius's slurred speech. His intoxicated state made no difference to a smitten Ilse as she and Julius talked and then danced to the American swing music that was played on the phonograph player.

"Ilse, my father is a boss at work," boomed Julius's voice. "But I want to be the boss. I live in his house, and he reminds me of this every day. He was a blacksmith, and now he works for the railroads. He got me a job with the railroads as an apprentice mechanic. I am the lowest man there, Ilse, but I make this promise! I will be the top man! Whatever it takes!"

Julius slapped both of his thighs in satisfaction of his declaration before he jumped on his chair. He threw his arms into the air and shouted, "I will make money, I will travel, I will have a beautiful wife and beautiful children. I will show all of them. And after I die and they bury me after a glorious procession down the Kaiserstrasse, they will all say Alfred Julius Walker was a great man!"

Ilse waved frantically for Julius to return to his seat, but it was too late. His inebriated admirers gathered around him and hoisted their clinking steins while they shouted "Prost." Julius took a final clumsy bow before he sat inches away from Ilse and took a deep breath that confirmed his exhaustion. Julius took out a handkerchief and wiped away the beads of sweat that trickled down the sides of his face before he burst into laughter. Soon Ilse and Julius fell forward in their chairs laughing so hard that tears came from their eyes. The sides of their heads gently touched. Julius placed a finger under Ilse's chin and, without saying a word, kissed Ilse Ettlinger.

A WALK

Weeks after Ilse and Julius met, they held hands as they walked down the Kaiserstrasse. The vision of three men in their distinctive Nazi Brownshirt uniforms getting out of a parked car caused the young couple to stop. The Nazis straightened each other's ties, swastika armbands, and caps before they locked arms and started marching toward the couple. Julius instinctively pushed Ilse behind him. Ilse's hand trembled at his back while he confidently nodded in response to the Nazi salutes and enthusiastic chorus of Heil Hitler. Julius and his friends had joked in the beer gardens about the Brownshirts and what they would do to them if there was a confrontation. Never afraid to fight, Julius knew on this occasion that talking would be a better option given Ilse's presence.

Although outnumbered and slowed by too many steins of beer, he could not control himself. "What a joke." The declaration of war found a fourth Brownshirt pushing past the wall of men.

"Hey you!" barked the disrespected thug. Ilse buried her face in Julius's back as the men glared at each other. Then inexplicably, the Brownshirt appeared to surrender. He placed his hands up in the air in front of a man who was clearly ready to fight. The Nazi lowered his hands slowly onto his victim's shoulders. "Julius Walker?"

Julius slowly unclenched his fists and answered, "Hans Tritschler?" The equally bizarre response left the men embracing in front of a confused Ilse and even more confused Brownshirts.

48

"Boys, this is Julius Walker. Our fathers worked together for years. Julius was my neighbor until we were twelve, thirteen years of age?" The old friend nodded in agreement as Hans looked at a silent Ilse and then back at Julius.

Julius looked at his friend. "So I see you are in the party. I never saw you in politics; soccer, beer, and girls, but never ever politics."

Hans spoke over the last words of Julius, "I am not in politics, Julius. I am in the SA There is a difference, my friend."

A preening Hans straightened his tie and pressed his tailored shirt against his flat stomach. "I was here in May when the führer spoke at the Festhalle. I looked for you, my friend, but you obviously moved." Julius nodded before the Nazi continued. "I heard from my parents that you are like our fathers, working for the railroads."

"Yes. It's hard work, but I think I have a good future, because the railroads have a good future. The economy is good, and in a few years I hope to become a supervisor and make some real money."

"You should think about things other than money," lectured Hans. "You should think about the SA and the future of the Aryans, the true Germans, my old friend."

One of the Nazi Brownshirts gave Julius a leaflet about the six Nazi Party candidates running for office in the upcoming May elections in Baden. "These true Germans need your votes: two farmers, one master artisan, a teacher, and two Nazi Party officials. They are good men," lectured Hans again. He put his hands back on the shoulders of Julius. "We need your help, my old friend."

While Hans gave one last embrace to a silent Julius, he whispered as he looked at Ilse, "Please give my best wishes to your parents and sister, Martha." There was one last smile between the men before Hans reminded Julius to vote and to "Think about what I said." When the Brownshirts were sufficiently far down the street, Julius looked at Ilse's shaken face. He answered the question that was never asked. "I don't care if it was strange; it was awkward for me too. Should I have introduced you?" Ilse was startled by Julius's aggressive tone until he put two fingers over his upper lip and gave a Nazi salute that left a laughing Ilse falling into Julius's arms. Two days later, when Ilse and Julius walked down the Kaiserstrasse, they could have cared less that Julius's friend and his Nazi Party emerged with only 2.9 percent of the votes cast in Karlsruhe.

During the ensuing months, Ilse's effortless white lies to her parents became an implicit affirmation that her faith and family had taken second place to her love for the skinny apprentice train mechanic. By the winter months of 1928 and 1929, the infrequent and awkward contacts between the once loving couple left Ilse unnerved. Panicked, she pushed for an explanation. "Ilse, what would you have me do when my supervisor tells me I am needed in Munich or I am needed in Berlin? I want to be the boss, Ilse, not the person who is told what to do." He tugged at his jaw. "You can't always be with the one you love."

The irony was not lost on Ilse, who was now the recipient of an endless string of transparent lies. Ilse's own lies ended when she finally told her parents about Julius. Ilse's futile effort at reconciliation with her parents left her with few options but to plead with the man she inexplicably loved. It was not until fourteen days before the birth of Heinz Walker on March 28, 1930, that Julius finally surrendered to Ilse's plea to marry her and therefore legitimize the birth of their child.

CHRISTMAS 1930

The familiar-sounding footsteps echoed as his thick legs slowly drove the one-inch-soled work boots onto the first step of the apartment building. The drumlike sound that announced his arrival banged fourteen more times until he paused at the second-floor landing to catch his breath. It had been less than two years since Ilse first met Julius. Even though he was still a young man of twenty-four, Julius looked ten years older from working many hours, smoking, and frequent hard drinking.

The boom of that first step initiated the unnecessary cleanup of the tiny fourth-floor attic apartment and a few quick brushes through Ilse's jet-black hair. It had been almost a month since she had seen him, and this unexpected Christmas Eve visit found Ilse alternatively smiling and trembling as she pulled at her simple gold wedding band. With the last boom Ilse clumsily unlocked the door while she tried to anticipate which version of her husband might be standing on the other side of the door.

"Good evening, Julius," said Ilse as the door squeaked open. He stood inside the frame of the doorway. Ilse gave him a polite kiss on the cheek while she removed his coat. He was drunk, but thankfully not the bad drunk that led to an argument and worse. He blinked his half-opened eyes on his way to the worn brown couch, where nine-month-old Heinz was sleeping. Ilse quickly loosened her tightly drawn apron before she timidly stepped toward her husband.

Ilse whispered, "He's sleeping. Please don't wake him, Julius. He has a cold and I finally..." The unhearing father picked up his snoring son and held him at arm's length. Julius smiled at the baby whose head fell backward. Ilse unthinkingly took Heinz and cradled the still sleeping baby in her arms. She studied Julius's sigh and the way he placed his hands on his hips for a sign of any perceived slight. Julius wiped his mouth with a dirty handkerchief while Ilse nervously returned her sleeping baby to the couch.

"Merry Christmas, Ilse," muttered Julius. "I have a Christmas present for you." Ilse's forehead wrinkled with three deep furrows while Julius placed a brown envelope on the only table in the apartment. He sat down and blew out the flame of the thick candle and rolled it over the envelope until the ripples disappeared. He carefully bent up the metal clasp of the envelope and pulled out the contents. "It's a photograph of you and one of Heinz. Do you like them, Ilse?"

"Yes, Julius, very much."

"Remember, Ilse? The photographer lent you the pearls to wear. You looked very beautiful that day, just like the day we met." He smiled at the images. "He is handsome like you, Ilse," he said, speaking with the slow slur of someone fighting to give the appearance that he is in control. Ilse blushed with the gift of the first compliment she had received in months, albeit one fostered by too many beers.

"Thank you for such a wonderful gift. It's too bad the stores will be closed tomorrow, because I would like to get some frames." Julius took out his filthy handkerchief and wiped his face. He searched for words that did not come. Ilse took advantage of the momentary pause. "Are you hungry?" asked Ilse while she ladled out some cold soup and placed it and a thick piece of stale bread on the table. Julius buried his face in the bowl and slurped away at his food.

Ilse placed a fist-size piece of coal in the stove and prodded it with a metal poker. She closed her eyes. "Julius, I want to thank you again for the wonderful Christmas present." Ilse cleared her throat. "And I have a present for you too. A Christmas present, and an early birthday present." She wiped away at the crumbless counter and tried to think of something else to clean as her audience finally picked up his head. Ilse turned to her husband and took off her loosened apron.

Julius's eyelids fought to remain open. "What are you talking about, Ilse?" There was no hint of emotion in his voice. He yawned. "I don't understand."

Ilse pressed her blouse against her stomach. "Heinz is going to have a brother or sister. You are going to be a father again in the middle of May. Maybe even on your birthday." She stammered out the last words, "So this is my present."

"Ilse, you have not worked since Heinz was born—my job barely pays enough for me, let alone all of you—I don't know how I can do this—two children and you. My God..." Julius's head fell back and his eyelids momentarily closed over pink eyes. His deep sigh stirred the sleeping baby. Julius jerked forward, placed his chin on his fists, and shook his head as he engaged in a private conversation. He spilled out the contents of a nearby box and pushed aside buttons and other odds and ends until he found a silver pen.

"What are you doing, Julius?" asked Ilse. There was no answer while he wrote on the back of the photograph of her. Ilse bit the nails on her right hand until Julius placed the pen down and smiled. "This is for you."

Ilse quivered while she read the few words. She shocked herself when she unthinkingly slapped Julius. Ilse anxiously twirled the rough edges of her gold wedding band up and looked at her waking baby. Her lips trembled. "Get out, Julius! Get out!"

While Julius wiped away the tiny droplets of blood from his right cheek, Ilse prayed that her emotional outburst would not be met with a like response. She backed into a corner of the small room and watched Julius stare at his rose-stained handkerchief before he placed the photographs in the envelope.

After Julius left the apartment on Christmas Eve 1930, the devastating realities of a future without Ilse's parents and a father for her children was almost more than she could bear. But she allowed herself little time for self-pity. Instead, she pushed herself to find employment as a seamstress and maid. She also humbled herself by accepting assistance of money, food, and clothing from her brother and ever-shrinking group of friends.

At the same time, Sophie's estrangement from Ilse was filled with painful irony given her own choices that resulted in the loss of family and an existence in a loveless marriage. Sophie's well-intentioned decision to keep secret from a young Ilse her own past and her initial deference to Isack's expulsion of Ilse left her uncertain. Eventually Sophie made a defying decision that drove a final wedge between herself and Isack. And with that decision made, she forged ahead with a loving relationship with Ilse and little Heinz. Emboldened by each stolen moment, Sophie repeated her own white lie to Ilse after each kiss good-bye. "I'm sure your father knows that I have been bringing you food, money, and clothing, but he doesn't ever say a word. I know he wants me here. Just write him a letter. Talk about the baby, about your pregnancy. I'm sure Poppa will make it right with you."

Years later on January 31, 1933, Isack, overwhelmed by the losses of family and country, sat silently in a café as the Knights of the Round Table ridiculed Adolph Hitler, the new chancellor of Germany.

THE SEPARATION

Ilse scanned the booths in the Platz for stale crusts of bread that were given to children. When Ilse heard the familiar "hello" she counted the number of weeks it had been since she had talked to Julius. "I understood you were working in Munich. What a surprise to see you here," said Ilse sarcastically.

"I was planning on stopping by to see you," answered Julius.

Ilse's teeth ground away as she listened to the beginning of another lie. "My parents told me they saw you and Heinz. They were happy to learn that your pregnancy is going well." An unresponsive Ilse sat on a nearby bench to rest her cramping legs. "Let's not avoid it, Ilse," pressed Julius. "The truth is we do need to talk. After my expenses there is little money left. We can't afford two children. I work..."

"What do you mean 'we'? I support your son, and with no help from you!"

"I don't want to fight with you," smiled Julius while the staring citizens of Karlsruhe walked by the arguing couple. "The truth is you have not done it alone. I know your mother and my parents have been helping you."

Ilse shook her head in disgust and massaged her legs. Julius moved closer to Ilse. "I came to Karlsruhe because my parents wanted to talk to me about Heinz. They have made an offer of help. A practical offer, until I get myself a better paying job with the railroads. Until I get myself more settled."

"What does that mean?" said Ilse while Heinz sucked on a piece of hard crust.

"My parents will take Heinz in for a while, until we figure this out. That way you can give the baby the attention it will need. Then, when I find myself in a better position, we can be together."

Ilse felt ill and covered her mouth. "We have no options," said Julius. He smiled once again at the passing strangers. "You know your father will never help."

"And you, Julius? Everyone but you! Your parents, my parents, me, but never you! You're only talking to me because of a chance meeting," interrupted Ilse.

An unnerved Julius squeezed Ilse's arm and snarled, "Be quiet."

"Heinz is right here. Doesn't the father want to hold him? Doesn't the father want to ask a question about his son?"

Julius dismissed the provocative questions. "I'll be in town until tomorrow. Tell my mother when she should come to the apartment."

In the early morning hours of May 17, 1931, Ilse's friend Helga Sprauer hurried to both Ilse's and Julius's parents' homes. Minutes later, Julius's mother, Luise Walker, charged up the stairs to the tiny attic apartment where Ilse was preparing to leave for the Jewish hospital. It was only minutes more before Sophie was embracing her anguished-looking daughter on the street in front of her apartment. The moon fell behind a single cloud in the sky. "Ilse, who is that with little Heinz?" asked Sophie as she released her daughter.

Ilse groaned with another contraction. "Please, Frau Ettlinger," cried Helga. "We need to get Ilse to the hospital!"

THE DIVORCE, 1934

In the months prior to the introduction of the many anti-Jewish laws of 1934 and 1935, 4,700 daily German newspapers favorably editorialized about the anticipated restrictions. The 1934 laws that made former friends suspicious of their Jewish neighbors also made the infrequent contacts between Heinz and his new little brother, Kurt, dangerous. Those circumstances forced Ilse to agree with the Walkers to end Kurt's attendance at a Catholic preschool where the laughing brothers were repeatedly scolded by the nuns for stealing apple slices. In the days that followed, Kurt was inconsolable as he cried for his best friend, Heinz.

She also understood that her visits to see Heinz in the Walkers' home, where Kurt received extra food and hand-me-down clothes, had to end. Nonetheless, Ilse made sure to keep the brothers of this fractured family together. "Thank you," said Ilse each time Helga brought Kurt to Heinz so the Walkers would be protected from the ever-increasing scrutiny of Ilse's presence.

It took only another year to make a wave of Ilse's hand to Heinz impossible. On September 15, 1935, the harsh Nuremberg Laws imposed further national restrictions on Germany's Jews. In part, the laws prohibited marriage between Jews and Germans and the displaying by Jews of the Reich flag. Two months later, the Reich's declaration that, "A Jew cannot be a Reich citizen. He is not entitled to vote on political matters; he cannot hold public office..." brought Hitler congratulations from throughout the world.

The 1934 German newspaper editorials left a fearful Ilse taking frequent walks past her parents' apartment. But she never had the courage to stop—until a Friday night in 1934, when a complicit Sophie opened the door. No words were spoken when Sophie nervously kissed Ilse and Kurt before she returned to her bedroom. Ilse placed Kurt on the floor and watched him run to the seated stranger with the closely cropped gray beard. Other than a stolen moment of seeing Kurt on the Kaiserstrasse with his mother or seeing him sitting by the pyramid on the Hitler-Platz, this was the first time Isack had been near his grandson. Nonetheless, he refused to acknowledge his expected guests while he pretended to read his newspaper and enjoy the last of his bread and boiled vegetables.

A reflective Ilse stood in the Spartan single-bedroom apartment. There was no telephone, no radio, and only the same few pieces of furniture from her childhood. She smiled at her father and his resourcefulness that allowed for the potbelly stove to be surrounded by stacks of newspapers, which doubled as fuel and toilet paper.

Ilse kissed Isack. "Good evening, Vater."

Isack pointed to the chair and then to the plate of bread while he continued to read. Ilse maintained her smile. "No thank you, Vater." The newspaper that covered Isack's face only intensified her anticipated apprehension. The chill went unnoticed by a three-and-a-half-year-old boy who happily ran in circles around the table. When a dizzy Kurt finally stopped, he climbed onto a chair and pointed at the newspaper.

"Opa Isack, Mutti?"

Before Ilse could answer, Kurt grabbed a piece of bread and took two quick bites. "Ask before you take, Kurt," said Ilse. Kurt seemed on the verge of tears as he slowly put the bread back.

"You cannot have a piece of bread," volunteered Isack while he methodically folded the newspaper. "But you can have two." Kurt's face went from devastation to confusion to a smile before the bread vanished with three quick bites. Isack asked his young guest, "Do you want to play with Gretel?" The feral cat that had followed Isack home only days earlier finally served a purpose, thought Isack. "She sleeps behind my desk. But be careful, she scratches."

Kurt threw himself on the floor and asked the sleeping cat, "Gretel, do you want to play?"

Ilse's shallow breaths returned to normal with her father's unexpected kindness. "So, Ilse, your mother tells me you wish to talk to me about a problem. A new problem, I should say," observed Isack. "My question is why don't you talk to your husband or his gentile parents?" Ilse's heart sank and her breathing became labored.

"Why do you come to me, a poor Jewish man who has nothing to offer? Your mother can confirm that, but as you can see, she is not here."

And so it began. Years of pent up anger came flooding out as Isack listed Ilse's violations of the Torah. Ilse said "Vater" three times before she was able to complete a sentence. "Vater, if it's all right with you, I would like to answer your question. Julius cannot help me with this problem." Ilse pushed the folded papers toward her father. Isack reached for his reading glasses. "I need help, Papa. Not just for me, but..." Ilse looked at Kurt, who was asleep on the floor next to a purring Gretel.

Julius Walker and Ilse had been reading the same newspapers that editorialized about the anticipated Reich laws. The laws determined that children who had at least two Jewish grandparents were to be considered Jews or Mischlinge of the first degree. Gentiles that married a Jew were also considered Jews. For Julius Walker, the establishment of these laws would become insurmountable roadblocks toward his singular goal of becoming the boss. Whatever hesitation had stopped Julius Walker from confronting those obstacles disappeared with his reading of an article published in a local Karlsruhe newspaper. The banner article about the Heidelberg man who obtained a divorce caught Julius Walker's attention. He made sure to give a copy to Ilse when he placed the official-looking documents in her hands. She read the brief story about the husband who received a divorce from his Jewish wife because he had "...not known the full concept of this race." Months after the March 3, 1934, ruling, when Ilse accepted the papers from Julius Walker, she knew she could no longer walk past her father's home.

Ilse tearfully looked at her sleeping son and then at her father. She stammered, "I know...I have disappointed you. I know that I have made mistakes, and I am paying for them now. I only see Heinz on the streets and even then I don't think he recognizes me." Ilse pulled out a picture of Heinz and placed it in front of Isack. "Vater, he is still yours. Just like Kurt is yours. Don't punish them because of my choices. Julius will get his divorce, but I want at least one of the boys. I have nothing. I have lost..." Her voice trailed off before she regained her composure. "Please help me."

"I will always love you, Ilse, but I can never forgive you. And you are correct. Kurt should not be punished." The old man tugged on his beard. "Yes, you can live in this house, but I will be Kurt's legal guardian. I will make the decisions about Kurt. You may be the mother, but this little one will not make the mistakes that you've made. So you tell your husband he can have his divorce. You tell him I will be the legal guardian of Kurt. Tell him that this Jewish boy stays with us. And as much as he wants to deny it, his Heinz is just like Kurt. The Ettlingers will not be afraid to say that these babies are Jews."

When a spying Sophie heard Isack stand up and push his chair away from the table, she cracked open her bedroom door. "But most of all, you tell Julius Walker that in the next election when his führer is defeated, you will take Heinz back. Julius Walker wants to be a big man and will do whatever it takes to succeed. Bodies on the street only become steps for him to walk up. So he says to himself, I can't be a big man, a successful man, if I'm married to a Jewess and have two little Mischlinge." Kurt stirred, and Isack lowered his voice. "So you give him his divorce and then you tell him I said to go to hell!"

In May 1933, months before Ilse met with her father, the union of the Reichsbahn's railway employees was shut down and its leaders were replaced by members of the Nazi Party. In that same year, all train employees, including those in the repair shops, were ordered to attend classes and speeches regarding Nazi ideology. Following the Nazification of railroad employees and the death of the eighty-six-year-old president of Germany, Paul Von Hindenburg, a vote was held on August 19, 1934, to approve the consolidation of the position of chancellor and president of Germany. With the approval of 90 percent of the German voters,

Hitler's goal of complete power over Germany was attained. The next day, Julius Walker, the man who wanted to be a boss and who had laughed at his old friend Nazi Brownshirt Hans Tritschler, became a civil servant of the Nazi railways. Julius Walker glanced at his observant supervisors and repeated his oath as a member of the Nazi Brownshirts:

"I swear: I will be obedient to the leader of the German state and people, Adolph Hitler, to observe the law, and to conscientiously fulfill my duties, so help me God!"

THE STOLEN APPLE

After Ilse's plea for help was accepted at the minimal cost of her own independence and the extraordinary cost of transferring Kurt's legal guardianship to her father, she settled into a secure life in her parents' apartment. For Isack, his solitary days over the ensuing months ended each night with a silent dinner with his daughter, grandson, and the occasional boarders making their way out of Germany. Sophie isolated herself even more by retreating for days to the only bedroom in the apartment. Her curious behavior left an independent Kurt alone for hours, where he was content to entertain himself by watching a hissing Gretel terrorize dogs that dared to walk past the first-floor apartment window. It tore at Ilse to see the once-loving relationship that Sophie had with Kurt inexplicably disintegrate into a scream of "Leave my things alone!" or "Get out of my room!" Kurt responded to the frequent outbursts by mimicking Isack when he mumbled in Yiddish, "Such a Verbissener."

No longer free to make any important decisions about Kurt or her own life, Ilse maintained a low profile. She contributed her meager earnings as a maid and seamstress to the family, shopped for food, prepared meals, cleaned the apartment, and washed clothes on a washboard at the cold water tap in the kitchen sink. More importantly, Ilse made sure to spend time with Kurt. Each Sunday Ilse took heated water from the black potbelly stove and poured it over a screaming Kurt while he sat in a metal tub. "Close your eyes, Kurtela. You don't want any soap to get in your eyes!" laughed Ilse. But no time was more special for an exhausted Ilse than when she sang Kurt's favorite folk songs before they fell asleep and dreamed of better times.

On rare occasions when Kurt went with his mother to clean the homes of generous, rich Jewish families, he did not need dreams to enjoy a fresh salad and something he only saw on important Jewish holidays, chicken. For an undemanding Kurt, a hissing Gretel, a few marbles, a top that he pushed along the cobblestone road in front of his home, and a single treasured copy of his Max and Moritz comic book left him both content and oblivious to the complicated world he lived in.

But no matter how oblivious Kurt was to the world, he could not escape Isack's gruff demeanor, leaving him and his mother unquestionably compliant. After Kurt moved into his grandparents' home he was immediately enrolled into a Jewish preschool where he received used clothes and a morning meal of bread and schmaltz seasoned with salt. Before Kurt's enrollment in preschool, Isack brought him to the Jewish hospital in Karlsruhe. Hours later, a terrified Kurt ran into his mother's arms.

Isack declared, "The mohel was away and this could not wait! Now with this circumcision, Kurt has entered into a covenant with Abraham to begin his journey to become a good Jew. And with this covenant, there will be no gentiles living in this house!" Tears of the only person who did not understand the meaning of what had occurred filled the room.

Months later, when Kurt sat upon a moist mound of dirt, he saw a vague outline of a chunky middle-aged man pacing back and forth in the darkness. "I'm sorry. I know…" said Kurt just before five fat fingers grabbed at his shirt and lifted him in the air. The man, who had heard enough, felt for the shadowy area of the nearby open four-foot door and threw Kurt into the tiny room. After Kurt came to a rest atop the mound of spoiled vegetables, he spit dirt and blood from his mouth as he spoke. "But I …" was all he was able to say before the slamming door made it so black in Kurt's tiny prison that he could not see his hand. With his heart racing, Kurt crawled toward a gray sliver of light and placed his ear against the splintery door where the sounds of the wheezing man's mutterings, "Fucking Jews and Gypsies" eventually faded with each step taken up the stairs. "No, no!" cried Kurt.

When the growling refrain of "Fucking Jews and Gypsies" woke Kurt hours later, he knew the recent past had not been a dream. His muscles tensed when a bear-sized hand carried him up the stairs and dragged him like a sack of potatoes out of the small store and onto a side street off the Kaiserstrasse. Tearful and filthy, Kurt ran past laughing spectators until, mercifully, he pushed opened the front door to his apartment building. Afraid to enter his apartment, Kurt hid in the small alcove repeating, "Opa, Mutti, I'm sorry."

When Kurt looked through the small glass panel of the apartment building door he could seek Isack approaching. He wiped his blackened face in a hopeless effort to avoid the inevitable question.

"My God! What is it this time?" asked an exasperated Isack upon seeing his filthy grandson. Kurt buried his head in his lap in a childlike hope that Isack might disappear. The Ettlinger mode of communication, silence, found the old man waving Kurt into the apartment and then to the kitchen sink, where he began to wash Kurt's face.

Kurt wished his grandfather would speak, eliminating the painful silence that preceded his inevitable punishment. But it was Kurt who finally spoke as tears began to dot his muddy clothes. "It was about a stolen apple, Opa," said Kurt haltingly. Isack listened intently to the story about the apple, the store owner, the run home, and then finally a promise to never do it again. The old man rubbed his hands against the back of his neck while Kurt trembled. Isack pointed to his old chair with the faded blue cushion.

Blinded by tears, Kurt could not see that the patriarch of the family was shaken by the fear he witnessed in Kurt. Isack tried to call upon the wisdom he thought he once had as a young father. Instead, he turned his back on Kurt, because he knew the truth, he was afraid. Isack searched for the right words to replace one awkward sentence after another until he looked at Kurt's gray face.

"Kurt..."

"Yes, Opa?"

"Have you ever seen my library?"

Kurt's "no" to the bizarre question saw Isack extending an open hand that was slowly filled. "This may look like a desk, but I can assure you that it is not just a desk. Each drawer holds the most important documents and papers in the world."

In that moment, Kurt's fears vanished with the pronouncement that the desk was so much more than what it appeared to be. Kurt swept his hand over the library. "What kind of papers does it have, Opa?" Kurt took a step away from the piece of furniture that he had seen every day for over a year. "Treasure maps, Opa?"

Kurt was startled by his grandfather's laughing response. "No treasure maps. But there are photographs of my family and records of the Ettlingers that go back to 1714 in Ettlingen." Isack saw that Kurt was disappointed with his answer. He corrected himself with his faded recollection of "...at least one treasure map buried under all of my other papers." Kurt's face lit up with excitement from the extracted promise that no one could know about the maps other than Kurt and his grandfather.

"What other papers do you have, Opa?" asked Kurt.

Tapping fingers and a momentary look out the window that somehow triggered memories of the past preceded Isack's response. "Kurt, do you like fairy tales?" Kurt did not answer. Instead, he watched his grandfather pull back the creaking roll top of the desk, exposing the numerous cubbyholes and stacks of books. Isack pointed once again to his old chair. Kurt sprinted to it while Isack pored over the books until an "ah yes!" filled the room. Isack opened the familiar book of *Grimm's Fairy Tales* and skimmed through the faded yellow pages.

"This one is my favorite, Kurt," smiled Isack before he joined Kurt. "It's called Hansel and Gretel." Isack gently ran his fingers over the familiar pages. The unexpected pause saw Kurt shaking his grandfather's arm. Isack looked momentarily at Kurt before he read. "Close to a large forest there lived a woodcutter with his wife and two children. The boy was called Hansel and the girl was called Gretel." Kurt's smile remained until a sense of sadness overtook him with the turning of the last page. The old man took Kurt's finger and pointed at the last few words. Slowly they read, "...So all their troubles came to an end, and they lived together as happily as possible."

Kurt was thankful for the long pause that allowed him to inspect the simple drawing of the scary witch. When Kurt picked his head up to begin his request to read the story one more time, he saw a single tear climbing down the wrinkles on his grandfather's face. Kurt pulled Isack's face into a smile before he kissed him. "Opa, it is not a sad story. It is a happy story. Everything will be all right with them."

HEINRICH WEIL,
AUGUST 9, 1936

When the car pulled up to the apartment building at Markgrafenstrasse 1, Kurt turned to his best friend and yelled, "Opa, I think they are here!" An anxious Sophie and Ilse quickly finished putting the holiday dishes on the table, while an indifferent-appearing Isack closed the squeaky drawer to his library. Kurt jumped onto the window ledge like an American cowboy and kicked his right arm and leg until he gained the attention of the arguing couple.

"Good afternoon. I'm Kurt Walker," squealed Kurt's introduction while Gretel crawled over his shoulders and purred uncharacteristically like a domestic house cat. "Opa, they have a car and it is blue!" screamed Kurt.

"Shush, Kurt," said Isack. "Enough! Now come away from that window and throw Gretel in the bedroom."

After a hissing Gretel was thrown behind the closing door, Kurt ran to the front door and wrapped his hands around the worn knob. When the expectant knock was heard, an impatient Kurt looked to Isack, who gave the nod that allowed him to open the door. Isack tugged at his sleeves and pulled at his tie before he shook hands with his brother-in-law, Heinrich, and kissed his sister-in-law, Lina. The silence between family members who had not seen each other in years ended with Isack's proud announcement, "This is my grandson, Kurt."

Kurt mimicked his grandfather and threw his hand out, which was warmly received by his great-uncle Heinrich Weil. Isack looked back and nodded at a waiting Ilse and Sophie. They rushed to a welcoming Heinrich while Lina acknowledged Kurt with a stiff smile. Heinrich brushed the hair off of Ilse's face. He glowed over her. "Still the most beautiful girl in the world! Time has not changed that!"

"Thank you, Onkel. It's so wonderful to see you after all these years," said Ilse, who buried her smiling face into Heinrich's chest. And while Ilse talked with Heinrich, Sophie approached Lina, who stood away from the small group.

"So good to see you too," said Sophie as she briefly embraced her sister-in-law. Sophie could feel Lina's muscles tighten through her thin expensive silk blouse before she awkwardly stepped away.

An observant Isack called out to Kurt. "Why don't you go outside and play with your friend Fritz?"

Kurt pulled at the coat of his grandfather's black synagogue suit. "But Opa, they just got here. I want to visit too."

Isack looked into Kurt's eyes. "You already ate. I am not asking you. Now please do as I say." Kurt's shoulders dropped. He grabbed his Max and Moritz comic book and stomped out of the apartment. Seconds after his echoing statement of displeasure ended, a barefoot Kurt crawled back to the closed door. He pressed his face firmly against the wooden floor and jealously watched the moving shoes while he tried to listen to the muffled conversations.

The money Isack borrowed to ensure the Sabbathlike feast of dumpling soup, preserved pike, tongue with peas, roast goose salad with hardboiled eggs, dessert, and coffee brought forth the compliments he desired. Upon completion of the satisfying meal that told Heinrich and Lina Weil just how well Isack Ettlinger was doing, came the stiff conversation between people burdened by the past. When Lina excused herself to go to the communal bathroom, the sound of Lina's approaching shoes barely gave Kurt enough time to hide in the alcove just outside the apartment. When the door opened, Kurt heard his grandmother do something he had not heard her do in months. Sophie laughed, "Yes, Ilse, Heinrich did call me Mutti Sophie."

However, with Lina's return, the room once again became cold and uninviting. Heinrich's eyes caught those of his sister as he attempted to rescue the moment. "So I am leaving on the twelfth for America."

"Yes, how exciting," smiled Sophie, who waved the two-week-old letter from her brother that told of his departure.

"I'm so happy that we can spend this time together before the train takes me to Cherbourg," continued Heinrich as he received a glaring stare from his wife. Heinrich twisted in his chair. "How long do you think it will take to get to the Bahnhof from here, Isack?"

"Thirty minutes if you have to walk, but I understand," grinned Isack, "that you have a blue vehicle, so it should only take a few minutes."

Heinrich attacked another uncomfortable moment of silence. "Then after I arrive in America, Lina and Rolf will follow me in December. Hopefully by then I will have secured employment and housing. I fully…"

Lina insincerely apologized for interrupting her husband. "I never asked Ilse, but how is your Kurt doing? You know, it's a shame that Rolf and Kurt have never met." This time Lina did not apologize for interrupting an answer that she had no interest in. "Isack, did you know last summer we sent Rolf to Switzerland for French lessons at Lausanne's Ecole de Commerce? If Kurt is inclined, you should consider it."

Isack's silence both fulfilled his promise to Sophie and dismissed Lina. He looked at his brother-in-law.

"I saw in the *Sign of the Flame,* how the Nazis wrote about your influence with your employer," said Isack. "It's so nice to know that the Stuttgart headquarters of the Singer Sewing Company is not run by its Aryan president who is a former World War I U-boat commander but by a powerful, behind-the-scenes Vollblutjude, full-blooded Jew, such as yourself."

Heinrich sarcastically added, "You know when they did the census in 1933, the Reich proudly proclaimed that there were sixty-seven million Germans, of which only four hundred thousand were German Jews. Isack, you were always good with numbers, what is that? Less than one percent? So I ask you, how could so few be the cause of Germany's problems? We truly are the supermen of Germany."

"You are wrong, Heinrich. Not Germany but the world!" answered Isack as the men savored a hearty laugh. "But you know, Heinrich, with every superman that leaves Germany it does leave the rest of us a little weaker. You are a veteran, wealthy and educated. They won't do anything to you. Even simple Jews like me have learned to be content with our lives. Remember, while we are proud to be Jews, we are also proud to be Germans regardless of what he says."

Heinrich refused to be drawn into a debate. He also refused to discuss his recent meeting in Paris, the European headquarters for the Singer Company, which sealed his fate. The reality was that the Nazis had won Heinrich's dismissal. The Singer Company's options for Heinrich in Budapest, Hungary, and Ankara, Turkey, were dismissed by him as unrealistic. An offer as a store manager in Jaffa was also dismissed when his visit to the store during an outbreak of conflict between Jews and Arabs resulted in his witnessing two Jews being shot in front of the location. Heinrich's eventual request for a transfer to America was denied given the ongoing economic depression and his poor command of English. Ultimately, this newly unemployed German Jewish veteran of World War I, who was determined to get his family out of Germany, was left with no option other than to accept the offer of a yearlong severance at $25 per week.

A seething Lina advanced a defense of sorts for her husband. "Did you know that Heinrich is going on the *Aquitania* to America and in first class? The ship has a movie theater. It's the sister ship of the *Queen Mary*. You have heard about the *Queen Mary*, Isack?"

Isack exploded, "They can't do a thing to a war hero. Yet alone a war hero wounded in defense of Germany." Isack stood up and pointed at Heinrich. "You were born in Germany. They are no better than you. Your home is Germany!"

"You can't be serious, Isack," said a shocked Heinrich. "Do you actually believe it is safe here? I think we can agree that last year's Nuremburg laws did not help us!"

"Things have been fine recently," answered Isack.

"Fine?" shouted Heinrich. "Wait until the Olympics are over in Berlin. Did you see how they took down the 'Jews Not

Welcome' signs? They want to impress the world with the achievements of a Third Reich that does not want to deal with the Jewish distraction. So what do they do? They take down a few signs. Yesterday I heard on the radio that Hitler refused to shake hands with the American Negro Jesse Owens after he won his third gold medal. I hope he wins more and drags the German flag on the ground.

"How can you say fine, Isack? In 1933, when our great führer came to power, he immediately started taking our rights away. In '34, the Jews were removed from the stock exchanges and then last year with the Nuremburg laws...why, we can't even vote. Isack, we aren't Germans anymore. We aren't citizens. In three years we lost everything that was gained in the prior two hundred years. You are no better off than when the margrave invited the Jews to become his subjects. And if you want to gamble with your life, fine, but..." He stopped in midsentence and drew a cautious breath. "And if you think Kurt's father will be here to protect all of you, then you are a fool," exclaimed Heinrich as Ilse and Sophie held hands under the table.

Kurt wondered why his unspoken-of father would be able to help. When the legs of the chairs scraped against the floor, followed seconds later by the unmistakable sounds of clicking shoes, a trapped Kurt stood at the opening door. Isack's voice spilled out into the hallway. "Please, leave whenever you want..."

Sophie and Ilse begged the men to sit down and enjoy their dessert while a barefoot Kurt ran down the hallway and out onto the street. He dragged his hand down the side of the enormous blue car until he saw fourteen-year-old Rolf pick his head up from his book. The cousins waved at each other until Lina brushed past Kurt on her way into the car.

"Are you going so soon, Onkel?" asked Kurt upon seeing his flustered uncle. Lina screamed from inside the car, "Now!"

Heinrich touched Kurt's shoulder as the driver's door violently flew open. He looked back at his wife and then at Kurt. "I hope to see you again, Kurt." An even louder "Now!" ended the brief exchange before the car, containing a waving Rolf, sped away.

On December 31, 1936, well after the Olympics concluded and the "Jews Not Welcome" signs were returned in full view of the German people, Lina and Rolf Weil arrived in the United States of America. Within a few days they were reunited with Heinrich in their new home in the Hyde Park neighborhood of Chicago, Illinois.

KRISTALLNACHT, THE NIGHT OF BROKEN GLASS, NOVEMBER 9–10, 1938

"We haven't a Pfennig. Can you send us something to Lodz?"

Postcard sent from Berta Grynszpan to her brother, Herschel Grynszpan, dated October 31, 1938

In the weeks before November 9, 1938, the limited portions of bread, jam, and milk provided by Kurt's Jewish school ensured an almost 100 percent attendance by the hungry children. Strangely, Stanislaw, one of Kurt's few friends, had been missing in the days leading up to November 9. After Kurt left school that day, he arrived at the stoop of his friend's apartment building. His repeated screams of "Stan" went unanswered. Annoyed, Kurt trudged to the third-floor apartment where he looked at the unreachable worn metal door knocker that hung at apartment number 5. Kurt's gentle kicks to the door brought no response. He placed the extra jam sandwich for Stan on the floor and pressed his back against the door while he sent his favorite red-and-blue marble pinging against the wall in the narrow hallway. "If Stan moved, why didn't he tell me?" questioned Kurt before he bit into the sandwich.

When Kurt finally arrived home, his anxious grandfather met him on his way downstairs from the apartment of Gustav, the barber. "Kurt, where have you been?" screamed Isack as he dragged Kurt into their apartment. "Enough with you in the streets alone! I want you home immediately after school! No more without your Opa!"

The frenetic old man's family gathered around Isack while he hung thick blankets over the windows. "I just heard on the radio in Gustav's apartment," panted Isack, "that vom Rath, a diplomat, was murdered in France. Himmler called the shooting a Jewish-inspired world conspiracy against Germany." Isack spoke quickly as he hammered the last nails. "He said that unless all the Jews turn in their firearms, they will be placed in protective custody." Isack sat down in the darkened room and wiped the sweat from his face. "Now all of you listen to me," whispered Isack as he stared at Kurt. "We do not go outside for a few days. We stay in the apartment. I talked to Gustav. He will go to the market for us until it's safe."

"Safe for what, Opa?" asked Kurt.

On October 16, 1938, the Polish government issued a decree that passports of Polish citizens were to be rescinded by the end of October unless a special permit granting reentry into Poland was obtained. The Polish government's intentional delay in the processing of the necessary papers for its Jews, who had lived in Germany for decades, was part of a developing strategy to deport them to the island of Madagascar. These actions drew close scrutiny from the Reich government that declared it would not be the dumping ground for the unwanted.

Days before Kurt went looking for Stan, Adolph Hitler ordered the expulsion of Polish Jews living in Germany. With no notice, terrorized Polish Jews were taken at the point of a bayonet to the Bahnhofs of Germany. During the methodical processing,

Nazi authorities and former neighbors seized every piece of the Jews' forfeited personal property. By the second day, the German Reich reported that twelve thousand Jews were abandoned at a Polish border town in what became known as the Zbaszyn Deportation.

On November 4, 1938, an outraged seventeen-year-old Polish Jew, Herschel Grynszpan, sat in Paris reading a Yiddish newspaper's graphic accounting of suicides and horrific living conditions resulting from the massive deportation. On the following Sunday morning, Grynszpan went to 61 Rue du Faubourg Saint Martin and entered gunsmith M. Carpe's store, A La Fine Lane, the Sharp Blade, and purchased a gun. On Monday, November 7, at 9:30 a.m. he took a train to the German embassy at 78 Rue de Lille armed with a 6.35 caliber gun loaded with five bullets. When Grynszpan was greeted by Third Secretary Ernst vom Rath under the pretext of providing documents, he pointed his pistol with the price tag of 235 francs still attached by a red string. He screamed, "You are a filthy Boche, and here in the name of twelve thousand persecuted Jews are your documents."

Of the five shots fired by a shaking Grynszpan, two of them hit his intended target. On the evening of November 9, 1938, German radio observed two minutes of silence after announcing that Ernst vom Rath had succumbed to his wounds from the Jewish assassin, Herschel Grynszpan. Six days earlier, Herschel Grynszpan had received a postcard from his sister, Bertha, who was stranded at the German Polish border. The brief note stated in part,

```
"...A police van brought all of us right away
to the Rusthaus. All were brought there. We
were not told what it was about, but we saw that
```

everything was finished for us.... We don't have a Pfenning. Can you send us something to Lodz?"

The murder of the German diplomat became the pretext for the events that terrorized all the Jews of Germany over the next twenty-four hours. The meticulously planned national offensive was led in Karlsruhe by college professor Mikuleit. Later, his fame brought him free beers and applause in the local cafés and beer halls, but only after he first recreated that moment at 2:00 a.m. when he assembled the flying squads of enthusiastic Nazi Brownshirts thugs. He regaled each audience with how he demanded silence from his SA men regarding the "...Most Urgent Telegram from Munich..."

He dramatically produced from the breast pocket of his crisp uniform the original telegram from that night to each subsequent applauding crowd before he continued with his performance.

"I know you have all heard the rumors on this, the fifteenth anniversary of the führer's failed Nazi putsch. I will read to you orders I received tonight.

"Re: Measures against Jews tonight

Following the attempt on the life of Secretary of the Legation vom Rath in Paris, demonstrations against Jews are to be expected in all parts of the Reich in the course of the coming night, November 910, 1938. The instructions below are to be applied in dealing with these events:...

a) Only such measures are to be taken as do not endanger German lives or property (i.e.,

```
synagogues are to be burned down only where
there  is  no  danger  of  fire  in  neighboring
buildings).

b) Places of business and apartments belong-
ing to Jews may be destroyed, but not looted...
Special care is to be taken that the Jews ar-
rested in accordance with these instructions
are not ill-treated...

    Richard Heydrich
    SS Gruppenführer"
```

Despite the order to use "special care," centuries-old anti-Jewish hatred, fueled by the Treaty of Versailles and anti-Jewish laws that legitimized a Jewish second class, Karlsruhe's Nazi Brownshirts became even more ferocious. The results were the destruction of Jewish property, the arrest and indiscriminate beating of Jewish men, and the detention of women until their husbands turned themselves in to the Nazis. For the terrified Ettlingers, secreted away in their apartment, a night of constant screams, sounds of breaking glass, and the smell of thick, acrid smoke left them waiting for the inevitable kick at their door. Thankfully, an imprisoned Kurt would not be burdened by the memories of humiliated Jews reading from Hitler's autobiography or being forced to urinate on the smoldering walls of the Ettlinger synagogue, bonfires consuming prayer books and Torah scrolls, or laughing Brownshirts striking the skull of a fleeing Jew. Nor would Kurt have the memories of weeping Christians witnessing a tragedy that forever defined Germany.

Inexplicably, while the rampaging squadrons of Nazi Brownshirts carried out their orders, there was never a kick at the Ettlingers' door. Two days after the flames smoldered and the screams ended, Kurt learned that his uncle Julius, along with hundreds of other Jewish men, some older than seventy years of age, was arrested. Continually beaten and deprived of food and water by armed guards until 11:00 p.m. on the evening of November 10, Julius and some of the other men were transferred to various camps such as Dachau, Buchenwald, and Sachsenhausen for an undetermined period of hard labor. During the twenty-four hours of the pogrom, ninety-one German Jews were killed and more than thirty thousand were arrested. Of the approximate three thousand Jews that were sent to the camps, two thousand were released over the next few months. Fortunately Kurt's uncle Julius was not among the one thousand Jews that were murdered. Upon his return home, a different Julius discovered a Karlsruhe where its Jews looked at the ground when they walked and where they were forbidden to go to the theater, concerts, movies, amusement parks, or drive automobiles.

In addition to the human loss, 7,500 Jewish shops and countless Jewish homes lay in ruins, along with 265 synagogues, including Isack's synagogue in Eppingen. By September 29, 1939, except for furniture manufacturer Reutlinger & Co., all of the larger Karlsruhe Jewish businesses, including the only Jewish hotel, the Nassauer Hof, had changed ownership to proper Aryans. The remaining ninety-two small Jewish businesses that employed 230 people, such as the woman's clothing store Sofie Wolf-Fortlouis, Maas Bakery, dentist Dr. Acker, and the bookstore Bielefeld'sche Hofbuchhandlung, were so badly vandalized that they never reopened.

In the days following the pogrom, Gustav Schroeder brought food and news for his neighbors who remained hidden behind their blanketed windows. The news disclosed the irony that Germany's Jews were fined one billion marks for the damage that occurred on November 9 and 10, 1938.

Adolph Hitler avoided any personal acknowledgment with what became known as Kristallnacht, other than a telegram he sent to the parents of German diplomat Ernst vom Rath on November 9, 1938:

```
"To Herr and Frau vom Rath, Paris

Please accept my sincere sympathies on the
grievous loss with which you have been afflict-
ed as a result of the cowardly assassination of
your son.

                Adolf Hitler"
```

In the days following Kurt's search for his friend Stan, Kurt had unknowingly lived through and witnessed the beginning of the Holocaust.

SARAH AND ISRAEL

"Jews may be given only such given names as are listed in the Guidelines on the Use of Given Names issued by the Reich Minister of the Interior....Insofar as Jews have other given names than those which may be given to Jews... they are obligated, beginning January 1, 1939, to assume an additional given name, namely the given name Israel in the case of males and the given name Sarah in the case of females. August 17, 1938."

On a late December day in 1938, Ilse made her way to the police station located just outside the Hitler-Platz. When Kurt ran up the steps of the massive brown fortresslike building at Beiertheimer Allee 16, Ilse uncharacteristically yelled. Kurt froze until Ilse dragged him down the stairs under the indifferent eyes of the Friday morning pedestrians.

"Kurt, I told you when we left home that you are to stay with me! Now if I have to tell Opa you did not listen to me—Do you want me to tell Opa?" Ilse pushed Kurt's chin up. "One last time, when we go inside, you sit down where I tell you to and you say nothing."

Ilse pulled open the door and pointed to the bench where a somber Kurt sat alone. She approached the police officer, who immediately chastised her. "I'm sorry," answered Ilse. "I know I should not have waited, but my parents have been ill and..." The officer dismissed her with a wave of his hand. He pulled out a preprinted form and began an inquiry he had done hundreds of times before.

"Is that one yours?" asked the officer. Ilse's "yes" brought a startled Kurt to his feet. Ilse mouthed "stay!" before she followed the officer to the white backdrop. Kurt craned his neck and watched his mother straighten her colorful scarf just before the flash from the camera temporarily blinded her. The bored officer grunted, and an obedient Ilse walked back to the counter where her ink-stained fingers were rolled back and forth in the allotted space on the form. The bureaucrat was like a machine sliding the completed form into a file while he simultaneously grabbed for another.

"I see from your work permit that you are a maid?"

"Yes."

"Birthplace?"

"Rastatt, sir."

"Present address?"

"Markgrafenstrasse one, first floor, sir."

"Do you have any specialized skills?"

"Well, sir, I am a very good cook and seamstress."

"Marital status?"

"I am divorced, sir."

"Maiden name?" asked the officer as he scrutinized for the first time Ilse's papers.

"Ettlinger, E-T-T..."

"Don't insult me. I know how to spell," said the officer. He looked past Ilse. "Your son, how old is he?"

"Eight, sir."

"And the boy's father?"

Ilse's hand shook as she signed Ilse Sarah Walker for the second time on the form. "Julius Walker."

The officer continued to stare at Kurt. "And this one, he is your only child?"

Ilse's eyes burned in the direction of Kurt before she turned toward the officer and smiled. "Unfortunately, yes."

A week later, on January 6, 1939, Ilse returned to the police station and picked up her identification card that was valid until January 6, 1944. She provided her last name, and the documents were flung across the counter. Ilse barely took a step before the officer reprimanded her for turning her back on him. Her lips tightened while she completed an immediate about-face.

"I remember you," said the Nazi. He slowly drew out each word. "Divorced from Julius Walker and you have only one child?" A bitter copper taste filled her mouth.

"Yes, sir."

"Bring your papers back to me," said the Nazi. He looked at Ilse while he stamped an image of an eagle and swastika on her new identification card. She felt as if she was going to pass out as the Nazi continued his long, hard stare. "You have to keep this with you at all times to be official, Ilse Sarah Walker. We want you to be official, Ilse Sarah Walker. Don't we?"

THE CONVERSATION

On April 20, 1939, Adolph Hitler's fiftieth birthday, the Nazis in Karlsruhe used the occasion to recruit and register boys from ten to fourteen into the Deutsches Jungvolk, or German Youth.

Kurt, transfixed, pushed through the crowd of emotional parents on the Hitler-Platz. He envied the solemn group of uniformed boys with ornate daggers at their sides who stood on the stage. Kurt raised his feet unconsciously while the boys marched toward the Blood Banner, a flag that had been symbolically dipped in the blood of those who had made the ultimate sacrifice for the Nazi Party. Seconds later, each boy grasped the Blood Banner with his left hand and raised three fingers on his right hand. The senior Nazi official administered the oath as the ceremony came to an end:

"In the presence of this Blood Banner, which represents our Führer, I swear to devote all my energies and my strength to the Savior of our Country, Adolph Hitler. I am willing and ready to give up my life for him, so help me God."

Hitler's newest Nazis, bathed in applause, marched off the stage singing the Horst Wessel Nazi anthem:

"Clear the streets for the brown battalions,
Clear the streets for the storm troopers!
Already millions look with hope to the swastika
The day of freedom and bread is dawning!..."

Suddenly Kurt ran past the crowd until the angry chorus no longer blocked his ability to recall happy memories. He dropped to his knees and sucked in the reviving cool air until the vision of a neighbor putting him in a bicycle basket for the thirty-minute ride to a small farm became clear. He closed his eyes tight. Kurt was at the farm pulling potatoes from the ground before catching a rabbit for dinner. His eyes closed tighter, and Uncle Julius placed Kurt in an empty coffin that sat on a wagon in the cemetery where he worked. Seconds later, Kurt and Julius were flying past startled mourners. Kurt grinned with the memory of his mother hitting his uncle a day later, when he returned home with bedbugs from sleeping in a flophouse that Julius called home.

When Kurt opened his eyes, he looked up at the nearby hill. He was sitting on his mother's lap while the slow cable car took them up the steep Turmberg. Kurt closed his eyes for the last time. It was two years earlier, and he had snuck into the local movie theater outside the Marktplatz where he watched the explosion of colors from Disney's *Snow White*, the only movie he had ever seen. When he opened his eyes, a seven-year-old Kurt was singing his rendition of "Heigh-Ho," "We Dig, Dig, Dig…" to his grandfather.

Repeatedly, a stoic Kurt called upon those memories when the unshakable pain of the real world grabbed him. More often than not, a solitary Kurt could not defeat the daily reminders of pain, such as Sophie's increasingly bizarre and disquieting ramblings that left her and Kurt strangers. However, he took great solace in his relationship with his grandfather, a relationship that had been born from the seeds of a stolen apple. It was a blessing and a gift of unconditional love. He saw in his grandfather the noble attributes of faith and patriotism that he admired, respected, and desired.

But what endeared Kurt to Isack was his grandfather's closely guarded sense of humor. Each morning when Isack woke Kurt he whispered, "Are you hungry?" This brought the same sleepy nod of yes and the same whispered response, "But Kurt, last night I brought you a lox and bagel sandwich. Don't you remember eating it?" The laughter that began each morning became one of the many moments of a life's journey that drew them closer.

In the months following Kristallnacht, Germany reverted to an indifferent tolerance toward its remaining Jews. Its focus was directed to a looming war. Even Karlsruhe's local newspapers that reported about Adolph Hitler's stay at the Germania Hotel on May 17, 1939, mentioned nothing about its Jews but only Hitler's tour of the defensive west wall between Karlsruhe and Kehl. It was in an environment of patriotism and nationalism after Germany's invasion of Poland on September 1, 1939, that Isack begrudgingly said yes to Kurt's request to spend Christmas 1939 with his next door neighbor and friend, Fritz Schückle. "Remember, Kurt. I do this only because Fritz's father just returned from the front and he is the one that invited you."

When the war started, Isack's struggle between his pride in the true Germany and his Jewish faith was not unique to him, especially given the 150,000 Mischlinge who fought for Germany in World War II. Although most Mischlinge became members of the regular army, or Wehrmacht, some rose to become generals, admirals, navy ship captains, and fighter pilots. When a more aggressive policy to remove these men from their military service was implemented, many sought exemptions under the process of Deutschblütig. These applications for exemptions, which were personally reviewed by Hitler, ended with his attempted assassination on July 20, 1944.

Mischling Kurt Walker was filled with pride as he saluted the brave German soldiers who gave him a piece of bread in the Hitler-Platz before they left for battle in France. It was that same pride that saw Kurt and Fritz standing before Fritz's uniformed father on Christmas 1939, singing about Germany's victorious aerial bombing over London on September 7, 1939:

"Today we want to sing a song
And we want to drink some cool wine
And the glasses clink together
And it must happen
Give me your soft hand
Live well my darling
Live well my darling
Live well because we are traveling against England."

Kurt's singing of that patriotic song often acted as the key to the door that allowed him to walk past the "Jews Forbidden" signs and into the zoo and the many other prohibited places in Karlsruhe. Whenever Kurt took one of his frequent walks with his Jewish-looking grandfather, there was no song that could open the prohibited door. This was especially true in early October 1940, when they passed the zoo entrance and the sounds of a growling lion.

Isack responded to the unusual edgy silence. "We sit down here and you can ask me what you want, Kurt." Isack touched his forehead to Kurt's and looked him straight in the eye in a silly and disarming way. Not this time, thought Kurt. He turned away and watched some pigeons running toward a discarded piece of paper.

"Many times," said Kurt as he gathered his thoughts, "I have asked Mutti about my father, and Heinz. She always says that I should not ask about them. Opa, I am so happy that I live with you, but I don't understand this. I know I must have a father…" Isack tugged nervously on his beard. "Once when I was little, I was with Mutti and someone asked her about Heinz." Kurt twisted his body away from his grandfather. "Please don't tell Mutti I asked you, but why don't I live with my father and brother like other families?"

Now it was Isack who turned away. "Kurt, you know that your father divorced your mother almost six years ago…"

"But Opa, Mutti told me my father and my brother, Heinz, never met me. That seems strange to me. I mean, all I know about Heinz is his birthday." Kurt picked his head up. "Can't I see them at least once?"

"Kurt, you have to trust me. This is better left alone."

Kurt turned away as the first of many tears began to fall. "Opa, why do we even stay in Germany? Everyone has left, even Uncle Heinrich."

Isack wiped away Kurt's tears with his thumbs and delivered his long-ago prepared response. "Kurt, even if we wanted to leave, we don't have the money or the contacts that your uncle Heinrich had."

"But why does Mutti want to stay here? There is nothing here," argued Kurt.

Even Isack felt wounded for his daughter who had secured only one condition when she moved back with her parents—that they never leave Heinz.

"Kurt, I love you and so does your mother, and believe it or not so does Oma, but we will not discuss this anymore."

THE KNOCK ON THE DOOR

The first thing nine-year-old Kurt heard on the cool Tuesday morning of October 22, 1940, was Ilse whispering, "Kurt, wake up." With one eye partially open, a fuzzy vision of Kurt's grandfather appeared at the foot of the couch Kurt slept on. It took an anxious Ilse one final "Kurt!" before her sleepy son sat up in bed.

"Good morning, Herr Schückle. Are you home from the front so soon?" yawned Kurt. "I told Fritz my family is going to the rabbi's house for Succoth. When I get back, I will ask Opa if we can play."

"Kurt, that is not Herr Schückle," said Isack. He inched closer to his grandson.

Ilse followed her father and literally draped herself around her son until Kurt pushed at his mother. "Mutti, please stop squeezing my hand so hard, you're hurting me."

Kurt looked at his mother's trembling hand while the younger of the two soldiers reached into his pocket for his written orders. He read, "You have thirty minutes before we leave. You can each bring…"

"Leave? What do you mean leave? This is our home. Where are we going?" asked a forceful Isack. There was no answer from the young member of the Wehrmacht or the salt-and-pepper-haired soldier who sniffed the air in an effort to determine what had been planned for breakfast. "I want to show you something," said Isack. The undeterred salesman reached into the top drawer of his library and spoke with a self-assured voice.

"Look, look," pressed Isack. "This is me in my uniform. I am in the center of these other wounded German veterans." Isack looked at the blank faces of the men and then at Ilse and Kurt. "Trust me. That's me. I'm just older now," smiled Isack. He placed the picture over his chest. "I am a veteran like you. I fought. I killed. I was shot at. I was gassed. I did it all for Germany, and I would proudly do it again." He took a final step forward. "You see I am a German."

Kurt listened in amazement. He had not known that his grandfather, who would be sixty-six years old in eight days, had fought in World War I. Kurt wanted to ask how his grandfather had been wounded and a thousand other questions, but he was content to look at the picture that was now nervously slapping the side of Isack's leg. While the older soldier drifted toward the stale black bread, an undeterred Isack approached the younger soldier.

"What is your last name, friend?"

"Groner," answered the eighteen-year-old member of the Wehrmacht.

Isack's confidence soared. He placed the photo in the soldier's hand.

"I sent this to my wife while I was hospitalized." Isack paused dramatically. "You know, I served with a Groner from Berlin. He was about six feet tall, blond hair, just like you. He was very good with a rifle. Where is your family from, young man?"

The young soldier began to answer until the hungry soldier approached. He wiped away crumbs from his filthy uniform.

"You have thirty minutes before we leave. You can bring one suitcase each, no more than fifty kilos in weight, and only one hundred Reichsmarks. And yes, bring food and water for three days."

Kurt pulled on his mother's arm and whispered, "Where are we going, Mutti?"

The unmoved soldier answered, "The Bahnhofplatz."

The announcement coincided with Sophie shuffling past the startled soldiers. She exclaimed, "What do you mean the Bahnhof? Why would we want to go to the train station? Besides, we have no money for the train."

The lack of a response brought an angry look from Sophie. She glared at her wide-eyed husband. Ilse quickly pulled her mother into the bedroom while Isack did his best to distract the soldiers. "Young men, please. I want to show you something else," said Isack. He rummaged through the drawers of his library mumbling, "It's here, I know it," until he pulled out a faded blue box. "Look at these, my friends," said Isack. He pulled out his service medals and placed them over his heart. "I am a German! I fought for Germany! I bled for Germany! I am a German! We are all Germans! Yes?"

Ilse stifled her tears while a degraded Isack put his arms to his sides. He straightened his back and made sure that his fingers pointed with military-style precision to the ground while he sang a familiar marching song of soldiers going off to battle in World War I:

> "We, are united, one people, one army.
> In love and loyalty we get along.
> We stand together! All differences disappear

Wherever they had been;
Whether of high or low birth, whether Jew or Christian,
There is only one people in our land!
We fight together for the Kaiser and the Reich."

Isack marched toward the younger soldier, whose eyes he never stopped staring at. The soldier looked down and shuffled his black-booted feet, until the older member of the Wehrmacht walked between Isack and his uncomfortable companion. "You have thirty minutes. Whether you bring anything is not a concern for me."

Kurt waited for his grandfather to somehow fix the problem. The moment had clearly passed. Instead he was left to watch Isack place his medals back into the drawer of his library.

Ilse leaned over Kurt. "Put on both sets of clothes. Your pants, underwear, and socks. All of it."

"I cannot wear all of these clothes, Mutti. Why do..."

Isack's right foot crashed to the floor with such force that three Hanukkah candles rolled off the library and onto the floor near Kurt's sockless feet. Kurt felt the stares of the soldiers while his mother buttoned his second shirt and tied his only pair of shoes, which had been repaired with pieces of thick paper. The senior member of the Wehrmacht elbowed the younger soldier. "He looks like an onion with all those layers!" Once again the young soldier shifted his feet and looked at some nonexistent point of interest on the floor.

While the seconds of this insane moment literally ticked away, Isack and Ilse asked themselves, "Should I take photos? Bed linen, soap, pots, books? If they are taking us to Madagascar, should we bring warm weather clothes?"

While the packing continued, Kurt watched his seated grand-mother slowly rocking from side to side. Over recent months, Sophie's frequent bizarre behavior that left her screaming during rainstorms usually left Kurt unconcerned. But somehow this was different. "Mutti," whispered a pointing Kurt. Ilse put one hand on her hip and the other over her mouth. "Mutti, please," whispered an anxious Kurt again before Ilse went into her parents' room.

"Where are we going, Ilse?"

"I don't know, Mutti."

"Why are we going, Ilse?

"I don't know, Mutti."

"Then you should contact Heinrich."

"But Mutti, Onkel Heinrich is in America."

"Just do as I say, Ilse. Contact Heinrich and tell him Mutti Sophie wants to know what is happening. Trust me, Ilse, he will know. Promise me you will contact him."

She buttoned the last button on her mother's white blouse that she had made for her birthday. "I promise, Mutti."

Kurt remained seated on the couch listening to his mother until he heard the slamming front door to the apartment building. The soldiers remained motionless. Gustav Schroeder's deep voice called out. "Isack, when are you and Kurt coming for a haircut? Last night they had Kurt's favorite show, the *Yellow Wagon*, on the radio." His familiar throaty laughs that covered his footsteps were replaced by mock anger. "I had ten customers waiting, but I told them no. Isack and Kurt go first. You just can't…"

The barber's laughter abruptly ended with the soldiers' appearance at the Ettlinger door. Isack moved his head from side to side until he caught Gustav's eyes. No words were necessary. The barber paused for a moment before his arthritic knees allowed him to limp up the two flights of stairs.

The older soldier looked at his pocket watch as Gustav's door slammed shut. "Thirty minutes are up. Let's go." Groner ran to the apartment building door ahead of the line of Ettlingers and stood there as the cool fall air thankfully washed over him. The strange moment of civility was quickly lost. "Move your ass, Groner!" screamed one half of the military escort. "They know how to open a door!"

Isack placed Sophie's hand onto the belt of his coat and carried both of their bags out of the building while Kurt followed through the tiny opening of the closing door. The impatient civilian truck driver smirked as he started up the engine. Kurt could not take his eyes off its cargo, nine adults and one child that were partially hidden by the black cloud of foul-smelling fumes.

"Mutti, I thought it was just us. Are they taking everyone?"

Isack grabbed Kurt at the shoulder and whispered, "No one speaks but me. Do you understand, Kurt?" Kurt nodded as the fumes choked him. When only the last wisps remained, Kurt saw Fritz Schückle, along with his brother and sister, running down the steps of their next door apartment. Fritz joined the growing crowd and yelled, "Where are you going, Kurt? We are supposed to go to the Schloss."

Kurt let go of the handle of his bag and took a few steps toward Fritz until his path was blocked by Ilse.

"What is going on here?" yelled Fritz's mother, who joined the growing crowd. Fritz and his siblings ran to their bewildered mother, who pushed them behind her with a sweeping motion of her arms. "Ilse, what's happening?" cried out Frau Schückle.

Ilse put her fingers to her lips and mouthed no to her friend as a neatly attired member of the Gestapo walked through the parting crowd. "This is not any of your business. Stand back."

Frau Schückle swung her arms again and captured her children, who tried to pass in front of her. Her voice cracked. "Please...can you tell me what is happening to my friend?" Ilse put her fingers to her lips a second time as Isack pulled himself onto the truck that now held twelve people. Frau Schückle tried again to call out to her friend, but the words just trailed off. "Ilse, I don't understand..."

In reality, Frau Schückle and everyone else on the narrow street knew exactly what was happening. But for Kurt, it was not until he saw Frau Schückle crying on the street and a distraught Gustav hanging out the window of his apartment that it made some sense. He was nine years old and had seen sixty thousand Nazis marching down the Kaiserstrasse in 1936. He had witnessed the destructiveness of Kristallnacht in 1938 by the hated Nazi Brownshirts and watched the waving Nazi flags in the Hitler-Platz. But his grandfather had always told him not to worry, because they were Germans, and for Kurt, that had always been good enough.

The Yiddish-speaking prisoner standing next to him on the truck grumbled the obvious truth, "We have Hitler's Nazis to thank for this day."

When the truck finally pulled away, Fritz, dressed in his uniform of black lederhosen, dark shirt, and distinctive Hitler Youth silver belt buckle, ran into the middle of the street and screamed, "Kurt."

By the end of October 22, 1940, when the truth filled the streets of Karlsruhe, the Schückles learned they had witnessed one tiny part of the mass expulsion of 945 Jews from Karlsruhe.

THE BAHNHOF

After the truck pulled away, the driver reveled in his momentary fame. Over the next two hours he proceeded slowly down the Kaiserstrasse and past the faces pressed firmly against the store windows. His self-declared importance ended when a soldier drove the butt end of his rifle onto the bed of the truck and screamed, "Old man, move this truck or you can join our friends back here." The angry driver punched the accelerator before he made a sweeping turn into the Adolf-Hitler-Platz, where he became part of a long convoy of trucks that proceeded past the pyramid, the massive Protestant church, and the city hall.

When the convoy finally stopped in the center of the Marktplatz, the citizens of Karlsruhe became quiet amid the sounds of the huge Nazi flags snapping in the wind. Seconds after Kurt looked up at the spinning golden boy weather vane, a growing chorus of "Juden-frei, Juden-frei, Juden-frei" filled the Marktplatz. The minority of people who refused to produce a Nazi salute or join in the chorus of hate silently walked away in disgust as the last of ten rings from the church bells was struck.

Kurt pulled at his grandfather's coat. "I don't understand. What did we do, Opa?"

The salt-and-pepper-haired soldier stroked Kurt's head. "It's because you are a Jew, my boy!"

The one-mile route south to the Bahnhof should have taken ten minutes under normal circumstances, but of course these were not normal circumstances. The stop-and-go movement of the trucks, clouds of black, acrid exhaust fumes, and increasing stress caused some of the unwilling cargo to collapse and then lapse in and out of consciousness.

"Kurt, stop staring," said Isack. He pushed down Kurt's arm that was pointing at an old woman whose eyes had rolled up into her skull.

"But Opa, she does not have eyes…"

"She is just sick and she has a family standing next to her," whispered Isack angrily. "And they don't need you pointing. There has been enough of that already."

Thirty minutes later when Kurt finally arrived at the Bahnhofplatz, hundreds of people were standing in front of the huge gray structure. "Get out! Get out!" screamed the soldiers. Each person dealt with the indignity of the moment in his own way. Merchant Jakob Altman wept as his wife passed him their six children, including day-old Paulina. The ninety-two-year-old wheelchair-bound Josephine Leavis, whose son, Dr. Otto Leavis, had been president of the Senate, graciously thanked those who carried her crippled body from a truck.

When Kurt made his way to the rear of the empty truck, he jumped without hesitation into the comforting bear hug from his grandfather. Isack pushed Kurt's head onto his shoulder and repeated his instructions from earlier in the day. "I want you to promise me that you will not say anything while we are here." The simple "yes" brought one last hug and kiss from Isack before he placed Kurt on the ground.

Hours later, Kurt snuck one last look at his exhausted family before he faded into the forest of people on the train platform.

"I heard him say they are taking us to Madagascar," said the young woman as she rocked her newborn to sleep.

"Always with Madagascar," replied her husband. "The rabbi does not know everything, and if he did, we would not be here." The exasperated man threw his hands up in the air. "Why now? In a few more weeks I'm sure we would have gotten the sponsorship affidavit from Uncle Herman in New York."

The young mother placed the baby's head on her shoulder. "If you want to make a speech, I would tell you to run for office, but then you know, we can't vote."

The husband reached for his baby. "But I don't have my tools with me. How am I supposed to make a living? Besides, the baby…"

Kurt snaked his way past the arguing couple and through the obstacle course of people until he tripped over a pristine piece of leather luggage with gold stitching. While Kurt pulled himself up, he could not stop staring at the owner's bowler hat, which was tipped at a stylish angle, and the black tie that stood out against his crisp white shirt. The silver-haired man, whose opulent attire spoke to his upper status in better times, still commanded respect as his family nodded in concurrence with his running narrative.

"… and I have lived in Karlsruhe all of my sixty years. In the middle of the night when they were sick and when I should have been with my family, they called me and I went. It made no difference to me who they were. I was there for them. Now I am treated like…"

A young stranger put his finger in the doctor's face and spit in a controlled rage the rest of the doctor's sentence. "They treated you like a Jew, you fool. You think you are better than the rest of us? Better than me because I dig ditches? Before today you thought you were a German doctor who was better than me, a stupid, unemployed ditch digger. Now you know that you and I are the same. There are no more doctors or ditch diggers today. We are not even Germans. We are only Jews. The only difference between us is that I knew this day was coming and I could not leave, and you didn't know this was day was coming and you could have left."

Kurt followed the enraged man until he saw a group of twenty Orthodox Jews with their gray hair poking out from under their caps. The sight of the old men facing southeast toward Jerusalem as they chanted a prayer drew a reassured Kurt like a magnet. Kurt knew that since he had not made his Bar Mitzvah, he would be excluded from joining the men. However, as the prayer came to a conclusion, Kurt put his cap on and bent at the waist and dipped at his knees like the old Jews. Confident that no one was watching him, Kurt mumbled his own limited version of Hebrew as the last few words of the prayer were recited:

"You cause the wind to blow and the rain to fall.
You sustain the living with loving-kindness and with mercy, renew life.
You support the falling, heal the sick, free the captives and remember those who have passed on. Who can compare to You, Almighty God? Who resembles You, the Source of life and death, the Source of blossoming hope?
You are faithful in giving life to all. Praised are You, Who renews life."

When the men disbursed, Kurt heard the familiar voice of his annoyed rabbi.

"Where is your Opa? You should not be here alone."

"Why, I think he walked away from me to find Mutti, Rabbi."

There would be no punishment for the obvious lie. Instead, the rabbi limped toward the neatly attired doctor. Neither the doctor nor the rabbi could do anything for the elderly woman who had just collapsed or her husband whose tears fell on his dying wife. Kurt fled to the far end of the platform, but there seemed no escape from the endless dramas. He hid behind a pillar listening to the dangerous statements from the group of animated young men, which included the defiant ditch digger.

"So you think the ten of us can overpower the SS, the police, and the soldiers? Are you insane? Do you want us to die?"

"I have a knife," said the ditch digger.

"So do I," joined another young man.

"Well, hopefully they will stand in line quietly for an hour while you two hack away at them. Then what? We all go back to our homes and pretend everything will be fine?" argued another.

"My grandfather is blind, my wife is pregnant, and I have no money. I will take my chances where they take us. So they send us to Madagascar or South Africa. If we all stick together we can get some money and get to America or Mexico or..." responded another.

"Listen to me," answered the angry knife-wielding man. "We have all gone to the same schools. We have all helped each other.

Karl is my brother-in-law, Max married Peter's sister. We need to stay together."

"You are telling me to leave my parents. To leave everything I have?" questioned another.

"Don't you understand? We don't have anything. My God! Whatever we have is in our bags. Please don't tell me that you agree with this blind little boy who wants to be protected by his mother and father?"

Kurt crawled from behind the pillar to see two men flashing their knives in the tight circle of friends. Moments later, he watched in amazement as the two men jumped from the platform and ran down the tracks. Kurt looked back at the remaining crying men who quickly vanished into the crowd while he tried to comprehend what was happening.

Neither Kurt, his grandfather, the doctor, the fleeing men, nor anyone else on the platform knew the real truth: they were all part of the Wagner-Burkel Action. Overseen by two local Nazi activists, and done with the support of higher authorities, this first mass deportation of German Jews out of Germany began at 7:00 a.m. on the morning of October 22, 1940. By the close of the day, the coordinated systematic assault resulted in the removal by seven special trains from the southwestern states of Baden, Württemberg, Palatinate, and Saar of 6,538 German Jews from Germany. Richard Heydrich, chief of the security police and the SS, the same man who had previously written the emergency memo that had been delivered to the Karlsruhe college professor Mikuleit in anticipation of Kristallnacht, wrote of the Wagner-Burkel Action:

"The deportation of the Jews was conducted throughout Baden and Pfalz without incident. The general population was hardly aware of the operation. Heads of relevant authorities will deal with seizures of Jewish property, its disposition and utilization. Jews in mixed marriages were not deported."

During the evening of October 22, 1940, Adolph Hitler was personally notified that the state of Baden was finally "Judenrein," cleansed of Jews.

LEAVING KARLSRUHE

An hour after Kurt started his journey on the platform; he smiled as he slid next to his sleeping grandfather. Kurt's good fortune ended when he strained to hear the whispers, "Kurtela, I will not say anything because you already know the words, yes?"

"I'm sorry, Opa," answered a startled Kurt.

Isack bit his lower lip as he pulled himself up on his arthritic elbows and kissed Kurt on the forehead. "Try to sleep."

Two hours later, the sound of squealing train wheels ended Kurt's dream of Gretel hissing at a pack of fleeing dogs. Isack squeezed Kurt into his arms and turned his face away from the long line of passenger cars filled with blank faces and machine gun-toting German soldiers. Isack's concerns about the train quickly ended when he tried to warn Sophie and Ilse, but he was too late.

"Pick her up and move to the train now!" screamed the advancing soldier. Kurt and his grandfather watched in horror as a defenseless Sophie raised her arms to defend against the inevitable blow. "Get up! Get up, Oma!" yelled Kurt as the soldier ran past Sophie and drove the butt end of his rifle into a stranger's back.

"Get up now," yelled the attacker to his bloody victim while screams of "Move! Move! Move!" flooded the station.

"Take your mother's hand. We all stay together," ordered Isack. "Never let go of Mutti's hand and never stop looking at me."

It was 11:00 p.m. when Kurt and his family finally entered the train. Kurt stared at his grandfather's watch that dangled from his torn pocket until the doors to the train burst open and the uniformed man in black gabardine breeches appeared. The mere presence of the feared Gestapo officer produced the requisite tension he clearly enjoyed. He cleared his throat with a sense of theater before proudly announcing his name and rank. His distinct accent made it clear that he was educated and from northern Germany, but only he cared about that part of his resume.

"If the shuttered windows do not stay closed, you will be killed. If you attempt to escape, you will be killed." The officer scanned the train and pointed to a slender man sitting at the far end of the car. "You there, come here please," smiled the member of the Gestapo. The man looked at his wife while the other Jews said a selfish prayer of thanks. The chosen one swallowed several times, but no words came out of his mouth.

"Yes, you. Now come here please and join me," followed the friendly sounding request. The seated man escaped from his wife's grip and walked to the head of the train. "Sir," smiled the officer. "If you had asked me to come to you I would have, out of respect, removed my hat."

The quivering man reached for his simple frayed hat and buried it in his pocket as the officer shook his hand. "Your occupation and name?"

"Why..." stuttered the man. "I am a carpenter and my name is Jakob Breuer. I worked for..."

"No, not just to me, talk to our friends," interrupted the officer. He spun the man around. "Now my friend, please, one more time." The Gestapo officer placed his arm around the man. "My friends, this is Jakob Breuer and he is a carpenter." The officer bowed to the carpenter's sobbing wife, who watched as her husband was ushered outside the train. When the carpenter and Gestapo officer reentered the car, they did so to the sounds of Jakob's weeping wife.

"Before you today stands my friend, Herr Breuer. He is now head of this car. If there are any problems, please talk with Herr Breuer. Now I assume there will not be any, but if I have any problems I will communicate with Herr Breuer. I am sure you agree with me that this will make things more efficient. I will leave you for now and Herr Breuer will have a few words for you. Finally, there are some changes. If the shutters are opened or someone attempts to escape, Herr Breuer will be shot."

THE TRAIN RIDE

After the train slowly pulled out of the Karlsruhe station for the seventy-mile trek to the south, it did not take long for tears to be replaced with the rustling sounds of unconscious bodies. Hours later when Kurt awoke on the train floor, he looked once again at the dangling pocket watch of his grandfather. It was 5:00 a.m. when he slowly pushed open the shutters. Kurt's eyes squinted at the approaching sign. "I know Freiberg. That's where Oma is from," thought Kurt.

Kurt shook his mother. "Mutti, I think we are stopping in Freiberg," whispered Kurt. Contrary to the Gestapo officer's orders, the awakening Jews peeled back the curtains that covered the shutters. Kurt watched Sophie's sad eyes become electric. She pushed her face against the window while the distraught carpenter ran to the center of the car and begged for the shutters to be closed.

"This is good," interrupted a man. "Freiburg is only thirty miles to the Swiss border. When I worked, I traveled to Zurich constantly. Our prayers have been answered. The Nazis are taking us to Switzerland and then maybe to America."

Even Jakob joined in a round of quiet applause as the train lumbered into the Freiburg station. "Close the shutters! We do not want our friends to have any reason to be upset with us," announced a cautious Jakob.

The ensuing minutes of silence ended when loudspeakers barked out a series of orders. The impatient ones hurried to the exit doors while Kurt asked, "Opa, why would they say get on the train when we are already on the train?"

"No, no, no," warned Jakob to the Jews who opened the shutters that revealed a large number of people approaching the train.

"My God!" shouted the horrified passengers as bloodied Jews were pushed and punched toward the train. The shocking vision quickly ended when an SS officer pounded his fist against the window. Almost instantaneously the shutters were closed and the Jews retreated to their seats. "We are still going to Switzerland. This does not change anything," shouted a lone confident voice. But this time there was no applause while 350 Jews from Freiburg were loaded onto the train.

"Now we know it is not just the Jews from Karlsruhe. They are getting rid of all of us," answered the few who were brave enough to whisper.

"But to where?" came another courageous whisper.

"If it is to the east that means Poland and death," followed another whisper.

There was little time to digest what had been said given the sickening thuds of people being beaten in the train car ahead. Kurt cowered behind his grandfather and watched the shadowy figures beat the defenseless Jews while the SS screamed, "Hand over your watches and money." In the resulting pandemonium, Isack draped his body over Kurt.

"Opa, please do not be unhappy with me," said Kurt, who flinched with each crashing sound.

Isack's grip over Kurt tightened. "Why would I be unhappy with you?"

Kurt looked ahead at the car filled with screaming people. Isack tried again. "Why would you ever think I would be unhappy with you?"

"Opa, I heard what you said to the soldiers when you showed them the photograph and your medals. I..." Kurt's voice trailed off against a backdrop of the unrelenting screams.

"Kurt, say what you want," said Isack, who cared only about distracting Kurt from the inevitable.

"You fought for Germany, you love Germany, Opa." Kurt paused. "I hate Germany. I hate the Germans. And I hope we never go back to Germany...Please don't be unhappy with me, Opa, but I never want to go back to Karlsruhe or Germany, and if you make me go back, I hope I get to kill Germans." He looked his grandfather in the eyes. "I am not a German anymore."

Isack's futile attempt at a thoughtful response ended when the train began its violent movement forward. Although he was uncertain what direction the train was heading, it was clear that the Nazi flashlights no longer burned and the screams from the car ahead stopped. Hours later, when the train approached the city of Breisach located near the Rhine River, the border between Germany and France, it was apparent that the Jews were heading away from Poland and the black rumors of death.

The emotionally spent Jews, most of whom had never left Germany, proceeded past the tributaries of the Rhine, the Doller, and Ill Rivers before they came to the town of Mulhouse, located twenty miles into France. Mulhouse and the surrounding villages, which had long been a source of conflict between France and Germany, were, from 1871 to 1914, part of the German Empire. However, with the support of President Woodrow Wilson after World War I, the region emerged as the short-lived Republic of Alsace-Lorraine. Its subsequent annexation by France in 1918 left Mulhouse and the former Republic of Alsace-Lorraine under the control of France, until Germany's victory over France on June 25, 1940.

While the train lumbered to a stop, Kurt could have cared less about the politics of the region as the loudspeaker blared the familiar warning, "Keep the blinds shut, or you will be shot. If you attempt to escape, you will be shot."

When the train eventually stopped in Mulhouse, the feared Gestapo officer appeared once again. He gazed over the bowed heads and curled his trigger finger. Jakob, the reluctant captain, walked to the head of the car and without breaking stride followed the Gestapo officer out the door. When a solitary Jakob returned, he barely made it into the car before his sobbing wife wilted into his arms.

Jacob gathered his thoughts and did his best to comfort his distraught wife before he spoke. "I have good news. We are all going to get some food and water." The confused looks and blank stares left Jakob crestfallen. "Didn't you hear me? There will be soup and bread for everyone. I saw the food myself." He walked up and down the aisle repeating the good news until the stony faces began to smile. With the hopeful mood of the train restored, Jakob took a long breath. "I have been instructed to collect everyone's Reichsmarks so that they can be exchanged for French francs."

"What do you mean?" grumbled the Jews.

Jakob pulled his cap from his head and called to his wife. "Hannah, please collect the money." Jakob placed the cap in his wife's hand while Kurt watched Jakob's money spill into it. "You see, we all have to do it. Please do as I ask. None of us want any problems." Jakob's wife clung to her husband's arm. He walked down the train apologizing as each mark was dropped in his cap. "And when the food is brought here," said Jakob, "you are not to say anything. Never speak! Never say a word in German."

One of the other few young men in the train stood up. "Jakob, what are you talking about? This is insane."

Jakob did not respond, because there was nothing he could say. He took his last steps to the door. "Who speaks French?" When three hands slowly rose, he pointed to the men. "You have just volunteered under the orders of the Gestapo." The men fearfully followed Jakob to the door. "Now when they come in here, if anyone forces you to talk, even if it is the Gestapo, you are to say that we are Jews deported from Alsace-Lorraine. You understand? Not Germany!" He placed documents in each man's hand. "These are identification papers. Memorize the names. And remember, none of us are Germans."

With Jakob gone, the three men distributed the food and water under the eyes of the frustrated French civilians, whose repeated questions went unanswered. It would be another three hours before Jakob stood in the middle of the train car and spoke in hushed tones. "I have your money."

"What is this?" shouted the white-bearded man. "There should be two thousand francs! You cheated me. You gave me only four hundred francs! This is not acceptable!"

Jakob threw some francs at the man and screamed, "Just because we are in France, did you think they would stop stealing from us?"

While the Jews argued, they were unaware that the last car of the train that housed the Nazis was being detached from the rest of the train. It would not be until the next morning when the train moved southwest from Mulhouse toward Besancon that it was clear to the Jews that the German soldiers and SS were gone. It took even longer for the Vichy French to realize that they had been tricked into accepting a sign-draped train of 1,200 German Jews that read, "Jews from Alsace-Lorraine."

"The Accused's Section IVD4 participated in the execution of this deportation, too, by organizing the transport of Jews in sealed carriages. Moreover the Accused personally played an additional part at a critical part when the French had to be convinced that they would allow the entry of the trains into the unoccupied area of Francesomething which they were not obligated to permit by the terms of the armistice (T37, p143; t637). In his testimony, he told the Court how he succeeded in convincing the French station master at the border railway station...and thus succeeded in casting the Jews across the border (Session 77, vol. IV, ppXXXX26-30)."

Judgment of the Accused: Adolf Eichmann, son of Karl Eichmann, in the District Court of Jerusalem Case No. 40/61

OLORON-SAINTE-MARIE

After the train lumbered west past the towns of Besancon, Lyons, Nîmes, and Toulouse, Isack joined the group of elderly men. He listened briefly before he spoke. "My friends," said the salesman, who looked at Kurt. "I agree with Samuel. The French have just lost a war. What do they want with us? Every day we are on this train it costs them money and men to guard us. Spain has also finished a war. What do they want with us? Spain and France are parts of Germany just like Alsace-Lorraine. We know that Germany does not want us. Why would they want us as neighbors in France or Spain?" Isack paused. "My friends, there could be worse places, but we are going to America!" An excited Kurt followed the lead of the others and clumsily repeated "New York, Philadelphia, Chicago, Milwaukee, Brooklyn, and Boston."

Later in the day and after the sun fell behind the Pyrenees Mountains, rain began to pelt the windows of the train. Continuous dark clouds that blocked the moon at night and sun during the following days left Kurt in a black tunnel that proceeded for hundreds of miles. The unintended benefit of the depressing blackness was a sleep that distracted him from his surroundings. That was until, in the evening of October 25, 1940, the train's wheels locked and tossed Kurt out of the arms of his mother.

When the doors of the train opened, two uniformed men entered screaming, "Sortez, apportez vos baggages!" Kurt shrunk into his mother's arms. The panicked passengers looked at

Jakob, who slowly stood up. "I think they want us outside with our baggage."

While the screams of "Sortez" continued, Kurt was drawn to the black-uniformed men with pistols at their sides, unusual hats, and tailored overcoats that glistened from the rain. Kurt reached slowly for his imaginary pistol until the screams of "Move, everyone out now" in poor German caused everyone to jump to their feet. Kurt, the last person to leave the train, looked out the open door in disbelief at the sight of hundreds, if not thousands, of people standing in the rain. He remained there for only seconds before he jumped into the mud and ran toward his jubilant family and into the arms of his uncle Julius.

The emotional reunion was quickly interrupted as more screaming, uniformed men waved the crowd of Jews toward the small train station. The windblown sign above the station read "Oloron-Sainte-Marie."

German efficiency allowed for the identification, removal, and transportation of its Jews. This was in stark contrast with the attempted transport of this newly formed village. The conspiracy of silence by the Nazis ensured that the Vichy government had no plan to deal with the mostly elderly, sick, fatigued, and hungry Jews who stood in the rain.

The rain painfully slapped at Kurt's face while Julius, Ilse, and Isack stood over him like human umbrellas. He listened intently to his uncle's familiar story of expulsion from Karlsruhe, until an apologetic Kurt interrupted his family. "Opa, Mutti, when are we going home? When do we go back to Karlsruhe? And what about Gretel?" Isack dropped to his knees, put his forehead on Kurt's, and confidently declared, "Soon, Kurtela, soon." Ilse, whose tears were hidden by the rain, joined in this unique moment of Ettlinger solidarity and repeated her father's statement of fact.

Julius steadied his father, and Kurt gritted his teeth as Isack placed his full weight on him. After Isack rose to his feet, he wiped away the clumps of mud on his knees, making sure to never take his eyes off Kurt. Then, with his teeth chattering from the chill of the night, he kissed Kurt and said, "Ganna gut, ganna gut, everything will be fine."

After Kurt returned to the protection of his human umbrellas, bolts of lightning transformed the area around the train station to a bright, sunny day. In that brief moment, Kurt saw his forgotten grandmother sitting on her luggage only feet away. The image of her alone left him guilt ridden. To Kurt, his unapproachable grandmother had always looked severe, unhappy, and angry, but with the vision of her collapsed felt hat hanging around her ears he felt sadness. With each subsequent lightning bolt that lit up the sky, Sophie's flat and expressionless face remained unchanged as tufts of wet gray hair swung violently over her eyes. Her unfocused gaze in the direction of Kurt was accompanied by her familiar sway from side to side. Kurt raised his hands to his face and waved them in unison as he waited thirty seconds for the sky to light up again. In the brief seconds of light that eventually followed, he saw something that he had not seen in years, something he would never see again, a smiling Sophie.

LEAVING
OLORON-SAINTE-MARIE

The freezing wet French police waved their batons at the approaching rusty trucks. The lucky Jews, forty or fifty at a time, eagerly crammed into the stained, canvas-topped vehicles that afforded them a brief respite on their way to freedom. For those not afforded such a luxury, their spirits could not be dampened while they waited in lines trying to once again pronounce New York, Philadelphia, Chicago, Milwaukee, Brooklyn, and Boston. An energized Kurt shivered while he sounded out "Feel-oh-deal-fee-ha" before he looked back at an approaching train.

Kurt pulled hard on his uncle's coat. Julius picked Kurt up and placed him on his shoulder. The crowd mumbled, "What is this? Are we going back home?" A disgusted French policeman glared at the unexpected train. He angrily pointed his baton at his superior. "If there are any more, I'm going back home."

The senior officer quelled the minimutiny with a look not too dissimilar from that of an unhappy parent to a petulant child. He cautiously approached a police officer who jumped from the stopping train. The unnerved captain accepted the written order, while hundreds more disoriented Jews fell out onto the muddy area around the station.

Kurt's uncle lowered Kurt to the ground and swatted away at the baton of a nearby officer before he placed his hands and knees into the muddy ground at the rear of a truck. He swore in German before he motioned to his mother, who held onto Isack and Ilse while she climbed into the uncovered truck for the eleven-mile trip.

After two hours, Kurt heard the mutterings of people farther down the line of trucks. "Mutti, what is that?" said Kurt as a two-inch pool of water rolled back and forth over his disintegrating shoes. But there was no answer from his mother or any of the other people pointing at the sign that sharpened under the glow from the weak headlights. Kurt pulled at the wet collar of his mother's coat and whispered, "Mutti, I don't understand this. What is Camp de Gurs and why are we here?"

A bearded and wounded Isack Ettlinger outside a hospital during WWI

A pregnant Ilse holds Heinz.

Camp de Gurs

Heinz prepares to dive into a swimming pool on the day his father dies

Ilse Walker Christmas 1930

Julis Walker in striped shirt drinking with friends

Julius Walker approximately 1940

Kurt and Jolene winter 1942

Kurt "Welker" is honored in the press

Kurt Wagner at Anshe Emet Synagogue 2012

Kurt with some of the children transferred from Camp de Gurs to Maison des Pupilles. Kurt is behind the left shoulder of the boy in the beret. The "Little Grey Man" stands in the center

Kurt, Fritz and Fritz's siblings in Karlsruhe

Kurt, Rolf Weil and Heinz in America

Kurt's mother and Uncle Julius

Last picture taken of Kurt and Ilse

Lina and Heinrich Weil.

Photo taken by Alice Resch of the boys chosen to
leave Maison des Pupilles for America.
Left to right are Ernst and Richard Weilheimer, Rolf
Hess, Hugo Schiller, Hjalmar Mauer and Kurt.

The Wagners and Kurt

WAG & BELLE
25th Anniversary
1920-1945

Wags' and Belle's wedding day.

Kurt and his family, summer of 2013.
Left to right are Ben and Marrian Walker and their daughter Jenny
and Kurt and Marilyn Wagner and their two sons, Stuart and Irvin

PART II
FRANCE

CAMP DE GURS

-ASYLUM versus REFUGEES-

Spain and France's natural border, the Pyrenees Mountains, with its vast deposits of granite and limestone, spans 270 miles from the Bay of Biscay at the northeast corner of Spain to the Mediterranean Sea to the east. Formed 150 million years ago from a single block of the earth's crust with peaks rising to heights greater than 11,000 feet, the mountains could not deter a unique sense of fraternity between the two nations. In southwest France lived some of those very people in the small town of Gurs. The only notoriety for this farming community of 502 people came from the fact that Lourdes, a place of miraculous healings, was fifty-four miles to the southeast. The complicated set of events that allowed Camp de Gurs to be built and, more importantly, for its gate to open on the evening of October 25, 1940, began more than two decades earlier with World War I.

The cost of World War I for France was over 1,300,000 dead, 3,000,000 wounded, and a birth rate that plummeted. By 1919, France had only half of the able-bodied nineteen- to twenty-one-year-olds it had before the war. The resulting shortage of three million workers was, by necessity, filled by foreigners whose presence over time caused the French to resent its once-needed guests.

Years later, in 1934, one million French people were left unemployed as a result of the worldwide depression. This was at a time when France maintained its long-standing tenet that it was an island of asylum for the disaffected of Europe. This noble concept, which emanated from an ancient notion of providing an inviolable place of refuge and protection, was continually tested throughout the prewar years of the 1930s. The growing tension between the French and foreigners eventually gave way to antiforeigner legislation that challenged France's long-standing principle of being the conscience of Europe. In the years before the great depression, those seeking political asylum or work in France were referred to as aliens or foreigners. By the end of the 1930s, with the emergence of Hitler's Germany, the transparent euphemisms were discarded for a simpler direct label, Jews.

In March 1938, after the annexation of Austria by Germany, thousands of Austrians fled their native country. They became part of the 180,000 German-speaking refugees who entered France to escape Hitler's Germany. Many were Jews who entered illegally. Months later, with the world on the brink of war, France once again declared new laws that would maintain its position as the conscience of Europe. Although the clear statement in the preamble of new legislation declared that France was a place of refuge, the actual laws made an expulsion order of an alien or foreigner almost impossible to appeal. These laws manifested the changing and conflicted psyche of the French.

France's struggle with its foreigners continued with its July 20, 1939, order that all foreign men of draft age, including Jews, register for the military draft. Six weeks later, on September 4, 1939, the day after France declared war against Germany, men from Austria and Germany from the ages of seventeen to fifty were ordered interned. Then in the spring of 1940, twenty-five thousand more German and Austrian foreigners were interned. The antiforeigner sentiment was directed toward the German and Austrian Jews whose presence, it was argued, was the cause of its continuing financial despair and its involvement in yet another world war. This sentiment was legitimized in the summer of 1940 when France instituted laws that sanctioned anti-Semitic excesses in the press. In October 1940, the French government, without any pressure from its Nazi victors, enacted laws that excluded Jews from the military, the judiciary, civil service, newspapers, movies, and radio. Finally, Algerian Jews who had been granted French citizenship in 1871 saw this right taken away. The process of going from a host nation of political asylum to anti-Jew had taken less than ten years.

-THE SPANISH CIVIL WAR-

In July 1936, after many months of unrest in Spain, nationalistic generals of Spain, led by Francisco Franco, began an uprising against the Republic of Spain. In the early months of the junta, Franco asked for and received assistance from "His Excellency Benito Mussolini, Head of Government, Duce of Fascism, and Founder of the Empire" and Chancellor Adolf Hitler. Soon the German Luftwaffe and Italian Air Force would be bombing civilians in Madrid and Barcelona.

On April 1, 1939, Spain ended its bloody civil war with the victory of Generalissimo Francisco Franco's forces over the Spanish Republic. The 500,000 deaths from the war became an impetus for 450,000 civilians and soldiers to flee Spain. There were few options for those trying to escape from a country surrounded mostly by water, other than France, the "Island of Asylum." One group attempting to escape, the International Brigade, was comprised of many Jewish communists. The 32,000 soldiers who made up the brigade came from fifty-three nations, including the Abraham Lincoln Brigade of America. By February 9, 1939, with the end of the civil war imminent, some members of the brigade collected near the border between Spain and France. When the physically and mentally depleted brigadists arrived at the border, they were met by armed French police who refused their entry into France.

The small Basque communities attempted to reach out to help, but on the whole the native French people had come to have a strong dislike for the newest assemblage of foreigners. Their government asked one simple question: What is to be done with these thousands of refugees massing at our border? Unbeknownst to those fleeing Spain, and the French police guarding them, was the fact that the French government had begun to construct holding camps. Future camps such as Camp Barcaré would have seventy thousand refugees pass through it, while Argelés and Saint Cyrien would eventually process forty thousand and thirty thousand refugees respectively. Over time, other refugees would find themselves in a camp named after the small nearby town of Gurs.

-THE CAMP-

The design and construction of Camp de Gurs by the company of Lombardi and Morello came under the management of the French Department of Roadways and Bridges. The political rhetoric of the time made it appear that Gurs had been carefully chosen because of its close proximity to the main road that served not only Gurs but the small towns of Préchacq-Josbaig and Dognen and the train station at Oloron-Sainte-Marie, only seven and a half miles away. The decision makers assumed that the farming community of Gurs would be receptive to a camp built on wetlands, which were unsuitable for either crops or grazing cattle. The hostile opposition of the one thousand people from Gurs and the surrounding small towns emanated from something other than the loss of clay soil on a flood plain.

Georges Mendiondou, the mayor of Oloron-Sainte-Marie, was appointed the administrator of the Gurs project. He argued that the town of Oloron-Sainte-Marie would benefit by the thousands of people passing through with money to spend. He also speculated that he might personally benefit from this short-term undertaking. The fact that the newly appointed administrator of the project was the only popularly elected official in the region who favored the construction of the camp drew a cynical eye from the local population. The cynics' beliefs were confirmed when they read on February 11, 1940, in the *Pyrenees Patriot* about, "...habitual criminals, murderers and torturers..." who were to be placed in the camp. Mayor Mendiondou's March 11 response to the editorial in the *Patriot* addressing the "humanitarian reasons" that justified the camp and the resulting prosperity fell on deaf ears. The *Patriot* dismissed Mendiondou's arguments and continued to report about the negative consequences of a camp that would bring typhoid fever from the internment of an "army guilty of international crimes." Also, it was argued, the lack of phones in the area made it difficult to alert the police when the criminals escaped.

While the citizens' grievances were aired in the press, Mayor Mendiondou carried out his simple directives to facilitate the internment of nineteen thousand people for six months. On February 27, 1939, with picks, shovels, saws, and hammers, six hundred laborers started to construct Camp de Gurs. The camp's 195.21 acres measured 1.2 miles in length and .3 miles wide. A 19-foot-wide asphalt road ran the entire length of the camp. Thirteen separate prisons called ilot, or islands, were constructed six to the left and seven to the right off this single main road. Each ilot, enclosed by barbed wire and a separate gate, contained approximately thirty distinct barracks. By virtue of this design, the ilots became separate camps within the larger Camp de Gurs. Three miles of railway tracks were laid so that carts powered by horses or by hand could haul materials throughout the expansive camp. Four thousand feet of drainage ditches were dug to accommodate the fifty inches of annual rainfall.

The simple design and construction of the barracks was taken from the warfare experiences of the French army during World War I. It was understood that the 1939 internee version would, like the World War I version, have a short life. Each barrack, with an intended capacity of approximately fifty to sixty people, was seventy-eight feet in length, eight feet in height, and thirteen feet wide. It was constructed of unsuitable, newly cut wood.

When completed, the barracks appeared like rows of neatly lined giant dog kennels. The single entry door and three wooden hatches were the only source of natural light and ventilation. On both sides of the exterior of the barracks were wooden walls that flared out to the ground, like the sides of a triangle. This design provided strength to the structure and a pathway to divert the heavy seasonal rain. Separated by fifteen feet, each of the thirteen ilots were surrounded by an eight-foot-high double fence of barbed wire and an additional nine rows of fence that encircling the entire camp. With a total of 428 barracks, 382 for the refugees and 46 for guards and administration, Camp de Gurs became the largest of the camps to be constructed by the French government.

Forty-two days after construction began, Camp de Gurs was declared completed. On April 4, 1939, the military camp commandant welcomed the first refugees into the camp. When nine hundred fighters from the International Brigades marched six across into Camp de Gurs with their wounded comrades on litters, they protested that the camp was not complete. Their numbers afforded the French government the free labor that ultimately completed the construction of the camp. These workers included many artists whose skills allowed for elegant numbers and letters to appear over the sterile barrack doors and ilot entrances. On April 25, 1939, the camp was formally turned over to military authorities. By August 31, 1939, Camp de Gurs had taken in 6,555 Basques, 6,808 International Brigadists, 5,397 pilots, and 5,760 Spaniards. The camp that had been constructed to hold 19,000 people for up to six months had swollen to a total of 24,520 people.

The internees were keenly aware of their political standing and immediately claimed refugee status and requested asylum. To appease the surrounding communities, the minister of the interior sent a correspondence to the mayors in the area. He confirmed that no asylum would be given to an "interned army." Demoralized by their incarceration, the internees pursued a plan to revive their collective spirit and regain their humanity. The internees consisted of people whose varying interests in the arts, politics, science, and trades made this goal a reality. After seeking approval from the camp commander, a barrack from each ilot was assigned for cultural programs. The prisoners developed their own distinct and varied programs, such as painting, sculpting, weaving, and choral groups. Professors of the arts and history gave lectures in the open air, while daily chess tournaments flourished. Still others enjoyed the camp's self-published newspaper. At the forefront of these cultural programs were the proud brigadists who recognized they had accomplished something under difficult circumstances.

In anticipation of the 150th anniversary of the French Revolution, the heads of the cultural commission for all the ilots proposed a celebration. The brigadists took the lead, and soon gymnasts were tumbling and forming human pyramids. Instruments from the surrounding towns of Pau and Oloron-Sainte-Marie were obtained for the newly formed marching band. On July 14, 1939, the celebration began with a parade. Led by Yugoslav Brigadist Milevic and followed by three columns of marching brigadists, the former soldiers marched onto the parade ground carrying the flag of France. In the blazing heat, these bare-chested defeated warriors marched past a seated group of French military dignitaries. As Milevic approached the honorees, he screamed an order of "eyes right!"

The celebration concluded when thousands of internees rose in unison and sang in French the French national anthem, "La Marseillaise":

> "Arise, children of the fatherland
> The day of glory has arrived!
> Against us the tyranny
> The bloodied banner is raised.
> Do you hear in the countryside?
> The roar of those ferocious soldiers?
> They come right here among us
> To slaughter our sons and wives!"

Upon the completion of the first verse, the French military, with their salutes still firmly in place, unashamedly cried. Days later the internees read of the reported celebration in a local newspaper. They reveled in the fact that their pride and dignity had been both restored and acknowledged.

In July 1939, the last pre-World War II Tour de France took place. The cultural commission for the camp knew that the cyclists would have to go past the camp on their way from Salies-de-Béarn to Pau. On July 16, 1939, permission was granted to the brigadists to watch the cyclists speed by on their test of endurance. A day later, they stood at the first row of barbed wire as the front runners of the eighth stage of the 1939 Tour de France approached. The newly energized cyclists pushed themselves when they heard the passionate brigadists shout, "They are coming! They are coming!"

Then with an order of "now!" the brigadists pulled out from under their shirts sheets of paper with single letters written on them. The sheets were raised to chest height as the leader of the Tour de France, twenty-five-year-old Frenchman René Vietto, flew down the road. Upon seeing the human telegram, the communist cyclist slowed his bike and raised a clenched fist as he read:

"The fighters for freedom salute the prisoners of the road."

As the clenched fist of René Vietto punched the air, the prisoners responded with a booming chorus of cheers. The price for Vietto's recognition of these fighters was costly; René Vietto would come in second place in the 1939 Tour de France, the last Tour de France to take place until 1947.

On Sunday, September 3, 1939, at 5:00 p.m., France declared war on Germany as a result of its invasion into Poland two days earlier. The unintended consequence of the declaration of war was the significant reduction of French resources and men being utilized at Camp de Gurs and the other camps in the region. France was left with few alternatives; the prisoners in Camp de Gurs would have to be released. By May 1940 the mainly Spanish population in Camp de Gurs that had numbered almost 25,000 fighters and civilians in August 1939 numbered approximately 1,500. However, with the displacement of German and Austrian women from Belgium into France as a result of the May 10, 1940, Nazi invasion and the May 15, 1940, French arrest of mostly Jewish women, the population of Gurs increased. On May 21, 1940, over five hundred foreign nationals arrived at Camp de Gurs. A day later 3,500 Spanish refugees from deactivated work units arrived, followed a month later by nine hundred French political prisoners.

By the end of June 1940, Camp de Gurs's population swelled to fifteen thousand people as a result of the French government's desire to house a variety of "les indésirables." No sympathy was afforded this new group of internees. Ironically, many were stateless German Jews who had fled to France, "The Island of Asylum." The array of people incarcerated in addition to the German Jews included French communists, pacifists who refused to work in the war industry, people sympathetic to the Nazi cause, homosexuals, prostitutes, Gypsies, other stateless people, and common prisoners awaiting trial.

The significant increase in the camp's population was short-lived as a result of the signing of the armistice between France and Nazi Germany. With Camp de Gurs's remaining resources drained, most of the internees were freed by the overwhelmed and newly constituted Vichy civilian authorities. The remaining population of two thousand Spaniards found work outside of the camp and were no longer under any real control by the Vichy. This was not true for the remaining 980 Jewish women who remained interned and under the control of the Vichy.

-THE WAR-

Not even the Nazis expected its army could, within six weeks, reach the Pyrenees Mountains and thereby defeat what had been thought to be the most powerful army in Europe. With the war lost, France signed on June 21, 1940, at Compiègne a cease-fire agreement with Nazi Germany. The site had been specifically chosen because it had been the same location where Germany had signed the armistice confirming the terms of its defeat in World War I. On November 11, 1918, the representatives of the warring nations met in a dining car that had been built by the Wagon-Lits Company and subsequently converted to an office on wheels.

On June 19, 1940, Hitler directed army engineers to demolish the wall of the museum where the same railway car was displayed. After the last remnants of the wall fell, the railway car was brought to Compiègne. At 3:00 p.m. on June 21, 1940, the heels of Hitler's knee-high black leather boots clicked away as he slowly walked the last 250 yards toward the railway car. As the June sun streamed through the forest of elm, oak, cypress, and pine trees, the assembled press reported that Hitler's face was filled with "scorn, anger, hate, and revenge."

The führer's pace slowed to savor the last few steps while his World War I Iron Cross, which he had been nominated for by Jewish Lieutenant Hugo Gutman, bounced against his deep-gray double-breasted uniform. Then abruptly he stopped, before walking to a granite block. He read the inscription before he entered railroad car 2419D at 3:23 p.m.:

"HERE ON THE ELEVENTH OF NOVEMBER 1918 SUCCUMBED THE CRIMINAL PRIDE OF THE GERMAN EMPIRE — VANQUISHED BY THE FREE PEOPLE WHICH IT TRIED TO ENSLAVE"

At 3:42 p.m. Hitler exited the railway car. He enthusiastically slapped his thigh as he strode down the path back to a waiting Mercedes while a German band played "Deutschland, Deutschland über Alles" and the Horst Wessel song of the Nazis. Three days later, Hitler ordered the site of the armistice signing to be destroyed with dynamite.

The armistice agreement created a geographically divided France. A German-occupied zone to the north established Paris as its capital. A southern unoccupied zone was to be governed by the French in Vichy. Article 3 of the armistice granted authority to the French over their country but submissive to the occupying power of Germany. Accordingly, France had no real power. France's agreement with the devil required the Vichy government to maintain and operate the many camps of southwest France. The Vichy had neither the money nor the desire to maintain camps that had already fallen into a total state of disrepair. Additionally, pursuant to the armistice agreement and anti-Semitic laws of October 1940, France agreed to turn over to the Nazi government any German and Austrian nationals identified by the Nazis. A German commission identified over seven hundred nationals that were to be returned to their native countries of Germany and Austria. At the same time, French military commanders in charge of the camps in southwest France transferred their power to the Vichy government. However, in a final act of defiance, the commanders destroyed the records of their internees.

-MADAGASCAR-

In 1937, both France and Poland had begun to investigate through formal commissions the prospects of transferring its Jews to Madagascar, a French colony annexed by France in 1896. On November 12, 1938, three days after Kristallnacht, the president of the Reichstag, Hermann Göring, presented to the German Cabinet Adolf Hitler's vague proposal of Jewish immigration to Madagascar. This bizarre plan moved ahead when the Reichsbank president, Hjalmar Schacht, tried to acquire international loans from London for the purpose of sending Germany's Jews to this island off the southeast coast of Africa. In December 1939, German Foreign Minister Joachim von Ribbentrop included as a component of a peace proposal to the pope the emigration of the Jews to Madagascar. In May 1940, Heinrich Himmler, the leader of the dreaded protection squads known as the SS, or Schutzstaffel, presented the status of a Madagascar Plan to Hitler. The Jews would be sent to "a colony in Africa or elsewhere," to which the führer responded, "...very good and correct."

Franz Rademacher, the head of the Jewish Department of the Foreign Affairs Ministry, was ordered to develop a plan for the "approaching victory" over France in which "...France must make the island of Madagascar available for the solution of the Jewish question..." The written plan closed as follows:

"This arrangement would prevent the possible establishment in Palestine by the Jews of a Vatican state of their own, and the opportunity for them to exploit for their own purposes the symbolic importance which Jerusalem has for the Christian and Mohammedan parts of the world. Moreover, the Jews will remain in German hands as a pledge for the future good behavior of the members of their race in America.

Use can be made for propaganda purposes of the generosity shown by Germany in permitting cultural, economic, administrative and legal

self-administration to the Jews; it can be em-
phasized at the same time that our German sense
of responsibility toward the world forbids us
to make the gift of a sovereign state to a race
which has had no independent state for thousands of years: this would still require the
test of history."

Britain's refusal to easily succumb to the Nazis' war machine and Hitler's invasion of the Soviet Union in the fall of 1940 diverted attention away from the Madagascar Plan. By January 1942, with Germany fighting a world war, the Madagascar Plan was ultimately replaced with a horrific alternative developed in the Wannsee Conference. But before the implementation of the plans developed in the Wannsee Conference, the victorious Nazis inspected the southern, or Vichy, zone of France. Located within the southern zone were many camps that could be used until the Madagascar Plan was fully implemented. One of those decaying camps was called Camp de Gurs. The location and existence of Camp de Gurs and its sister camps was not lost upon France's Nazi victors when the time came to deport 6,538 German Jews from the Baden, Pfalz, and Saarland regions.

Pursuant to the armistice agreement, the Vichy government agreed to receive all deported Jews from the newly annexed former French region of Alsace-Lorraine. Local Nazi activists in the southwest region of Germany, Governor Robert Wagner of Baden, the former Nazi Party leader who had operated a floundering Nazi Party out of his tiny apartment in Karlsruhe in 1925, and Governor Josef Bürckel of Saarland made inquiries about an almost empty Camp de Gurs. Their inquiries were the impetus for the deportation of thousands of German Jews during the

Jewish holiday of Succoth. This unprecedented action became known as the Bürckel-Wagner action.

Almost four years after Kurt's deportation from Karlsruhe on October 22, 1940, in a train draped with a sign that read "Jews from Alsace-Lorraine," Governor Josef Bürckel was awarded the German Order. This was the highest decoration the Nazi Party could award for services to the Reich. Shortly thereafter, on September 28, 1944, the former governor of Saarland committed suicide. On August 18, 1946, after having been found guilty of multiple crimes by a French military court in Strasbourg, the former governor of Baden and eventual governor of Alsace-Lorraine, Robert Wagner, was executed by a firing squad.

The plight of the 60,559 people who found their way through the main gate of Camp de Gurs would be heard through the voices of 3,370 prisoners who were eventually liberated on August 26, 1944, and for a few others who escaped.

Ilse Ettlinger tightened her arm around Kurt in the back of the truck and answered, "I don't know what Camp de Gurs is, and I don't know why we are here."

THE SEPARATION

"Q. Toward the end of 1940 you were arrested, Dr. Grueber, were you not?

A. I was arrested on 19 December 1940. I assume that it was in conjunction with the Gurs action. I was never interrogated...

Q. When you refer to the Gurs action, you mean the Jews of Baden, Palatinate and Saar areas?

A. These Jews were brought to the "Camp de Gurs." It is in the foothills of the Pyrenees. It was a cantonment previously used for Red Spanish prisoners. The accommodation was under the most terrible hygienic and sanitary conditions, and the treatment meted out by the French guards was no better than that of German guards.

Q. Dr. Grueber, you connected your arrest with the Jewish Camp de Gurs action? Were you in touch later with the Jews from there?

A. ...We received the most terrible reports from Camp de Gurs, much worse than the reports about people deported to Poland. There was absolutely nothing there above all no medicines, no medical supplies..."

estimony at the trial of Adolf Eichmann on May 16, 1961, by Dr. Heinrich Karl Ernst Grueber, who in 1939 was a parson in Karlsdorf in the eastern suburb of Berlin. In 1964, the Righteous Among the Nations award for non-Jews who risked their lives to rescue Jewish people during the Holocaust was awarded to Dr. Heinrich Karl Ernst Grueber.

When the truck came to a stop past the gate at Camp de Gurs, Kurt was greeted with a cordial request in perfect German, "Please get out." Kurt's search for the youthful-sounding man hidden by the darkness yielded nothing. "Men and boys over the age of thirteen, get out," continued the calm voice. The bizarre request to the unresponsive Jews left the man suddenly shrieking. "Get out! I want to get out of this rain! I'm not asking anymore! Now move!" In the panic-stricken moments that followed, Kurt felt a sense of sadness for the man whose last scream was followed by a pathetic, drawn-out "Please." The moment of compassion ended when Kurt was blinded by the flashlight of a French policeman.

When the light momentarily exposed the sad face, Kurt and the others could see that Jakob had been rewarded with yet another job he clearly did not want. "What's happening, Jakob?" cried the frantic Jews. "Why are they splitting up the families? This is not Poland! We went west!" There was no answer from the carpenter who retreated into darkness.

While the unanswered questions continued, an enraged Julius glared at a French officer whose black leather-gloved hand reached for his pistol. "Julius, don't!" screamed Isack, who watched his son acknowledge the threat by throwing his luggage into the filthy pool of water. Julius's controlled anger did not, however, stop him from jumping into the same filth that sprayed the officer's pants. Isack nervously chewed the hairs of his untrimmed beard as he slid from the truck. He thanked God that at least on this night, the screaming policeman had not noticed Julius's act of disrespect.

"My God," uttered Isack with the first of four bolts of cracking lightning that revealed hundreds of faceless figures aimlessly walking toward rows of eerie structures. Isack, weakened by a lack of food and sleep, shook his head. He dismissed the images and shouted out Kurt's name.

Kurt looked at his mother, who held onto a fragile Sophie. "What are you doing, Poppa? He is a baby!" shouted Ilse just before Kurt jumped into the old man's arms.

"I am the boy's legal guardian. No more needs to be said," shouted Isack.

"Monsieur, Monsieur," shrieked Ilse to the policeman as the screams of the families being torn from each other's arms went on around her. Ilse spoke calmly, but unfortunately in German. "My son is only nine. Not thirteen." There was no response until Ilse raised nine shaking fingers and pointed to Kurt. The police officer pointed to Kurt and back to a smiling Ilse. She nodded yes before he grabbed Kurt from Isack's arms and dropped him onto the bed of the truck. Isack screamed out Kurt's name until the blackness of Camp de Gurs swallowed up the moving truck.

Stunned, Kurt fell to the floor of the truck filled with howling women and crying children that, inexplicably, after fifteen minutes, turned around and went back the way it had come. Ilse and Kurt helped Sophie to her feet. She mumbled, "I want to see what is happening here." When the lights of the truck lit up the mountain of luggage, Kurt yelled, "Mutti—Opa and Onkel are gone!"

As the truck proceeded past the luggage and a solitary Jakob, a hysterical woman on the truck screamed, "I see the entrance! They are taking us out of the camp and keeping the men for the labor camps!" The statement of impending death strangely quieted the group so that only the sounds of the rain pinging on the truck were heard. Kurt looked at the terrified faces and placed his hands over his ears as he readied himself for the next set of screams.

"Please get out," said the German-speaking woman after the truck came to a stop. There were no protests from the women and Kurt, who followed the dim glow from the flashlight that allowed him to safely jump to the muddy road. When he rose to his feet to thank the woman, Jakob's wife was already gone.

ILOT K-BARRACK 3

When the empty truck pulled away, its spinning wheels spit out tiny beads of mud onto the stateless Jews. The numbed travelers did not bother to wipe away the black streaks that bled on their clothing. A muddied Kurt thought only of his grandfather until a short, hollow-cheeked woman limped past him. The curious-looking woman waved her arm wildly while she leaned on her umbrella crutch, trying to yell above the noise from the storm. In a fusion of French, Yiddish, and German she announced to the people who collapsed around her, "My name is Eve." Her obvious French accent caught everyone off guard. "Please, this way, my dears. Everything will be all right, and your luggage, don't worry about it. The Spaniards will collect it later."

Kurt tugged at his prescient mother, who quickly apologized after she snapped, "I don't know why Spaniards would be here, Kurt. I am more concerned about Opa and Onkel and leaving for America."

The woman tried to complete her introductions, but she and the others turned their backs to avoid the powerful tramontane that howled over the unseen Pyrenees Mountains. When the winds finally passed, she turned to the group. "This way, my dears." The Jews remained still amid the slop that crept over their ankles. It took a series of waves from Eve's crutch and her comforting words before the thirty strangers tentatively followed her to the French guard, whose World War I rifle hung lazily over his shoulder.

"Mutti, look," said Kurt, pointing above the barbed wire gate where a faded but once elegant-looking letter K flashed under a flickering light.

Eve cupped her hands around her mouth. "The French call it an ilot. In German it means island." The group muttered "Insel?" while another guard emerged from his tiny wooden cylinder guardhouse and opened the gate. Eve walked up to a nameless professor's wife, took her hand, and placed it on the shoulder of the anonymous janitor's wife standing in front of her. The raindrops cut at her face while she took the hand of one of the few children and placed it on the thick wool coat of the banker's wife.

"Like the elephants," said Eve, who swung her umbrella back and forth in front of a terrorized three-year-old girl. After a chain of people had been formed, she returned to the front of the line and shouted in Hebrew, "Acharay! Acharay!"

Ilse, Sophie, and Kurt, who had become the tail of the elephant, listened to Eve's warning. "There is no asphalt or cobblestones ahead, just a muddy path. I have a light and I promise to go slowly, but you must not let go of each other."

But by the time Kurt started to move, Eve and her flashlight had disappeared around a corner. Kurt probed the ground with the heels of his water-logged shoes as the path slowly disintegrated into a muddy bog that came up to his thighs. Even though his mother was next to him, he wanted to scream, but the shriek that followed did not come from him. After the moaning woman was freed from the quicksandlike mud, Eve, undeterred once again, shouted "Acharay!" Moments later, she pointed her blinking light into the darkness, while ghostly and unseen cries blanketed the

Jews. "It's just the tramontane," said Eve unconvincingly before she disappeared into Barrack 3.

After Kurt took his first steps into the dark room, Eve hooked her umbrella onto the wet rope handle of the door and pulled it shut. When her light shined into the room, Kurt saw twenty drenched, muddy women and children huddled into a corner of the narrow room. Eve shuffled to the center of the room. Then with a single wave of her arm, she invited the women and children to gather around the unlit rusty stove. Eve leaned on her crutch and spoke while Kurt followed her waving light. The room, thick with rat droppings and tracked in mud, had six hatch-shaped windows and numerous holes in the roof. Rainwater spilled onto the decaying wooden floor while a single broken light bulb swung from a wooden beam.

"My name is Eve Rosenberg. But please call me Evie. I am from Paris. I was arrested in Paris and brought here on June 21, 1940. I am what the French consider an undesirable, because I am a communist. Worse than that, I am a Jewish communist." She nonchalantly opened her umbrella as a steady stream of water fell on her. "I know you all have many questions, and I apologize, I will not have many answers. A few hours ago some of us were told by the administrator of this camp that you would be arriving. His angry reaction causes me to believe that no one here knew you were arriving until a very short time ago."

The elderly woman who had fallen shivered in her coat of mud. She raised her hand. "Please, you say here. Where is here? A few days ago I was in my bed in Karlsruhe and now I'm here. I don't know why..."

Evie cleared her throat. "We all know why we are all here. I can tell you that you are in a camp just outside the village of Gurs in the southwest of France." She pointed with her open umbrella. "We are about twenty-five miles from the border of Spain. The few Spaniards that were here when I arrived told me that this camp was built for their countrymen who were escaping the war. They were twenty or thirty thousand here at one time. Today there are maybe two to three thousand. I understand that maybe a few thousand more are arriving here tonight. What happens to them, to you, to me, I wish I knew."

The elderly woman's hand waved again. "We understand that we are to be sent to Madagascar, Mexico, or possibly America. I have family there and…"

The others joined in that Gurs had to be a holding camp in preparation of the last part of their journey. It was only after the five-foot-tall Evie rattled her umbrella against the exposed beams in the ceiling did the group quiet. "You see," yelled Evie. "I have learned from you. I didn't know of this. I have family in America too. I can only pray that this is correct." There were many more questions, but at least on that night, there were no more answers. Evie closed her umbrella and hobbled to the barrack door. "I must return to the trucks and the Moche. I promise we will talk again. God bless you all."

"Wait, wait, wait," cried one of the women as the tramontane ripped open the door.

"What about food, blankets, water, our luggage? We have had nothing since Mulhouse," shouted another voice in the black room.

The panicked group surrounded Evie, who pulled a candle out of her pocket. She lit it and gave it to one of the women before she inched toward the door that banged against the side of the building. "Please believe me when I say that I'm sure tomorrow will bring answers to all of our questions."

The fat unlit candle was quickly relit. Ilse helped Sophie to the ground while a woman packed fresh mud between one of the many gaps in the walls. Too tired to stand, Kurt collapsed where he had been standing and watched his mother squeeze dirty water from Sophie's clothing before she and the other women began to insulate the walls with mud and talk of exotic places such as Madagascar, Mexico, America, and, from some, a return to Karlsruhe.

And when the talk ended, Ilse picked up a sleepy Kurt. "Mutti, when do we see Opa?"

"Kurt, everything will be fine. But some things…" began Ilse as the candle went out from another blast of cold air. "I'm sure we will see Opa tomorrow."

Kurt patted the outline of his mother's face. "Mutti, I think when we go to America we should get a dog. One day in the Platz I saw a man walking a dog. I asked him what kind of dog it was and he told me it was a toy collie. I think we should get a toy collie. It would be good for the family."

While Kurt's wrinkled fingertips walked up and down his mother's face, he could feel her smile. It was only seconds more before Kurt was asleep just as October 25, 1940, came to an end in Barrack 3 of Ilot K of Camp de Gurs, located at the base of the Pyrenees Mountains. Ilse shook the motionless body of her son before she allowed herself one indulgence, a flood of tears.

By the time of Kurt's deportation, Germany's 1,400 anti-Jewish laws had been effective in forcing many Jews to leave their country. For those that hung on to the bitter end, such as the 6,538 Jews from southwestern Germany, of which 60 percent were women, 40 percent were over the age of sixty, and 10 percent were over the age of seventy-five, they had no practical or psychological preparation for Camp de Gurs.

"...This was done in accordance with the proposal of the governors of the districts....In the reports found in the Germany Foreign Ministry (T674), we read the customary cruelty in carrying out this deportation....They were put into the Gurs camp under the worst possible circumstances (Session 41, vol. II, p. 699)."

Judgment of the accused and architect of the Holocaust: Adolf, son of Karl Adolf Eichmann, who was hung on May 31, 1962. In the District Court of Jerusalem Case No. 40/61

THE FIRST MORNING

Mutti, Mutti," whispered Kurt to his unresponsive mother. He looked at the shattered crystal lens of Ilse's watch. It was 5:30 a.m. Driven by curiosity and years of independence, Kurt put on his squishy shoes and coat before he took his first steps past the warped door of Barrack 3. There was total silence. Back in Karlsruhe, regardless of the time, there were always some sounds; the clopping of a horse-drawn wagon, drunks singing outside the front door of his apartment building, or one of the neighborhood prostitutes screaming.

The observation became irrelevant when seconds later his feet disappeared into the muddy path. "How could I forget the mud," said a disgusted Kurt. He grabbed a dead branch and feverishly began to dig. After a freed Kurt, with his stick in hand, fought his way down the narrow paths, his youthful energy was quickly sapped. "Only a minute," he said to himself before he rested his head against one of the dilapidated barracks.

"Mutti, where is Papa? I want to go home," cried a pathetic voice from behind the flimsy wall. "Mutti, I am hungry. Why can't I have some milk, some bread, some jam," wept another. Still only a child himself, Kurt ran from the voices until he looked out onto the same road that the clench-fisted Frenchman René Vietto had ridden on one year earlier in the Tour de France.

"Now I can see," said a four-foot-tall Kurt as he ran to the top of a six-foot-tall wooden platform. He steadied himself on his toes with his stick and carefully straddled the three gaping holes in a futile attempt to see his grandfather and uncle. Dejected, Kurt plopped down on the platform until in the distance he saw a lone French policeman walking down a path enclosed by two walls of barbed wire. Excited by the mere presence of another person, Kurt hid behind the barracks until he was within feet of the wire. Slowly he raised the stick to his shoulder and pulled the imaginary trigger at the smiling police officer who casually walked past him. It was not until Kurt fired that first shot that the memories of the main road, the trucks, the barbed wire gate, Eve Rosenburg, and the guard returned.

When Kurt reached the eight-foot-tall barbed wire wall located at the main road, he carefully grabbed the wire. No longer hidden by the darkness of the prior night, countless other barracks appeared. While Kurt tightened his grip around one of the grotesque wirelike ribbons that appeared to wrap around the nearby snow-capped Pyrenees Mountains, a tall, rifle-toting French policeman emerged from his tiny guardhouse.

Kurt looked at the dour face of the enormous man. Cautiously he slipped his hand through the wire. "Bonjour?" asked Kurt. The guard's stern face faded slowly as he placed a peanut-size wrapper into Kurt's tiny hand. The giant pointed to himself and spoke the only German he knew, "Mein Name ist Paul." Kurt answered, "My name is Kurt Walker."

Kurt's "danke, danke, danke" could barely be heard as he tore at the wrapper. In seconds he was biting the piece of candy in half. The unexpected gift slid from cheek to cheek as Kurt delicately rewrapped the remaining half. Kurt's cheeks ballooned with each slide of the cool peppermint while he leaned contently against the wooden pole of the gate.

Encouraged by the gift and the minimiracle of communication, Kurt carefully poked his head between the ribbons of wire and watched Paul walk to the center of the road. In seconds he was opening the gate in front of a saluting Kurt. Almost immediately Kurt's right shoe was flying down the narrow road after he kicked at an imaginary soccer ball. But Kurt could have cared less as his sock tore away on the rough asphalt road. His carefree attitude ended when he noticed the twelve blackened wooden towers along the road and the wet and bored policemen standing with their rifles pointing into the vacant ilots.

Paul walked toward Kurt laughing. "Rue Moche, Rue Moche." Kurt repeated "Moche" until he recalled the umbrella lady saying the same thing the night before. Kurt grinned. "Ah, Moche." Paul slapped Kurt on the shoulders and answered, "Oui, oui, vous l'aves." It would not take long for Kurt and the other recently expelled Jews to appreciate the humor of the Parisian internees, such as Eve Rosenburg, who had sarcastically christened the asphalt road Moche because it meant "ugly" in French and rhymed with the famous and exclusive Avenue Hoche in Paris.

While Kurt picked the last bits of mud from his shoes, hundreds more barracks slowly began to appear under the low gray skies. "Paul, where are all the people from the train?" Paul's rolled shoulders and expressive eyebrows made it clear he did not understand. Kurt pulled on his imaginary beard. "Juden? Juden?"

"Oui, oui, Juifs—là et là et là et là," answered Paul while he swung his arm in a circle.

"Opa! Opa!" yelled Kurt, who jumped in a futile attempt to look down the over-one-mile-long Moche. Kurt's personal guard's quiet laughter quickly dissolved when Kurt ended up fifty yards down the road. The continuous screams of "Kurt" that woke the guards finally ended when Kurt, with his open coat flapping like wings, ran toward a relieved Paul. He rubbed Kurt's dirty hair and said, "Mon meilleur à vous, mon ami Kurt." Kurt paused for only a moment before he looked at the big man. "Paul, mein bestes zu Ihnen, mein freund."

DEATH

On the morning of October 26, 1940, the camp administrator privately acknowledged that the responsibility for the impending disaster in Camp de Gurs would fall at his feet. Unwilling to accept the repercussions, the politically savvy bureaucrat appointed civil servant Raoul Gruel, a tall, stout man with a loud voice, to be his first assistant in charge of the overall operation. In the first days after Kurt's arrival, Helga Holbrook, a representative from the Quakers relief organization, approached Gruel with an offer to take over the distribution of the meager food rations. She never forgot Gruel's response. "It is completely unnecessary. Why should the Jews be better off than the French people? No one in France has enough food!"

Later that day, Helga reported to the Quakers' headquarters about the "...hypocrite who practically needed a wheelbarrow to cart his stomach around!" Her refusal to accept his angry denial led her to contact André Jeane-Faure, the administrator for all of the camps in southwestern France. Her success in obtaining the eventual reversal of Gruel's decision, which she personally published to Gruel, inspired him over the succeeding months to do as little as possible. His governing of Camp de Gurs, which culminated in his efficient winding down of the camp in the important summer months of 1942, was rewarded with his promotion to the rank of sous-préfet and the nickname of Gruel the Cruel by the internees. Ironically, by September 1943, Gruel would be imprisoned in what he deemed retribution for the French underground's theft of all of the weapons in Camp de Gurs. The

French citizens in post-World War II agreed with Gruel and elected him for ten years to the position of lord-mayor of Bidos, a suburb of Oloron.

Gruel knew by the end of October 1940 that there were no plans for the imprisoned Jews in Camp de Gurs, the worst of the twenty-seven camps operating in the south of France. Given the emerging crisis, Gruel instituted the 1939 camp model developed for the fleeing Spanish. He ordered each barrack and ilot to elect its own leaders. The simple directive that led to the election of Pforzheim native Fräulein Kaufman as the head of Ilot K meant that Camp de Gurs was looking less like a temporary camp.

For those who bravely tried to be leaders and boost the spirits of the others in the first days, they eventually succumbed to the desperate conditions and wept uncontrollably. In those early days Ilse struck a mother's promise with herself—she would never let Kurt see her cry. Despite Kurt's lofty opinion of his strong mother, Ilse viewed herself as a fraud who kept hidden the emotional toll of both caring for a mother who silently rocked back and forth and an independent child who ran free in the camp. Nonetheless, in this place of desperation, Ilse measured herself only by whether she could provide Kurt with a sense of the impossible, that everything was all right.

After the Jews arrival in Gurs, their health quickly declined. Their overcrowded living conditions worsened under an unrelenting infestation of fleas, bedbugs, lice, and rats, leaving the most vulnerable, the ill and elderly, with horrible untreated bleeding blisters and infections. In the late morning of October 28, 1940, while Kurt leapt down the muddy path of the last row in Ilot K, he heard shrill screams coming from his barrack. He imagined the worst as he peeled back the brittle door that revealed the gray faces of the women and the Spanish men picking up the rigid body covered in its own excrement. Kurt took advantage of a distracted Ilse and followed the impromptu funeral cortege to the Moche, where the Spaniards placed the stiffened body into a wagon. His mouth fell open when the wagon, pulled by a gray swayback horse, violently tipped from side to side while the woman's feet seemed to defiantly kick her protestation to the cemetery.

"Kurt, when she failed to get up in the morning no one wanted to disturb her," began the uneasy conversation later that night. Kurt threw some old newspapers about the exploits of the 1939 Tour de France into the rusty stove. "She had been sick like all of us. We all thought it was better to let her sleep than have her greet another gray morning without any food. When we realized what had happened…" Ilse's voice started to crack, "…the religious ones prayed that this first death in Gurs be the last one before we leave."

In Karlsruhe a phone call, newspaper article, or even a rumor started in the Platz or synagogue allowed for the fluid dissemination of information in the city of 100,000 people. But in Camp de Gurs, the events in one barrack remained unknown to those in the same ilot. This was especially true for those in Barrack 3 who asked, "Did anyone know that on October 28, 1940, sixty-two-year-old Karlsruhe native Elsie Frantz was the first person to die in Camp de Gurs?"

Before Kurt's arrival in Gurs, the camp's death book that recorded mostly Spanish names had been collecting dust. On October 28, 1940, a new page in the book was literally turned to record Elsie Frantz's death. Contrary to the belief of those confined to Barrack 3, the death of Elsie Frantz had not been the first. This false assumption would also be true for other internees who believed that they too had witnessed the first death in Camp de Gurs. The death book confirmed that the average age of the nine men and four women who died on that day was almost seventy-five.

For the surviving Spaniards who remained in Gurs, the October deaths became a blessing given the Vichy government's need to hire gravediggers and coffin makers. Absent of any tools, gravediggers used rocks, pieces of discarded wood, and their hands to claw away at the porous ground until a thin wooden coffin, weighted by rocks, sank to the bottom of a watery hole. The few stunned family members who were allowed to attend the mass burial stood in muck up to their knees and stared at the sinking coffins. As rumors of even more deaths brought on by dysentery, malnutrition, and untreated preexisting medical conditions became a reality, the internees of Camp de Gurs began in greater numbers to congregate at the barbed wire of their ilots to watch the single gray swayback horse pull the body-filled wagon down the Moche.

OCTOBER 31, 1940

On the last day of October 1940, as Kurt and a few other children looked for Paul and a piece of peppermint candy, the faint sounds of approaching airplanes bounced off the nearby mountains. While the droning sounds muffled by the low clouds grew louder, the cautious children squeezed under the wire. Liberated, they played an impromptu game of tag, until a little girl pointed to a slow-moving column of sputtering trucks. Kurt waved to Paul, who along with the other French guards stood on the running boards of the trucks. There was a real sense of excitement given Kurt's realization that the recent gossip was true: they were getting out of Camp de Gurs.

While the trucks drew closer, furious waves from the guards forced the children back under the wire. When the line of twenty canvas-covered trucks came to a stop, Kurt could not decide whether he should wait or run back to his mother with the good news. Ultimately the decision was made for him when he saw a piece of luggage sailing from the back of one of the trucks. Paul waved again at the children to leave, but Kurt could barely raise his foot from the thick mud before another piece of luggage sailed onto the Moche with a sickening thud.

When Kurt burst into Barrack 3, he yelled, "Mutti, Mutti. On the road…"

An exasperated Ilse put her hand over Kurt's trembling lips. "Look at you, Kurt! You are wet and filthy. I've told you that you can go where you want, but I have no way of keeping you dry and clean." Ilse slowly removed her hand from her son's mouth. "Take your clothes off. Do it now! You can put my coat on while they dry, but no more, Kurt. I don't have the energy for this anymore."

Kurt shivered. "Mutti, please…" Ilse responded with an Isack stare, but Kurt could not be stopped. "You don't understand. They are coming on the trucks. I saw them!" Ilse pulled off Kurt's muddy shoes and pretended not to hear Kurt's whispering questions. "Why are more people coming here, Mutti? I thought we were leaving. I thought we were going to America."

"Stop it, Kurt!" answered Ilse. The others encircled mother and son.

The newly elected barrack chief put on her formerly elegant fur coat. "The boy has seen something," said Rebecca calmly as she tried to diffuse the rising anxiety. "Maybe the boy is wrong. Maybe he is right. For all we know it's our husbands and sons. We have not heard a word from them."

Kurt was not alone as he nodded. "Mutti, maybe she is right. I didn't even think to look for Opa or Onkel Julius."

"Why would the Vichy bring more people to a place where there is no food, clean water, beds, or medicine?" asked Rebecca on her way to the door. "They want us gone." The succinct observation ended with the barrack chief putting on her stylish sheepskin gloves while she made a final self-assured pronouncement. "I will see for myself."

In reality, what Kurt had seen on October 31, 1940, were 7,010 Jews and other "undesirables" from the camps of Saint-Cyprien, Rivesaltes, Recebedou, Noe, and Les Milles in southwestern France being dumped into Camp de Gurs.

JOHANNA

Given the looming disaster, the eventual chief rabbi of Camp de Gurs, Leo Ansbacher, and ten other rabbinical scholars were granted permission to move about the camp with one single insurmountable directive; revive the spirits of thousands of desperate Jews. But even the rabbis agreed that it was the early November request by the Spanish women for help to prepare soup that finally lifted everyone's spirits. Kurt took his mother's hand and followed the excited women to the open kitchen, where they watched grunting Spanish men hang six huge scarred 250-liter pots onto the finger-thick black metal wire. Excitement intensified after wood salvaged from barracks was stacked and then lit beneath the cloudy water-filled pots. Spontaneous cheers erupted as bags of six-month-old pebble-hard lentils, beans, and a few colorless carrots, potatoes, and onions were thrown into the boiling water.

Rabbi Ansbacher walked down the lines of women, shaking their hands. "God has answered our prayers," said the rabbi as soup, filled with maggots and other dead insects, was ladled into the dirt-rubbed bowls. The thankful women drank the hot, cloudy water and chewed on the rubbery beans and, if lucky, a piece of stringy horsemeat.

"Ilse," screamed the mud-encrusted woman who labored toward the huge kettles where Ilse helped. Ilse dropped the wooden paddle into the pot before she ran into the arms of her father's sister, seventy-six-year-old Johanna.

"I am so sorry about Onkel Jonas, Tante. I didn't have the money for the train," said a tearful Ilse as she and her aunt tightened their comforting embrace.

"We were married in 1887. We had a good life, three wonderful children. But I am happy he is not alive to see this." Ilse nodded in agreement with the candid assessment.

"Kurt?" asked Ilse's aunt cautiously.

"Yes, he is here in the barrack with Mutti."

"And Isack and Julius—have you heard from them?"

"Not seen since the night we arrived," answered Ilse.

"Our barrack's chief said that they may start giving out travel permits for family members to visit the other ilots, Ilse, but only six per day." Ilse's aunt's cautious questioning continued. "And with your parents, better, I hope?"

Ilse answered nonresponsively. "I don't think you will recognize Mutti anymore. Her mind seems somewhere else."

"And Isack?"

"Tante, we talked about this when Kurt and I visited you years ago. Nothing has changed. Poppa will always hate me…"

"Ilse, I know your poppa can be harsh, but he loves you. Don't ever forget that. He wanted the best for you. He wanted a better life for you than the one he had. That's the dream of all parents. He just doesn't know how to…"

"Please, Tante, I know I have been a disappointment to Poppa and Mutti—the loss of Heinz, my marriage, and the divorce. I understand it all. And I know most of all that I am a bad Jew, especially in Poppa's eyes." Ilse did not bother to whisper her most private thoughts amid the disinterested crowd. "But Tante, where has their faith gotten them? My lack of faith and their faithful observance have found us in the same place." Ilse's hands were shaking. "I know he is your brother and I know you love him, but…"

Johanna gently rubbed Ilse's arm. "We will have time to talk about this, so let me just enjoy the fact that I found you."

Ilse's apology was graciously interrupted by her aunt. "You never told me about Kurt. Tell me about your baby."

Ilse's eyes lit up. "He is not a baby. He's all grown up, nine years old. You can put my Kurt anywhere, even here, and he would be fine."

Ilse happily went on about Kurt until she found herself apologizing again. "I enjoy talking about my Kurt, maybe a little too much." The two women giggled like schoolgirls as they strolled along the razor sharp wire.

"And for you, Tante?"

"I told Selma that she was wrong, but it turns out she was the smart one. She's been in America since April in a place called Brooklyn, New York," said Johanna. Her voice trailed off.

"What about Hedwig and Frieda?"

"Unfortunately, they are here." Ilse looked across the Moche into the soup line forming in Ilot L. "So sad for the family to finally be together in this place."

With their arms linked, the women slogged back to the soup line where Johanna waited for the right moment. "I must also tell you that I saw Sophie's sister, Jenny."

"My God," smiled Ilse. "What barrack? Is she in good health? This will be so good for Mutti."

Johanna grabbed the warm bowl of watery lentil soup with her arthritic hands. Ilse tried again. "Tante, how is she? Well, I hope? And Tante Irma; is she here?"

Johanna picked at the dead bugs and then set the bowl on her lap. "It has been difficult for all of us, but it has been especially hard for Jenny. She told me that when the Nazis came for her and Irma at the house in Freiberg..."

Johanna's hands shook and the watery soup spilled over the edges of the bowl. "What is it, Tante? What did she say?"

"When the Nazis came for them they were told that they had only thirty minutes to pack."

"Yes, they said the same thing to us. We barely had..." Johanna meant no disrespect to Ilse, but she continued talking over her niece in a flat monotone voice. "Your Tanten did as they were told. They went to their rooms to gather their things. Jenny told me after five minutes she heard a crash coming from Irma's room. She surprised herself when she pushed the Nazis away from the broken window." The single tear from her aunt brought with it a long, awkward, silent moment that found Ilse's shaking hand being held by her aunt.

"Jenny told me that she started to run out of the building, but the Nazis told her that if she left she would be not allowed back in her own home. It's so painful to think she went through all of that alone. But she stayed and packed a few things before three brave Nazis escorted her out of that beautiful home, past the crowd that had gathered around Irma's body. They would not even let her stop to touch her sister, to say a prayer, nothing. But she did not cry. Jenny refused to give them that. Your Tante got into the truck packed with Jews. And that was it. They left. Thankfully some of the men whispered Kaddish as they drove off with Irma lying in the street like a piece of garbage. I think, Ilse, maybe it was good that they took us out of Germany. These Nazis are not human…"

Johanna stumbled with a request for forgiveness. Ilse picked pieces of mud from her aunt's hair and stated in few words the truth of her destroyed relationship with her father. "Now you understand why Father hates me."

"Ilse, your father does not hate you. I only hope you come to learn that and understand him." Johanna moved toward breaking the solemn promise she had made long ago. "Life has not been easy for your parents. They each have lost so much because of their own choices. Ilse, don't you ever ask yourself why you never see your Mutti's family?"

"Yes," followed the meek response. "I heard the arguments when I was small, when their bedroom door was closed. It was always about Tante Lina and Onkel Heinrich causing problems and that Mutti never received her dowry. It was not fair that they had to get married by themselves. Poppa and Mutti have been through so much…"

Ilse rose to her feet and kissed her aunt. "Tante, come with me. I will bring you to Mutti and Kurt. That is, if he is there," said a suddenly upbeat Ilse. "If Mutti sees you, maybe she will feel better. She has not been herself for years, and all of this has made things worse. You can talk about the old days with her. I have to believe there were some good times. Weren't there, Tante?" asked Ilse during their short walk.

"Mutti," said Ilse in the nearly empty barrack.

Sophie, wincing in pain, pushed herself into a seated position. She put her hands up to her eyes to adjust to the stream of dull light coming from the open door. Her unfriendly voice snarled, "Who is that, Ilse?"

Ilse helped Johanna to the floor where the two old women embraced. "How is my little sister-in-law?" smiled Johanna.

"You look terrible," answered Sophie while the women stroked each other's hair.

"I look terrible? You're lucky I didn't bring my mirror," laughed Johanna.

THE OFFER

After the chief for Ilot K walked into Barrack 3, she took her officious-looking rock gavel and clanged away at the unlit stove. "I bring good news from the administration office. On November 17, 1940, Herr Gruel advised the ilot chiefs that Camp de Gurs will no longer be a concentration camp. So starting today Camp de Gurs is a shelter center." The chief's mocking laughter over the changed status was derisively cheered until she once again banged her rock gavel. She pulled out a scrap of paper and read, "Would the following women please follow me outside?"

"You're right," whispered Ilse to a woman who recalled Rabbi Ansbacher's desire to form various committees similar to those established by the Spaniards.

"So how does a group of three seamstresses, a nurse, and a teacher help the rabbi with the committees?" asked one of the women after they exited the barrack.

"Didn't your barrack chief talk to you?"

The confused women looked at each other. "I'm here to discuss the status of your children," stated the chief. There was no response to the provocative statement other than the defensive stares of protective mothers. Nonetheless, she pushed ahead. "Apparently efforts have been underway to transfer children to safe houses throughout France. A request has been made to get fifty children out of this camp. Although there are very few specifics, there will be schooling, proper medical attention, and better food."

The women's mouths fell open and their eyes turned to a wet pink. "I apologize, but I didn't realize you knew nothing about this. I must also apologize, but I need your answers now." The thin veneer of confidence from the chief began to crack. She spoke haltingly. "I'm a mother too, but this appears to be a chance for your children."

"Frau Kaufman, please help me to understand," asked the teacher before she ran back to the barrack. "But what happens if we end up in America or go back home? If we stay here awhile longer, can my Rebecca come back? Can my husband and I visit her? Could she be sent back to Germany without us? Please help me to understand, because dear God, I don't."

Before the chief could answer, the nurse angrily spit out, "You ask me to give you my baby without talking to my husband. You can't tell me anything about where my child is going or for how long, and then you say I need to give you my answer now!" She buried her crying face into Ilse's shoulder and whimpered, "No more, enough!" before she too ran back to the barrack.

One by one the remaining women left without a word being said, until Ilse stood alone in front of the uncomfortable messenger. When the sad eyes of the chief finally looked up, she nervously unrolled the list. "It's Ilse Walker?" Although Ilse did not answer, more importantly, she did not run back to the barrack.

"The honest answer is I don't know how to respond to most of the questions you want to ask me. I promise you I will know more. Your child," asked the chief as she looked at the paper "is Kurt and he is nine years old?" Ilse stared at the muddy ground. "I can tell you that Kurt will remain in France and will be watched over by a number of organizations, including the Quakers and the OSE. I wish I had more to tell you, but..." The chief put her hands on Ilse's shoulders. "What do you want me to tell them about Kurt?"

In the moment of sheer panic that followed the question, Ilse's choices throughout her life passed before her. She cynically checked off each one. Ilse could not recall a single choice that was not fraught with self-doubt and, in hindsight, correct. The words "not again, not again" rang like a bell inside her head while she relived the moment when baby Heinz was taken from her.

"Ilse, I have almost twenty more barracks to visit. I know this is difficult, and I wish I could help you, but honestly I don't know what to say..."

"When do I have to tell you?" asked Ilse.

"Ilse, didn't you hear me? I need to know now. The Quakers will be here by the end of the day. There are documents that need to be completed and they will want to talk to you."

Ilse paced along the worn path near the barbed wire. She acknowledged Paul's smile and, like many other internees, unashamedly spoke out loud to herself. "How do I contact Poppa to get his permission? He will say I should not have made such a decision without his approval." Ilse rested her head on the wire. "I need to respect that he could have said no when I needed his help."

Later that evening, Ilse wrapped Kurt's face with a piece of torn cloth to fight off the imminent attack of biting lice and bedbugs. No longer a novice in the camp, she neither screamed nor jumped but simply gathered her thoughts as she looked at a hanging blouse coated with bugs. Ilse walked toward the thick flickering candle with a stubby pencil in her hand and a torn border from an old newspaper. The simple note ended, "Please do not hate me, Poppa. I love you, Ilse."

After the note was completed, Ilse buried it in her luggage.

DECEMBER 4, 1940,
THE FUNERAL

Julius Hammel was honored in early November when the rabbis of Camp de Gurs asked him to ensure that chevra kadisha, the burial of Jews in accordance with Jewish law, be followed. His acceptance was lauded by the rabbis, since the tending to the dead was an act for which the deceased could never say thank you and for which there were no ulterior motives.

Weeks later, when Julius Hammel stood on the dirt floor in the small, windowless shack on the cemetery grounds, he prayed that God relieve him of his duties. His unanswered prayers left him rubbing a rag with the last few drops from his precious bottle of cologne. He tied it over his face and began the process of bathing the body. Since there was not enough tachrichim, or shrouds of pure white cotton, to dress the man in accordance with Jewish law, he placed ten small pieces of linen over the body while his female counterpart prepared the bodies of the women with twelve pieces of linen. His body lurched forward with dry heaves as he washed the clothing stained by human waste.

While he completed his solitary work, the shomereim, or watchers, stood outside the shack to honor the deceased by guarding his body until its burial. In better times, the shomereim refused to eat or drink while they carried out their duties so as not to disrespect those that had died. But in Gurs, even this rite could not be observed since they were already starving. After Julius Hammel rubbed his wet hands on his pants, he rested on a small wooden bench and prayed for the dead man and his family. When his prayer ended, he dropped his head, read the body tag, and sarcastically said to God, "I'm so tired. Maybe you can take me to be with my new friend, Julius Ettlinger."

When Kurt, Ilse, and Sophie returned from the outdoor kitchen they were immediately met by the barrack chief. "Sophie," said the direct, red-eyed chief. "Your son died on December first. You and your family received permission to attend the funeral today." Sophie's usually flat and expressionless face convulsed. She yelled for Kurt to help her to the ground while tears bled from her vacant eyes.

A sober Kurt whispered to his mother, "Does that mean Opa is here?" A focused Ilse did not answer Kurt; instead, she put Elsie Frantz's winter coat over her mother's coat. On December 4, 1940, three generations of Ettlingers raised their funeral passports to Paul before they came upon the first major improvement in Gurs, the rock-paved path that led to the cimetière.

When Kurt began that solemn walk neither he nor his family knew that Julius Ettlinger had been one of thirty-six Jews to die in Gurs over the prior three days. One of the people who did know the truth of the many deaths was the clerk for Camp de Gurs. His recording of deaths began with eighty-five-year-old Moritz Khuen and concluded with a baby boy whose life ended on the same day he was born. The clerk recorded the baby's name simply as Vogelsang, since the hysterical mother was unable to give the dead child a first name.

"Kurt, you stay here. Oma will come with me while I'll look for Opa," said the single-minded Ilse, who hurried past the simple wood archway.

When his mother was out of sight, Kurt passed under the archway. Soon he stood among the many open graves and scores of people who had also received permission to go the cemetery. This included the weeping families of brothers Max and Felix Benjamin from Köln and eighty-three-year-old Johanna Meyer. The sight of the pained family watching the brothers' thin pine caskets being lowered into the watery graves quickly became too much for Kurt.

"Rabbi, Rabbi," called Ilse as Kurt threw his arms around his unquestioning mother. The rabbi shook Ilse's hand. "Who are you here for?"

"My brother, my mother's son," answered Ilse. She drew Sophie closer to her.

"His name?" asked the rabbi.

Ilse looked at her unresponsive mother. "Julius Ettlinger."

"I know this name, but the body is not here yet."

With the last few words barely out of the rabbi's mouth, Kurt screamed and ran past the muddy gravediggers, mourners, and stacked caskets. He was deaf to the scolding admonitions from the angry rabbis as he jumped into the arms of the raggedly clothed man. "We thought you were dead!" cried Kurt.

The confused rabbi, who had only seconds before been praying with Sophie, held her from collapsing as a screaming Ilse followed Kurt through the mud. "Mutti, Mutti," squealed Kurt as his legs dangled above the cemetery grounds in the embrace of his uncle Julius.

"They told us you were dead," cried Ilse while her brother's impromptu dance brought angry stares.

179

"You there," shouted another rabbi. "Be respectful in this solemn place!" The rabbi dismissed her shivering apology that was drowned out by the joyous cries from her slowly approaching mother.

"We didn't know if you were here, and then we were told that you were dead, and now this," shouted the happy group that tried to move away from the words of Kaddish that seemed to come from all corners of the cemetery.

"I wasn't sure where you were either," answered Julius as he kissed his mother. "I told the rabbis I worked in the cemeteries back home. So here I am each day. I get a little more food that I can share." Julius dropped Kurt to the mud and pulled Ilse closer. He whispered, "There are so many people dying every day. Hundreds have already died." He kissed his mother again. "We hear that the ilots for the women have it worse than the men. Our ilot has some bed frames, straw, and even a few chairs. Some of the Spaniards are even selling food for those that can afford it."

While Julius continued to talk, Kurt asked, "Onkel, where is Opa?" Ilse picked nervously at one of the many scabs on her hand.

"I got him a job working here. He is my assistant," said a self-mocking Julius, who puffed out his chest before he ran back into the crowd. After he returned with a frail-looking Isack Ettlinger, Kurt's muddy shoes dangled above the cemetery grounds while Isack stroked Kurt's unkempt hair. Ilse grabbed at her mother's hand as Isack walked the last steps alone. His gentle hug and polite kisses on their foreheads allowed him to keep his emotions in check as he made small talk about their health during the awkward reunion. Julius put his arm around his father and attempted to inject some black humor. "Poppa, Ilse was told that I was being buried today."

"You didn't tell them?" asked Isack.

Isack cleared his voice. "My brother Julius died. I saw him the morning after we arrived. He was already sick. Just two more weeks and we would have celebrated his seventieth birthday." Isack's voice remained strong. "So now it is just me and Johanna. We are all that is left from Eppingen."

"Poppa, we saw Johanna. She is here! She is here with all of us in the camp," said Ilse as she stroked her father's arm.

"Johanna, here in Gurs?" muttered Isack while the rabbi tapped him on the shoulder.

Seconds later he felt a familiar embrace and heard an old woman say, "You were always my favorite, my baby brother." Isack thought he would collapse, but of course there could be no sign of weakness, only the indulgence of a quick kiss before the Spaniards brought the casket of Julius Ettlinger to a water-filled grave. Isack looked into the teary eyes of Johanna before he took her hand and walked up to each family member with a pocketknife and made a jagged three-and-a-half-inch tear on the fraying clothing near their hearts. He alone would ensure that the symbolic ritual of K'riah be completed. When he made the last cut he prayed:

"Blessed are You Lord our God, King of the Universe, the True Judge."

Upon the conclusion of the prayer, the poorly built casket sank to the bottom of the grave while the Ettlingers were joined in prayer by the families of Max and Felix Benjamin and Johanna Meyers:

"Glorified and sanctified be God's great name throughout the world which He has created according to His will. May He establish His Kingdom in your lifetime and during your days, and within the life of the entire House of Israel, speedily and soon; and say, Amen…"

As the last words of Kaddish were chanted, Isack saw that Ilse had not joined in the prayer. He let go of Kurt's and Johanna's hands before he presented Ilse with a spoon that would have to suffice for the mitzvah, or doing of a good deed, for his dead brother. She placed three spoonfuls of dirt into the open grave before she unthinkingly gave the spoon directly to Kurt. Isack seethed, and the rabbi grabbed her arm.

"No, no, Kurt is a mourner. He cannot touch the shovel directly. To do so would allow the death of Julius to be contagious. Place it back in the dirt!" ordered the annoyed rabbi.

After the Ettlingers exited past the wooden arch, Isack whispered to Ilse, "I heard you gave permission to the Quakers for Kurt to leave the camp. Is it true?"

A panicked Ilse looked for an unnecessary escape from the false allegation. Had her mother seen the undelivered note she had written to her father? "Yes, I talked to them, Poppa, but…"

"You had no right to do that. You may be the mother, but I make the decisions about Kurt. I should not have to remind you of that." Isack's voice became louder. "The fact that the papers are back in Karlsruhe does not change a thing."

"Poppa, please, until a few moments ago I didn't even know you were alive, let alone here in Gurs. Yes, I did talk to the ilot chief about Kurt, but I told them no. I swear on the life of Kurt, Poppa." Isack stood silent. "But Poppa," said Ilse, who had returned to her subservient persona. "But what do you think? Maybe we need to get him out of here. The anti-Jewish laws here in France…They hate us too."

"You don't understand," snapped Isack. "Things are getting better here. In the last few days there have been some drugs for the sick in the hospital, and I understand that some of the barracks have started getting electricity. Besides, it will not be long before we all leave here. But none of that matters. Regarding Kurt, I make the decisions, not you. We do not discuss any more!"

DESPAIR

"In its work of national reconstruction the government from the very beginning was bound to study the problems of the Jews as well as that of certain aliens, who, after abusing our hospitality, contributed to our defeat in no small measure. In all fields and especially in the public service...the influence of Jews has made itself felt, insulating and finally decomposing.

All observers agree in noting the baneful effects of their activity in the course of the recent years, during which they had a preponderant part in the direction of our affairs. The facts are there and they command the action of the government to which has fallen the pathetic task of French restoration."

"Vichy to Penalize Jews for Defeat," *New York Times* article dated October 18, 1940, in which the preamble to the first Statut des Juifs is cited

Before Kurt's expulsion to France, numerous unaffiliated organizations were aiding both the French and non-French people impacted by the war. However, by the middle of December 1940, their efforts had no real effect on the issues of malnutrition and disease that were pervasive in the camps in southwestern France. Amazingly, the important consolidation of these groups came about as a result of the October 1940 French codification of the anti-Jewish sentiment that Jews were "un-French."

While Kurt and his family languished in Gurs, Rabbi René Hirschler, a native of Marseille and the grand rabbi of Strasbourg, brought together nine Jewish organizations to assess the conditions in the camps. These disparate groups finally joined together to form a single group known as the Central Committee. Only Solidarity, a Jewish Communist organization, refused to join, because of its unwillingness to have the appearance of cooperating with the Nazis. Nonetheless, through the leadership of Rabbi Hirschler, the Central Committee began the complicated process of providing clothing, medicine, food, and other relief to the camps that were under the watchful eye of the Nazis and Vichy.

The process of consolidation culminated on November 20, 1940, when representatives from a total of twenty-four additional groups met in Nîmes, France. Among the groups present in addition to the Central Committee was the American Friends Service Committee, more commonly known as the Quakers. The emergence of the Nîmes Committee coincided with the justified harsh attacks on the Vichy government by the international press. This was especially true in the United States and Switzerland, where the press reported that revolts in some of the camps in the fall of 1940 were quelled with a "...disproportionate amount of violence." Due to continuing worldwide pressures, the Vichy military eventually relented and granted various organizations under the Nîmes committee access to the camps for humanitarian purposes. In January 1941, the Vichy agreed that all internees could be released as long as they continued the process of emigration, but only after they guaranteed the impossible, their ability to pay a 1,200 franc per month stipend.

On December 20, 1940, the Quaker relief work in Gurs, led by its representatives Andrée Salomon and Dr. Joseph Millner, began in earnest. Milk was distributed to children and pregnant women while nurses began the ominous task of tending to the sick and dying. Eight days later workers arrived with beans, rice, lentils, lard, and clothing, and although their presence was greatly appreciated, it was too late for the twenty to thirty people dying each day from typhoid and meningitis.

The Quakers, a Christian-based religion founded in the middle of the seventeenth century in England, was notable in part for its members' refusal to attend established churches, take oaths of office, pay tithes, or bear arms. Two and a half centuries after its formation, the AFSC, a US-based Quaker aid society, was established in Philadelphia in response to the human tragedy occurring in Europe during World War I.

```
"Although they will neither take up arms or
make ammunition or participate in any way in the
destructive aspects of warfare, the Quakers as-
sembled at the meetings of the Religious Society
of Friends, at the Friends Meeting House at
Fifteenth Street and Rutherford Place, decided
yesterday to organize a unit of 500 Quakers to
go abroad and assist their French and English
brethren in restoring devastated homes behind
the fighting line in France..."
```

"QUAKERS TO WORK BEHIND FIRING LINE," *New York Times*, May 30, 1917

The 1917 America Quaker founder, Rufus Jones, and his followers searched for a way that conscientious objectors could provide nonmilitary services to civilian victims of the war. Their collective acts of charity that provided wartime care and medical services for civilians in France in 1917 and the feeding of one million starving children in Germany and Austria in 1918 would not be forgotten. Years later, while Nazi Germany readied itself for war, the Quakers pursued their traditions of pacifism, social equality, and integrity by operating child feeding programs in Spain during its civil war. When the Quakers followed thousands of Spanish into the newly constructed internment camps in southern France, they continued their selfless work. True to their words, the Nazi and Vichy governments had not forgotten the acts of charity by the Quakers during World War I. They allowed in 1940 an old friend's request to enter Camp de Gurs.

When the fifty-seven employees of the Quakers began to oversee the relief for the camps, they were tested just as they had been in World War I. At that time, it became politically necessary to condemn Britain's blockade of food to Germany. Similarly, in order to function in World War II, the Quakers remained silent when 80 percent of the relief supplies arriving in their Marseille headquarters were stolen by the Nazis.

Undaunted, the Quakers persevered in their acquisition of rice from Egypt, fish and sugar from Portugal, and milk from Switzerland. Some supporters' donations were publicly acknowledged, such as the $10,000 gift made by the American Book of the Month Club. However, the astute Quakers made sure to conceal donations from obvious Jewish organizations, companies, or individuals, such as the $1 million gift from the American movie studio of Metro-Goldwyn-Mayer. Because of those efforts as of Christmas 1940, the camp administrator for Gurs proudly published to the world's press that the Jews of Gurs were consuming

1,200 calories of food per day. The Quakers quietly reported the truth back to their headquarters. The mounting deaths from malnutrition in Gurs resulted from a starvation diet of seven hundred calories per day.

By early January 1941, Rabbi Leo Ansbacher, the rabbi of Camp de Gurs, began to implement the Spanish model in Gurs. He lifted the internees' emotional and religious spirits by entering every ilot on the Sabbath to pray. He ensured that each ilot had a separate barrack that served as a cultural center and synagogue. The same barrack served as a post office to send and receive mail, both within and outside of the camp. He also implemented a 10 percent tax on all money received, a one-half-franc tax on small packages and one-franc tax on large packages so that additional food, clothing and medicine could be procured. And with that extra money the rabbi directed his brother, Max, to make black market purchases of vegetables, flour, and figs for the children and those suffering from severe malnutrition.

In addition to the converted synagogues in each ilot, a hut at the camp's entrance was appropriated for the camp's rabbinate of Jewish scholars. This yeshiva, or school for Talmudic studies, was named Bnei Brak in honor of an Ultra-Orthodox Jewish settlement just east of Tel Aviv, Israel. It became a home for classes in Jewish history and the Talmud and a setting for weddings, circumcisions, and Bar Mitzvahs. However, by the close of January 1941, the reality of Gurs had infected the internees with a sense of utter hopelessness. The dire conditions were endless: a persistent tramontane, improper sanitation, polluted drinking water, and a lack of medicine and food. And through it all, Ilse impatiently waited for the well-intentioned rabbis and Quakers to save her child.

The patience of the hopeful Quakers was equally tested given their failed efforts to remove any children from the camps. The first glimmer of real hope occurred on February 23, 1941, when the Quakers obtained the approval to release fifty children from the camps. The first children were to come from Camp de Gurs.

```
"'I went to see the Gurs Camp,' he (Red Cross
official F. Sahlman) said, 'to see how living
conditions were and I was shocked at the hous-
ing problem. In one small shack without windows
and virtually no ventilation I found 150 people.
I had to use my flashlight to pick my way about
the hut without treading on the refugees....When
6,000 Jewish Germans arrived...the commander of
the camp received no increase in his food al-
lowance. If this situation...continues many will
die for lack of nourishment....'"
```

"GURS CAMP SHOCKS RED CROSS OFFICER, French Administration said to Be Doing Its Best With Inadequate Supplies," *New York Times*, Steve Fulton of the United Press, December 28, 1940

Rabbi Hirschler eventually ascended to the chaplain general of the all of the camps of southern France. In March 1943, Rabbi Hirschler was murdered in the Austrian death camp of Ebensee.

A SECOND OFFER

"Three of the camps visited on the first day were...Recebedou...Noe, and Vernet....The people complained mostly about not being able to get swiftly to America....Some said they felt almost happy to be there after their experiences at Gurs, farther down in the Pyrenees, from where they had been evacuated. We did not see Gurs..."

Chicago Tribune, David Darrah, April 4, 1941

"Are Ilse and Kurt Walker here?" said the woman whose clean clothes and healthy appearance made her stand out from the suspicious Jews in Barrack 3. Ilse pressed her face deep into her luggage.

"I am a social worker with the OSE (Oeuvre de Secours Aux Enfants, or Children's Aid Society), a French Jewish child care agency, working with the Quakers in Toulouse."

Ilse felt the unrelenting stares. "Yes, my name is Ilse Walker. Kurt went to the post office to see if he got a letter from his Opa. What's this about?" The volume of each word rose as both of her hands reflexively balled into fists and rhythmically struck the sides of her legs. Gossip, good or bad, was the only form of distraction in the camp, and this time Ilse was center stage.

"Please, may I call you Ilse?" asked the social worker, who put out her unaccepted hand. The worker felt the same uncomfortable stares. "There is nothing wrong. I just wish to talk to you. Can we go outside? Would you like a cigarette?"

"I don't smoke anymore," said Ilse. She took the thick communal coat that had belonged to Elsie Frantz and placed it over the cloth coat she wore twenty-four hours a day.

With her minor victory accomplished, the worker took a final look at the disappointed faces before she repeated her earlier question, "Do you mind if I call you Ilse?"

"No," said Ilse anxiously.

"I'm Andrée Salomon, but please call me Andrée." Ilse picked nervously at her scabbed hand that seemed to never heal.

"Do you recall talking some weeks ago about some of the children leaving Gurs? Are you interested?" asked Andrée directly.

Ilse's hand quickly became speckled with fresh blood. "The fifty children were already chosen. I saw the list posted in the camp yesterday," answered Ilse.

"That's true, but eight of the children are not going any longer. It was just too difficult." Over the prior hours in which Andrée had begun the same conversation, she had witnessed mostly tears, but with Ilse there was only silence.

Relying on her poor German, Andrée proceeded cautiously. "Ilse, if you are still interested, I can have the necessary papers prepared."

Ilse gulped for air. "My father is the legal guardian for my Kurt, and he was so angry because he thought I had...He was furious with me, just furious," mumbled Ilse.

"Ilse, I'm sorry, but I…"

"My father is the legal guardian. He is the one to make the decision. You need to talk to him."

"When did he become the guardian? I am not sure I understand. You are the mother?"

"Yes, I'm Kurt's mother."

"Well, that's why I am talking to you."

Ilse wiped away the tiny beads of perspiration that dotted her upper lip. "In 1934, when Kurt's father divorced me, my father was given legal guardianship of Kurt. It was just better that way."

"Who cares about what a court did in Germany? Germany does not even recognize you as a citizen. You are imprisoned here in France," said the incredulous worker.

"It's not about Germany or the courts. He is my father," responded Ilse.

"But my concern is what you want to do for Kurt?" asked a still confused Andrée.

"Andrée, they will not keep us here forever. It has only been a few months and things are already getting better because of Rabbi Ansbacher and the Quakers. Besides, we hear rumors about being sent to the United States, Madagascar, or even going back home. What if Kurt is brought to an unsafe place? What kind of a parent would that make me?" Ilse looked at Andrée's shocked face.

"Ilse, this is about Kurt, not your father. I understand the choice is not an easy one. I am uncomfortable even asking parents the question." She paused. "But I ask you. What is it that you want to do?"

Ilse's voice fought to remain strong. "I am tired of having to make these decisions about my boys!"

Andrée looked at the brief information listing Kurt as an only child. "Ilse, I have upset you and I apologize. My coming here was to bring good news for you and Kurt. Please accept my apology. All of the families of the original fifty children said yes, and then some of those same families said no. No parent should ever have to give up a child."

Andrée's words stung at Ilse, who immediately thought of Heinz. "Whatever you decide will be the correct decision, but I do need an answer. The children leave on February twenty-sixth."

After Andrée walked out of the ilot, she waved a final good-bye as Kurt marched his last steps on the Moche. After he raised his arm to complete a formal salute to Paul, a rolled-up piece of paper began to cartwheel down the road.

"I believe this must be yours, sir," said Andrée to a racing Kurt.

"Merci, Madame," responded Kurt before he marched past Paul. Never one to walk, Kurt raced to Ilse, who barely had enough time to catch the skin and bones that had become her son. She bent Kurt backward so that his long hair slapped at the ground, while the infectious laughter of mother and son left Paul and Andrée laughing. When Ilse finally placed Kurt back on the ground, she was energized.

"Kurt, where were you? I thought you went to see if you got a letter from Opa," laughed Ilse.

"I stopped to see my Spaniard friend after I went to the post office. He finished a painting of me." Kurt unrolled the paper and proudly displayed the portrait.

"Mutti, he is going to do another one of me riding a horse for Opa. If you look on the bottom, it has his name and today's date, February 24, 1941. Do you like it, Mutti?"

"Of course I do!"

"And Mutti, you won't believe this. He did not want anything for it. He said that's what friends do, because it's the right thing to do," smiled Kurt.

ADIEU, CAMP DE GURS,
ADIEU, OUR MAMAS,
ADIEU, OUR PAPAS

"...Despite the severe food restrictions, the problem is a moral one...Some of the women where the inmates swarmed about the correspondents became hysterical.... Many believed that the correspondents were an international committee to investigate their cases. Even when they knew they were only correspondents, that knowledge brought a breath of hope. ...The internees took every opportunity to thrust notes and written pleas on the visitors. Nearly every one of them, it appears from their statements, dreams of being able to go to the United States. They are thinking of the United States now as the country of Liberty, which used to be their conception of France."

"REFUGEES SUFFER IN FRENCH CAMPS," Lansing Warren, wireless to the *New York Times*, Vichy, France, March 28, 1941

On Wednesday morning, February 26, 1941, while Kurt stretched on the former mattress of straw that had become a bag of dust, he was unaware that Ilse had stayed up the entire night to remember every moment of their lives together. Over those hours she repeatedly asked of a sleeping Kurt, "Do you remember when…" Then, with the arrival of the faint morning light, sheer terror ripped at Ilse. She cupped her hands over her mouth to deaden her cries. Ilse whimpered, "No parent should have to give up one child, let alone two." When her moment of self-pity passed, Ilse gently shook Kurt. "It's time to wake up. I have a treat for you," sang the immediately transformed Ilse.

Kurt watched his mother remove a thick piece of bread from a sheet of newspaper before she placed it onto the blazing potbelly stove. While the wonderful smell of the toasting bread filled the barrack, Ilse pulled a small jar of jam from her coat. "And for my Kurtela, I have something special if he gets dressed," giggled Ilse.

The others tried to give Kurt and his mother their privacy, but they stole each moment as if it was theirs. Kurt smiled as Ilse whipped the jam with a handmade spoon in the bowl made from a sardine can. His smile grew when his mother dipped her finger into the frothy delicacy and then generously spread its contents onto the warm bread. Quickly he was chomping away at his treat while Ilse glanced at the fractured lens on her watch. She whispered to Kurt, who immediately dropped to his knees and kissed his sleeping grandmother. Seconds later the emotional women and children of Barrack 3 hugged and kissed Kurt while they offered their prayers for a safe journey.

After a quick wave to Paul, Kurt dragged his mother down the Moche. When he spotted the small groups of people walking slowly toward a stopped truck, Kurt looked at his mother. She kissed him and said, "Yes."

"Opa! Opa!" screamed Kurt until Isack captured Kurt in his arms. Isack's angry eyes burned in the direction of Ilse before he became lost in his private moment. He was oblivious to the infectious sounds of laughter that brought the community of Gurs out from their barracks. A kneeling father looked into his child's face for the first time in four months. A seven-year-old girl sat in her mother's lap while another mother and father walked in circles with their ten-year-old son. The witnesses clung to the barbed wire and waved filthy rags as they called out to the children. The uninhibited children ran from ilot to ilot in an unchoreographed ballet. Their brief moments at the wire that allowed a kiss, smile, or hug ended with, "Write to me. Make sure you study. I will see you soon. Be good. I love you."

Walter Kirchmeyer, Hannah Moses, and Maria Dafner were, at thirteen years of age, the oldest of the children on the Moche that day. They tearfully listened to the simple instructions from their parents that they had to watch out for the little ones. The youngest child to leave, sixteen-month-old Victor Friedman, thankfully had no memories of his mother, collapsed on the Moche.

Ilse kept her distance on the muddy shoulder of the road. She watched Andrée Salomon whispering to the Cohns, the husband and wife escorts for the children. Ilse's muscles grew taut as she watched them drape an arm around a parent's shoulder. It's starting, thought Ilse. The Cohns ushered the Adlers and their four children, including five-year-old twins Siegfried and Martha, to the truck. The Adlers took some comfort that they were among seven sets of parents whose children left Gurs with at least one sibling.

While Ilse inched toward Isack and Kurt, Lilly and Max Weilheimer were tapped on their shoulders. It was time for their two boys, nine-year-old Richard and five-year-old Ernst. Ilse could not take her eyes off a smiling Richard, who never let go of his little brother's hand. Moments later Lilly Weilheimer painfully lifted Ernst onto the truck. She took great comfort in knowing that her boys were unaware that she was dying from cancer.

The distraction of the Weilheimer boys left Ilse unprepared for the gentle caress around her shoulder. "Frau Walker," whispered Madame Salomon. "Do you need any help?"

Kurt's startled mother answered, "No, we are fine."

Kurt looked at his unemotional mother and grandfather. "I thought this was a good thing, Mutti, Opa. Why is everyone crying?" asked Kurt. Ilse and Isack, who had not said a word to each other, looked at each other's expressionless faces. They hoped one of them would be able to answer the question, but the only words they heard came from the screaming one-armed truck driver, "Quakers have to go!"

Isack placed the palms of his hands under Kurt's chin while the last of the crying children were carried to the truck.

"Listen to me, Kurt," said Isack.

"Yes, Opa," answered Kurt to his businesslike grandfather.

"Remember...remember," started and stopped Isack. "Remember to be a good boy and study. But most of all, promise me that you will be a good Jew. If you are not a good Jew, you cannot be a good boy, and then you can never become a good man. You must lead a holy life, a Jewish life. And when the gentiles see you, they will say if that is the way a Jew acts, then Judaism must be a wonderful religion and the Jews must be good people. Promise me, Kurt, that you will be a good Jew." Although his businessman's voice was forceful, it was almost as if Kurt's grandfather was begging him.

Isack never took his tired brown eyes off of Kurt's face while he grunted his way to his feet. After he straightened his tie, pulled at the cuffs of his dirty gray shirt, and closed his eyes, Isack prayed:

"We praise you, Adonai our God, for having kept us alive and sustained us and enabled us to reach this day. We give thanks for the wondrous privilege of seeing our Kurt grow day by day, week by week, and year by year. For the health and strength you have given Kurt, for the mind and spirit with which you have endowed him, for his ability to elicit and return love. For all these precious gifts, we thank you.

"Watch over Kurt, O God, and may the teachings of our heritage guide Kurt throughout his life, and may he lead a life worthy of your blessings."

When Isack finally opened his eyes, it was clear that he had unsuccessfully fought back the tears that exposed him, at least in his mind, as being weak. Ilse could not hear the conversation between her father and Kurt, but she could see that Isack was crying. She promised herself that neither Kurt nor her father would ever see her cry.

"Don't worry, Opa. I promise you. I will be a good boy and a good Jew. Ganna gut!" answered Kurt confidently.

"Ganna gut, Kurt," quivered Isack.

With a final look from Madame Salomon, Ilse moved slowly toward Isack and Kurt. Isack pulled a picture postcard from his coat pocket that he had sent to Sophie years earlier. His long beard, erect posture, and crisp uniform presented the image he wanted Kurt to remember, not the old crying man that stood before him. "This is for you so you never forget your Opa," said Isack. Kurt's eyes lit up as he accepted the same photograph Isack had shown the soldiers in their apartment back in Karlsruhe.

Ilse took Kurt's hand and walked him the short distance to the rear of the truck where the whimpers and cries injured every adult. "Kurt, I wish I had more to give you," said Ilse after she placed a small leather wallet in Kurt's pocket. "I put some photographs in the wallet so you won't forget your Mutti."

"But Mutti," asked Kurt incredulously, "Opa said the same thing. How can I forget you when we will all be together?" Ilse and Isack looked at each other amid the continuing cries until the one-armed Quaker picked up Kurt with his good arm and placed him in the truck. The families of the children stood at the rear of the moving truck as the older children led the others in song:

> "Must I then, must I then leave the village today, village today.
> While you, my love, stay there?
> When I come, when I come, when I come back again, come back again,
> I'll return, my love to you, to you.
> May I always come to you, my dear,
> For I know no joy but with you.
> When I come, when I come, when I come back again, back again,
> I'll return, my love, to you."

When the song ended, the older girls sang in French:

"Adieu Camp de Gurs, adieu our mamas, adieu our papas."

The original eight children who refused to leave Gurs—twelve-year-old Margot Jankelevicz, seven-year-old Selina Bodenheimer, seven-year-old Karl Hauszman, thirteen-year-old Suse Levy, eleven-year-old Leonore-Therese Sondheimer, eight-year-old Beate Stern, five-year-old Suse Stern, and thirteen-year-old Ilse Weissmann—were murdered in the Nazi killing camps. Gunther Hauszman, unlike his younger brother, Karl, left Camp de Gurs on February 26, 1941. He returned to Gurs at the age of thirteen in the summer of 1942. The emotionally driven desire to see his family cost Gunther Hauszman his life.

LA MAISON DES PUPILLES

After Andrée Salomon collapsed in the bouncing truck, she thought of Helga Holbrook, the Dutch head of the Quakers. Andrée, nicknamed the Scarlet Pimpernel by Helga because she seemed to be everywhere, was given the gut-wrenching task of getting the children out of Camp de Gurs. In those early days after Kurt was interned in Gurs, it was Helga who searched for a location to house the children. It was she who obtained the necessary finances and, most importantly, through a byzantine process, the required paperwork for each child. By the close of 1940, when Helga located La Maison des Pupilles, the onetime home for tubercular children was a refuge for approximately fifty French war orphans. Her desperate negotiations obligated the Quakers and the other relief organizations from the Nîmes committee to become financially responsible not only for the children of Gurs but for supplementing the food and clothing of the French children. Helga's poker face left the representative from La Maison unaware that she had no idea where to acquire the money to house and feed one hundred children.

When the truck filled with forty-eight strangers passed through the opened gate at Camp de Gurs, not a word was said until they arrived at the Oloron-Sainte-Marie train station. "This is the station they took us to. I wonder," whispered one of the older girls, "if they are they taking us back to Germany?" Kurt's eyes bounced back and forth between the mumblings of the children and the adults who spoke in hushed tones. If a trip back to Germany was part of the plan, Kurt would not be part of it.

His time spent thinking about his escape ended when the rain forced everyone into the tiny station. Kurt forced his way past the sad children until he slid next to a boy who unashamedly laughed out loud while reading his book. Kurt peered over the boy's shoulder, who read:

```
"...'Tis a dreadful thing to tell
That on Max and Moritz fell!
All they did this book rehearses,
Both in pictures and in verses."
```

The boy's animated and high-pitched nasal reading as Moritz left Kurt doubled over in laughter. It took only a few more seconds before Kurt's infectious laughter left both of them unable to look at each other. The laughing ended when Kurt elbowed the boy in acknowledgment of the unwanted stares of the children, the Cohns, and the Scarlet Pimpernel.

"What's your name, Moritz?" whispered Kurt.

The boy pointed his finger. "I don't always want to be Moritz. You have to be him next time. I want to be the boss sometimes!"

Kurt looked at the hand that was almost touching his face, pumped it, and answered, "Agreed!"

"And my name is not Moritz, it's Hugo Schiller. I'm from Grünsfeld. What about you?"

"Kurt Walker and I'm from Karlsruhe."

After the introductions were completed, the boys returned to Max and Moritz's *A Juvenile History of Seven Tricks*. Head to head, they sat lost in the adventures of the two boys. Hugo, a few inches shorter than Kurt and with his blond hair and blue eyes, would, under normal circumstances, have borne no resemblance to Kurt. However, the two nine-year-old boys were indistinguishable from each other since their skinny bodies were covered with filth. They smelled like the waste they had lived in for the past four months. Their matted hair, a breeding ground for the many blood-sucking bugs that lived in Gurs, left itchy raw scabs on their skin and droplets of dry blood on their clothing that stood out against their pale gray skin. They wore the same mask of unhealthiness that made all the children from Gurs appear to be from the same family.

"Children, children we must hurry. The train is here," shouted Madame Salomon. Her unacknowledged warnings required the strong arm of Herr Cohn to literally grab Kurt and Hugo.

"Where are we going?" asked the boys simultaneously. The simple question was answered with a quick knuckle to their heads. And as they raced each other to the train, the painful blow from the knuckle could not wipe away the smiles of the new friends. The boredom of the ninety-mile train ride brought the boys some needed rest before they arrived in the town of Saint Gaudens and the trucks that took them south to the mountain town of Aspet. Two hours later, well after the sun hid behind the Pyrenees Mountains, the trucks climbed the last steep incline under a canopy of huge leafless trees.

"Children, wake up," said Madame Salomon as she placed sixteen-month-old Victor Friedman in the arms of Frau Cohn. "Please be patient. I know the trucks are old and the road is steep, but I promise, we will be there soon."

A final series of hard turns brought the trucks to a flat, brick-paved courtyard 2,200 feet above sea level. Exhausted, hungry, and disoriented, the children emerged from the trucks into a night even blacker than what they had experienced in Gurs. Kurt strained his eyes in the direction of the light bleeding through the huge, rectangular burnt-orange wooden shutters of the main building. His squinting finally ended when the headlights of the second truck illuminated the two-story-tall dirty white stucco building. It had a clay tile roof, windows framed by red bricks, and a balcony that ran the length of the building.

While the reticent children exited the trucks, Kurt kicked at pebbles that painfully poked through the newspaper-lined soles of his shoes, until he came upon Madame Salomon, the Cohns, and a male stranger. When Andrée observed Kurt and the other approaching children, she ushered the quarrelling adults past the rich brown wood-and-glass door. When she returned alone to the courtyard, her tense smile did little to allay the speculation from the children. "Madame Salomon, are the Nazis coming for us?" cried the children.

"My God, children, no," answered Andrée. "You have nothing to be afraid of," assured Andrée as she glared at the Cohns and the stranger. Kurt and Hugo jumped onto a chairlike stump to watch the adults, who were quickly surrounded by the children.

"Madame is correct," joined the Cohns. "There are no problems. In fact, I have some very good news. We are going to the kitchen to have some bread and milk. Not powdered, but real milk."

Kurt and Hugo jumped to the ground and joined the cheering children. They followed the Cohns to a single-story building just off the courtyard where they received copies of an eleven-page pamphlet, "MAISON DES PUPILLES D'ASPET." Kurt looked at the unintelligible French words until he motioned Hugo to look at the light streaming past the closing wooden shutters on the second floor. Hugo dismissed Kurt with a shrug. "It's nothing. Besides, if we stay here we won't get any milk." Kurt refused to move. Instead, he grabbed Hugo and pointed to the blackness at the rear of the property.

"Do you see that?" whispered Kurt. He pulled Hugo to the faint lines of barbed wire.

Hugo cupped his hands over Kurt's ear. "Do you see any guards?"

"They're lying to us. That must be what they were arguing about," responded Kurt.

Herr Cohn's knuckles flew off the heads of the boys. "Enough of that talk, you two. There is milk, bread, and cheese. If you want some, fine, if not, well, the choice is yours." The exhausted boys ran to the end of the line that brought them to the four long wooden tables, easily accommodating the already seated children.

After the three French girls employed by La Maison politely carried the pitchers of milk past Kurt and Hugo, the oldest of the girls pointed to herself and said, "Jacqueline Sallebert." He was sure she would put her fingers to her nose to avoid the smell of Gurs. To the contrary, she smiled before directing the boys to a table where she poured them each a glass of sweet, refreshing milk. Kurt's head fell back and white lines dribbled down his chin. Seconds later, his head bobbed and he drifted off to sleep. That was until Hugo placed a clean white plate close to their faces. An energized Kurt convulsed with laughter upon seeing his distorted, skeletonlike face, while Jacqueline discreetly opened all of the windows.

While the laughing continued, the adults continued their heated discussion in the courtyard. The stranger, Monsieur Couvot, the French director of Maison des Pupilles, was **still** in a state of shock with the news that the Cohns only had travel documents. They would have to return to Gurs the next day. His anger exploded again when Andrée advised Monsieur Couvot that she too would be leaving for Toulouse immediately. He stomped his foot like an ill-tempered child and snarled, "I can't take care of forty-eight more children without help." Monsieur Couvot pounded his fist in his hand. "You tell your Madame Holbrook this was not part of the agreement!"

When the Cohns walked back into the dining room they were pulled aside by Jacqueline. "The children keep raising their empty plates and glasses for more food. You must tell them that they cannot have any more food. They will become very ill."

"Not now, young lady," said Cohn curtly. He looked at the boys and girls while he spoke. "Madame Salomon has already left. I must tell you that my wife and I must leave tomorrow for Gurs. The director of the camp, Monsieur Couvot, will be in charge. Unfortunately, there is no one here who speaks German." A lying Cohn continued, "Someone who speaks German will be here soon to assist Monsieur Couvot. Now please gather your things."

After Cohn walked out of the dining room, the ragged children remained with Couvot. His phobia of bugs and angry mood ensured a long first night in Aspet for the children. Jacqueline acknowledged his curling finger before she led the children out of the dining room. Kurt lingered behind and grabbed at the few remaining pieces of crust until he was drawn out to the courtyard by the choruses of "Sales Boches! Sales Boches! Sales Boches!" He spun in a circle looking for the voices that hurled the insults. Suddenly the closed shutters on the second floor burst open, revealing the shadowy faces of the screaming French children.

Even if Kurt and the others had known that the verbal assault had come from children orphaned as a result of a warring sprint across France by the Nazis, their own anger would not have been tempered. The insults of "Nazis" were met with hate-filled responses of "Feiglinge," cowards. Couvot slapped his cane to the ground and ran into the building, while the Cohns tried to control the rock-throwing boys. Order was ultimately restored after Monsieur Couvot's cane brought about the painful screams from the French children. Even the Cohns could not resist a smile as they dragged the cheering children to a separate wing of the main building.

While the girls were ushered to the second floor, Cohn and Couvot directed the boys to the basement. A sense of exhilaration filled Kurt and the other victorious boys who walked beneath the eerie spider-webbed tentacles of the heating ducts. They followed Cohn's instructions and removed their clothes, while a disgusted Couvot stood his distance, watching Cohn take the soon-to-be-burned smelly rags out of the building. Jacqueline walked past the naked boys and tugged on a small rust-colored wheel until streams of hot water fell from pipes wrapped in real spider webs.

Kurt, who had not bathed in four months, screamed with delight as the refreshing water fell on him. Black filth from Gurs easily slid off the boys and trickled toward the director's shoes. Couvot's single grunt announced his exit. When the water was turned off, a shivering Kurt was pelted with a handful of delousing powder before he proceeded to Cohn's handheld hair clipper. Kurt spat out the foul combination of powder and bits of hair as he patted his stubby and scabbed head.

The sounds of a tapping cane, clicking heels, and harsh-sounding French words once again blasted throughout the basement. The room quieted, and Kurt inched closer to Hugo as the cane-waving Couvot reappeared. The boys instinctively tightened their protective circle as the last wisps of steam floated away. Couvot was rendered speechless at the vision of the sunken eyes, scab-covered bodies, and forest of bony limbs. The tip of his simple pine cane tapped the muddy floor ten times before he retreated to his office.

While Couvot placed his angry phone call to Helga Holbrook one hundred miles away in Toulouse, Kurt and the others put on their new ill-fitting clothes before they made their way to the main building. After months in Gurs, the sight of the large first-floor room filled with beds of real mattresses seemed unreal. Kurt ran his fingers over the crisp white sheets and thick blankets while Jacqueline pantomimed that each boy was to place his few possessions into a cubbyhole. They did as instructed before following her into the bathroom where each boy received a new toothbrush. Surrounded by glistening porcelain sinks, Kurt watched Jacqueline dip a toothbrush into a home brew of hydrogen peroxide and baking soda. Kurt joined the other boys and vigorously began to brush his teeth while blood oozed from his gums. He felt like a member of royalty.

The new prince laughed until Hugo slapped his head. One, two, and finally three tiny parasites fell into the sink. Kurt wanted to retaliate against Hugo, but instead he grabbed at the sides of the sink and closed his eyes as violent stomach cramps doubled him over in pain. When the last bit of pain faded, he looked into a huge mirror that hung over the row of sinks. He had laughed at his eerie circuslike image in the dinner plate, but now there was no laughter. He stuck his tongue out and pulled at his face to make sure he was looking at himself. Ill from dysentery, malnutrition, and more, Kurt had no idea he looked so bizarre until he saw his shaved head, oozing scabs, red eyes, and frail physique.

After Kurt returned to the dormitory, Jacqueline closed the burnt-orange shutters, turned off the light, and wished the boys, "Bonne nuit." Kurt stood alone in the corner and silently prayed for a quick return to Gurs.

THE FIRST DAY IN ASPET

In the morning, Kurt and Hugo slid onto the cold wooden floor, creeping past empty beds and others crowded with sleeping children. Seconds later, the sounds from the opening window alerted the others, who tumbled toward the sight of the rising sun. Kurt pointed toward the single four-foot-high row of wire that separated the courtyard from a pasture where twenty light brown cows were feeding.

"That's the wire from last night, Hugo. There are no guards here!" smiled Kurt.

"You're right," whispered Hugo as the boys' stick arms pushed past them. They oohed and ahhed pointing to the bluest sky that they had ever seen and the reds, yellows, and greens from the early blooming flowers. Kurt followed the older boys out of the building, past a few who remained asleep. In reality, they were not asleep, but too embarrassed to do anything that might expose their secret—urine-soaked sheets. This common occurrence in those first days, which Jacqueline and the other La Maison girls unsuccessfully hid from the administrator, became a source of annoyance for the strict Couvot. His insensitive and punitive treatment forced the traumatized offender to stand in the courtyard with a urine-soaked sheet wrapped around his neck before each victim completed a walk to and from the center of town. At least on that first day, Jacqueline's beautiful smile and "bon jour, bon jour" allowed the humiliated but otherwise unpunished children to join the others in the courtyard. Nonetheless, it took little time for the children to rename Couvot "the Goat."

While the children listened to the angry and unintelligible words of the Goat in the courtyard, they grudgingly accepted that they had been lured to Aspet by lies and empty promises of toys, schooling, activities, and books. Their black mood intensified with their thirty-day restriction to their rooms. Even if an explanation in German of the necessary quarantine to minimize the transmission of disease had been understood, the disheartened children knew the real truth: their confinement was punishment for some violation issued that morning by the perpetually angry Couvot.

Unlike the other children who left behind a mother and father in Gurs, Kurt's separation from his less than traditional family and few friends found him better prepared to deal with the first days at La Maison. Notwithstanding that, Kurt found great solace in being with the other children under circumstances that united him in a way that he could have never appreciated.

On March 11, 1941, the Quakers' office in Toulouse received a radiogram "VIA MACKAY RADIO" from its Philadelphia headquarters. The radiogram stated in part, "...You will identify children selected to Consul for quota visas. We anticipate no difficulty..." However, on April 26, 1941, Marseille-headquartered American Vice Consulate Hiram "Harry" Bingham Jr. IV was summarily relieved of his position by Breckenridge Long, the assistant secretary of state for America and the individual in charge of visas.

"The trip to Gurs was made on November 27, 1940 in the company of Dr. Donald Lowrie, Chairman

of the coordinating committee of twenty organizations doing work in the camps, including American Friends Service Committee, Secours
Suisse aux Enfants and Union des Societes O.S.E
the barracks appeared to be old and somewhat
dilapidated and weather-beaten. Judging by the
few little pipes with smoke escaping, only a
small proportion of the buildings could have
been heated.The oldest inmate is 104 years old.
Several babies were born in the past few weeks.

Each person received about 350 grams of bread
each morning which had to last all day. Such
other food as was obtainable was put in a soup
the soup was often cold or filled with sand and
dirt before reaching the barracks furthest from
the kitchen.

The latrines consisted of outhouses raised
over an open row of exposed garbage cans.To be
reached one had to brave the outside cold and
walk over 50 to 100 yards of muddy ground. Such
washing as was possible might be done in long
uncovered wooden troughs

Deaths listed in one day:

4 from chronic heart disease,7 old people, 1
45 yr old woman from malnutrition, 1 16 year
old diabetic patient, 1 baby of 4 months, 1 two
year old child from enteritis, 1 16 year old
from polycephalitis, 1 40 year old woman from
lung trouble

There is some reason to believe, according to one well-informed Frenchman, that the Germans wish conditions in the camps to be "hard" and will endeavor to keep them so by dumping thousands of new refugees from Germany and the occupied part of France into the unoccupied zone where they must complicate the whole problem. By doing so their own concentration camps in Germany would appear in a favorable light, particularly as regards sanitation."

Memorandum to the Honorable Secretary of State, Washington, D.C., by Vice Consul Hiram Bingham Jr. December 20, 1940

Since Bingham's appointment in 1939, he issued 2,500 visas to Jews instead of the few hundred he had been authorized. In addition to the issuance of these gifts of life, he hid Jews in his own home and provided them with disguises. He also claimed others as members of his family and purchased false documents in order to save them. Some were scientists, authors, or famous public figures like Marc Chagall. But most were ordinary people who, because of a lack of money and influence, would feel the greatest impact from the dismissal of the Schindler of France. Bingham's eventual transfer to Portugal and then Argentina halted his truly heroic efforts to save the fleeing Jews. His dismissal also had devastating consequences for the Marseille-headquartered Quakers who were trying to protect Kurt Walker and forty-seven other German Jews living in Aspet.

Unknown to the Quakers and even Bingham, the procedure for obtaining visas by late 1940 had been crippled months earlier. In June 1940, controversial Breckinridge Long established a plan to limit the number of visas available to Jews. An intradepartment memo stated:

"We can delay and effectively stop for a temporary period of indefinite length the number of immigrants into the United States. We could do this by simply advising our consuls to put every obstacle in the way and to require additional evidence and to resort to various administrative devices which would postpone and postpone and postpone the granting of visas."

Pursuant to his directive, the ability to leave France for the United States became a tortuous process in which an exit visa, a transit visa, affidavits of support, moral and political affidavits, certificates of good behavior, and paid tickets for a ship going to the United States were required. In the post-Kristallnacht year, 1939, Jewish immigration to America reached 43,450. Under Long's supervision, the numbers dropped to 4,705 from July 1942 to June 1943. In furtherance of Long's plan, he misrepresented to the US government by over 300,000 the actual number of refugees that had been admitted into the United States. After the exposure of this lie and numerous other misdeeds by Breckenridge Long in restricting refugees into the United State, he was finally removed, albeit too late, from his position in 1944.

"Commenting on reports that Camp Gurs...was about to be closed and its prisoners interned in other camps, Dr. Boris Gourevich, vice president of the Union for the Protection of the Human Person, announced yesterday that the camp was still in operation and that according to latest

reports, there were still between 12,000 and
15,000 refugees.

The organization...has succeeded in obtaining
modifications under which refugees at Camp Gurs
could be released.... Such request must be made
by the prisoners themselves, who must prove
they have sufficient means to cover their living expenses.

The sum of 1,200 Francs a month to cover the
expenses for each refugee must be deposited for
a number of months and persons released from
Camp Gurs are allowed to receive financial help.

All releases obtained through such a method are only temporary... and would not entitle
released persons to work or stay in France.
They must continue their efforts to leave the
country."

"Camp Gurs Not Yet Closed – Group Here Gets Easier Terms for
Refugees' Release," *New York Times*, April 4, 1941

ALICE RESCH

"In June 1940 I ended up with the Quaker delegation in Toulouse in the South of France. In October I was almost knocked off by a typhoid fever, and came back to work at the end of February 1941, only to find my work had been taken by my co-workers, so I felt more than lost and useless....Mr. Couvot (or 'the little gray man' as we baptized him) Telephoned in despair to us: Do send someone to help me out, someone who who at least speaks German! ... Helga came to me: "You are wailing because your work has been taken over by the rest of us, now I have a wonderful job for you! Go to Aspet and look after the Gurs children until the Cohns obtain their release from the camp. Do you think I was grateful? Oh no! I protested violently!! But Helga, I have no experience with children whatsoever apart from looking after an occasional sick child in the hospital You MUST not ask this of me! ! "I was scared stiff -But well, I was the only one available at that moment, so off I went, with a desperate prayer: Oh God, you just HAVE to help me! And, so he did-"

Letter from Alice Resch dated January 2, 1990

When Couvot heard the revving engine from the 1937 two-seater blue Simca, his sprint from his second-floor bedroom allowed him to arrive at the courtyard before the vehicle. It was Saturday evening on March 1, 1940, when the tall woman nodded yes to Couvot's "Alice?" After thirty seconds of disconnected ramblings, Couvot abruptly stopped. He had asked for someone who spoke German. Maybe the new arrivals from Gurs could speak with this woman, but how could he? Alice was amused with the obvious desperation that washed over Couvot's face before he collapsed into the tree-stump chair. She let her host linger a few moments more until she spoke in French, "I also speak Danish, German, Norwegian, and English."

A rush of color returned to his sallow face before Couvot pulled Alice through the front door of the dining room yelling, "Jacqueline! Bring the children!"

Alice looked at her trembling hand that told the truth behind her false bravado. Her search for words that would comfort the children ended with the sounds of their thundering steps. Their oddly shaped bodies, mottled skin, and shaved heads took Alice's breath. Thankfully her blank look went unrecognized in the room of the smiling children, who understood that the blond stranger was there for them.

Alice stared at the line of children that wrapped around the room: boys to the left, girls to the right, and Couvot in the center. When the sounds of the shuffling feet and whispering children finally ended, everyone stood like sentries guarding their new guest. Couvot placed his finger to his lips. The rehearsed children watched Couvot raise both hands, and when his arms fell to his side, the children sang out, "Bonsoir, Madame Resch."

Alice bathed in the warm applause. After the room returned to silence, she responded. "My name is Alice Resch, and your mothers and fathers have asked me to stay with you..." Alice was never able to complete her thought. The children gathered around her and gently touched her arms. Bent at the waist to ensure that every child could be at eye level with her, Alice did her best to answer the barrage of questions. Everyone liked her immediately. She was young and pretty, and when she smiled, they all knew she meant it. And when she asked a question, it was only because she cared.

While the excited children pushed to get closer to Alice, she saw Kurt standing at the far end of the room rubbing his shaved head. His eyes quickly looked to the floor. Alice, draped in children, slid over to Kurt. "And what is your name, young man?"

Kurt's face turned a tomato red until Hugo pushed his way through the children. "This is my friend Kurt Walker. He is from Karlsruhe. He is nine like me, but shy."

"Stop," argued Kurt. "I can do it myself." Kurt took a long, deep breath. "My name is Kurt Walker. I am from Karlsruhe, and I am nine years old like Hugo."

Alice kissed Kurt's scab-covered head before she spoke. "I understand from Monsieur Couvot that all of you have stayed up late to greet me, so I am sure everyone must be tired." She turned to Kurt. "I wonder if you, Kurt Walker from Karlsruhe, can show me where all of you stay?"

Kurt stuck out his chin at Hugo. "This way, Fräulein Resch," said Kurt as he dragged Alice past the blinking shutters of the French children and a relieved Monsieur Couvot.

After Alice walked the girls to the second floor, she hurried to the first floor where the boys quietly waited. Alice looked at her steady hand and thought, maybe I can do this. She took charge and divided the boys into two groups. The youngest, which included Kurt; Hugo; the Weilheimer brothers, Richard and Ernst; Rolf Hess; and Hjalmar Mauer, were placed in one room. In the instant before the light was turned off, Alice saw the terrified faces of children. When her shaking hand turned the lights back on, she saw five-year-old Richard Adler in his brother's arms crying for Martha, his twin sister, and Ernst Weilheimer's weeping face buried in his brother's chest.

These poor babies, thought Alice before she fled the room and climbed up the wooden steps to the second floor. Hidden from everyone, she selfishly began a conversation with God in which she asked to be removed from La Maison des Pupilles. When Alice returned to the little boys' room she did so carrying rope, bed sheets, and her luggage. The puzzled boys watched her take a shoe off and pound some nails into the walls. Alice looked mischievously out of the corner of her eye while she tied off the ends of the rope on the nails and threw some bed sheets over the taut five-foot-high rope. Then, with a bit of flair, she pulled apart the sheets before walking into the triangular-shaped space. She counted to ten before she parted the sheets.

"What do you boys think? Personally, I think it will do quite nicely. Now who can help bring my luggage into my bedroom?" laughed Alice.

Kurt took one step forward, but stopped when he saw no one else move. "No helpers?" Alice dragged her luggage past the sheets. She put her hands on her hips and asked, "Who here can sing?" Giggles followed as Alice put her finger on the nose of each boy while asking, "You? You? You?"

Hugo climbed onto a bed and proclaimed, "I am Hugo Schiller, and I am the best singer in Aspet!"

Alice made an exaggerated frown and lowered her voice. "I don't believe you! Do you know 'Yesterday Evening I Went Out'?"

"Every German knows that song," answered Hugo, who mocked Alice by placing his hands on his hips.

The laughing boys watched Alice put her hands back on her hips. "Prove it, Hugo! I do not believe you," countered Alice, who slowly sat cross-legged on the floor. Hugo's beautiful soprano voice captivated Alice.

> "Yesterday evening, I went out
> I went to the forest
> A little rabbit sat in the bush…"

When the last note faded, Kurt ran from the corner of the room and joined the others who slapped Hugo on his back. Alice composed herself. "I will be back in a moment, boys, but please get in your beds. I need to check on the girls." When she returned to the brightly lit room, she found Rolf Hess, Hjalmar Mauer, Hugo, the Weilheimer brothers, and Kurt asleep in one bed. Before Alice turned off the lights, she dragged five empty beds next to her wall of sheets and filled them with limp bodies. She completed one last prayer. It was a prayer that would be answered many months later.

FIRST MORING FOR ALICE

The next morning, Alice awoke at 5:30 a.m. She dressed and ate before waking the children at 7:00 a.m. And so began her uncomplicated morning routine, where after breakfast Alice looked to the skies to determine how the remaining hours of the day were to be filled. Unpleasant weather meant a day in the small detached gymnasium, where games of tag, schooling without books, and singing occurred. In good weather, which meant anything other than a downpour, Alice and the children took long hikes in the surrounding mountains.

After the first week, a physically exhausted Alice answered the knocks at the massive front door of La Maison des Pupilles. Jules Frey, an Austrian Jewish refugee on the run, had carefully investigated La Maison before Alice opened the door. His shock of blond hair and Aryan features had allowed him to walk unmolested to La Maison des Pupilles, where he begged Alice for work in exchange for food and housing. "Thank you, God," shouted Alice before pulling him into the kitchen. His obvious enthusiasm over a plate of bread and preserves sealed the deal of his twenty-four-hour days that included soccer, hiking, and occasional excursions into the village's café for a treat of homemade soda pop.

Over the following days, Alice came to enjoy the fatiguing marches where silly songs could be heard echoing throughout the Pyrenees Mountains. "Listen to me, children," whispered Jules. "I understand you have been learning some French songs."

He looked over his shoulder for a nonexistent spy. "But you are not French!" His whisper rose to a scream. "The French are losers! You are winners!" Jules dropped to one knee. "Gather round me. I sang this song when I was in the army. It is a song for winners." The children cheered on Jules's deep baritone cry of "No more French songs!" before he sang:

"Oona Irrigori nasti onke ji onka ja
O nicko egooham punka
O nicko ego o chama punkaaunka unka…"

When his song was completed, Jules sat on the ground staring at the collective look of confusion. In an instant, he became buried under the weight of the hysterically laughing children. After Jules staggered to his feet like a drunk, his voice thundered that the nonsensical song of made up words "Is your song!" Three hours later, when the singing children, linked arm in arm, climbed the last bit of the steep road to La Maison, they were greeted by the Little Gray Man yelling for quiet from his office window. Alice waved her threatening finger at Jules, but he would have none of it. To the contrary, he encouraged the children that day and every day thereafter to sing loudly as they marched past the waving cane of Couvot.

Such joyous moments continued into the night when Alice listened to the voices of the little boys just outside her wall of sheets. Hugo talked about his home that had a shower in it and his father, the former mayor of his hometown of Grünsfeld and owner of Rosenbusch & Company. Also he described how, under the threat of the Nazis, his father was forced to give up his position as mayor and sell the family business for nothing. Rolf proudly described his school, where he flourished. Richard spoke of how he and his brother searched for shrapnel from exploded bombs.

When the interrupting boys finally let Hjalmar have his turn, he talked endlessly about the shape and smell of each vegetable harvested from the family garden. But most of all they talked about the many friends and family they had left behind in Gurs and Germany.

"Kurt, you never say a word," observed the boys one night. Alice slowly sat up to hear the soft-spoken Kurt.

The boys pushed for an answer. "You don't always have to be so shy, Kurt."

"I'm not shy, it's just…It's just that I was falling asleep."

"He is from Karlsruhe," answered Hugo.

"Stop it, Hugo!" yelled Kurt. "My family lived in a beautiful apartment. I had my own bedroom. My grandfather is a salesman, and my father…he is in America. He worked for the Singer Sewing Company before he was transferred to America. My family was supposed to follow him after he found us a home, but that didn't happen. So now we wait, I guess." His abbreviated history went unchallenged while the others whispered about seeing their temples being burned by the Nazis and Brownshirts, the train ride, the lack of food, and the dead and dying in Gurs. Alice moved closer to her wall even though the boys had ended any effort to keep quiet.

"I never want to go back to Germany," spit out Richard.

Hugo looked at Richard in amazement. "How can you say that? I want to go back, and when I do, I want to kill every Nazi and Brownshirt."

Hjalmar stood up on his bed and pointed at Hugo. "He's right! We should go back and kill them all." Alice rolled back onto her bed in tears. Soon the repeated nightly memories became her own and connected her to the little boys in a way that forever changed all of their lives. And when she was confident that the boys who guarded her bedroom were asleep, she kissed them and whispered, "I love you. I am your friend, and you never have to be afraid. I will protect you."

"In the evenings, after the light was out, you were allowed to talk quietly for a while. I went to bed at the same time and lay mouse still in my corner listening to the talk of my little boys you were talking about your parents, your mothers and the dreadful experiences of the last years. Can you imagine what I felt I wanted to take every one of my little boys in my arms."

Letter from Alice Resch dated October 11, 1989

KURT AND ALICE

"...Kurt Walker. The latter was a funny nine year old with a great sense of humor, so that whenever he opened his mouth the others fell laughing. When they were naughty...I might put on my most angry face and say that if you don't stop I'll box your ears. Then Kurt quick as a flash and very quietly would say if you are not quiet I'll box your ears, and we all had a laugh."

Undated letter from Alice Resch

Two weeks into Alice's assignment, a waving Kurt ran toward her while the other children chased after Jules in the farmer's pasture. Kurt jumped onto the tree-stump chair in the courtyard and balanced on one foot while Alice held his hands. "Fräulein Resch, do you think you can take me for a drive in your car?"

"Kurt, you know that gas is difficult to get and is so expensive."

"My uncle Heinrich has been in America for four years and is very wealthy. He's president of the Singer Company. Maybe he can buy some for you."

"Oh, he must be the one that your father works for?" asked Alice innocently.

Kurt pretended not to hear Alice. He jumped from the stump. "I know my mother has written to him for help many times. He must be very busy. When he sends Mutti the money, I will ask her to send me some francs. Then maybe we can go for a ride."

Alice embraced Kurt. "I think it is more important that your mother keeps those francs. But for now, why don't we just sit in the car." Kurt's face lit up.

"How old are you?" asked Kurt after he slid behind the steering wheel. Alice threw her head back in mock anger. "Don't you know you are not supposed to ask a woman her age?"

"But you know my age," answered Kurt directly.

Alice laughed, "Thirty-two."

He inched closer to her. "You aren't Jewish, are you?"

She played along and whispered back, "No."

"Then why are you here with us?" asked Kurt. "I mean, if I was as old as you, I wouldn't want to be here. I would rather go where it's fun. Besides, the older girls told us you don't have any children and you aren't married. If you stay with us, how will you ever get married?"

Alice's hand slowly crept over her smile. "How about if I just tell you some things about myself and then you tell me some things about you?"

"Fine," said Kurt as he shook Alice's hand. "But I should get Hugo so you don't have to repeat everything."

Once again Alice's hand crept over her mouth. "How about this time just you and I talk? I will be happy to tell Hugo my fascinating life story a second time." Kurt placed his hands back on the wheel. "I was born on December 14, 1908, in Chicago, Illinois."

Kurt interrupted, "You mean Chicago, America? That's where my uncle Heinrich lives."

"Yes, Kurt, Chicago, America." Kurt pulled on the stick shift and made an engine sound with his lips. "Look out the windshield at the mountains, Kurt. Chicago is as flat as the Pyrenees are high. I don't remember much of Chicago since I left when I was very young. I do remember downtown Chicago, it's like a Platz. They have trains that run on tracks thirty, forty feet off the ground. The trains go in a circle next to very tall buildings called skyscrapers. On foggy days you can't even see the tops of the buildings."

"What else?" said Kurt, spellbound.

"When I was four years old I was with my mother on one of the train platforms. There was a very bad fire, and my mother picked me up and carried me like a bag of potatoes under her arms. She ran downstairs into the street filled with screaming people, smoke, and firemen. It was all very exciting."

Kurt gunned the car's engine. "You look like an athlete. Do you like sports?" asked Alice.

Kurt squinted at mountains that turned into Chicago skyscrapers before he answered, "Of course, soccer!"

"Well, in America, they play baseball. No soccer. When I was a baby, my father took me to their baseball championship, which is called the World Series. Chicago's team was called the Cubs, I think. Anyway, they were always in the World Series when I was little. I hope you get to go to Chicago one day. Maybe when the war is over, you and I will go to Chicago and see the Cubs in another World Series."

"I would like that very much. What else about Chicago, Fräulein Resch?"

"That's it, Kurt. When I was six, my mother, father, brother, and I went to live in the tiny village of Tysedall, Norway. It was so far away from everything that you had to take a boat to reach it. Father ran a power station. His success allowed me to live a very good life. In fact, we were the first family to have a car. Can you imagine that I didn't even know about the war until it was over, Kurt? The entire world is at war, and Mother and Father were somehow able to hide it. Unfortunately, after the war Mother lost her hearing during the flu epidemic, but she continued to read and study foreign languages, as did Father. It's because of them that I learned different languages." Momentarily Alice became lost in her own perfect memories, before she said, "Enough about me, Kurt."

"No, no, no. That's only up to the time when you were little. Then what happened?"

"My God, Kurt, you make me laugh. Are you sure you just don't want to get out of the car?"

"No, no, no," begged Kurt.

"When I was eighteen," continued Alice, "I spent a year abroad. I entertained myself at the best restaurants, the theater, the opera, and nightclubs. I must tell you I was a very good dancer. In Paris I went to museums and the Eiffel Tower just like the tourists, but I have to admit that I was a little afraid because I was alone. I ended up with a nursing degree from the American

Hospital in Paris. Then back home to Oslo for more schooling in physical therapy, another trip back to Paris and eventually to Vienna to work as a nurse. When I went back to Paris, I was a private nurse to millionaires, politicians, and actors. I traveled with them and lived in their mansions. I even went to America on the *Queen Mary.*"

"Why would you leave all of that?" questioned an amazed Kurt.

"The honest answer is I was not happy. It certainly was all very exciting, but everything changed for me after the Nazis burned the temples and invaded France. Then one day I met Helga Holbrook from the Quakers."

Kurt rolled up the driver's window. He pulled out the pictures from the black leather wallet his mother had given him. "This is my Opa, and this one is of me and my Mutti in Karlsruhe."

"He is so handsome in his uniform, and your mother, she is so beautiful. What about your father, sisters, brothers? Tell me about your family."

"There is no one," said Kurt.

"That's impossible, Kurt. You have to have parents and grandparents."

Kurt looked at the Pyrenees. "They are dead. All of them."

"Please forgive me, but..." Alice bit her lip while maneuvering her way through the first of many guarded and cautious conversations with Kurt.

"Kurt, do you see the tall mountain that still has snow on it?" Kurt barely moved. "It's called Mount Cagire. To the left is the

Chapelle de Miege-Coste. It was built in the middle of the fif-teenth century. I will borrow Couvot's binoculars one day so you can see the wooden Black Madonna on top of it. The Madonna calls upon God for help against war, plague, and famine."

Kurt ended his tearful silence. "Please don't be upset with me, Fräulein Resch, but I think maybe she should pray a little harder."

"Well, Kurt," said Alice, "maybe we should all try to pray a little harder."

"I think that's a good idea, but before I do anything I need to talk to Hugo and my Opa. In a few more years I will have my Bar Mitzvah. I don't think my Opa will want me praying there." Alice said nothing about Kurt's curious reference to a supposedly dead grandfather.

"I think as long as you pray, that's the most important thing. I don't think you should worry about where you do it," answered Alice.

"Can I ask you something else, Fräulein Resch? I don't un-derstand why you were afraid to be alone in Paris when all those people lived in the same city as you?"

"It is not about being alone, Kurt. It was about not having friends and family with you. When you were in Karlsruhe, wasn't it more fun to play with your friends and be with your family? You never wanted to be alone, did you?"

GOOD-BYE, ANGEL OF ASPET

"I cannot understand that you can remember meafter all, I stayed with the Aspet children for such a short time and you were so young."

Letter from Alice Resch dated January 2, 1990

Alice's "Good night, girls" a month after her arrival at La Maison alerted the boys to end their late night wrestling match. The boys, who had once nervously huddled together in their dark bedroom, had changed dramatically over the prior month. Their hair had grown out, weight was gained, and ashen faces had been replaced with a ruddy healthy complexion. Bed sheets once stained with urine and clothes dotted with blood from oozing scabs were gone. And through it all, Alice refused to acknowledge any role in accomplishing those changes. Most remarkably, Alice also refused to accept that she alone had transformed the forty-eight strangers into a true family of brothers and sisters.

Alice slowed her pace when she heard the sound of laughing snoring coming from the darkened room. Alice turned on the light. "Oh no, I got here too late to give my sleeping kleine Jungen some candy."

"What candy?" shouted Ernst. The others complained, "That's not fair, Fräulein Resch."

"My boys, I have good news for you," said Alice as she hugged Ernst. "Hopefully you all remember the Cohns. Well, they are coming here tomorrow."

"Why do we need the Cohns?" asked Rolf, who suddenly stopped laughing.

The boys protectively gathered around Alice. Her voice cracked. "The Quakers are going to send me to help some other children."

Hjmalar pulled on Alice's hand. "We don't want the Cohns. We want you," protested the boys. Alice watched Kurt climb back into bed. She sat down next to him while the others clung to her like leaves on a branch.

"When are you leaving?" asked Richard.

Alice called upon all of her strength. "Tomorrow morning." She continued to reassure them, but in reality, after they heard "Tomorrow morning," they stopped listening and retreated to two beds instead of their individual beds. She pushed Kurt's hair off his forehead. "Kurt, please, I beg you. I beg all of you to not be upset with me."

Kurt whispered, "Every night you tell me that you love me and that we are friends, and now you are leaving me. I don't understand any of this. I would never leave you."

Alice stroked Kurt's wet face.

"Boys, the only children I have are here. I don't want to leave any of you—"

"Then don't!" cried the boys.

Kurt whispered again, "Please don't leave. I promise I will try harder. I will do whatever you want me to do."

Alice placed his head in her hands and looked at him incredulously. "Try harder at what? You are a wonderful boy."

"Whatever you want me to do...I know I can be better," begged Kurt.

"Dear Fraulein Resch,

We children think of you very often and of all the good things you did for us. Much has changed. We have a school now and a female French teacher who understands German. We learn French from her. We also learned English from a gentleman who lives in the village. We had our second English lessonRecently the home accepted 63 children from Toulouse who are to stay here for vacation. There has been quite a commotion because of this. We all hope you will come and visit us."

Letter dated July 21, 1941, to Alice Resch and signed by Kurt Walker and the children of Aspet

THE FINAL OFFER

"Dear little Kurt, even if I do not write very often, my thoughts are constantly with you. I see from your letter that you would like to go to America. If it comes to that, I shall try some way or the other to see you again, to speak with you. May God see to it that you go toward a good future and I hope you will enjoy it as much as you like the home you are in at present.

It is getting dark here already and the Jewish holidays are about to begin.

I am looking forward to hearing from you soon. With fond kisses from your loving Momma.... Opa's birthday is on October 30."

Letter from Ilse to Kurt dated October 1, 1941, and approved by Gurs Censor No. 4.

When Andrée Salomon and Ilse embraced on January 27, 1942, they happily acknowledged that the accommodating weather permitted a walk down the paths in Ilot K.

"You know the Americans are finally in the war," began Andrée.

"There are rumors in the camp, but it's impossible to know what truth is here," responded Ilse. "Our contact with the world comes from a little boy who works in Gruel's office and listens to the radio."

"The papers in Toulouse say the Japanese attacked the Americans on some island in the Pacific. Two days later, the Germans declared war on America. The war is not just Europe anymore. The world is at war, and it sounds like the Americans are in trouble."

"What does all that mean for us? It's over a year that we have all been here." Ilse paused before she answered her own question. "I admit that I'm sick of hearing about Madagascar, but is that even a possibility anymore?"

"Presiding Judge: The document will be marked N14.

(Defense lawyer, Dr. Servatius reads) "Envoy Bielfeld has informed me of your communication of 10 February indicating that the Fuehrer has decided that the Jews are not to be deported to Madagascar, but to the East. Madagascar is no longer to be considered a part of the Final Solution.

Trial of Adolf Eichmann, June 26, 1961."

"I have no idea about Madagascar. Honestly..."

"But then I must assume you did not come here to talk about politics?" interrupted Ilse.

Ilse pointed at the commissary. "This place is for the rich ones who can afford extra food and toiletries at the expense of the poor ones who have nothing."

Andrée waved away Ilse's apology for being angry before returning to her reason for being in Gurs. "From the beginning, Ilse, the goal for the Quakers was to get the children out of the camps. If there were other opportunities, we explored them. In fact, last summer we had the children take passport photos just in case. Kurt told us he wrote to you about going to America." Andrée took Ilse's hand. "We are talking about a few of the children going."

"When, Andrée?"

"Things may never happen, especially with America getting into the war. But we have to be able to move quickly." Ilse's prolonged barking cough gave Andrée an excuse to seek some privacy in the relative comfort of one of the barracks that had been appropriated by the Quakers. "Ilse, I brought some real tea," said Andrée. She wadded up some balls of paper and started a fire. The sweet aroma of brewing tea quickly filled the room.

"Thank you for my trip to heaven," said Ilse.

Andrée refilled the empty cup. "Ilse, I think we can get Kurt out. I know you wrote him about America and you said yes. I also remember you telling me you had family in America, an uncle…"

Ilse interrupted Andrée upon hearing that her rich uncle Heinrich might hold the key to Kurt going to America. "Once I was a good Jew, daughter, wife, and mother. And if I was honest with myself I would have to agree that my successes in life have been few. Since I have been here, most of my time is spent thinking of my children and what I could do for them. If I had extra food or money, I'd give it to them. I would give my life for them. I remember the first time you talked to me about my Kurt and how some of the families refused to send their children to Aspet.

I must tell you that I thought they were correct. I did not want to send my Kurt away. But now I know I did the right thing. If he had stayed here with me that would have been selfish. I think you would never say it, but I assume you agree with that?"

Andrée's slight nod comforted Ilse. She chose her next words very carefully. "Those parents who did not want to give up their children would die for them too. But they could not say yes, go to Aspet. I know two things. We have nothing and we will stay here until the war is over. I must tell you I am an expert at letting go. So tell Kurt his mother says he should go and that we will be together in America, or Mexico or Palestine or wherever else he goes."

"But Ilse, I can't promise you will be together with Kurt. I don't want to lie to you."

"I'm not asking you to lie. I am asking you to tell him exactly what I said, Andrée."

"And your father?"

"I am asking you to tell Kurt what I said, not what my father wants. Please, Andrée, help me to be good at something."

Andrée lit two cigarettes before she removed a question-naire titled, "A REMPLIR EN QUATRE EXEMPLAIRES ALA MACHINE A ECRIRE" from her bag.

Andrée quickly went over sections I and II that required basic information about Kurt before she moved on to section III.

"Kurt speaks some French now in addition to German?"

"Yes."

"And where were you born?"

"Rastatt, Germany."

"Birthdate?"

"January 14, 1906."

"Did you have a profession?"

"I was a dressmaker in Karlsruhe."

"And Kurt's father's name?"

Ilse looked into the emptied cup of tea. "Why do you need that?"

"The simple answer is that the form requires it. Besides, his father has rights just like you. Maybe we can speed this process up or have other options if we involve Kurt's father."

Ilse sucked hard on her cigarette.

"The father?"

Ilse closed her eyes. "Julius Walker."

She shifted uncomfortably as Andrée wrote the answers to each of the remaining questions.

"Karlsruhe, Germany, on May 19, 1907—Railroad mechanic—German—Protestant—Divorced 1934—He's remarried and lives in Stuttgart, Germany." When Andrée finally picked her head up, she was taken aback, if only momentarily, by the hard stare from Ilse. Move on, move on, thought Andrée.

"In section four, you have to identify someone to make decisions regarding Kurt." Andrée protected herself by looking at the form as she spoke quickly. "You know, Ilse—in case something happens to you?"

There was no hesitation. "My father, Isack Loeb Ettlinger."

"I also have to read something to you." The tension was palpable until Ilse burst into laughter when Andrée read "A LIRE TRES SOIGNEUSEMENT ET A SIGNER A L'ENFROIT INDIQUE." When Andrée finished reading the formal legal release of the Quakers from any liability in the event Kurt was killed or injured during his escaped from France, Ilse placed her hand over her heart. Still chuckling, she said, "I promise I will not sue."

Andrée was grateful for Ilse's attempt to diffuse the sober atmosphere. "Well then, Ilse, no more questions from me. Your turn—do you have any for me?"

"The children, how are they chosen?"

"We simply don't know. There is no procedure in place yet, and there may never be. There are so many issues, such as visas, quota restrictions from countries, and money from the family to defray costs. Also we have to investigate transportation availability, the health of the child, and whether there is a willing family member that can take the child. There are probably a hundred other things we haven't even thought of."

"You know," said Ilse haltingly, "I am a woman with little formal education, who knows no important people. I have no money to help pay for Kurt's expenses, and I have no family in America that I can rely upon to take Kurt.

"...We still have not had anything from Uncle Heinrich...My Little Kurt, I have to give you some sad news that your Oma died of weakness. You know she loved you so much and always wanted to see you again. She kept all of your

```
letters and spent much time re-reading them. It
is three weeks now since dear Oma died and dear
Opa is also ill. My thoughts are with you, my
dear Kurt. Would to God we could all still be
together..."
```

Letter from Ilse to Kurt and approved by Gurs Censor No. 2

Ilse's sigh belied a voice that desperately tried to project strength. "I don't mean to burden you. Every day you must hear complaints from everyone." Ilse shook her head. "Yours is a job that I would not want for anything in the world."

"What are you talking about, Ilse?"

"Andrée, you are all I have. You have the power. You know the people. You know how to get the money. You know the words that need to be said." Ilse held onto Andrée's hands. "I need you to save my son. Talk to Alice, to the ones that have the power."

Andrée had spent much of her waking hours trying to persuade anxious parents to let their children go. Ironically, it was she who was filled with anxiety. "Ilse, you told me you have another child, a boy, as I recall. Why can't Kurt just go with his brother?"

Ilse pulled out a worn envelope and removed a photograph of a smiling Ilse with a one-year-old baby sitting on her lap. "That's Kurt's brother, Heinz. He was born on March 28, 1930, in Karlsruhe. He still lives in Karlsruhe with his father's parents."

"But Ilse, this is great news. The Quakers can try to contact the grandparents and the father." Andréewas ecstatic, but it was clear that Ilse was not paying attention to her.

Until Ilse interrupted Andrée, she had never been able to utter the dangerous truth, "...that there would be no help coming from the Nazi Brownshirt father of Kurt." Ilse sat back in her chair while Andrée examined the picture. "Kurt is here because he is a Jew and my Heinz is in Karlsruhe because he is not," said Ilse. She clicked her brittle nails on the wooden table. "Two weeks before Heinz was born, my husband honored me with a marriage proposal," said Ilse, dripping with sarcasm. "I am embarrassed to say this so many years later, but I loved Julius and sometimes even today, I think he loved me and our make-believe family. After my Heinz was born, Julius was working in Berlin, Munich, and small towns all over Germany. Honestly, I don't know if that was true. All I know is that there was no money and no help from him.

"I was a good seamstress, and I did my best to support myself and Heinz. His parents helped a little, and my mother tried so hard. But they weren't happy. How could they? One said, how terrible, my daughter, the Orthodox Jewess, is with a Christian, and the other said, how terrible, my Christian son is with the Orthodox Jewess.

Before I met Kurt's father, most of my friends were married and had children. They had what I never had growing up and what I wanted as an adult. I just wanted to be part of a real family...I was so naïve and selfish. When I met Julius I was so certain he was the one. And when I had Heinz, I was the happiest person in the world.

I never could have imagined my selfish choices would bring so much pain to my boys. Please don't think badly of me, but I wish they were never born. Two brothers—without each other—without a mother and a father. Every day of their lives they have been punished because I could not save them."

Andrée was numb. Her mind raced to come up with some response that would attempt to heal the open wound that Ilse had become. "But you did nothing wrong," said Andrée tearfully.

"Andrée, do you think my boys would hold me blameless if they knew the truth or, God forbid, when they are older and learn what I did to them? Do you honestly think they will say that the pregnant Jew who married a Nazi German Brownshirt is not responsible for what happened to them? That they will say my mother was only a little bit wrong?"

After Andrée returned to Toulouse, she placed a single piece of thin typing paper in a typewriter. When she finished, Andrée read her memo that was created as a result of an extracted promise from Ilse to show it to no one other than Alice Resch.

```
"WALKER, Kurt

    The child is a result of a mixed marriage...
The father registered to the Nazi Party and
is a Brownshirt, had renounced his wife and
two children. Kurt has a brother who stayed in
Germany with his maternal parents.

    The divorce having been pronounced official,
the mother raised her children thanks to her
work. Expelled to France with the youngest son
(the oldest succeed in escaping expulsion). She
was interned with him. The boy was freed by the
Quakers who placed him at Aspet. The mother is
still interned. Kurt is a sweet boy, intelligent
```

and well raised. He considers himself Jewish and judges the conduct of his father harshly. The mother would like him to be raised in a Jewish family not necessarily orthodox.

Present address of mother: Mrs. Walker Camp de Gurs BP. France."

AMERICA?

Alice approached the solitary sweating boy kicking a soccer ball. "How is my Kurt? I understand you and Hugo got the leads in the play about the French baker. I would have loved to see you boys dancing and singing in your white uniforms and tall hats."

"Fräulein Resch," screamed Kurt.

"Kurt, you almost squeezed the life out of me! I haven't seen you in months and now look at you! You are a man!"

Kurt threw off his coat, rolled up his sleeves, and proudly displayed his tightly flexed biceps. "When we play tug of war, I am always the last man! We never lose!"

"That must be from all the good food," laughed Alice on that late March day in 1942.

"I don't like the blood pudding ever since I saw them kill the cow. The French children say it is good for us, but I'd rather eat almost anything else," said Kurt, gagging.

Alice pretended to take his picture with her hands. "And your French, Kurt?"

"C'est un jour joli. Mon nom est Kurt Walker. Quel est votre nom?"

Alice had a look of feigned shock. "Mon nom est Alice Resch. Est-ce que vous êtes heureux ici dans Aspet?

"Oui. Trés beaucoup."

"Comment voudriez-vous aller en Amérique?"

Kurt kicked the soccer ball against the chair stump. "What do you mean, how would I like to go to America?"

"I mean just that, Kurt. I think we can get you to America. You still want to go, don't you?"

"Yes, but who is going?" said Kurt. He pawed at the ground with wooden soles that had been artfully attached to a pair of reclaimed leather shoes.

Alice looked at Mount Cagire and dismissed her naïve wish that Kurt would not question her. "Kurt, I don't know. Things are changing all the time."

"I don't understand. We all came here together and have been together for a long time. I don't think it's such a good idea to break us apart. And what about my family?"

"They will not be going, at least not yet. For now, the Quakers are helping to get the children out. Kurt, I know you wrote to your mother some time ago and you said you wanted to go to America? You have to remember that, Kurt."

"I said that." His trembling lips acknowledged a once distant dream becoming a reality.

"Kurt, you can't stay in Aspet for the rest of your life. This is a wonderful place. I know all of you have become very close, but this is not your home."

"But Madame, you don't understand," argued Kurt. "Karl Landau conducts the services on the Sabbath for us. We eat together, we play together. Why, we still take our monthly showers together to save hot water." Kurt fell silent. He wanted to tell her how they gambled for crusts of bread when they played cards, and about the thousands of marble matches that had been won and lost. He wanted to tell her how the girls faked fights to distract the farmers so the other children could steal unripe apples, corn, and chestnuts used to feed pigs. He wanted to describe how they took turns hiding Couvot's paddle that enforced his strict rules. He wanted to talk about when Ernst had a chest cold and was treated with hot bags of sand that burned him. Even the youngest girls took turns putting medication on his wounds. Kurt wanted to tell Alice everything. But most of all, he wanted to tell Alice that the others were his family and La Maison des Pupilles was his home, but he didn't.

"Kurt, you have been here over a year. There is a war going on, and many people are being killed every day. The safety for all of you…We simply don't know what the future holds for any of you children." Alice put her arm around Kurt. "Madame Salomon spoke to your mother not long ago and she wants America for you."

"What about Opa? What does he say? I need to speak to him about this."

"Your Opa loves you. He wants you to be safe, and staying here will not be safe."

"Yes, but I still think I need to talk to him, Madame," said the soft-spoken ten-year-old boy.

Kurt's fingernails dug into his arms. "When I was in Karlsruhe I would walk with my mother on the Kaiserstrasse. Most of the time, we just looked in the windows of the stores since we didn't

247

have the money to buy anything. Mutti made up a game. We would look in the windows and wish for something. She wanted a new pot to make me spaetzle or leather to make me lederhosen. Mutti always wanted things for me, never herself. I wished for a toy, a new Max and Moritz book, or marbles. One day I was with Mutti, her friend, Frau Schückle, and her daughter. They lived next to us."

Kurt's fingernails dug deeper into his arm. "We stopped in front of a store window and the little girl pointed to a plain wooden box. I asked her why she wanted a box. She whispered that it was a wishing box and that you didn't have to buy it to make a wish. You just had to close your eyes, make a wish, and it will come true. But you couldn't say what the wish was or it wouldn't come true."

"I'm sorry, Kurt, but I don't understand," said Alice.

"I never told my Opa about this because I was afraid he would be upset with me."

"Your Opa is a good man. He could never be upset with you, especially about a wishing box."

The tips of Kurt's interlocked fingers turned white. He moved closer to Alice. "Please do not tell Opa about this, but every time I went by the store window after that day, I would close my eyes and make a wish. The last time was the day they took us away and we drove down the Kaiserstrasse. I always made the same wish, even if there was something in the window that I really wanted." Haltingly, Kurt declared, "I'm so ashamed—but Fritz's sister was right—if you wished—it would come true."

Alice gently pulled Kurt's hands away from his face. "Was it America? Is that what you wished for, Kurt?"

"It was not just America," said Kurt. "It was that I only wished for myself. I never thought about my family..."

"Dear Lord, Kurt. You did nothing wrong. Your family wants what you want. This is a good thing. Look at me, Kurt. I promise you will be with your family." Alice pulled Kurt closer and refused to let him go until she gained control of her own emotions. "Kurt, what did you tell me that your Opa used to say to you when you were sad?"

"Ganna gut, he always said ganna gut."

"Well then," followed the strong voice of Alice, "Ganna gut, ganna gut."

ILSE AND ALICE,
APRIL 13, 1942

After Alice entered Camp de Gurs, she learned that Ilse was working in the infirmary in Ilot J. While Alice looked around the crowded infirmary, she tried in vain to recall the photos of Kurt's mother. She approached the thin man with a broken stethoscope. "Doctor, I'm looking for an Ilse Walker. I understand she works here."

"Well, she is here," said the confused doctor. "You walked right past her."

Alice walked to the foot of the fragile bed. "Ilse Walker?"

"Yes. Who are you?" answered the raspy voice.

"My name is Alice Resch. I'm with the Quakers."

"Alice Resch, I know all about you." Ilse spoke through the interruptions of an annoying months-long cough. "Kurt wrote about you. You let him drive your car while you told him all about yourself."

Alice was clearly shocked. "Kurt actually wrote about that? That was more than a year ago, but yes, I remember."

Ilse pulled herself up against the rough wooden planks of the infirmary wall. "He wrote that the children call you the Angel of Aspet and that you look like a statute of a woman they see up in the mountains. Kurt said that even when you left, they would look up at the statute and say that they didn't have to worry, because you were still watching them."

Alice lost focus given the sight of a clearly sick Ilse and the emotional recollections. "You should not be embarrassed. Kurt obviously loves you. All of them do. You have done so much for them."

"That's kind of you, but I spent so little time with the children."

"You don't have to be a doctor to save someone's life, Alice."

Alice politely dismissed the compliment by changing the conversation. "How long have you been here in the infirmary? I don't think Kurt knows you are here."

"I haven't written to Kurt in a long time. I didn't want him to be concerned. In December it started with a cold or flu that just wouldn't go away. By the end of February, the beginning of March, I was transferred here. They think it's typhoid. Everyone here is sick, but the truth is I feel much better. It's just that I can't seem to get my strength back and shake this fever. And even with the fine cuisine here, it is a little difficult to put on the weight I've lost." The black humor of Gurs left both women laughing until the doctor glared at them.

"I had typhoid myself," whispered Alice. "It took me four months before I was well enough to return to work and the children. Hopefully you will have as much good fortune as I did."

"Maybe we should wish a healthy dose of typhoid and good fortune on the führer and his friends," said Ilse. The women's laughter drew another stare.

"Do you remember when Andrée was here around Christmas?"

"Of course," said Ilse. Alice removed a document from her briefcase.

"The last time I saw this, it was blank," wheezed Ilse. She gently slid her fingers over Kurt's photograph and tiny fingerprints. She muttered, "I feel so guilty that I've not written to my little Kurtela. He looks so angry."

"I have a copy for you to keep," said Alice, who took a pen from her briefcase and pointed to the places on the form where Ilse was to sign. Ilse, inconsolable, picked up the pen in one hand and the photo in her other hand. She fell back on the straw dust mattress. Alice hurried to the doctor who gave her a cup of boiled water and a pill that had been cut into thirds. The former nurse pulled Ilse forward and placed the glass at her mouth. "Thank you, Alice. Thank you for everything," said Ilse.

Alice gently laid her patient down. "So what happens with my Kurt?" asked Ilse.

"We don't know when, but we think we can get him and a few others to America."

"Aren't they all getting out?"

"Not yet."

"Who decides?" questioned Ilse.

Alice shrugged her shoulders, pushing aside the inquiry.

"But Alice, what happens when they find out that I have no one to take care of him in America?"

"Once he gets to America it's no longer a problem. The problem is making sure we get him to America." Alice placed a moist washcloth on Ilse's perspiring forehead. The former strangers sat quietly while Alice held onto Ilse's wrist and snuck a look at her watch.

"Once a nurse always a nurse?" chuckled Ilse.

Alice cleared her throat while the uneasy laughter came to an end. "You asked me when Kurt might leave. We don't know, but two weeks ago I received a hysterical phone call from the director in Aspet, Monsieur Couvot. He told me that the police came to Aspet at six in the morning and removed five of the children. They were taken to their parents who had been transferred to Rivesaltes from Gurs. Fortunately, through our contacts with the Vichy, the children were returned. Although we received the word of the police that they will leave the children alone, the truth is we can't trust them. We need to get them out of not just Aspet but France."

Alice never told Ilse that Kurt, Ernest and Richard Weilheimer, Rolf Hess, Hugo Schiller, and Hjalmar Mauer, the same boys who slept outside Alice's wall of sheets in La Maison des Pupilles, had been chosen weeks earlier to be the first children to leave Aspet. Alice also never disclosed to Ilse how her own tearful nights of listening to the little boys' compelling stories had moved her to make a decision that forever changed all of their lives.

"Alice, I'm sorry to burden you with this, but I need you to do one more thing for me," said an exhausted Ilse.

"Please, whatever you want me to do," offered Alice.

"Go to my father and tell him what I have done. I want him to know what I did, that I said yes. Can you please do that?"

Alice bent over Kurt's sleeping mother, kissed both of her cheeks, and whispered to Ilse.

"Hurry up," urged Jacqueline on a late May morning in 1942. Kurt finished his breakfast of watered-down café au lait soaked with bread and dusted with a few precious crystals of sugar. "Always the last one," grinned Jacqueline. The noise from the courtyard poured in through the barely opened windows. Kurt stood on his chair to see Alice surrounded by the children. Increasing pressures to supply food and medicine for the camps, and the added responsibilities of getting the children out of France, made this visit an unexpected joyful event.

Seconds after Kurt's sighting of Alice, he ran toward her yelling, "Madame Resch."

Alice put her hands on her hips and exclaimed, "I said to myself, where is my Kurt? Has he forgotten me?" Kurt put his hands on his hips and made a sour-looking face before Alice scooped him up in her arms.

After Alice passed out cookies, she listened intently to the younger girls' complaints of being bossed by the older girls and which of the children were boyfriend and girlfriend. Eventually she gave them good-bye hugs and kisses. Alice begged herself to not linger, but she could not help taking one last look at the children who dispersed throughout the pasture. This was true for everyone except Hugo and Kurt, who stood alone by the barbed wire watching Alice's every move. "My little boys," muttered Alice before she cried out, "Come here, my Max and Moritz!" She whispered, "I need you two to do me a favor. I see that the Weilheimers, Rolf, and Hjalmar are out in the pasture. I did not say a proper good-bye to them and..."

But before she completed her request, Kurt and Hugo were sprinting like cowboys attempting to round up some stray cattle. They dragged each laughing boy back to Alice. When the six boys were finally assembled, Alice combed their hair as she spoke. "I was thinking that since I am going away for a while, I would like a picture of my boys. Now Richard, Hugo, and Kurt, stand in the back," pointed Alice. She reached into her car for her camera and looked through the lens. "Don't just stand there! Smile and put your arms around each other. You are the brothers of Aspet." The boys chanted "brothers, brothers, brothers," as Alice proclaimed, "Fantastique."

While Alice slowly drove away from the group of waving boys, she was certain of only one thing: she would never again see Rolf, Hjalmar, Richard, Ernst, Hugo, or Kurt.

NEW YORK

On Friday morning, May 29, 1942, Monsieur Couvot dialed number 17. "Doctor Jaureguiberry, the boys need certificates that they are healthy and…"

In the late afternoon on the next day, Kurt, Hugo, the Weilheimer brothers, Rolf Hess, and Hjalmar Mauer returned to La Maison from Dr. Jaureguiberry's office. When they spilled out of the car driven by Jules Frey, their frustration at having missed another soccer game made great theater for the other children. They rolled on the ground like a bunch of drunken sailors, striking each other's vaccinated arms. Couvot's cane clicked away until Jules placed an envelope into his hands. He immediately returned to his desk and placed the medical records into six stacks. The certification stated that each child, "...est en bonne santé et ne présente aucun symptom de maladie contagieuse." Couvot grinned. "Yes, this is good."

"It's the Goat!" whispered the boys when the sounds of the clicking cane were heard in the courtyard. Each boy made sure to inflict one last punch before they followed the disapproving Couvot and his waving cane to his office. Three to a chair, they watched an unemotional Couvot while they waited for their lecture and certain paddling.

"I have news. You are going." The unresponsive reaction by the fluent French-speaking German children was unsatisfying. "You always ask me questions. I never have an answer, but now I do. Don't you understand? All of you are leaving."

Richard pulled Ernst onto his lap while Rolf and Hjalmar grabbed at Hugo's hands. Kurt stared into Couvot's eyes.

"We don't know when, but it will be before the middle of August. Things are still being finalized with the Quakers, but you are going."

"Are we all going?" asked Hugo.

"No. Just you boys, Lore Bauer, and Eva Herz."

Kurt rose from his chair. "I don't think Madame Resch knows about this. She would never let this happen."

"But Kurt, it was Madame Resch who picked…" Couvot abruptly stopped. "You boys, Lore, and Eva are the first to go! I don't have to answer to you." Couvot's lips quivered. "None of you can stay here anymore. It's simply not safe. Now go outside and play."

"I don't understand," said Richard. "If it is not safe for us, it can't be safe for the others."

"Enough," said the Goat before he slapped his cane on his desk.

The silent procession ended when Kurt and Hugo knocked at Monsieur Couvot's closed door. His annoyed "Vous pouvez entrer" found the boys once again sitting in front of him. "Excuse me, Monsieur Couvot, but Kurt and I wanted to know where are we going?"

Couvot picked up his head and pulled off his reading glasses that covered his surprisingly red and swollen eyes. "America. You boys are going to America."

A CAR RIDE – JUNE 4, 1942

On June 5, 1942, widower Max Weilheimer secured a one-day release from Camp de Gurs to see his sons, Richard and Ernst. Although he remained crestfallen after his return to Gurs, he sought out each of the parents of the children in Aspet. When his gentle shakes woke Ilse from her sleep, he apologized. "Frau Walker, my name is Max Weilheimer. Your boy, Kurt, is in Aspet with my Richard and Ernst. I wanted to tell you that I was in Aspet yesterday." His halting speech made her tremble beneath the sheet that allowed her some modesty. "I never got to see my boys. They were gone…"

One day earlier, Kurt and seven other children were driven to Toulouse, some sixty miles away. There were no long good-byes, songs, or tears as there had been when Kurt left Gurs. To the contrary, Couvot wanted it to be just a normal day when Kurt waved his final good-bye to the courtyard filled with his brothers and sisters. While Kurt sat in the car on that hot summer day and Max Weilheimer sat holding Ilse's hand in the infirmary in Gurs, the ferocious engine of the final solution became fully engaged. It forever obliterated the lines separating the Nazi regime and its complicit Vichy partner.

When Kurt got out of the car across the street from the train station in Toulouse and looked at the former two-story shoelace factory at 16 Boulevard Bonrepos, he read the sign, "Quakers Americains." He recalled how Alice said the sign might have said Quakers Americains, but there was only one Quaker and one

American in the Toulouse office. His smile grew when Harriet Marple introduced herself. "Fräulein Resch spoke about you. You are the rich one and the only American," said Kurt.

The unpretentious laughter that preceded her "guilty!" contradicted the appearance of the wealthy American, whose deep-blue eyes, stylish gray hair, and tailored clothes made her look like European royalty. The inviting wave of her hand led the obedient children up the squeaky wooden stairway to the second-floor offices.

"You must all be hungry," insisted Harriet Marple. "I am going down the street to get a present. Perhaps some pastries?"

After the excited children were left alone in the breezy room, seven-year-old Hjalmar explored a desk weighted down by an assortment of paperweights, pens, and stacks of papers. He craned his neck to read the upside-down letters of his name on one of the files. A second later, he was bouncing on a chair and reading out loud in French. There was a sense of excitement as the others crowded around the same desk.

Kurt ran to the bottom of the stairs and yelled, "No one is coming!" When he charged into the room, Kurt spotted the lone file. He plopped himself down on the second-floor landing and began to examine the few sheets of onionskin paper. "I remember when they took that picture of me last summer," said Kurt, grinning.

"July 16, 1941 letter from Ilse Censor No. 9

Dear little Kurt, are you managing to learn a lot of French? I was very surprised to hear that they had taken photos of you. If you can let

us have a picture, please do so, as something
to remind us of you. We are very much looking
forward to it..."

With his fingers, Kurt combed his thick brown hair away
from his eyes while he pushed and pulled at his mouth. He only
stopped when he was satisfied that he mirrored the angry-look-
ing face in the one-year-old photo. He rubbed his arm as he read
Dr. Jaureguiberry's certification of the shots he received. His
growing excitement over each little treasure made it impossible
for him to read more than a few words at a time. He unfolded
a single piece of paper that began, "Kurt is a nice boy...
clever...good pupil."

"Wait till I show this to Hugo. He thinks he's the best student," said Kurt as he punched the air in celebration.

"Quakers liberated him and was sent to Aspet."

"I would like to take Opa and Mutti to Aspet. I think they
would like it," reflected Kurt before he placed the paper only inches away from his face. He mumbled slowly when he read "frère,"
the French word for brother in the memo Andrée Salomon had
prepared immediately after interviewing his mother. His eyes
darted back and forth.

"Brother stayed in Germany...Jewish mother
married Christian...railroad mechanic...divorced...
Father registered to the Nazi party and is a
Brownshirt"

The muffled laughter from the children reading about themselves filled the hallway while Kurt read:

"...June 7, 1942, Emigration Registration Form, WALKER Kurt Aspet. Father Julius Walker, Stuttgart, Germany, Aryan. Brother, Heinz Walker, Karlsruhe Germany, Aryan."

Kurt whimpered, "My father and brother are Nazis and I am not a Jew!"

ESCAPE TO MARSEILLE

The next morning, the crammed car proceeded east toward Narbonne, north along the coast to Nîmes, and finally to Marseille, eighty miles away. After it came to a midday stop near some nameless fishing village, the children ran to the sea. "Not too far! Stay close by for lunch," screamed the driver to the splashing children.

Kurt swore at the red-billed Audouin's seagulls picking at the remains of dead fish. He removed his thick wooden-soled shoes and ran toward the scavengers. His arms pumped and glistened with sweat, and when he could run no more, he collapsed onto the warm sand. He never felt more alone. He covered his weeping eyes from the brilliant sun. When a hazy sleep took him away from the endless images of his Nazi father and brother, Kurt found no respite as he shouted, "No, no, no" to the Nazis who hid behind the advancing clouds.

"Why are you here by yourself with these crazy birds, Kurt? The driver bought us some food," shrieked Hugo. Kurt returned to the reality of the sandy beach. Sweat bled through Hugo's shirt while he pulled Kurt's arm. "Aren't you hungry? We have to hurry or there will be nothing left!" puffed Hugo.

"Hugo, are we best friends?" asked Kurt, shielding his eyes from the intense sun that bounced off the water.

Hugo pulled harder on Kurt's arm. "Enough with these stupid questions, Kurt! I want to eat!"

Kurt pushed Hugo away. "Listen to me," yelled Kurt. "I need to know! Are we best friends? It's a simple question."

Hugo pushed Kurt into the foamy water. "Of course we are best friends. We're Max and Moritz." Hugo shook his head. "Sometimes you are so strange, Kurt."

"Why are we best friends?" screamed Kurt. He grabbed at Hugo. "We aren't Max and Moritz! That's not an answer—they aren't real. We are real. I want to tell you something, and I can only tell it to my best friend. Are you my best friend?"

Kurt balled up the collar of Hugo's opened shirt in his fists and pulled him closer. "Tell me why we are best friends!" They stood inches apart.

"I never had a brother, Kurt. We are more than best friends, we are brothers. We are brothers forever."

"No matter what?" asked Kurt while Hjalmar ran toward them in the foamy water. Kurt and Hugo placed their hands on each other's shoulders. They looked like wrestlers ready to spar.

"If we are brothers, nothing can ever change that? If you are a brother, you are always a brother, no matter what?"

Hugo's body tensed under the bizarre questioning. Kurt waved off a slowing Hjalmar. He pulled Hugo closer. "No matter what, Hugo?"

"We will always be brothers, Kurt—no matter what happens."

MARSEILLE

By virtue of the surrender of Paris in June 1940, six million French citizens and refugees fled from the advancing Nazi army. The Quakers, part of the mass exodus, retreated to Marseille to open their new headquarters. The former Greek settlement, long before the summer of 1942, had become an international city known for its diverse ethnic groups, striking water views, museums, and magnificent restaurants. On October 9, 1934, the filmed assassination of King Alexander of Yugoslavia and the death of his assassin by a sword-wielding French policeman reinforced Marseille's unseemly but well deserved notoriety as the Chicago of France.

Prior to France's surrender to the Nazis, 190,000 displaced persons arrived in Marseille in the summer of 1939. They hoped to take advantage of the city's most significant asset, its harbor of ships. But with their arrival, the city's infrastructure, government, and citizenry of Marseille were taxed beyond its means. Severe rationing of food, gasoline, medical supplies, and clothing resulted in a surging black market. Freedom became another commodity in a city where angry newspapers spewed Nazi propaganda. It also became a perilous place for the fleeing foreign and stateless Jews who, because of a failure to secure a residence permit and safe conduct pass, were subject to arrest and random police roundups.

Although initially isolated from the war, the 625,000 residents of the oldest city in France felt its consequences on June 1 and

2 when thirty people died from German Luftwaffe bombs. On June 21, Italian bombers killed another 140 people. The blame for Marseille's dead fell at the feet of the foreigners and refugees who were alleged to have dragged France into another war. This was confirmed in July 1942, when a new ordinance made it illegal for Marseille's foreigners and refugees to stay in a hotel for more than five days. Ironically, four hotels, Hotel Bompard, Hotel du Levant, Hotel Atlantique, and Hotel Terminus des Ports, ultimately became internment camps for Jews.

On a black, moonless night, when Kurt got out of the car near the top of the white limestone cliffs, he looked down on the city of Marseille and the port of the former French Empire. The eerie vision of the international city left Kurt watching the tiny lights flickering until a waiting French husband and wife ushered the exhausted children into a two-hundred-year-old single-story building. A candle flame exposed the three decaying rooms that seemed to be one heavy rain away from collapsing. The famished children's surroundings went unacknowledged when they were welcomed with a meal of bread, cold pig's feet, tripe, and lard.

Hours later when Kurt awoke on a dirt floor, he dismissed the warnings from the absent couple to never leave the building without an escort. "What are you doing out here alone, Kurt?" said Hugo. Kurt pointed to the sun rising over the south side of the Old Port and the largest city he had ever seen.

"Yeah, it's a little bigger than the Rappenwort pool in Karlsruhe you told me about," chuckled Hugo.

"And what about that?" asked Kurt. He pointed to the highest point in Marseille, the landmark 1864 gold-domed basilica, Notre Dame de la Garde. He looked at the impressive thirty-seven-foot-tall statute of the Virgin Mary holding her baby atop the basilica. Kurt thought of the Black Madonna outside La Maison that had watched the children each day for the prior sixteen months.

"What did you say? You always mumble," yawned Hugo.

"I was just thinking of something Madame Resch told me about the Madonna and praying," answered Kurt. He looked back at the thousands of buildings crammed together and the Mediterranean Sea that stretched out as far as he could see. The silence ended when the rest of the children stumbled out of the shack.

"Hey, look at that," exclaimed Hugo. He pointed to the kilometer-wide main road, the Canebiere, and the huge transporter bridge that spanned the opening of the harbor. The wide-eyed children watched the huge gondola, suspended by cables, flying just feet above the water.

"I helped to build that. We call it the Eiffel Tower of Marseille. It's only one of five transporter bridges in France," blurted out the old Jewish man who shuffled toward the distracted children. Kurt thought of the prior night's warning to not leave the shack. "Don't worry. I'm a friend," said the leathery-skinned Frenchman who passed out bread and cheese from his burlap sack. He continued his minihistory lesson. "We finished it on December 15, 1905. Each tower weighs 240 tons and reaches 280 feet into the air. They are connected by a 540-foot pedestrian bridge at the very top of the towers. In fact, I helped hang the cables from the bridge to those gondolas." The man proudly stuck out his chest. "It takes only one and a half minutes to transport the passengers across the harbor. And you will not believe this, but at the top of tower, over there on the left, is a turtle-shaped restaurant that serves the most fantastic meals…"

Over the next days, the old man brought food and history lessons of his beloved bridge. And after he left, the bored, shirtless, shoeless boys, with pants rolled to their knees, withdrew to the hills singing, "Oona irrigori nasti onke ji onka ja…" The tedium of those days came to an end on June 23, 1943.

"No, no, no," whispered Lore. She grabbed at Rolf's arm. "They said don't answer the door."

"She's right, Rolf," whispered the others. They retreated until they were stopped by the collapsing rear wall. When the door opened, a middle-aged skinny man standing next to a woman in a faded flower dress and wide black belt appeared before them.

The muffled cries of "My Hugo, my Hugo" quickly ended when the man wrapped his arms around his wife and Hugo. It was obvious that Kurt was looking at Hugo's parents, but what did this emotional reunion mean? Was the war over? Had they somehow escaped? More importantly, where was his family? He ran past the united family and onto the empty road. Kurt kicked at the ground. When he returned to the shack he heard Hugo's father say, "Look, Selma! My baby is gone."

"I don't understand," wept Hugo. "Are we going back to Gurs?"

There was no answer. Instead, Selma and Oskar Schiller looked at the faces memorized from the photographs they had seen days earlier when most of the parents met with Andrée and Alice. Hugo introduced his parents to each child. The children glowed amid the kisses and hugs as a tearful Hugo said, "This is my brother...and this is my sister..."

"The Weilheimer boys! Richard and Ernst," said Hugo's father in a booming voice. "Your father told us he had been to Aspet to see you. That's how we learned that you had already left." Ernst burst into tears with the stunning news that they had lost an opportunity to see their father. "Please boys—girls," stammered Oskar Schiller. He grabbed for pieces of peppermint candy from his pockets. "Please, we have good news for all of you. Your mothers, your fathers, they will all be here."

While the children erupted into applause, Hugo walked his parents to a dark corner in the room. "This is my best friend, Kurt." A huge smile wrapped around Kurt's face. Hugo's mother kissed Kurt, and Oskar Schiller placed five pieces of the sweet treats into Kurt's hand. Kurt popped them into his mouth and said what sounded like thank you.

"So this is the famous Kurt Walker of Karlsruhe that you write about?" asked an elated Frau Schiller. Hugo put his arm around Kurt.

Kurt broke into an even larger smile made comical by his puffy cheeks. "That's me," mumbled Kurt.

"Well, Kurt of Karlsruhe," said Selma Schiller, "it's my pleasure to finally meet you."

Her brief conversation with Kurt ended with the children's questions. "Is my entire family coming? Are we all going to America? When are the others from Aspet coming?"

Oskar Schiller looked at his wife. "Unfortunately, we will not be leaving with you on this trip. But all of your families are continuing to do whatever they can to make sure that they will be with you in America."

The satisfied children talked among themselves while Hugo's father looked at his watch, aware of each precious second that he and his wife would have with their son. And as much as Hugo's parents wanted to stay with the children, they rushed out of the shack with their son.

An hour later, the children heard the first of many more welcome knocks. Eva, whose seventh birthday was the next day, received an early birthday present when her parents walked through the door. Thirty minutes later, it was eight-year-old Lore's turn to be swept up in the arms of her parents. The emotional reunions went on for another two hours, until only Kurt and Hjalmar remained. The ecstatic boys dragged a broken chair to the closed door where they picked at their cheese and bread and talked about their own reunions that were minutes away.

After an anxious hour passed, Hjalmar jumped from the chair and dug into his waiting piece of luggage. "Got it," said Hjalmar proudly. "This is for you." Kurt looked at the almost two-year-old picture of eight-year-old Hjalmar's smiling face. Kurt's confused look was misinterpreted by Hjalmar. "But Kurt, I have nothing else to give to you."

"No, you don't understand...I have nothing to give you. Besides, when we get to America we will be together, so..."

The three successive knocks that preceded the opening door stopped Kurt. "Mutti, Papa!" screamed Hjalmar. Kurt stood by and smiled as his brother was repeatedly thrown into the air. When Hjalmar's feet finally rested on the ground, he turned to Kurt. "Mutti, Papa, this is..." But Kurt was gone. Hjalmar ran to the empty rooms and then to the opened window where he yelled, "Kurt, Kurt, Kurt!"

"We will meet your friend later," smiled Hjalmar's father. He gave his son a handful of peppermint candies that were promptly placed on Kurt's luggage.

When Kurt awoke outside the next morning, he watched the sun break over the horizon. The surprised old man who had provided history lessons explained, "They told me it wasn't necessary to bring any food, because..."

Kurt walked purposefully past the man who cautioned him, "Don't do it." Kurt put on his shirt, rolled down his pant legs, and began his angry walk toward the harbor. He sat for hours, watching the sun-scarred men dividing up the catches of fish, seahorses, eels, and octopus before throwing them into the blood-stained wooden bins. Then, for hours more, Kurt walked alone on the narrow roads off the Canebiere, past the flapping clothes that had been hung out of windows to dry, and through the toxic smell of mildew and dead fish. Just as in Karlsruhe, where his solitary walks found him drowning in unanswered questions, he struggled with a new question: what had he done to cause the absence of his mother and grandfather?

On August 22, 1944, three days before the liberation of Paris, the old man's beloved transporter bridge was destroyed by retreating Nazis.

GREETINGS

"Good morning, boys and girls," said the French stranger on the early morning of June 25, 1942. "I hope you had a pleasant evening. I also hope that you will be happy with the news that I bring you from the Quakers. Everything is ready. I have a car to take you to the dock."

The children responded with a defiant chorus of, "We can't leave yet. My parents are coming!" Dripping with sweat from the early morning heat, the Frenchman looked at his watch. "Children, I'm sorry that you are upset, but it is time to leave. This is not something that we are going to discuss."

Kurt said nothing. He picked up his luggage while the horrified children watched the driver grab their luggage. Richard pounded the table. "My brother and I are not leaving. We are staying until our father comes for us!"

Kurt stood at the open door. "We don't have a choice. Besides, what are we staying for? Our parents want us to leave."

Lore, inconsolable, screamed, "You're the only one whose family doesn't care." The painful words stung Kurt, but he had long ago come to the same conclusion during the hours he spent alone on the narrow streets off the Canebiere.

"Shut up, Lore!" yelled Hugo. "You don't know anything. Kurt's family could be walking up the road right now."

Kurt merely waved at Lore on his way to the car that had been eaten away by years of salt air. Moments later the angry children filed out of the shack and into the car. It bounced down the mountain toward another crumbling shack where stateless Jews eleven-year-old Willie Wolpert from Vienna, fourteen-year-old Eva, sixteen-year-old Arthur Kantor from Vienna, and a fourteen-year-old girl from Saint Paul, Minnesota, Josette Boglio, piled into the car. There were no introductions. To the contrary, eyes looked straight ahead and mouths tightened. The car of frightened children coasted down the steep road past the oldest hotel in France, the Grand Mercure Marseille Beauvau Vieux Port, a place where Chopin stayed and past the laurel, cypress, and olive trees, and finally onto the same Canebiere where the King of Yugoslavia had been assassinated.

When the car finally stopped, the children, stacked like cords of wood, fell out onto the boulevard. They quickly gathered their luggage as they fought to keep up with the fast-walking driver. He greeted forty-year-old lawyer Frederick Mayer-Alberti, Mauritas Kahn from Saint Petersburg, Russia, and twenty-year-old nurse Paula Pfeifer from Frankenthal, Germany. The brief introductions, which drew little attention on the crowded Canebiere, confirmed that these were the children's escorts from the American European Children's Bureau.

"And who is this little one?" asked the nervous driver to a screaming child.

"My boy, Jean Frederic. He was born in Gaudérin, France," said Alberti. His inviting smile, white teeth, and slicked back shiny black hair gave the appearance of what Kurt thought an American movie star looked like.

"Oh yes, I know Gaudérin well," said the driver, who scrutinized each passing stranger. While the men continued to talk, Kurt was drawn to the mother who was trying to comfort her son. Her short curly black hair dripped with sweat as she sang, danced, and spun the little boy, until the laughing child dropped his rattle. Kurt picked up the toy and handed it to the woman. Her simple thank you startled Kurt.

"You speak German," observed Kurt.

The mother put her son on the ground and grabbed Kurt's hand. "Yes, and Hebrew, French, and English. And where are you from?"

"Karlsruhe," chuckled Kurt as the little boy tried to crawl up into his arms.

"Illse, who is your friend?" said Mr. Alberti as the rusty car bounced down the Canebiere.

"Why, this is Jean's new big brother, Kurt," laughed Illse.

Kurt's eyes glowed as he pulled at the mother's dress. "My mother's name is Ilse, and I have a big brother too. His name is…"

"Kurt, let's talk about them after we get aboard," interrupted Mr. Alberti. "It's time to go."

IMERETHIE II

It was 8:30 a.m. when Kurt sat down next to Hugo and read each painted letter on the hull of the *I-M-E-R-E-T-H-I-E*. Kurt walked to the posted notice. "Hugo—the ship's not leaving until late afternoon." Hugo grunted an indiscernible acknowledgement while Kurt grabbed at the bars of the locked gate that led to the 3,713-ton French ship. Kurt refused to look at Hugo. His red eyes, staring at the cargo ship's double masts, single black funnel, and white hull, confirmed the reality that, like Hugo, he too was thinking of his family.

After the *Imerethie II* was built in 1924, its owner, the Marseille Campagnie de Navigation Parquet, became the first company to schedule service between Marseille and its important North African neighbor to the south, Morocco. The company's growth allowed it to open a chain of hotels in Morocco and purchase other cargo ships in order to import Moroccan fruits and vegetables to France. But more importantly for the children, the company's long-standing business connections between Marseille and Morocco, a French protectorate since 1912, would hopefully draw no special interest from either the Vichy or Nazis.

"Good morning, boys and girls," began the invitation to join the escort. "My name is Frederick Alberti, and this is Paula Pfeifer and Mauritas Kahn. We would very much like to join you on your trip to America." He reached for his son, whose repeated spinning and falling to the ground brought a needed round of laughter from the children. "This little one is my boy, Jean. Some of you have already met my wife, Illse." He put his arm around his wife. "I expect my wife is going to be busy with my son, but if you have any concerns or questions, we are all here to help you." He clapped his hands together in front of the disheartened children. "Good then. It's time to go to America."

When Kurt took his first steps toward the opening gate, a cautious collective breath was taken by many people in Europe and America who had taken on the final complicated process of obtaining for Kurt on June 10, 1942, sauf-conduit no. 3761 and on June 16, 1942, immigration visa no. 1892.

Hours after the children followed the instructions to go to the lowest deck on the *Imerethie II*, they heard short bursts from the ship's horn. At the same time, Kurt felt an almost imperceptible swing as he lay in his hammock. No words were said before Hugo, Richard, and Ernst rushed past Kurt on their way to a metal ladder. "It's moving, it's moving," shrieked Rolf as he watched the sprinting boys run down the hallway for one last chance to see their parents. They strained to push open the heavy metal door.

"This way!" yelled Kurt to the others, who frantically followed him up the ladder. The ship's horn sounded again as Kurt, the Weilheimers, and Hugo made their way onto the deck where the brilliant sunlight temporarily blinded them. Kurt cupped his hands around his eyes. He made his way to the railing where he joined the others and screamed, "Opa, Mutti, is that you?" to the tiny faceless figures waving in the distance.

While a tug boat slowly pushed the *Imerethie II* past the pedestrian bridge and out of the harbor, the weeping parents of the brothers and sisters of Aspet stood at the dock waving good-bye. Hours later the parents wrote to their children.

LETTER FROM THE PARENTS OF HUGO SCHILLER

"Hotel de Levant
Marseille, June 25, 1942

My Dear Hugo,

It is 9:00 o'clock in the evening. We just finished our dinner and we were talking about last
evening which was one of the most beautiful
ones in my life. The great love and kindness
which the Quakers and OSE have rendered to you
and us, we will never forget and we will be
grateful to them forever. I don't want to miss
mentioning the excellent and plentiful dinner.
For the first time since my internment on Oct.
25, 1940, was my hunger completely satisfied.
This morning we tried one more time to see you
on board, but it was in vain. Now we know that
you departed at 4 o'clock in the afternoon
and will arrive safely with God's help. When
you sail into Casablanca this letter will be
waiting for you and we hope it will make you
glad. On Sundaywe have to return to Gurs. Be
well and stay as you are, only learn to speak
up a little louder. Many cordial greetings and
kisses,

Your Loving Papale.

The dear Papale has already written everything.
Be as diligent and as good as ever and be reminded that your mother told you that you can

accomplish anything, just be courageous and not bashful. Write to us often and do not forget us.

Cordial greetings and kisses,

Your loving Muttel"

LETTER FROM THE FATHER OF RICHARD AND ERNST WEILHEIMER

"Friday, June 26, 1942

My Cherished Children!

I went in the afternoon to the jetty on the harbor and saw the Imerethie II anchored there. But I could only come to the gate, some 200 meters away from the ship....At 4:00 o'clock, I saw the gangplank retracted and anchor pulled, and shortly after, your ship was towed out by a small tugboat...soon the boat was out of sight... So my dear, good children, I again wish you all the best and above all, good health. Travel with God. May he protect you and keep you well. May he provide you with a joyous future filled with good luck and may he allow you to grow into healthy, Jewish youngsters who can stand tall among men in this difficult world....I pray to God daily for you and your voyage which will hopefully be good. Take care of yourselves, especially in the heat, and you, my dear Richard, always look after dear Ernst. All will become right with God's help. You don't have to be so serious, my dear Richard....Now my beloved boys,

stay well, and write to me as often as it is
my greatest joy and only wish to hear from you
soon again.

Regards and kisses, your loving Papi.

My address in Gurs remains the same as before.
Good Shabbos!

And at the same time

A good Week

I will continue to collect stamps for you."

Five days before these letters were written; Adolf Eichmann issued the Nazi's "Final Order" for the destruction of the Jews. On Thursday morning, August 6, 1942, Oskar and Selma Schiller were two of one thousand prisoners transferred via train transport number 17 from Camp de Gurs to Drancy, a city just outside of Paris. Oskar and Selma Schiller were part of the first convoy of Jews from the unoccupied French zone who had been handed over by the Vichy authorities to the Nazis. On August 10, 1942, at 8:55 a.m., the parents of Hugo, Oskar and Selma Schiller, were transferred from Drancy to Auschwitz, Poland, where they were murdered by the Nazis.

On Tuesday morning, February 26, 1943, the father of Richard and Ernst, Max Weilheimer, was transferred from Camp de Gurs to Drancy. On March 4, 1943, Max Weilheimer and 1,002 other Jews were transferred from Drancy via train transport number 50. The records remain unclear as to whether he ultimately arrived in Maidenak, Sobibor, or Auschwitz. In March 1943, Max Weilheimer was murdered by the Nazis.

Kurt Walker was the only child who did not receive a letter.

On August 22, 1944, three days before the liberation of Paris and ten days after "Operation Dragoon," the Allied invasion into southern France, the *Imerethie II* was scuttled and sunk by the retreating Nazis in the harbor at Marseille.

ISACK AND ILSE

"As I hear from your dear mother, I know
that you are well. I can say the same about
myself. I would love to go to America, but I'm
sorry that my papers are not ready. Stay well
and behave yourself and don't ever forget us.
As soon as I can come to you, I will look for
you. I am sorry at this moment this is not the
case. Please write to Uncle Simon and Selma
Intrudl. Mr. Simon Roos, 618 E. 15 Brooklyn,
N.Y. Your grandfather is better again and so is
Julius. Please tell Uncle Simon that he should
hurry up that I can come soon too. I am sure it
is beautiful there and you will like it. Also
dear Kurt, I say good-bye to you and hope that
we will see each other soon again. Have a good
trip. You will be heartily greeted from your
Aunt Frieda."

Letter dated August 6, 1942, from Frieda Friedmann. By the end
of August 1942, Frieda Friedmann was murdered by the Nazis.

On August 6, 1942, Gurs became one of the first camps in
southwestern France to be tested under the expulsion order issued by the Vichy and Nazis. Days earlier, a rumor of the
imminent transfer of the Gurs Jews resulted in most of the internees packing their bags for the next part of their vague journey. While the drama of early August began to unfold, Isack

Ettlinger's weeks-long request for a pass to leave his ilot was approved. After he waved his pass at the disinterested guard, Isack shuffled onto the Moche and then to the same infirmary door that he had opened seven months earlier when he said good-bye to his wife. During the intervening months, the physical changes in Isack were obvious. He had lost twenty additional pounds, what remained of his salt-and-pepper hair had turned a snowflake white, and his once erect posture was bent forward from debilitating arthritis.

The frail-looking salesman stood outside the closed door under the blazing sun. He slowly and methodically tugged at his sleeves before he raked both hands across his beard to ensure that no hair was out of place. "How did it come to this?" asked Isack. He prayed, "Please, God, help me." Isack shook his head violently in an attempt to bring himself back to reality and, more importantly, to exorcise the indulgence of self-pity that he loathed in others. He painfully threw back his shoulders and straightened his frayed tie while he grunted with his first step into the infirmary.

Isack took only two more steps before he grabbed for his handkerchief. The stale air, combined with the intense smell of urine and feces, made it difficult for him to breathe. Isack wanted to run as he looked at the poor souls who were too weak to swat at the persistent flies that dotted their faces. Slowly and deliberately he walked down the aisle created by the ten beds to his left and right. With each step forward, the spongy wooden floor bowed under his weight. He whispered to the nurse out of respect to the old women waiting to die, "My name is Isack Ettlinger. I am here to see my daughter, Ilse Walker. She had been in Ilot K, but I don't see her here."

The monotony of death, constant illness, and perceived futility of the nurse's best efforts brought a flat response. "I just arrived here from the camp in Rivesaltes. Your daughter must have been sent back to her ilot. If you contact the head of the ilot, maybe she can help you to get a pass to see your daughter."

Isack silently protested, "Surely Ilse could have sent me a letter or gotten some word to me that she was back in her barrack. Nothing changes. No respect." His shoulders bent forward once again and his chest heaved in disgust. The planks moaned his early exit, until Isack stopped and nervously pulled at his beard. He looked at the motionless body with long black-gray hair that partially hid the woman's gaunt face. He whimpered, "Gott in Himmel!" as he looked at the image of his wife that lay on the flimsy wooden bed that easily supported the dying woman. Isack slid his glasses off and shuffled the last few feet where he threw himself on his daughter and wept.

NYASSA

fter the *Imerethie II* steamed south past the Axis-controlled island of Corsica and the Italian island of Sardinia, it finally anchored in the port of La Goulette, near Tunis, Tunisia, the last Nazi base in Africa. After a few hours, the *Imerethie II* proceeded west along the northern coast of Africa until it anchored at the damaged dock at Oran, Algeria, the site of the Vichy government's victorious battle over the British in July 1940. By the fourth day, the *Imerethie II* continued at ten knots west until it reached the narrowest part of the Strait of Gibraltar, the imaginary line that divides the Mediterranean Sea and Atlantic Ocean. While hundreds of dolphins played in the ship's wake, Kurt shadowed the crew who pointed to the southern coastline of Morocco.

"I heard the sailors, Hugo," said Kurt, panting. "It's Casablanca—that's where we're headed."

Known as the White City from its connections with Spain and Portugal when it was called Casa Blanca, or White House, the Quakers' destination for the children was chosen because the ruler of the mostly Muslim nation of Morocco, Sultan Mohammad V, had, contrary to the Vichy, protected its small minority of Jews against anti-Semitic laws. Unknown to the Quakers, its time sensitive plans with the US Committee for the Care of European Children were occurring at the same time the Americans and British had been working on Operation Torch, the code name for the invasion plans into North Africa. Thankfully for Kurt, the invasion of 125,000 American, British, and free French troops would not land on the beaches of Morocco and Algeria until November 9, 1942.

After the ship docked, Kurt ran down the gangplank into the largest port in North Africa and the second-largest city in Morocco. His open mouth and bulging eyes made him look comical as braying donkeys packed with ksra made of barley, grains, tomatoes, potatoes, onions, garlic, peppers, squash, fruits, and rugs lumbered past him. The smell of cayenne, cumin, licorice, coriander seeds, ginger, and fish permeated the air in the sweltering ninety-five-degree heat while peculiar-sounding dialects of Arabic and Berber along with French and English and stranger-sounding music spilled out from the crowded stalls of the Moroccan bazaar. While Kurt gawked at this strange new world, he was oblivious to the pointing and gossiping men in long djellabas, white robes.

When the muezzin called the Muslims to noon prayer, the resulting empty streets eased the concerned chaperones. They quickly followed the simple map to a building in the center of town. When they opened the ornate door to the dirt-floored dormitory room cooled by huge ceiling fans, the children shouted with happiness. They bounced on the first beds they had seen since they left Aspet. Soon their stomachs were filled with sweet mint tea, couscous, thick pastries, roasted lamb, and chicken with lemons and olives.

The next morning the children joined their escort, Youseff, a local policeman, for a tour of the city. They reveled in their freedom while they watched a puppet show in a nearby park, drank sweet citrus drinks, and talked with their new friend about their journey from Germany. When the children finished applauding at the end of the show, they could have cared less that they had been abandoned by their companion, who wanted nothing to do with Jews. Savvy beyond their years and fluent in French, the children made sure to tell the Albertis that Youseff would be available to escort them wherever they wanted to go. This lie that allowed Casablanca to become Kurt's personal playground ended on July 12, 1942, when the Marseille children and an additional contingent of seventeen Spanish children were taken to the port in Casablanca.

Hugo pulled Kurt out of the long line of angry and frustrated escaping Jews. They watched the tanned, uncaring French sailors diving off the docked Vichy submarines *La Pschye, Oreade,* and *Amphitrite.* Their dreams of joining the sailors, who would be killed a few months later by US aircraft in Operation Torch, quickly ended when a surprisingly stern Illse Alberti walked over to the boys.

"Please don't leave the line!" ordered Illse Alberti before she dragged Kurt and Hugo back into a line of hundreds of people from all over the world waiting to board the *Nyassa.* She breathed deeply to calm herself while she placed the identification cards around their necks. "Kurt, you are number thirty-four, and Hugo, you are number thirty. Do you boys understand? Never take them off and stay together!"

The ship's formal christening on April 21, 1906, was preceded by a news release that proudly declared that the 8,980-ton ship built for North German Lloyd Company had accommodations for 108 first-class passengers, 106 second-class passengers, and 1,828 third-class passengers. In fine print, the release also announced that third-class passengers of this "luxury liner" would have to bring their own food, silverware, and linen and sleep on cots.

Eight years later, on July 23, 1914, the *Nyassa*, whose usual destination was the Far East, was forced to take refuge in Lisbon, Portugal, due to the outbreak of World War I. The ship remained there until 1916, when she was formally seized by Portugal and re-named *Tras-Os-Montes.* Reborn in 1924, she was sold to Companhia Nacional de Navegacao, a Lisbon company founded in 1881, and once again renamed the *Nyassa.* Over the many years leading up to World War II, her ability to accommodate passengers was dra-matically reduced as she was refitted for uses other than those of a passenger ship. This was confirmed on March 17, 1942, when the German submarine *U-106* sank two British merchant ships that were part of a convoy north of Cape Verde Island in the mid-Atlantic Ocean, three hundred miles off the west coast of Africa. Shipmaster Harry Bourne McHugh and forty-one crew members of the *Andalusian,* one of the sunken merchant ships, gratefully welcomed the *Nyassa*'s heroic response to their call for help and the crew's safe return to Funchal, Portugal. No less thankful were the thousands more fleeing from Europe who would also never forget the efforts of the *Nyassa* and its crew.

The citizens of the United States of America first became aware of the *Nyassa* when the *New York Times* reported on December 5, 1940, about the first of its fourteen dangerous voyages to America. The headline's bold black print, "Portuguese Ship Brings 458 Here From War-Stricken Countries" easily seduced its readers with the dramatic description of sub-zero tempera-tures that froze the *Nyassa*'s steering, rescuing tugboats, and the subsequent placement of its passengers under quarantine.

The front-page article was accompanied by photos of stern faces and sad eyes that tried to look away from obtrusive photog-raphers and reporters who wanted to paint a picture of war torn

Europe. Most passengers, such as the Viennese composer of "The Chocolate Soldier" and "The Dream Waltz," Oscar Strauss, said nothing to the reporters as light bulbs flashed away. However, when pressed by persistent American journalists, German Dr. Hartog and his wife told how they had been in the camps in southwestern France. In a flat voice Dr. Hartog told how, without food and water, he had been transported in cattle cars from camp to camp where he bore witness to a total of twelve suicides. The *Time*'s reporter closed with how the doctor's best efforts to treat an epidemic of cholera within the camps nonetheless resulted in many deaths. "We dug shallow graves with our hands and cremated those we could," said Dr. Hartog.

Four and a half months later, on April 26, 1941, the *New York Times* wrote for a second time about the exploits of the *Nyassa*:

```
"TINY LINER BRINGS 816 FROM EUROPE

...While they grumbled at the lack of ventila-
tion, the darkness and the fact that standing
room was so scarce that many of them passed the
time between meals lying in their bunks, the
refugees were fairly unanimous in expressing
delight over their escape from Europe.

Some complained at the unsanitary conditions
resulting from the assignment of one lavatory
to 200 passengers, and several said they had
been defrauded in Portugal by speculators who
extracted bonuses before passage on the ship
could be obtained...

The only American on board, Miss Dorothy Muckley,
declared the people in Germany where she spent
```

a considerable time had been surprised when the war extended for more than a year. She said the food conditions in Germany were not acute and that the people seem satisfied.

....Another passenger was Henry van de Voort, 25, a Netherlands lawyer...said that traveling conditions on the Nyassa were 'abominable' and that there were several clashes between the passengers, whose tempers cracked because of the conditions."

On August 10, 1941, the *New York Times* dramatically declared, "Ship Snaps Her Mast on Brooklyn Bridge; Steel Section Bent as Nyassa Brings 690." The short article noted that the seventeen-day trip was uneventful for the 690 passengers, except for a "...mild thrill..." when a ten-foot section of the hollow steel mast of the ship was bent over by the under span of the Brooklyn Bridge. It would be many months later, after the United States of America was engaged in World War II, that its press once again reported on the exploits of the *Nyassa*.

In 1951, the *Nyassa* was scrapped in the Blyth shipyards in England.

PART III
AMERICA

BALTIMORE

"REFUGEES AT CANTON Refugees from Europe line the docks of the Portuguese steamer, Nyassa docked at lower Canton today."

Baltimore Sun, Thursday, July 30, 1942

In contrast with the organized chaos of Kurt's departure from Vichy, France, his arrival in America had been prepared with military precision. The exacting July 29, 1942, twenty-paragraph memo from the director of the US Committee for Care of European Children, Robert Lang, entitled "Fifth Sailing," was impressive in its scope and detail.

"...Upon arrival in Baltimore we will go to the Hotel Emmerson....Thereafter we will go to the Coast Guard Station to obtain cards of identification, then to the office of Dichman, Wright & Pugh at the Kaiser Building for deck passes.

Upon arrival in Baltimore, Miss Levy will telephone Mr. Charles James, Penn. R.R. Passenger Div. Agent. At the present time the arrangements are that the group will take train 154 leaving Baltimore 3:46 on Friday and arriving in New York at 9:00 p.m....

As soon as we receive word that the boat is docking, Miss Levy will telephone Miss Ward of the Monumental Motor Tours ... and notify her approximately what time the buses would be at the pier to transport the children and adults to Penn. Railroad terminal. ...

Upon the boat's docking, Miss Levy and Mr. Bobe will obtain permission, if possible to go on board. Miss Lang will do the following:

Arrange with the escorts to have the children bring off their own luggage.

Arrange with the escorts for a meeting in New York.

Clear the children through Government officials.

Ms. Marcuse will have made arrangements for box lunches to be distributed to the children at the pier, and pending the hour of the train's departure and the children's release, will make arrangements for supper at a restaurant near Penn. Railroad Station.

Miss Olsen will take her U.S. Committee arm bands and will distribute those to staff before we leave for the pier...

As soon as the children are released from the pier, all members of the staff will help with the luggage.

Mr. Levy will call Ms. Ward again (Broadway 6200) and make sure that the buses will arrive at the pier.

Ms. Levy will call Mr. James again and notify him as to the exact time that we will arrive at the Railroad Station.

Upon arrival at the station, Miss Olsen will pay the bus driver the sum of $12.60 as prearranged. ...

Miss Levy will telephone Mr. Askwith, Campus Coach Co. (Murray Hill 2-1050) notifying him when the train will be arriving in New York so that he can arrange to have the bus waiting there....

Upon arrival at Penn Station, Miss Olsen and Miss Marcuse will take the children in the bus to Pleasantville.

Upon arrival there, Ms. Olsen will pay the driver $33.13 as pre-arranged.

Miss Marcuse will make arrangements for clothing."

When tugboats pushed the *Nyassa* into the Baltimore harbor on July 30, 1942, the atmosphere aboard ship was charged with excitement. Later that day, the *Baltimore Sun* reported about the Portuguese ship that had just arrived from war torn Europe, "...punctuated by a five day stop at Bermuda for inspection by British officials." The *New York Times* reported, "...that passenger...Mojesz Herman ... a refugee from Poland was attempting to smuggle $50,000 worth of gems into the United States."

Already weary after only eight months of war, most American readers quickly skipped over the article and muddy photograph of the crowded stern of the *Nyassa*, where a smiling number 34, Kurt Walker, peeked over the top railing and waved to America. His euphoria was matched by the other eight hundred passengers that included doctors, teachers, machinists, locksmiths, engineers, antiques dealers, musicians, lawyers, and a single acrobat who collectively represented virtually all of the nations of Europe and the Middle East. However, within seconds of Kurt being photographed, the refugees cowered when the armed agents of the Federal Bureau, Army and Navy Intelligence Services, Immigration Services, and the United States Coast Guard boarded the ship. Kurt grabbed for Hugo, who was swallowed up by a moving wall of people. The once-hopeful refugees' pleas in German, Polish, Russian, French, and broken English to not be sent back or beaten deafened the boarding Americans.

The pandemonium on deck drew challenging screams from the American dock workers, "Leave them alone." The captain of the *Nyassa* grabbed for his megaphone and pushed through the crowd yelling, "Be calm. No one is sending you back. The Americans are not here to hurt you."

Kurt's fear-filled eyes darted from face to face until he saw Hugo and most of the other children from Aspet clutching onto Mr. Alberti. Repeatedly he tried to punch through the demoralized people until Illse Alberti appeared and screamed, "No, stay with me, Kurt!" The mother and the child embraced until the shocked armed invaders holstered their weapons. The captain's reassuring instructions brought about a tentative sense of security. Although dehydrated and light-headed from the furnace-like heat and humidity that made it difficult to breathe, Kurt followed the instructions and descended toward the dock past the sick and elderly being removed on stretchers.

While Kurt's wooden-soled shoes clicked away on the dock, he smiled at the sight of the international Red Cross sign. His smile grew when the Red Cross worker presented him with a cup of chocolate milk and two chocolate doughnuts.

"You know, Hugo," said Kurt as he pointed to a sign. "I don't know what Baltimore is, but I think we are in America!"

"Mr. Samuel Finkelstein...came to the office this afternoon; he arrived on the Nyassa and came to inquire about the children....He came to know these children well and wanted to pass on whatever he knew of them...he thought that one parent was not Jewish, but he was told the boy was orthodox;...he was not placed at the kosher table..."

Memo to file from Lotte Marcuse dated August 6, 1942

PLEASANTVILLE

"...Only 375 were able to cross the ocean to freedom....Many had experienced life in crowded detention camps in southern France..."

Jacqueline Bernard regarding Pleasantville, New York, *The Children You Gave Us*, 1972

It was 11:00 p.m. when Kurt and the sleeping children completed the 220-mile bus ride from Penn Railway Station in New York. "Pleasantville," announced the driver to the awakening children, who called for the absent Albertis and Paula Pfeifer. In French and German they asked, "Where are they?" The unsatisfying shrug of the driver's shoulders stunned the children, who watched their luggage being thrown into a pile on the asphalt road.

The moonless night that revived Kurt's memories of his arrival in Gurs also hid the fact that he stood in the middle of numerous cottages positioned around a central square and an administration building. The meticulously maintained 150-acre education campus appeared just as it did in 1912, when its doors opened in order to find a better way to serve the diverse needs of Jewish children. With its opening, Pleasantville became the first cottage-style residential care center for children in America. By 1925 it was the first center for the psychiatric care of children in an institutional setting. Nine years later, concerned parents sent 105 German Jewish children from Hitler's Germany to Pleasantville. In that same year, a new organization, the German Jewish Children's Aid, later named the European Jewish Children's Bureau, was formed to find placements for those same children from Nazi Germany. Over the next six years its director of placement, Lotte Marcuse, worked to place many of these children in Pleasantville. However, during the years of the strict quotas imposed by Breckinridge Long, only 375 children found their way to Lotte Marcuse. One of those children was number 34, Kurt Walker.

THE INTERVIEW

The handwritten notes of the interview in Pleasantville with Kurt on August 4, 1942, were reduced to a one-and-a-half page single-spaced typed memorandum. The memo, which contained incorrect information about Kurt's grandmother, would, along with other seemingly insignificant error-filled documents, have long-term implications for Kurt's future. The memo stated in part:

"The Family

Father: Julius Walker, born in Germany
            1906

Mother: Ilse Walker, nee Ettlinger, born
            in Germany in 1905

Brother: Heinz Walker, born in Germany in
            1929

Kurt was born of a mixed marriage; his mother
is Jewish and his father is Protestant. Supported
his family by working as a railway mechanic, until 1934, under the pressure of the political developments in Germany, he divorced his wife. The
mother brought up her two boys by working as a
dressmaker. In October 1940, she and her younger
son, Kurt, were sent with the forced transport
into France where they were interned in Camp
de Gurs. The older boy, Heinz, happened to be

with the maternal grandmother at that time, and still remains in Germany with her. The grandfather, Isaac Ettlinger, accompanied his daughter and grandson into exile and is still in Gurs. Nothing is heard from the father; Kurt considers himself as Jewish, and judges his father's actions in divorcing his mother very severely. In February 1941, Kurt was released from Gurs and taken into the "Maison des Pupilles de la Nation" run by the French state at Aspet in the department of the Haute Garonne. His mother still remains in concentration camp at Gurs.

The Child

Kurt is a nice-looking boy with straight brown hair and brown eyes, quite poised and independent in his bearing. He is an interesting child, endowed with a lot of imagination and initiative and quite a droll sense of humor. Very self-reliant, able to take care of himself, inclined to fight quickly, he is the kind of child who never crieswho is too proud to cry. His school work is good and his powers of observation are especially acute. He is active in sports, and gives the impression of being full of spirit. He speaks French and German.

Kurt has a brother in Germany. He was not interested in talking about his brother or his family abroad. He gave the impression that he was not close with his brother, since his brother may be in the care of his father....He referred to himself as not having eaten meat in months because he was not supposed to eat it if it weren't kosher. He did not think he could eat meat if it were not kosher, if he lived with an un-kosher family."

Social History From France"

While Kurt sat across from the social worker, she reviewed Dr. Wilcox's three-day-old medical exam of a "Healthy Kurt" that noted his height as forty-nine and a half inches and a weight of sixty-two pounds. The worker took one last look at the photo of Kurt's angry face before she spoke.

"Yes please," said Kurt. He tore at the wrapper of Juicy Fruit gum while he admired his new shorts and leather-soled shoes. The German-speaking worker wrote, "...an attractive, young-ster, has dirty blond hair, rather fair complex-ion and sturdy, red cheeks."

"Kurt, I understand you gave up swimming to talk to me. So I would like to thank you. My name is Dorothy Davis, and I work for the Jewish Children's Bureau."

"They told me I can go swimming when we're done. Besides, my friends aren't going anywhere," smiled Kurt.

"So how are things going for you here in Pleasantville, Kurt?" asked the worker.

Kurt reached into his pocket. "I wrote a letter today to my mother. Can you mail it for me? I don't know how to do it. I only have stamps from France."

"I'd be happy to do that. In fact, I am going to our office in New York tomorrow and I will mail it for you. I bet your mother will love to get a letter from you," said Dorothy between her note taking.

"Why do you do that?" said Kurt.

"Do what?"

Kurt jumped from his chair and ran around the desk. He pointed to the sheet of paper that contained his name and sentences written in English.

"These are notes about our conversation. You're like a movie star in the cinema, and I'm like a newspaper reporter interviewing you."

Kurt was obviously pleased with his new lofty status. "Well then, you can ask me whatever you want."

"What have you enjoyed doing since you got here?"

"I like to swim. I wish I could swim all day. I also learned to roller skate. Last night a boy let me try his roller skates. I tried to do it, but it was too hard. So I only used one skate. I wanted to show him that I could beat him."

Dorothy clasped her hands together and grinned. "Well, is there anything else you like to do for fun? Books? Board games?"

"I don't like to read, except for Max and Moritz. I do like sports like basketball. Soccer is my favorite. And when I play, I like to win. I don't like to lose." Kurt puffed out his chest.

"Kurt, let's play a game, a different game," suggested the worker. "If you could pick any place to stay in America, where would that be?"

"That's easy. Right here in Pleasantville with Hugo and the Weilheimers. Well—I mean all of them."

"Well, let's pretend you could live anywhere other than here. Is there some other place you would like to live?"

"I guess I would have to say New York. New York is the best." Kurt spoke a mile a minute. "It has all the tallest buildings in the world, and I want to live in one of them and be way up in the sky. I think my family would like it here."

"I understand you have some relatives here in New York already, the Roos family. Would you want to stay with them, if that could be arranged?"

"No. No. No. That's not the family I'm talking about. I have their address, but I don't want to live with them. I'm sure the father does not want me in his home."

"I don't understand, Kurt."

Kurt clicked the heels of his new shoes. "Herr Roos is married to my mother's cousin. Besides, they haven't been in America long. They can't help me. I'm sure he will not want me."

"But Kurt, how can you be so sure? They may be very happy to take care of you."

Kurt folded his arms and clicked away as the worker wrote about the Roos family option, `"...quite disinterested..."`

"I think you know you can't stay here in Pleasantville until you are reunited with your family in Europe. We need to find a good place for you to stay. You need to be in a regular school and with a family. Not in a dormitory."

To the worker's surprise, Kurt immediately unfolded his arms. "I will go wherever you send me, but I need to be in a religious home and it has to be kosher."

The worker did not respond to Kurt's demand or ask why. She knew that finding a foster home alone would be difficult, but finding one that was orthodox would be almost impossible.

"So tell me about your family. I understand you have a brother. His name is Heinz?"

Kurt looked at the ceiling. "I don't want to talk about my family and especially about my brother or his father."

"What do you mean his father? Don't you have the same father?"

The worker playfully threw a balled up piece of paper at Kurt's head. "One more time. Don't you and your brother have the same father?"

"I have had nothing to do with them, and they have had nothing to do with me. And that's fine. They are the same. Let them have each other."

Dorothy opened Kurt's file and skimmed over the papers until Kurt began to speak.

"My Opa's name is Isack Ettlinger. He is a great man and a brave man. He fought in World War I. Most of all, he is a good Jew. He went to the synagogue all the time and he took me there until the Nazis...My Mutti is not so religious. But she is a good person. I spent a lot of time with my Opa. We would talk and take walks, and sometimes when I was little, he would take me with him when he had a beer with his cronies at a place not far away from our apartment. It's funny, but I can't remember the name of the beer garden anymore." Kurt fidgeted in the chair until Dorothy picked her head up from her pad of paper.

"Your Opa sounds like a wonderful man, Kurt. I can't wait to meet him."

Kurt finally looked down from the ceiling. "When I left Camp de Gurs to go to Aspet he even blessed me. Have you ever been blessed?" The worker shook her head no. "I think I must be very special. I don't know anyone who has ever been blessed."

Kurt cupped his hands around his face. "My Opa got down on his knees on the only road in the camp. We called it the Moche. I had not seen him in months, and he said, 'Kurtela, I have prayed to God that wherever you go, no danger will happen to you and that you will be a brave boy.' My Opa's prayers have helped me. I know this for sure. God is with me because of him. That's how I know nothing bad will happen to me, Hugo, Richard, and the others." Kurt looked back up at the ceiling. "And I know nothing will happen to my family as long as I honor my Opa's prayers."

"What prayers, Kurt?"

"My Opa prayed that I be a good Jew and to follow my faith. But I have not been able to study or follow the teachings of the Torah."

Kurt walked over to the worker and whispered, "I want to...I need to be a good Jew not just for myself but for my family."

"...On the whole, Kurt gives the impression of a rather, shy timid boy. His interest in athletics and games may come from a sense of insecurity in relation to the other boys of his age and size. There is a certain feeling of quietness and unhappiness about Kurt, as if he were a child of an unhappy home. It is my impression that Kurt may have felt some of the friction which resulted from religious grandparents and a mixed marriage. Kurt has a way of saying that everything is ganz gut. The pathetic way in which this is usually said might indicate that things are really otherwise.

Kurt also gives the impression that he will need lots of security and reassurance, as well as warmth, in order to meet his new environment. Kurt was one of the few children who wanted to stay on at Pleasantville....At this point this might indicate that Kurt is not quite ready to face the new problem of a foster home.

In the group Kurt was not outstanding. He was described as following the lead of the older boys and girls with respect to religious tendencies. Outside of religious matters, Kurt usually did as told. He was responsive to supervision. He mixed fairly well. He was average in cleanliness. There was no outstanding characteristic noted about him."

August 4, 1942, interview of Kurt Walker by caseworker Dorothy Davis

The day after the interview, Dorothy Davis went to the New York offices of the European Jewish Children's Bureau. She placed two blue thirty-cent stamps with Theodore Roosevelt's rendering in the upper right corner of a light brown envelope.

In the upper left corner she placed the return address, Suite 701, 139 Centre Street, New York, New York.

When Kurt's letter was received in Camp de Gurs on September 26, 1942, Censor No. 5 stamped the envelope, "RETUUR A L'ENVOYEUR" and drew lines through the words Madame Ilse Walker Illôt, Gurs (Basses Pyrenees) France. Months later, on January 15, 1943, a secretary for the European Jewish Children's Bureau glanced at an envelope that had been opened and reviewed pursuant to US protocol by USA inspector 147. She read the stamped words in French, "RETUUR A L'ENVOYEUR" and looked at the series of lines through Ilse Walker's name on the envelope before she mumbled, "Another return." The secretary pulled a pencil from her thick mop of hair and wrote "Kurt Walker" next to the Theodore Roosevelt stamps before she stamped January 15, 1943, on the envelope.

"Dear Mother:

After we landed in the harbor of Casablanca on the Nyassa we went to Bermuda where we searched for letters. Then we went on to Baltimore, a town in America and from there we took the train to New York. Then went two hours on the bus and arrived in a home at 11:00 in the evening. We were so tired that we fell asleep on the bus. When we arrived, we went to bed immediately and fell asleep.

After we woke up in the morning, we went for a bath and then for breakfast. We ate very wonderful food, as much white bread with butter and jam as we wanted, and milk as much as we could hold. I am very well off here and I have plenty to eat.

How is Grandpa and Uncle Julius? Many regards to Aunt Jennie and Aunt Freda. Now I will close. Greetings and many kisses from

Kurt"

GOOD-BYE

Prior to Kurt's arrival in Baltimore, significant efforts had been undertaken regarding the potential foster placement for the children. For some, like Hugo and the Weilheimers, their American relatives had not only been located but, more importantly, were willing to take the boys. For others, such as Kurt, the only plan was to get him out of Vichy, France, before it was too late.

After Kurt completed his interview on August 4, 1942, he ran into his room yelling, "Let's go for a swim." There was no response from Hugo, who was sitting alone on the floor squeezing a piece of paper that contained the simple note, "Good-bye, Richard and Ernst." Kurt's mind flooded with memories of the past eighteen months where he saw the birth of a family that was as strong as one tied by blood. Kurt, whose life had been hardened and defined by losses and separations well before October 22, 1940, wanted to escape from the devastating sight of Hugo's tears.

"Hugo, I don't understand. Where are Richard and Ernst?"

"I don't know," answered Hugo as he folded his arms over his eyes.

"Mrs. Davis will know. But we need to tell her that we want to stay here until our families come for us!"

Hugo rolled onto his bed and stared at the cinder block wall. "Kurt, we will always be friends. We will always find each other no matter what happens. The Nazis can't get us here."

"What are you talking about, Hugo? We are brothers! You told me that on the beach. Brothers stay together!" Kurt's shrill voice shouted, "We don't speak English. We don't have money. All we have is each other. You promised me!"

On the evening of August 6, Kurt entered the cafeteria for dinner after having spent the day with Dorothy Davis in the New York offices of the German Jewish Bureau. He put his tray of food down and scanned the room before he ran past Dorothy Davis. It took him only a few minutes before he held the piece of paper lying on his pillow. It read, "Good-bye from your brother, Hugo."

```
"ESCORT'S REPORT                    AUGUST 17, 1942

HUGO SCHILLER AND KURT WALKER

Mr. Kahn said they seemed always to get along
but there is so little he noticed that he could
not give detailed reaction to each...Hugo always
beamed when one looked at him kindly."
```

THE SELLING OF KURT

"August 5, 1942

Miss Dora Margolis, Acting Director
Jewish Child Welfare Association
6 North Russell Street,
Boston, Mass.

Re: Guenther Bodenheimer

Kurt Walker

Dear Miss Margolis:

I am sending you the material on Guenther Bodenheimer; unfortunately there are no photographs available at this time. If there were they would show you a rather short stocky boy with nice features, brown hair, light eyes and quite a mischievous expression. We have cleaned him up as far as possible and when he arrives in Boston he will have presentable clothing, I can assure you.

...The history on Kurt Walker will, I hope, encourage you to try him. He, too, has an entirely negative medical report and is ready to go at any time.

We would very much like to send the children away from her before the end of the week but

since you won't be able to tell me definitely
before Friday whether or not you can take Kurt,
we will probably have to postpone the departure
until Monday. However, if you could take them on
Saturday that would be all right with us also....

Sincerely yours,

Lotte Marcuse

Director of Placements

August 5, 1942

Mr. Isadore Offenbach, Executive Director
Jewish Social Service
152 Temple Street
New Haven, Conn.

Dear Mr. Offenbach:

I am sending you material on Kurt Walker,
Hjalmar Mauer and Guenther Bodenheimer.

I am fairly certain of plans for Guenther
and for Hjalmar and it is possible that Kurt,
too, will be accepted by Friday. I would, however, appreciate it if you would let me know
whether there are any chances in New Haven and
should any of the plans fall through, I will
call you.

Sincerely yours,

Lotte Marcuse

Director of Placement"

On August 6, 1942, the Jewish Children's Bureau received two phone calls regarding the placement of Kurt Walker. The polite initial call from the Jewish Child Welfare Association made it clear that they had a strong preference for Guenther Bodenheimer. The blunt second phone call thirty minutes later from the Jewish Social Service in New Haven confirmed there would be no placement in Connecticut for Kurt Walker. "We would prefer a younger child."

"August 6, 1942

Mrs. Eleanor Schwartz
130 North Wells Street
Chicago, Illinois   Re: WALKER, Kurt

Dear Mrs. Schwartz:

No sooner have I written that I am "sold out" than I am coming with a request which is, however, still tentative. It is possible that I shall hear later in the day or tomorrow morning that Kurt Walker, about whom I am writing, may join one of the other boys somewhat younger than he for placement in the same city...and hope that you, too, will wire me in case there is any special reason for your request not to send this boy along.

Although I have still several requests for single children, from several communities, I hesitate to utilize them because it would mean a complete separation from the group without the substitute consolation that there is a family waiting at the other end. For this particular group, with its terrific anxieties and fears this seems just a little bit too much to bear...

Kurt seems a very normal child and quite self-reliant. I hope the material speaks for itself in the telegram which I am going to send you tomorrow. I shall give the details on the location of the car in which they will arrive. I assume that you will wish to take advantage of the week-end, so that I could not reach you on Saturday. However, if you want me to I trust you will include that in your wire tomorrow.

Sincerely yours,

Lotte Marcuse

Director of Placements

Air mail special delivery"

"Miss Lotte Marcuse
New York Association for Jewish Children
Pleasantville, New York Re: Nyassa Group

My dear Miss Marcuse:

In re: the postscript to your "special" of August 4, Monday arrival would be fine with me and I prefer morning arrival in order to have time to take Lore Bauer to the South Side and then Esther Strang to the far North side. We would take a single boy and I have a kosher (but not orthodox) foster home where I could make a temporary placement. This is the Mittlepunkt home where Arnold

Isaak lives and there is space available thru the month of August as Arnold is away at camp. I presume you've sent or will send a history on a boy if you have one you want us to take.

Please let me know as soon as you can when to expect them. If you wire after early Saturday morning, you had better wire me at home, the Churchill Hotel, 1255 N. State Street.

Yours sincerely,

Eleanor F. Schwartz

Director of Refugee Placement"

On August 7, 1942, Lotte Marcuse sent a Western Union telegram to Eleanor Schwartz. The first stated:

"SORRY OUR WIRE TRANSFER OMITTED KURT WALKER HE WILL COME ALONG"

In the late afternoon of August 8, 1942, a solitary Kurt broke the surface of the water in the Pleasantville pool. He shielded his eyes against the rays of the setting sun.

"How are you, Kurt?"

Kurt moved to his left where the sliver of shade from the standing woman allowed him to see. "Oh, it's you, Mrs. Davis. How are you?"

"Great. I see you are enjoying yourself, but would you mind coming out of the water for a moment? I need to talk to you." She reached for the dry towel sitting on the wooden bench and wrapped it around Kurt.

"Have you ever heard of Chicago, Kurt?" asked the worker.

"Sure. They have gangsters. Al somebody and it's by the Pacific Ocean."

"Well, that's great, Kurt," replied the worker, grinning. "It's a huge city just like New York. In fact, some say it's even better than New York." Her voice took a more serious tone as she dried Kurt's hair like a shoeshine boy. "I have some exciting news. We found a foster placement for you in Chicago. You are leaving tomorrow with Esther and Lore. What do you think?"

Kurt ran his fingers through his dry hair. "Last night the two older Spanish boys from the ship did not sleep in my room, so it was just me, Hjalmar, Guenther, and Rolf." Mrs. Davis did not interrupt Kurt, who had become adept at not answering her questions. "None of us could sleep because they were not in the room with us. One of them must have left a coat on a hook and we thought it was a person. We were so afraid that we slept in one bed. I think it must have been light outside when I finally fell asleep."

Kurt kicked at the water and stared at his distorted image until Mrs. Davis said, "Kurt, I'm sorry I don't understand."

"In Germany my mother always stayed with me until I fell asleep; and when they took us to France, I always slept next to my mother. And then in Aspet all of us slept together. If I have to sleep alone in Chicago I don't think I could do it. I would be just too afraid."

Dorothy reached for another towel and wrapped it around Kurt. He began to shiver as the sun hid behind a cloud. "Did you know, Mrs. Davis, when we came here on the *Nyassa*, this little boy told me that a woman died in his kitchen back in Germany? He also told me he saw many other dead bodies where he lived." Kurt looked through an opening in the towel that was wrapped around his head and asked, "If Esther and Lore are going with me does that mean that we are going to live together?"

"...Again indirectly, Kurt reacted as if foster home was frightening...he wanted to know if I would stay in Chicago...if I would live there.... I explained there would be someone like me in Chicago.

Kurt did not seem happy during the interview. Either he was upset about his foster placement and unable to express this or else, he was still under the influence of the experience of the previous evening.

Altho there may be anxieties around foster home placement, Kurt gives the impression that he will be able to overcome these anxieties.

Dorothy Davis

Caseworker

August 8, 1942"

On Sunday, August 9, 1942, at exactly 2:47 p.m., Kurt, four other children, and Dorothy Davis left Pleasantville for Grand Central Station in New York. Upon their arrival, they boarded car 379 at 4:20 p.m. for an anticipated 8:20 a.m. arrival at the LaSalle Station in Chicago.

AUGUST 6, 1942–CAMP DE GURS

During the last weeks of July 1942, Theodore Dannecker, the director of the Jewish Affairs for the Gestapo in occupied France, ordered the camp directors in southwest France to restrict visits and reinforce security. Days later, on August 5, 1942, a confidential directive was issued by René Bousquet, the secretary general of the French police, to the regional prefects of the Vichy zone. With certain exceptions, it was ordered that all Jews who had entered France after January 1, 1936, were to be collected and transported to various countries, including Germany, before September 15, 1942.

On August 6, 1942, Ilse awoke to a commotion on the Moche. She slowly hung her black-and-blue legs over the side of the bed to avoid the dizzy spells that frequently accompanied any quick movements. Although her health had improved since she had seen Isack, her teeth still chattered even as the morning temperature approached ninety degrees. Ilse grabbed her stained and ragged bathrobe that had been pieced together from discarded scraps of cloth during the prior winter. She draped it over her shoulders and walked out of the barrack. Her salt-and-pepper frizzy hair poked out from her scarf and fell across the translucent skin on her face. Ilse clung to the barbed wire while some Jews were removed from their ilots. She looked at Paul, "Transfyrer Noe? Recebedou? Rivesaltes?"

"Je ne sais pas," answered Paul as Gruel waved his hands above his shoulders. Minutes later, the first of 525 women and 475 men, from forty-six to sixty years of age, walked past her.

What Ilse and most of the world did not know at that moment was that pursuant to the July 31, 1941, order of Adolf Hitler, Reich Marshal Herman Göring issued a command to Reinhard Heydrich, second in command of the SS, to prepare "A general plan of the administrative material and financial measures necessary for carrying out the desired final solution of the Jewish question." In furtherance of this order, Heydrich convened a conference in the Berlin suburb of Wannsee on January 20, 1942.

Considered an unusual choice due to his rumored Jewish background, Heydrich nonetheless had realized a meteoric rise as one of the most dangerous members of the Nazi Party. Heydrich, who once shot at his image in a mirror as he screamed "Filthy Jew," was the personification of committed viciousness and, more importantly, the correct Nazi to fulfill his new assignment.

In attendance at the Wannsee Conference were fifteen of the top Nazi bureaucrats. They coordinated the final solution regarding the estimated eleven million Jews in Europe and the Soviet Union. In referring to the solution, Heydrich made clear the goal of the meeting:

"Instead of emigration, there is now a further possible solution to which the Fhrer has already signified his consentnamely deportation to the east..."

Ten days after the Wannsee Conference, Adolf Hitler spoke at the Sports Palace in Berlin and pressed forward with his fist pounding rhetoric just as he had in the Festhalle in Karlsruhe on March 3, 1928:

"...the war will not end as the Jews imagine it will, namely with the uprooting of the Aryans, but the result of this war will be the complete annihilation of the Jews.

Now for the first time they will not bleed other people to death, but for the first time the old Jewish law of an eye for an eye, a tooth for a tooth will be applied.

And world Jewry may as well know this the further these battles (of the war) spread, the more anti-Semitism will spread. It will find nourishment in every prison camp and in every family when it discovers the ultimate reason for the sacrifices it has to make. And the hour will come when the most evil universal enemy of all time will be finished, at least for a thousand years."

The lighting of the fuse that ensured the ferocity of the Nazis and the correctness of Ilse's decision to let Kurt leave for America began on May 27, 1942, with the assassination attempt of the thirty-eight-year-old chairman of the Wannsee Conference, Reinhard Heydrich. Two days later, 151 Jews in Berlin were executed in retribution for the actions of the Czech assassins. These acts of murder were followed by Hitler's June 10, 1942, order that the Czech village of Lidice be liquidated. This death sentence was fulfilled when every building in the town was flattened and 172 men and boys over the age of sixteen were brought out in groups of ten and murdered by firing squad. Then, on June 30, 1942, Adolf Eichmann issued the final incomprehensible order that both implemented the final solution of the Jews and honored Reinhard Heydrich's death at 4:30 a.m. on June 4, 1942.

Seven months after the Wannsee Conference and almost two months after Heydrich's death, Ilse clung to the wire outside the infirmary in Gurs. Unknowingly, she had witnessed the initial implementation of the Wannsee Conference. While hundreds walked by her on the Moche, she recalled the innocent and unanswered question asked by Kurt almost two years earlier, "Mutti, I don't understand what Camp de Gurs is and why we are here?" At the same time, two anonymous Jews, Oskar and Selma Schiller, dragged their luggage past her.

HUMBOLDT PARK

"8-10-42 Arrived Chicago and placed Kastel,
Albert-Irene, 2715 W. Thomas, Humboldt Park.
Telephone Brunswick 3636. Board rate $24.00"

First entry placed in Kurt Walker's file by the Jewish Children's
Bureau, Kurt Walker's legal guardian in America

The history of the Chicago Jewish community began with the influx of German Jews in the 1850's
and 1860's. Their fleeing of Germany was generally not perceived as associated with religious persecution, but instead was
sparked by the year of revolution across Europe in 1848. This began with the February revolution in France, which brought about
the toppling of King Louis Philippe and numerous acts of insur-
rection across German territories. These newly arrived German
Jews recognized that part of their ultimate economic and social
success would be attributed to their assimilation into the non-
Jewish German society that existed in Chicago. This assimilation
contributed to the growth of Reform Judaism or an adherence
to a less ritualistic or strict compliance with how Judaism had
been observed in Europe. For example, the Sabbath would now
be held on Sunday to better conform to the Christian work week.
By 1900, essentially every German Jew had become aligned with
this new Americanized practice of Judaism.

With the development of transportation in Europe at the
turn of the century, many Eastern European Jews, contrary to
the German Jewish experience, immigrated in part to America

because of severe anti-Semitism. This new wave of immigration brought to Chicago a group of Jews whose religious fervor and desire to practice a more traditional form of Judaism would be in conflict with the German Jews who had already settled and established themselves. These differing views created a severe conflict between the two groups over many issues, including how charity and assistance would be delivered to the Jewish community. Because the German Jewish aid organizations had been established earlier and were better funded, the European Jews by necessity sought help from this older and more entrenched community. The European Jews nonetheless felt wounded and humiliated in the process of asking for help, given the attitudes of these 'non-Jews.'

It is from this conflict that the Eastern European Jews of Chicago desired to develop organizations to help provide food and shelter for their less fortunate children. That desire, and the financial success among its community members over the coming years, allowed their efforts to become a reality in accordance with their Jewish faith. At the same time that this conflict of faith between the two groups became more strident, the emerging area of social work became more a part of the implementation of social services within this community. The practical effect for the Chicago German Jews was that less emphasis was placed on religion.

It became clear that a resolution of the differences between these two groups was required in order to better serve the needs of the Jewish community. This difficult process reached some initial success, when in 1937 the Jewish Children's Bureau, or JCB as it came to be known, came into existence as a result of the merger of two German Jewish organizations, the Chicago Home

321

for Jewish Orphans and the Jewish Home Finding Society. This merger dwarfed the ability of any remaining organizations to deliver services and raise funds.

The last remaining Eastern European Jewish organization from Chicago, the Marks Nathan Hall which was formed in 1906, finally merged with the Jewish Children's Bureau of Chicago. The emergence of this new and stronger institution at a time of war and the implementation of the final solution was fortuitous for the many children that would soon be walking through its doors in search of help..."

The Chicago representative for the Jewish Children's Bureau, Eleanor Frank, hugged Dorothy Davis while Kurt, Esther Strang, and Lore Bauer stood shoulder to shoulder on the train platform at Chicago's LaSalle Station. Kurt stood in the cavernous train station as the ear-shattering sounds of train engines, screaming porters, and hundreds of nearby conversations overwhelmed his senses. Miss Frank drew the children into a tight circle and placed her finger over her lips. In her limited German she did her best to make her point. "Nein, nein! Nein German!" The children nodded affirmatively in recognition that their mere presence might draw unwanted attention from Chicagoans who did not want to hear why Nazi refugees were in their city.

Miss Frank returned briefly to her hushed conversation with Dorothy before the children linked their arms. Slowly they followed the women onto LaSalle Street, where they were punched by Chicago's summer heat and humidity. The short, daunting walk past seemingly thousands of harried Chicagoans crisscrossing in front of them left Esther weeping.

"Esther, enough! You're fifteen. No one else is crying. Stop acting like a baby," said Kurt before he entered the huge American car. In the satisfying silence that followed, Kurt wished that Hugo could have seen him putting Esther in her place.

While the workers chatted, the car proceeded west past Jefferson and Des Plaines to Halsted. Kurt shielded his eyes and looked back at the huge skyscrapers that had made the sunny day appear so cloudy. He could not contain himself when he uttered his new American word learned in Pleasantville, "Wow!" The distraction from the sight of the huge buildings was short-lived as the car came to a stop in a south side residential neighborhood consisting of three-flat apartment buildings and postage stamp front lawns. Kurt could not keep his eyes off Esther, who was literally dragged through the front door of a gray-stone apartment building.

"It's Kurt and Lore, isn't it?" asked Miss Frank. Lore, trembling, was unable to answer. Kurt remained silent as half of his body hung out of the car that proceeded north on Lake Shore Drive, next to the shores of Lake Michigan. That was until he shouted "wow" upon seeing the Hellcats and Corsairs from Glenview Naval Air Station landing on the five-hundred-foot decks of two former passenger ships, the USS *Sable* and USS *Wolverine*.

Miss Frank pulled Kurt back into the car. "It's Kurt?"

Kurt followed a bouncy landing by a novice Hellcat pilot.

"He won't really understand, Eleanor. Just ask a question and I'll translate," said Dorothy.

"How old are you?" began the three-way conversation.

"Eleven last May."

"Well, my name is Eleanor Frank and I have been assigned to help you while you are here in Chicago." She pressed her business card in Kurt's hand. "Now it's official. You are my boss." Kurt touched the raised lettering while he separated each syllable as he read out loud,

```
HOME FINDING SOCIETY    MARKS NATHAN HALL

JEWISH CHILDREN'S BUREAU OF CHICAGO
130 North Wells Street (6)
Chicago, Illinois.
Telephone Franklin 9555
```

"I do the same thing that Mrs. Davis does for the European Jewish Children's Aid. The only difference is she is in New York and I am in Chicago. Do you have any questions for me?" Kurt wanted to ask a thousand questions, but answered, "Nein."

"Well, if you have any questions, you can call me or ask me whenever we see each other. If you look on the back of the card, I wrote down the address of your foster family, the Kastels. Their home is located in the northwest part of the city called Humboldt Park, 2715 West Thomas. Their phone number is Brunswick 3636."

Kurt repeated the German-sounding Humboldt Park while Miss Frank reviewed her notes about Mr. Kastel, "...a quiet, unobtrusive person" and Mrs. Kastel "...a vigorous, alert, intelligent and outgoing person..." before she continued. "You should be very happy to know that in addition to a number of synagogues in the neighborhood, the Kastels keep a kosher home. They also have two other foster children, a brother and sister from Germany who have been with the Kastels since October. Herbert is seventeen and Edith is twelve. I'm sure you will like them. They speak French and German just like you. They also speak English."

She refused to tell Kurt that the possible return of the Kastels' two former foster children who Mrs. Kastel `"...had become attached to"` would mean his immediate removal. Also, the stressed worker failed to disclose her own opinion that the Humboldt Park area was `"...not too good."`

Miss Frank continued to sell Kurt on his new home. "Mr. and Mrs. Kastel are in their thirties. Unfortunately, they speak no German, just Yiddish and some Russian. Do you speak any Russian, Kurt?" After Mrs. Davis answered no for Kurt, the Kastel biography continued. "And they also have a little girl, Jolene, who is three and a half years old. The wife's name is Irene and the father's name is Albert. He is an account manager for a large department store. You will like this, Kurt: he was going to be a professional baseball player, but his parents disapproved. So he went to law school before he made a career change. Do you know about baseball? About the Chicago Cubs?"

Kurt briefly smiled. He recalled Alice's hopes that one day they would attend a Cubs game together before he answered, "Nein."

"Mrs. Kastel's mother, Sarah Chelnitsky, lives with them. She owns a fish store in the neighborhood. Unfortunately, her husband was killed in a hit-and-run motor vehicle accident on his way to the store. Anyway, she keeps very long hours. So she probably won't be around much." The workers looked briefly at each other before Miss Frank asked, "Don't you have any questions, Kurt?"

Kurt said nothing as the car proceeded west onto Division Street. He was awestruck viewing the mostly commercial street that dwarfed the Kaiserstrasse back in Karlsruhe. "Wow," whispered Kurt upon seeing an endless wall of black, white, Hispanic, and Chinese men and women on the street. The workers chuckled as Kurt tried to read each passing street sign of Halsted, Ashland, Damen, and Western, while pointing at the laundries, butcher shops, movie theaters, and clothing stores.

"What's that?" yelled Kurt as he pointed at the large Humboldt Park sign at the corner of California and Division.

"We talked about that, Kurt," said Mrs. Davis. "The whole neighborhood that you are going to live in is called Humboldt Park. That's the park over there. It's over two hundred acres. It's beautiful. They have a velodrome, and every Wednesday night they have bicycle races in the bowl. They also have a pond where you can go swimming and take boat rides."

"Wow," mumbled Kurt. The car made a slow left turn at California and one final left turn onto Thomas Street, where it proceeded past playing children and the two and three-story apartment buildings that sat on 25-by-125-foot city lots.

"That's your new home, Kurt," pointed Dorothy. The squealing tires scraping along the curb became an unintended knock on the door to the neighborhood. Dorothy's crooked smile preceded her attempt at humor. "Well, Eleanor, I'm sure the JCB will be thrilled with that repair bill."

Eleanor's witty response was never heard by Dorothy, who rushed out of the car and toward the approaching people. "Good morning, Mrs. Kastel. How are you? And Herbert and Edith, how are the Manns?"

Lore inched closer to Kurt and grabbed his hand. Kurt understood "good morning," but other than that, he had no idea what was being said within the small group of people. Lore's grip tightened and then released as Dorothy opened the car door. Kurt walked hesitantly while he pretended to be unaware of the staring children that had stopped to look at the new kid. The Manns slapped Kurt on his back and eagerly shook his hand.

He looked back at Lore's panicked face. Short and stocky with thick curly black hair to her shoulders, Irene Kastel joined in the hand shaking while the Manns peppered Kurt with questions in English. It only took seconds for them to read Kurt's blank face before they repeated their questions in French.

Mrs. Davis excused herself for interrupting before she told Kurt that she had to take Lore to her foster placement. Unthinkingly, she was too candid with her good-bye. "Kurt, you are going to stay here for a little while, and then Miss Frank will get together with you to discuss our plans for you." She looked at her watch again and then at Lore. "And I have this present for you, a German-English dictionary. So between the dictionary and the Manns, everything should be good."

"But I thought this is where I am staying until I see my family again? Why would I only stay here for a little while?"

"This is a wonderful home, Kurt. Not only do you have the Kastels to take care of you, but you have the Mann children. That must make you happy." There was one final impatient look at her watch before she ran to the car. Lore locked eyes with Kurt until the moving car was out of sight. Kurt would never see Lore Bauer again.

"He was somewhat shy and fearful but did not cling to the worker when the worker indicated that worker had to leave."

August 10, 1942 entry into Kurt Walker JCB file

DRANCY AND PITCHIPOI

"They made up a word when we asked where we were going. I think it was Polish. It meant something like a place beyond, unknown."

Unknown prisoner from Drancy concentration camp, 1942

Located seven miles from Paris is the town of Drancy. In 1936, its thirty-five thousand citizens took great pride in the fact that the center of its town would be the future sight of a U-shaped five-story public housing complex. However, by October 1939, the uncompleted structure functioned as an internment camp for homosexuals and other undesirables. Under the control of the French military police, it also became an intolerable place for the sixty-five thousand Jews who passed through its walls until its liberation on August 17, 1944.

Drancy's ominous place in history grew darker on August 20, 1941, when 2,400 French military police surrounded the working-class Jewish neighborhood of the eleventh district, the alleged center of the emerging Jewish resistance. The subsequent first time arrest of French Jewish citizens concluded with short bus trips to the Drancy concentration camp. Four thousand men were crowded fifty to a room, where they were forced to sleep on concrete floors covered with bugs. The only toilet, a long latrine at one end of the courtyard, immediately became a bog of muck. Within days, these once-proud Frenchmen slogged past the disease-laden latrines to a garbage heap, where they picked through the vilest of waste for something to eat.

In an effort to attain control over of the explosive situation within the camp, the French police copied the Gurs experience and ordered prisoner elections to take place. The winners, who mirrored a caste system of prominent Jews, were anointed heads of the twenty-two staircases. They were responsible for distributing the meager supplies of food. For some, their higher profile brought them access to the black market where a bribe bought extra food and potential freedom. However, for those unable to secure freedom, their expanding duties became more insidious.

By September, a toxic combination of food shortages and spreading diseases that were reported as "physiological misery" brought about many deaths. Ironically, two months later, the fear of nearby German troops becoming infected with an outbreak of cholera or typhus resulted in the sick and inmates under the age of eighteen and over seventy being released. Then, on July 16–17, 1942, 4,500 French police arrested thirteen thousand Paris Jews in what became known as the Grande Raffle, the Big Round Up. For the first time, the arrestees included women and 4,115 children between the ages of two and fourteen. This incomprehensible act resulted in over one hundred suicides.

The arrested Jews were brought to the outdoor Velodrome d'Hiv, the winter cycle station located near the Eiffel Tower. In the beginning of August 1942, wary mothers watched as identification cards were hung around the necks of their children. In the panic that ensued, mothers and children were beaten with fists and clubs, while some of the children were removed from the velodrome and taken to Drancy. In the following days, when another dozen mothers lay dead from suicide, the flimsy identification cards that were often lost, traded, or thrown away resulted in the children's true identities being lost forever.

On August 8, 1942, when Kurt Walker learned from Dorothy Davis that he would be leaving Pleasantville for Chicago, Ilse Walker was packing her few possessions in the infirmary at Camp de Gurs. When Ilse heard her name being announced, she dragged her bag onto the Moche. Others hid in their barracks and behind latrines and attempted to escape or commit suicide. Paul tearfully watched Ilse and scores more walk by him on their forced march past hundreds of sunning eight-inch-long brown wall lizards. Although Paul and the guards were under strict orders from Gruel to do nothing, representatives from the Quakers distributed their meager supplies of water, fruit, cheese, and chocolate to the Jews. While Ilse proceeded to her unknown destination in the insufferable summer heat, she unsuccessfully called out for her father and brother. Hours later, she arrived at the Oloron train station, where she was joined by hundreds more, mostly elderly Jews from the other nearby camps. There would be no respite for Ilse as the screaming French police pushed her into a waiting cattle car for the five-hundred-mile journey to Drancy.

When the train arrived just outside of Paris, Ilse and the others were herded into trucks and buses. The nearby apartment dwellers in the five fifteen-story apartment buildings that surrounded the camp leaned out of their windows and watched Ilse hobble past French police armed with machine guns. After being searched by the Jewish head of a staircase, Ilse climbed four flights of stairs. She looked into the crowded room of seventy women and collapsed.

When she awoke the next evening, she forced herself to begin the arduous task of returning to the courtyard for her promised meager ration of bread and dirty water. Her head ached.

She grabbed at the wall and walked slowly sideways down the darkened staircase. When Ilse reached the third floor, she was already soaked in sweat. She began to weep uncontrollably, until she heard children crying. Ilse's swollen feet were barely able to take her to the next landing where two little boys sat clinging to each other. Ilse wiped her filthy hands on the remnants of her dress and turned around the smudged identification cards that hung around the necks of the boys.

She pointed at herself. "Ilse. Nom?" said Ilse. She touched the older boy of four.

"Jacques," cried the boy. He pointed to the younger boy. "Max."

Ilse pointed back and forth between the boys asking, "Frère?"

"Oui," said both boys.

"Mère?"

The younger boy laid his head in his brother's lap. They shook their heads. They had no mother. There was no hesitation by Ilse. She picked up the younger boy with her black-and-blue pencil-thin arms and held the hand of the older boy. She bounced up the stairs to the fourth floor, through the door less room, where she placed Max on the floor. Ilse took off the urine-stained clothes of the sleeping boy and placed them under his head while the older boy wiped away his tears. Ilse patted the floor amid the snores, cries, and conversations of the nearby women and repeated "Jacques" as if she was reading a poem.

When Ilse, reinvigorated, got up early the next morning, she hurried down the stairs to get food for the sleeping brothers. She quickly removed the scarf from atop her thinning hair and covered her gagging mouth as she approached the foul-smelling latrine and the nearby rubbish dump. The horrors in Gurs paled in comparison to the sight of people on their hands and knees picking through the garbage. She walked out of the line to the latrine in tears and turned away in an effort to collect herself until she heard a familiar voice call out, "Julius, I think I found something." Ilse wiped her eyes with her scarf and turned to the garbage dump. She stood still for the briefest of moments before she began the long walk toward her father and brother.

Beginning on March 27, 1942, and ending on August 17, 1944, seventy-three convoys carrying seventy-five thousand Jews left France. Fifty-nine convoys departed from the same small train station just outside of Drancy at Le Bourget. In conformance with Nazi procedure, a quadruplicate form was completed for each convoy. It identified the name, birth date, place of birth, and country of origin for each transported Jew. On August 12, 1942, the Jews in Drancy walked down the twenty-two staircases for the 5:00 a.m. roll call. The Jewish head of staircase seven looked down at a sheet of paper and read out the names that he had been forced to pick. With the roll call completed and the chosen ones identified, the Jews walked out of the camp into the waiting buses for their 8:55 a.m. departure at Le Bourget train station.

When each bus arrived with its machine gun-toting German officer, they were met by a small cadre of French police. The German officer in charge, Oberfeldwebel Moller, gave a familiar order that saw the compliant French police forcing the Jews into one of twenty-two empty cattle cars. Across the street from the station sat the crowded and popular café that was frequented by many French railway employees, who had grown accustomed to this occurrence. But others, whose disgust on this broiling August day clouded the soundness of their actions, swore at the armed French police while they delivered food and drink to the few Jews they could reach. After the Jews were crammed into cattle cars, the silent patrons of the café listened to the Jews chant Kaddish while others damned God.

Later that day, a telex was prepared by SS Heinrichson and signed by former theology student Heinz Röthke, the head of the anti-Jewish section of the Gestapo. The telex was delivered to Adolf Eichmann in Berlin. It identified the names, ages, and birthplace of every Jew in the transport. This included 508 Jews from Gurs, 173 from Recebedou, 161 from Noe, and 88 adult males from Vernet.

Among the 1,017 people who made up the childless convoy number 18, the second convoy of Jews leaving unoccupied France for the three-day trip to Pitchipoi, were the names of a single unmarried male, Julius Ettlinger, a widower, Isack Ettlinger, who was older than 984 of those on the convoy, and Ilse Walker, a divorced mother. Five days later, on August 17, 1942, 957 people departed from Drancy via the train station at Le Bourget in convoy number 20 for Pitchipoi. In one of the train cars were two motherless brothers from Paris, Jacques Karpensztring, born on May 25, 1936, and Max Karpensztring, born on April 14, 1939. By the end of World War II Pitchipoi's real name, Auschwitz, became synonymous with the Holocaust.

AMERICA, HERBERT,
AND FAITH

While Kurt watched Lore Bauer disappear with one last turn onto Division Street, Herbert hauled Kurt's disintegrating piece of luggage into the Kastels' six-room first-floor apartment. He pressed his face against the screen door and looked at an unmoving Kurt. Seconds later, when Kurt felt a touch on his shoulder, he drew back his fist. "Auntie Irene says that you are to sleep on the daybed in the dining room," said Herbert calmly. Kurt followed Herbert past little Jolene Kastel, asleep on a couch.

"Do you think they will mind if I sit on their daybed?" whispered Kurt.

"Why would they care, Kurt? Besides, I just told you that Auntie Irene said that's where you will be sleeping," answered Herbert. Kurt's red eyes began to glisten. "Kurt, it will be all right," whispered Herbert.

"What's wrong with him? I don't..." asked Herbert's sister, Edith. Kurt wanted to run past her or to tell her to shut up as he opened his clenched fist that held the worker's card, but he did nothing.

"Just leave him alone, Edith," interrupted Irene Kastel, who was trying to calm her waking daughter.

"Mommy, why is Herbert holding that boy's hands? And why is he crying? And who is he, Mommy?" yawned Jolene.

"I think he is a little sad, Jolene."

Thankfully, Kurt's embarrassment was minimized by Herbert's refusal to interpret Jolene's innocent observations. Jolene swung her legs over the couch before she rolled over onto her stomach and then onto the badly scarred wooden floors. She looked up at Kurt and kissed the palm of her hand while making a big "mmmmm" sound before she patted Kurt's leg and ran to the back of the house giggling. Kurt pulled Herbert to the side and whispered to him.

Herbert picked up a charging Jolene and kissed her while he interpreted for Kurt. "Auntie, Kurt doesn't want to sleep alone in the dining room."

"Well, tell him that's not possible, Herbert," answered Irene.

"I don't think that's it, Auntie."

Kurt pulled on his interpreter's arm and whispered again.

"Herbert, where do you stay? Can't I just stay with you? Ask her if I can stay with you. Please?" begged Kurt.

"Herbert, if my Yiddish was a little better I would know for sure what you boys are talking about, but if you don't care I don't care. But tell Kurt he has to try to be a big boy."

Herbert put Jolene on the ground and threw his arm around Kurt. Herbert smiled a yes that produced not only Kurt's first toothy grin in days but his first English sentence in Chicago, "Thank you, Mrs. Kastel."

Irene smiled back. "Herbert, why don't you take Kurt out for a walk—go by the school and the park. Show him around."

At five feet one, with dark brown hair and blue eyes, the diminutive seventeen-year-old Herbert Mann was a blessing for Kurt. His calming influence on Kurt in those first few hours at the Kastels' home and in the following days left Kurt in awe of Herbert. How did he do it? How did he become an American? His speech, clothing, confidence, and even the way he walked were what Kurt wanted. Quite simply, he wanted to be an American like Herbert Mann. Herbert playfully slapped Kurt on the back. "Stop staring at me. It's not polite. Let's go for a walk."

Edith pouted as she ran to the door. "Can I come too, Herbert?"

Herbert looked at Kurt and slammed the door shut. "Men only, Edith!"

The boys kicked a small rock turned soccer ball down the sidewalk and past the curious neighborhood children until Edith's shrill screams could no longer be heard. "Where are you from, Kurt?" asked Herbert.

"Karlsruhe."

"We were almost neighbors back home in Germany. Edith and I are from Steinbach am Donnersberg, just outside Mannheim. We were probably seventy miles to the north of you." It had been almost two years since Kurt had thought of Nazi Germany. He angirly dismissed the thought while he watched Herbert almost dance Chicago style down Thomas Street. Kurt looped his right thumb onto his pants pocket while he did his best to hit the same fluid stride as Herbert, who bounced his finger off his head in acknowledgement of the neighborhood boys playing catch. He really is an American, realized an admiring Kurt.

A ball slapped into a leather mitt. Herbert pointed to the boys and released his thumb from his pocket. Herbert began his lecture with one word: "Baseball."

Kurt released his thumb. "Yes, I know about baseball. I drove past a baseball park today—Comisky Park, the Chicago White Sox, right?"

"This is important, Kurt. In Humboldt Park, people only like the Cubs. Forget the Sox. They stink. You don't want any problems. If anyone asks, just say you like the Cubs," warned Herbert.

"That's fine with me. I have a friend in France, and she likes the Cubs. So I guess I like the Cubs too."

The boys, who had known each other no more than an hour, broke into huge grins. The hopeful American peppered the new American with questions. The answers from Herbert were short and precise.

"Lafayette School is where you will go. I counted it once. Five hundred steps from the front door."

"The winters get very cold and there is much more snow here than in Baden-Baden."

"Try to not speak German. Speak French until you learn English."

"Don't leave the neighborhood."

"Don't ever defend Germany." Kurt nodded and hung his thumb back on his pocket. "They don't understand that we are Jews. They think we are the same as the Nazis."

Kurt pointed to the windows of the nearby apartments. "What about all the flags, the ones with the stars? There are so many."

"The blue stars mean that a husband or son is fighting in the war."

"What about the gold stars?"

Herbert pulled his thumb out of his pocket. "That means the husband or son was killed fighting the Nazis."

The two refugees walked to the end of the block in silence until Herbert pulled a thin piece of paper out of his pocket. "Juicy Fruit?" Herbert unwrapped the piece of gum, tore it in half, and pretended to pull it from behind Kurt's ear."

Ah, Magie!" laughed Kurt until he received a stern look from his mentor.

"I mean it, Kurt. Magicien!" said Herbert in French.

"Magicien," repeated Kurt.

The boys smacked their lips in unison. "You see, Kurt," said Herbert, laughing. "That's why they call it Juicy Fruit." Hebert became serious and spoke from the wisdom of a true American. "You should know that the man that owns the Cubs makes the gum too. He's a millionaire."

While Herbert tutored his pupil, he could see Kurt's eyes growing. "In America, baseball plus gum and you get to be a millionaire."

The pupil whispered in French, "Herbert, do you like the Kastels?"

"Sure. They are nice enough."

"What about the father? Does he beat Mrs. Kastel or you or Edith? Does he get drunk? I'm pretty sure he will not like me."

"What are you talking about? You haven't even met him. He is a nice man. Why, I don't even think I have seen him drink anything other than coffee or water. You are crazy with that talk," said Herbert. He put his arm around Kurt. "Now let's just go in here, and stop with that talk," demanded Herbert. Kurt read the address above the door, 2745 W. Thomas.

"This is a very good place, Herbert," mumbled Kurt as the intoxicating smells and rainbow of colors from the candy store left him unable to move. Herbert, frustrated, drew Kurt close to his face and repeated his prior warning, "French not German. Never in German." Kurt followed Herbert's eyes toward the disinterested teenager who was working behind the counter. Moments later the boys ran to the curb with their overflowing bag of Tootsie Rolls, licorice, Red Hots, and Kits. Kurt placed his frayed cap on his head before he unwrapped a Tootsie Roll.

"Where is your hat, Herbert?" quizzed Kurt, who fell back onto the grass parkway.

"What?" answered Herbert as he threw a piece of black licorice into his mouth.

"Aren't you orthodox—I mean if you are orthodox, why isn't your head covered?"

"What are you talking about? It's only candy," questioned Herbert. "Besides we're not in temple. And no, I'm not orthodox. And neither are the Kastels."

Kurt looked suspiciously at a piece of licorice before he bit into it. "This is not good, Herbert. This is not good at all. We have to talk to them."

"Kurt, this is America. You're not in Germany anymore. The Jews are different here. Auntie told me when I first got here that Edith and I would have to try to fit in and be more American."

"I don't think so, Herbert. If we are Jews we have to follow the Torah. We have to keep our promises to be good Jews. What about you, Herbert? Don't you want to be a good Jew? Don't you want to follow the Torah?"

There was no response from Herbert, who chewed on a string of red licorice like a cowboy chewing on a piece of straw.

"Herbert, please forgive me," apologized Kurt for the indictment that momentarily silenced his new friend.

"My parents sent me and Edith to Paris in March of 1939 because of the Nazis. They stayed with my older brothers. By September 1941 it got bad, so Edith and I left. We ended up in Chicago with Auntie and Uncle. I was just like you when I got here. I spoke only German and French. Now look at me. I even have a Chicago accent. Through all of it I am still a Jew. Maybe not your kind of a Jew. And the only reason I am here today is because of the Quakers. They got me and Edith out. They saved our lives, and it had nothing to do with whether Edith and I were orthodox."

Kurt stopped chewing. "The Quakers saved me too. Not just me, but my friends. They got us out of Gurs in France."

Herbert dropped the bag of candy on the ground and pulled on Kurt's arm. "My family was in Gurs and then Rivesaltes."

The powerful information found Herbert instantaneously reduced to tears. "When were you in Gurs? Did you know my family? My brother, Eric, is twenty years old. He has light brown hair. My mother is Regina—she is short—fifty-five years old. My father, Luitold, has a mustache and wears glasses. He is fifty-three, no, fifty-four. Do you remember those names or anyone that looks like that, Kurt?"

"Herbert, I was only there a few months and I was in one of the women's ilots. So I didn't get to see many men. I hardly saw my Opa and Onkel. I'm sorry. I just don't know." Kurt could see how quickly Herbert's manic excitement was overtaken by the numbing disappointment of his answer. Kurt tried to repair the moment. "Herbert, now that I think about it, I believe I do remember your father. In fact, I think he may have been the head of one of the men's ilots."

Herbert appreciated the kind but transparent gesture. He regained his self-control and turned the clock back two minutes. "France was not bad for me and Edith. What about for you?"

"There was always enough food, clothes, and blankets. It was fine, I guess," answered Kurt falsely.

Herbert smiled with the knowledge that his family was not suffering. "I am so grateful to hear that. My sister and I have not received a letter from my parents in such a long time. To have you here, someone who was in the same camp with my family has made me so happy. Wait until I tell Edith!"

Decades later, Herbert and Edith Mann would learn that on September 9, 1942, at 8:50 a.m., Regina and Luitold Mann were part of one thousand Jews who left Drancy aboard convoy number 30. They were subsequently murdered in Auschwitz.

"And your family, Kurt? Your Vater and Mutti?" asked Herbert cheerfully.

Kurt unwrapped another Tootsie Roll. He answered unemotionally, "Mutti, Opa, and Onkel are still in Gurs. My Oma died in Gurs. And unfortunately my Vater died before I was born."

Herbert quickly changed the subject and broke his sacred rule when he asked in German. "And Bruder? Schwester?"

"No Bruder, no Schwester, just me."

The boys replaced the soccer ball stone with the empty bag of candy and kicked it back to the Kastel home in silence until Herbert opened the front door. "Herbert, your English is so good. Can you help me to talk to Mrs. Kastel?"

"Sure, but call her Auntie. 'Auntie' is Tante and 'uncle' is Onkel." Herbert slapped Kurt playfully on the back. "You should be proud! We just completed your first English lesson." Kurt did not smile. He looked over Herbert's shoulder and into the apartment.

"But you will help me?"

"Sure," said Herbert as the boys walked into the apartment. "Auntie, Kurt wants to talk to you."

"Yes, Kurt," said Irene in her deep voice. She grabbed her German dictionary and handwritten notebook of common German phrases.

"First of all, Auntie, I want to thank you for taking me into your home. And I don't want you to be upset with me, but I need to ask you about some things."

Irene put down her dictionary and notebook. She walked over to Kurt, who slid behind Herbert. Irene smiled as the seconds ticked by. "In order to say what you want, dear, you have to open your mouth."

"Auntie Irene, my Opa Isack is orthodox. He is in France now and we spent a lot of time together. I would very much like to stay here."

Herbert interrupted Kurt. "You are not saying anything. Just say what you want to say to Auntie. She won't bite."

"Auntie, I think he is nervous," said Herbert, stating the obvious.

Kurt curled his right thumb clumsily around his pants pocket. "I need to be in a kosher house."

"Kurt, this is a kosher house. On the Sabbath, we wash the floor and put paper on the floor," answered Irene.

Kurt continued. "But are there two sets of plates? Is the meat kosher? And I need to wear my cap at dinner. And I can't carry money or ride in cars or trains on Saturday." Herbert waved to Kurt to slow down. "I guess what I am saying, Auntie, is that I need to know if this is a problem, because if it is I can't stay here."

Irene looked at Herbert. "What happened to our shy, nervous boy, Herbert? Tell him he can follow Koshruss in this house."

In the weeks before school started in September, Kurt began his Americanization, Humboldt Park style. After breakfast each day Kurt and Herbert walked down the neighborhood streets before they ended up in the two-hundred-acre park with its fish-filled lagoons, hills for sliding in the winter, and impeccably manicured gardens. With Kurt's thumb properly looped in his pocket and his right foot striking the sidewalk just so, the duo took the same route east down Thomas until they came to Washtenaw, where they made another left turn north to Division. The daily lessons began with Herbert pointing until Kurt gave a correct answer that was rewarded with a celebratory slap to the back.

"Twenty-six thirty-nine?"

"The Harmony Movie Theater, Herbert. They have good popcorn!"

"Twenty-six forty-three?"

"Kastel Fish Market."

"I hope you like fish," laughed Herbert in French and English, "because it's fish every night. You will probably never see Auntie's mother, but when she is home you will know," laughed Herbert uncontrollably, clamping his nose.

Herbert's finger pointed again. "Twenty-six sixty?"

"Division Street Theater," exclaimed Kurt while he matched Herbert stride for stride.

"It's ten cents for a movie, Kurt. It's like the Harmony, but better. You get three features, cartoons, a chapter film, and RKO news. You can't beat it. And don't worry. We get an allowance of three dollars a month. So we can go here whenever we want as long as we ask Auntie."

Kurt nodded as he tried to absorb the important information. Herbert raised his finger again and called out the addresses.

"Twenty-seven hundred?"

"Five and Dime."

"Twenty-seven-oh-one?"

"Joe Pierce Delicatessen."

"Twenty-seven sixteen?"

"Heller Shoe Store?"

"Twenty-seven twenty-five?"

"Kahn Fish Market."

"Now listen to me, Kurt, and don't forget it. We don't go to the deli for hot dogs. They are really bad. We go to Art Pine's Hot Dogs at Twenty-Five Twenty-Four West Division." Kurt nodded once again as if his life depended on it.

Once again Herbert pointed and Kurt answered, "Twenty-seven thirty-six—barbershop, twenty-seven forty-three—billiards..."

OCTOBER 1, 1942

On October 1, 1942, Kurt's social worker, Eleanor Frank, completed her first quarterly report. The detailed report was based upon numerous interviews and phone calls with the Kastels, the Mann children, Kurt, and his teachers. Each quarterly report was sent to the German Jewish Children's Aid in New York, whose name change to the European Jewish Children's Aid reflected its ever-expanding population.

On September 9, 1942, Jolene Kastel ran to the knock at the door. "And how are we today?" asked Miss Frank. Jolene kissed her hand and patted it on the worker's leg before she ran laughing down the long hallway.

"The highlight of my day," laughed Eleanor to Irene, who emerged out of her bedroom. "And how is our Kurt doing?" inquired Miss Frank.

Irene pondered the simple question while walking to the kitchen to get some iced tea and cookies. "He is an interesting little boy," yelled Irene. "Between Herbert and Edith, my German dictionary, and Yiddish, we are communicating fairly well." Irene looked down the empty hallway before she spoke. "Other than the first day when he cried after you left, he has been fine. Unemotional is the best way I would describe him. To be honest with you, he doesn't act like an eleven-year-old. It's like Halloween and he's a forty-five-year-old man dressed up like a little kid. He told me he is orthodox and needs to follow all the rules, and most of all, he expects us to do the same. Kurt is very sincere and extremely disciplined about all of this. He wears his Cubs cap during meals and even when he eats just candy or gum. He goes through the ritual hand washing before every meal. I also heard him tell Herbert that he can't ride the bus, tear paper, or carry money on the Sabbath. So he has Herbert carry his money for him. And every night before he goes to sleep I can hear him praying."

The worker furiously wrote while Irene continued with her laundry list. "He did ask me if it was a sin to go to a movie if someone else pays. I said no, but he still hasn't been to a movie, let alone on the Sabbath."

"That makes sense, Irene. Before Kurt arrived in New York, we were aware of some of this information. But I thought once he got here it wouldn't be such a big part of his life. Obviously I was wrong."

"I have never seen a young person take his faith as seriously as Kurt. Herbert says he gets that from his grandfather. I think his name is Isack. Oh, by the way, Kurt received some letters from his family in New York he had written to when he first came here. He also got one from an aunt in a camp in France. She sent it to Marseille, but it was forwarded to somewhere in North Africa and then again to New York before Kurt got it." Irene sipped her lemonade before she started reading the first letter, which had been written six days after Ilse, Isack, and Julius were taken to Drancy.

"August 18, 1942
Camp de Gurs to Kurt Wagner in Marseille

Dear Kurt,

As I hear from your dear Mother, I know that
you are well. I can say the same about myself.
I would love to go to America, but I'm sorry
that my papers are not ready. Stay well and
behave yourself and don't ever forget us. As
soon as I come to you, I will look for you.
I am sorry at this moment this is not the
case. Please write to Uncle Simon and Thelma
Intrudl. Mr. Simon Roos, 618 E. 15 Brooklyn
NY. Your Grandfather is better again and so is
Julius. Please tell Uncle Simon that he should
hurry up that I can come soon too. I am sure
that it is beautiful there and you will like
it. Also dear Kurt I say good bye to you and
hope that we will see each other soon again.
Have a good trip. You will be heartily greeted
from your,

Aunt Friedl."

"After Kurt received this letter, I suggested he write to
the people in New York. Their name is Roos and they live
in Brooklyn. Anyway, Kurt got a letter back right away from
them."

"August 28, 1942

Kurt,

How happy we are to hear from you. Especially that you are healthy and now in the beautiful America. I can imagine that you like it here with a nice family. To drive a car, to go to the movies, to play ball, and all the many nice things. We are happy that you were able to come here. How is your mother and grandparents? We're sure that you got our address from your grandparents. Here is the address that we have for your Uncle Heinrich, 1162 E. 54th Place, Chicago, Illinois. I hope it is correct. Now school starts again soon and I think we will soon learn English. And you will be able to write an English letter. Do you know French? How old are you really? I hope you are a good boy, obedient, ambitious and hard working in school. And you only bring pleasure to the family Kastel. Can you still sing so nicely? Do you still remember Gerdi?

But now I will leave some space for Uncle Simon. Do write again soon and I greet you heartily and kiss you.

Your Cousin Selma..."

"We were aware of these relatives, but Kurt was adamant that Mr. Roos would not want anything to do with him. When I asked him why, he wouldn't give me an answer."

"That's funny, Eleanor. After we got this letter from the Roos family, I asked Kurt if he wanted me to call this Heinrich Weil. Kurt told me that this man is his grandmother's brother. She's the one who died in Gurs this past winter. Anyway, I told Kurt that his uncle is only ten miles from here. I thought he would be excited, but he was almost angry with me."

"April 2, 1941 from Ilse Walker Ilot K, Barrack 3, Censor No. 8

My Dear little Kurt!

...We have not had any news from Uncle Heinrich yet. We are hoping that he will be able to send us a parcel or let us have some money, as we have none left..."

"Anyway, I called this Heinrich Weil, and he came here last Sunday for about thirty minutes. When he said good-bye, he made a point of thanking me for taking care of Kurt. When I asked Kurt about the visit with his uncle, he did not want to talk to me about it."

"His cousin came to visit him on a Sunday...an obviously poor refugee, employed as a Fuller Brush salesman, came to see Kurt...Kurt did not seem to remember him..."

"Well, Kurt has obviously been though quite a bit," said the worker. "On the positive side he looks healthy. In fact, he looks like he has even put on some weight."

"In the beginning, Eleanor, he would never even ask for seconds. It got so bad that Herbert and Edith would put extra helpings on his plate. Now he will take seconds, but only after asking. That kid could be starving and he would never say a word."

"Anything else?"

"You know the Manns and Kurt call me and my husband Auntie and Uncle. But with Kurt I must tell you it's a little uncomfortable. Kurt said that there should be no difference between Jolene and the other kids in the house. He seems almost hurt about the way I treat my daughter and the way I deal with him. I was firm when I told him that I cared about him, but I also told him he was not my son and…"

Eleanor stopped writing. "And?"

"A couple of nights ago during dinner Herbert said out of nowhere that Kurt did not want to call me and my husband Auntie and Uncle. So Albert said, 'Kurt, what do you want call us?' Kurt got up from his chair, and of course he was very serious. Herbert was equally as serious. He said that Kurt wants to call me and my husband Mommy and Daddy. I was not that surprised, because I had heard from the neighbors that he refers to me and Albert as Mommy and Daddy. I just decided to leave it alone since he seems very sensitive about this."

"…Mrs. K has recognized that Kurt needs a feeling of security with the foster parents and…use them as a substitute for his parents… told Mrs. K he wanted to be her son…"

"So what did Kurt do after he said that, Irene?"

"He walked over to Albert and cleared his throat. And in English, he must have been practicing, he said, 'I want to marry Jolene when I grow up.' Then he points to Herbert, and Herbert tells us that Kurt says that if he marries Jolene then we can stay as a family, that"...Mr. K could be his 'father-in-law.'" That was it. He just went back to eating, and my husband I are just left staring at each other."

Eleanor never lifted her head from her pad of paper. "And what about the sleeping, any better?"

"I told him he was a big boy and had to stop sleeping with Herbert, but he said something strange to me." "...Kurt said to her that he still wished to be 'a little boy' and that he did not want to grow up to be any bigger than he was." "In fact, last night I made him sleep in the dining room. Kurt came into my bedroom and scared me half to death. He said he was afraid, and I asked of what? I could barely make out his face in the dark, but I think he was crying when he answered, 'The man.' He wouldn't say which man, and I was too exhausted to argue. So I told him he could go into Herbert's room."

Overwhelmed by the mountain of information, Eleanor stopped writing.

"Oh, I forgot to tell you, I talked to the rabbi at the synagogue. Kurt told him that it has been more than four years since he had been in a synagogue and he was very anxious to begin his studies..."

"That's great."

"That's not it. Kurt told the rabbi that his father was dead. The rabbi mentioned that Kurt seemed to be totally unfazed by his death. So when I saw Kurt later, I asked him about his father, since I thought he was alive. After Herbert translated for me, Kurt's face became so red. I don't know if he was angry or embarrassed, but he told me he knew it was a lie. I said to him that he should not lie, especially in the synagogue. Kurt seemed devastated when he realized what he had done. He just mumbled something to Herbert and that was it. Kurt just walked out of the room. I asked Herbert what that was about. Kurt said that he knew his father was living, but "...he might as well be dead and said that his father used to hit his mother and indicated a good deal of hostility toward him."

"Have you talked to Kurt about his family?"

"Yes. After you gave me the information a few days ago, I talked to Kurt and told him exactly what you said to me; that the Quakers tried to inform his family that he had arrived safely, but that they were no longer in Gurs. I just told him that they had moved and no one had their address."

"How did he react?"

"He really didn't. He asked if that means that the others in France went with his family, and I said yes. He seemed very reassured by that."

"It meant in all probability that Kurt's mother and grandfather had been among the refugees who were rounded up in France and returned to Germany or Poland for forced labor....When his cousin Heinrich came to visit the following day...Kurt simply told him that he had just learned that his mother had left France, that he did not know where she was, and that he was not to write to her anymore. Kurt did not question the foster mother any further about this."

"One last thing before the kids get home from school, Eleanor. Can we get Kurt's monthly allotment increased to twenty-five dollars per month? Things are so expensive because of the war."

"That should not be a problem," said Eleanor just as the front door swung open and Herbert, Edith, and Kurt walked in.

"So how are the students?" asked Miss Frank.

Kurt proudly responded, "How you are and well very?"

While the others laughed, Edith whispered to Kurt who tried again. "I mean, very well, and how are you?"

"Good job, Kurt," said Eleanor. Kurt put his Cubs hat on before he devoured an oatmeal raisin cookie and a glass of milk.

"Who first, Miss Frank?" asked Irene. The children jokingly pointed at each other.

"How about my friend, Kurt?" answered the worker.

Eleanor looked at her watch and then back to a crumbly faced Kurt. "Herbert, can you translate for Kurt? I am running out of time."

"Sure," said Herbert, but Kurt refused Herbert's assistance. He desperately wanted to speak for himself, but Kurt's limited vocabulary made his ability to answer even the simplest questions almost impossible.

"So how is school?" asked the worker.

"Good."

"Are you happy here with the Kastels?"

"Yes. Good."

"Do you still want to stay here?"

"Yes."

"Let's start again," said Eleanor after she motioned for Herbert to join them.

"How is school? Do you like Lafayette?"

"Kurt told the worker that he had three years of schooling in Germany and about three months in France. At the opening of the school year... he was placed in grade 2B. He was upset..."

"How are things with the Kastels?"

"He talked about girls and wedding rings. Seemed to have a need for information about family arrangements to increase his own sense of security...He is eager to please the Kastels..."

"Do you remember a couple of weeks ago I said you might not be staying with the Kastels?"

Kurt became panic stricken with the memory of his first day at the Kastels.

"...worker informed Kurt that he was going to stay with the K family. He seemed very pleased. I think he will be an interesting child to work with."

JCB REPORT JANUARY 29, 1943

"...No word from his family. Does not verbalize any great anxiety. Letter he sent to his mother immediately after he arrived in NY was returned to the Agency in January. This was told to Mrs. Kastel but not to Kurt. He understands that due to the War it is not possible to get mail from his mother nor to write to her and has not questioned whether his mother is in France. The returned letter means that the mother had left and not returned and that means she is probably in Poland."

JCB, January 29, 1943

Kurt looked at Herbert, sleeping. He peeled back Herbert's eyelid and whispered, "Are you awake?" Herbert responded just as he had done over the prior weeks. He rolled over in bed and pretended to be asleep. "Herbert, it's me," whimpered Kurt.

Herbert grunted, "Remember, only in English."

The tacit yes allowed Kurt to pull the heavy blanket over his freezing body while Herbert listened. "I get along better with the younger kids. I don't let it bother me when the older ones tease me when I play with the girls and the younger boys. The little kids don't call me names and are much nicer than the boys my age. Do they ever call you names? Do they call you Nazi, Herbert?"

"Kurt had attempted to blackmail Mrs. Kastel because she punished him for fighting with a boy. Kurt threatened to complain to the worker. Kurt was advised that this was not right and

357

Kurt understood. Kurt agreed that the punishment was correct. Kurt was occasionally teased
and was sensitive to this...Kurt acknowledged he
fought occasionally. His clothes had been torn
and worker reminded that this was war and had
to take care of things."

Herbert rolled over and looked at Kurt. "Edith said there was a problem when Auntie took you downtown."

"It was nothing," mumbled Kurt.

"In November the Kastels took the children
downtown to see the store windows. Kurt became hysterical and cried when he saw a clown
and needed considerable reassurance from Mrs.
Kastel."

MARCH 28, 1942, WHO AM I?

"Dear Heinz,

I am pleased by your letter and I hope that you will write more often in the new year and that you visit your parents. Now you can be pleased we have been skiing and had nice weather. We will get you some cheese and now you can have my skis, but I can't send them to you. Be a good boy and be thankful for Aunt Martha and especially don't ruin the skis. Also, I have a special knife from the boy scouts in America. I bought it very cheap and when you are older and more responsible and if you don't fight with Gerhardt you can have it. Best regards. We kiss you, your parents. Excuse my bad writing on this bad paper."

Letter from Julius Walker to his son, Heinz Walker, dated January 1, 1942

Come back to my house before you go home, Heinz. My Tante sent some chocolate. We can celebrate your birthday and the victory." Heinz did not answer Erich. He picked at the mud on his shoes on the soccer field until Erich repeatedly punched Heinz in the shoulder. "I would like to score a goal in a game just once, but you score a goal every game and then two on your birthday. Next time, save a goal for your friend and pass me the ball!"

Erich pretended he was a radio announcer describing Heinz's winning goal. Their laughing teammates gathered as the description of Heinz's victorious goal ended with, "Heinz's godlike abilities allowed him to bicycle kick the ball into the goal!" Heinz savored the moment as each boy gave a final congratulatory slap to Heinz's back before they scattered to their homes to listen to the war news on the radio.

"Can we walk to my house before you go home?" asked Erich, who received only an indifferent shrug from Heinz. Erich persisted. "You are the only friend my mother asks about. 'How is Heinz? He is such a fine young man.' She never sees you, but always asks about you. I should tell her how you didn't want to come to her home while my father is away fighting for Germany!" grinned Erich.

Erich raised his voice in mock anger and punched Heinz again. "So do you want some chocolate or not? I don't care about you. Just say yes so I can have an excuse to get some for myself," laughed Erich.

Heinz paused. "My father is here from Stuttgart for my birthday. I haven't seen him in a long time. I really should go home..."

"Heinz, he's not going anywhere. Stop at my house and say hello to my mother. Besides, they probably think we're still playing."

After the door to the apartment was pushed opened, Erich announced, "Mutti, I have a surprise for you. I brought home a refugee from the war who wants some chocolate."

"Erich, stop playing," demanded his mother. He took a few steps back into the darkened hallway before returning with the red-faced boy.

"Heinz Walker, I'm so happy to see you," exclaimed Erich's mother. She embraced Heinz as if he was her own son.

"I'm happy to see you too, Frau Sprauer."

When she finally released Heinz from her bear hug, she took a step back. To Erich, the moment seemed awkward and strange as his mother wiped away her tears. Her son groaned, "Mutti, it's only Heinz."

Erich's animated mother did not hear a word as she embraced Heinz again. "I was just talking to Erich about you. It has been too long. I'm surprised that you even remember me, Heinz."

Erich could not stop laughing. His mother's rapid-fire questions made Heinz's attempts to answer impossible. Suddenly she stopped in midquestion and tenderly pulled Heinz's face close and kissed him on his forehead. "It's so good to see you, Heinz. It really is." She brushed his hair off his face before she sprinted the few feet to the permanently rust-stained sink and curled her first finger back and forth.

"Mutti, we are not babies. You don't have to do that," shouted Erich as his mother began to wash their sweaty faces. Erich's mother complained about their dirty faces until she pointed at her son. "Erich, you should be more like Heinz. He's not complaining,"

Erich's mother winked at Heinz. "Your grandparents, how are they, Heinz? Well, I hope?"

"Yes. Thank you for asking."

"Please tell them I said hello."

Heinz closed his eyes as the refreshing cold washcloth jumped from one cheek to another. Suddenly Erich grabbed his mother's hand.

"Mutti, I forgot. It's Heinz's birthday, and I promised him some of Tante's chocolate!"

Erich's mother made one final wipe on Heinz's face. "It's been so long since I've seen you, let alone talked to you. It must be four or five years since I waved to you and your Oma on the Kaiserstrasse. I'm not even sure either one of you saw me," lamented Erich's mother. She pulled out the round red tin of Scho-Ka-Kola from a kitchen drawer. Erich ripped open the lid that revealed the eight triangular pieces that formed a perfect circle of chocolate. It took only seconds for the chocolate aroma to fill the room and for Erich to devour his first and then second piece.

"Erich, slow down, and Heinz, please take a piece. Take as much as you want and take the tin too. I'm sure your Oma will find some use for it." Heinz beamed with his first bite that confirmed that his birthday could not get any better.

"You know, Heinz," said Erich. "My Tante wrote that the Scho-Ka-Kola is given to the Luftwaffe in their rations. Mutti, what did she call it?" Before she could answer, Erich hurried to his mother's bedroom. "Here is the letter, Heinz. They call it Flyer Chocolate, because it has caffeine from cocoa and roasted coffee. It gives the pilots extra energy. That way they can fly for hours." Erich pleaded with his mother, "Maybe you should ask Tante to send us more chocolate. That way if I had some before the soccer games, I could be the star instead of Heinz."

Erich's mother's shaking head indicated a definitive no as she occupied herself with busywork while the boys transformed themselves into fighter pilots. They pushed their chairs next to each other as their vibrating lips powered the engines of their Messerschmitts on their bombing mission to London. Erich's mother laughed. "You sound more like horses." While Erich gorged himself, Heinz happily accepted Frau Sprauer's caring questions about girls, school, and his goals after the war.

"Heinz, I know it is your birthday, but do you think your grandparents would allow you to stay for dinner?"

"That would be great, Frau Sprauer. I would enjoy that."

"You can't stay," interrupted Erich, who spun the empty candy metal tin like a top.

"Erich, stop that!" said his annoyed mother.

"But Mutti, Heinz told me his father is here for his birthday."

"Is this true, Heinz? Is your father in Karlsruhe?"

"I'm sorry. I forgot to mention it to you."

Frau Sprauer sat down at the table and crossed and uncrossed her legs. "Well then, if your father is here, we will have to make it for another time."

When the first wave of nausea from the Scho-Ka-Kola struck Erich, he ran to the common bathroom for the building. Erich's mother and Heinz burst into laughter as the sounds of vomiting exploded from down the hallway. "Shh, Heinz—if we can hear him he can hear us."

Heinz twisted in his chair. "Please don't be insulted, but you seem to have been staring at me since I came here. Are you upset with me, because..."

"Oh my—no, it's just that I'm so happy to see you," answered Frau Sprauer. "I am being so rude, Heinz. You must be thirsty. Let me get you something to drink." The room remained silent until a brightly colored dancing couple spun out of the chalet cuckoo clock and past the hand painted woodsman to the sounds of "Edelweiss." It was 5:00 p.m. Heinz's thoughts turned to his birthday dinner, the father he had not seen in months, and his soon-to-be angry grandfather.

When Frau Sprauer returned to the small circular table, her eyes moistened while she tapped along with the last notes of "Edelweiss." She grabbed Heinz's hand. "You have Ilse's eyes, Heinz."

"What do you mean?"

"Just that. You have your mother's eyes. Even more than Kurt."

"What do you mean Ilse and Kurt, Frau Sprauer?"

The few additional questions that were cautiously answered ended with a tearful apology from Erich's mother. "Heinz, I'm so sorry—I just assumed you knew."

When Heinz ran out of the apartment, the torrent of emotions—fear, anger, sadness, and disgust—made him oblivious to the fact that his best friend, Erich, stunned, had been sitting outside the open door of the apartment.

"Beloved Family!

During my night shift, I have just a little spare time to write. Before I say anything, dear

Mother, thank you for the stockings. We were very pleased that you think of us when you have so little... I have been very pleased to learn that Heinz has been working during the war since manpower is needed. I was disappointed to learn from Father that Heinz already wanted to quit and go back to school."

Letter from Julius Walker dated February 11, 1943

At the same time Heinz learned the sobering truth of his family, Kurt eagerly thanked the mailman for the February 1943 *Reader's Digest* magazine. He threw himself on the couch and read out loud the titles of the war-themed articles, "'My Blood is in the War,' 'A Grandstand View of Jap Naval Disaster,' 'Preparing Our Fliers for Combat,' and 'How the North African Campaign Was Organized.'" When he came to the article "Remember Us" by Ben Hecht, Kurt pushed himself to understand the three-page article and short biography about the author's books, movies, and first play, *The Front Page*. He bounced back and forth between the short sentences and his ever-present Webster dictionary. His heart raced when he read, "All the victims of the German adventure will be there to pass sentenceall but the one: the Jew."

He opened and closed the magazine until he finally read, "Of these 6,000,000 Jews almost a third have already been massacred by Germans....Remember us. In the town of Freiburg in the Black Forest two hundred of us were hanged and left dangling out of our kitchen windows to watch our synagogue burn and our rabbi being flogged to death....

Remember us who were put in the freight trains
that left France..."

Kurt felt ill as Jolene ran to the opening door, kissed the
worker's hand, and patted her leg.

"And how is my Kurt today?" asked a smiling Miss Frank.

HAPPY BIRTHDAY

The tenants in the four-story apartment building could smell the familiar prewar delicacies of potato soup, black forest ham, egg noodles, and sheet cake covered with a fruit topping coming from Heinz's grandparents' apartment. "Heinz, I didn't hear you," said his grandmother. She placed the last dinner plate on the table while Heinz stood at the door.

Christian Walker looked at his wife for only a moment before the confused patriarch approached Heinz. Christian's partial deafness from years of banging away at train engines unintentionally escalated the tension. He yelled, "Heinz, what's wrong? Did you hurt yourself in the soccer match?"

Heinz screamed, "Opa! There is nothing wrong with me! The problem is you! All of you!" Julius Walker hurried out of the only bedroom in the apartment. He placed the birthday presents of skis and a knife on the floor before he walked tentatively toward his son. "And you! You are the worst! This is your fault," continued a screaming Heinz. The back of Heinz's head repeatedly struck the closed door. He whimpered his assault. "Where is my mother, Father? Not your wife that you referred to as my mother in your letters, but my real mother, Ilse Ettlinger."

Julius looked at his parents. The banging sounds grew louder. "I know everything. I know the truth. She told me everything. I could have had a family." With each word, Julius Walker took a step backward until his back was at the end of the small apartment. "We are your family, and I am your Opa," said Christian, who tried to diffuse the explosive situation. But it was clear that Heinz's growing anger made any effort to have a conversation impossible. Christian looked long and hard at his mute son before he spoke again. "We tried to do the right thing, Heinz. We wanted to protect you. These have been difficult times."

Heinz's grandfather had anxiously awaited this moment over the prior years. He had hoped, as he had told his wife, "That it will be later than sooner, and hopefully after I am gone." So many years had come and gone in which Heinz had walked innocently through a life filled with mine fields. Christian was mindful that through it all, he had to protect Heinz.

"Protect me, or you?" came the inconsolable and painful response.

Christian's voice was barely audible. "We tried to do the right thing."

While Julius Walker finally moved past his weeping mother and defeated father he extended an olive branch. "We are family, son. I love you. Please listen…"

Rage dismissed Heinz's short-lived fear. He walked toward his father and drove his finger into his chest. "Son!" spit out Heinz. "I know everything. Erich's mother told me. She is more of a family to me than you have ever been. She told me how she brought a little boy here to get my old clothing and that I would play with him and have meals together. She told me that Oma made him Schnecken and Opa put him on his knee and sang to him. That was until I got to be too old, too old to remember him. That little boy's grandparents are Isack and Sophie Ettlinger—my grandparents. That little boy also has an uncle named Julius—my uncle Julius." Heinz screamed his unrelenting attack. "You know who I am talking about, Father? That little boy's name is Kurt. Kurt Walker. Walker, just like me! Just like Oma! Just like Opa! Just like you, Father! My brother, your son—isn't he in our family?"

Heinz's grandparents begged, "Whisper, so that the neighbors don't hear our business."

The request brought more screams that became disturbingly unintelligible. Heinz gasped for air. "You want me to be quiet— just as you've been to me? No! There will be no more quiet! My father that loves me, is it true you married my mother fourteen days before I was born?" Heinz looked at his silent father in disgust. "You never wanted me. I am no more a son to you than Kurt is."

"I love you, Heinz," cried Julius.

"They were all here for years." Heinz raised his arm and pointed out the window. "They lived right there on Markgrafenstrasse. We could have saved them. But none of you did anything." Heinz slapped his father's arm away. "Where is my mother, Ilse? Where are my grandparents, Sophie and Isack, and my uncle Julius?"

No answers to the damning questions could have controlled Heinz's unmitigated rage, but they tried. "It was complicated— you would not understand—you were special." Heinz became infuriated. He pulled at the faucet in the kitchen sink and let the cold water run directly on his face, until his shirt and coat were drenched. He felt faint while he watched his approaching father in the reflection of the window. Heinz turned around. "One last thing, my Nazi father, my Brownshirt father. When were you going to tell me my mother is a Jew? And that I am a Jew? The truth is you hate my Jewish brother! You hate my Jewish mother! That you hate me!"

And with that last bit of vitriol spit at Julius Walker, Heinz collapsed in the arms of his father. Unlike twelve years earlier when he held his nine-month-old son in a small apartment on Christmas Eve 1930, Julius Walker did not smile when his son's head fell uncomfortably backward. "I should leave, Opa, Mutti," said Julius Walker while he laid his son on the couch. Before Julius left, he completed a discussion that had begun years earlier. "He is thirteen today and we all know the truth. It should have already been done. If Frau Sprauer said something, others have already gossiped. There must be no questions about who Heinz is—that he is special. It's important for all of us. He needs to do it!"

The next morning, Christian fulfilled the first of two promises he had made with Heinz. They walked to the Nazi headquarters in Karlsruhe. The grandfather and grandson energetically responded in kind to the uniformed man's crisp Nazi salute and enthusiastic "Heil Hitler." Christian cleared his throat. "Some years ago, sir, I believe in October 1940, some people were taken from Karlsruhe."

"Yes," said the Nazi. Heinz felt his grandfather's painful squeeze of his hand before the man walked away. He returned with Willi Worch, the former Karlsruhe brewer who, from 1932 until the end of the war, was the NSDAP district leader of Karlsruhe. Christian let go of Heinz's hand and produced another crisp salute and slight bend at the waist. "Good morning, sir, I am trying to verify if Ilse and Kurt Walker were in a group of people who were taken from Karlsruhe in October 1940, and if so, sir, where they might be today. I—"

"If you are so concerned about these Jews," interrupted Worch, "I believe I can help you. You and the boy can simply ask them yourself, or better, you can take their place. Now, would you like me to arrange this?" There was no answer other than a final bow at the waist. After Christian and Heinz left the Nazi headquarters, they never discussed Kurt or Ilse again.

On April 20, 1943, Adolph Hitler's fifty-fourth birthday, Christian fulfilled his second promise. It began with his anxious prodding of Heinz to quickly change from his school clothes into his new dark shorts and dark, long-sleeve shirt. When Heinz walked onto the stage, he was indistinguishable from the other boys who stood in perfect military formation beneath the huge Nazi flag, framed by photographs of the führer. When Heinz's name was called, like Erich Sprauer, he gripped the Blood Banner with his left hand and raised three fingers on his right hand and recited the oath:

"In the presence of this Blood Banner, which represents our Fuehrer, I swear to devote all my energies and my strength to the Savior of our country, Adolf Hitler. I am willing and ready to give up my life for him, so help me God."

The assembled friends and family that included Christian and Luise Walker nervously cheered when Heinz completed his initiation into the Jungvolk. He was now a proud trial member of the Hitlerjugend, or Hitler Youth.

During the probationary period over the next year, Heinz demonstrated his physical prowess in athletic events and passed the required written tests to establish his mastery of Nazi ideology. At the Nazis' request, his grandfather provided Heinz's Ahnenpass, an official document from the government and baptismal records that proved his racial purity as an Aryan. Christian also made sure that Heinz attended the home evenings in cellars and basements run by the Hitlerjugend, where he sang Nazi songs, memorized passionate anti-Jewish slogans, and listened to speeches on official Nazi radios. And when Heinz received one of the many badges that honored his journey toward becoming a true Nazi, it was Christian who made sure that they were sewn onto his uniform.

One year later on Adolph Hitler's next birthday, and after Heinz had attained the age of fourteen, Heinz's commitment was once again rewarded when he was admitted into the Hitlerjugend. After he repeated his oath and received the coveted dagger with the Nazi emblem, "Blut und Ehre," "Blood and Honor," his journey toward becoming a true Nazi was realized.

THE DIVE

The twelve-hour night shift afforded Julius Walker an escape from the stifling hot summer months of 1943, and an early morning return to his wife, newspaper, breakfast, and hopefully, a long sleep. It was sleep that allowed him to escape, if only temporarily, from his past.

"Dear Heinz:

You have to keep working. Things will not always go your way.

...Your father's efforts have been in vain, but we will all be together in the end. Because of the war we all have problems, like trying to obtain food, you should know this as true. But now because of the war everyone is being murdered. All of this has been for nothing. Other ones that have higher aims seem satisfied by the war. My happiness comes from working, but more from trying to have a good life. I hope we are alive at the end of the war. I hope you have a good evening and a good life.

Best regards from Julius and Luise"

Letter from Julius Walker dated February 11, 1943

On a regular basis, Julius received vivid letters from his parents regarding the devastating bombings in Karlsruhe. No amount of sleep allowed Julius to escape from the haunting images described in those letters.

The first cracks in the impenetrable walls of the Reich began with the 1942 British morale bombings of highly populated German city centers and working-class residences. This culminated in the one thousand bomber raid in Cologne on May 30, 1942, and the devastating July 27, 1942, fire bombings in Hamburg. By the summer of 1942, the insulated civilians of Karlsruhe, a place where Wild Bill Cody and Annie Oakley had once entertained, had not yet felt the terror of war. Nonetheless, the citizens of Karlsruhe lived in constant fear from the reports of nearby bombings and the memories of June 22, 1916, when French war planes dropped forty bombs on Karlsruhe. A monument dedicated to the 260 people who died, including seventy-one children who were visiting a circus, remained a constant reminder of the inevitable costs of war. More than two decades later, in September 1942, the memories became reality for Karlsruhe when seventy-three lives were lost and another seven hundred citizens were injured by the first eight-thousand-pound British blockbuster bomb ever dropped during the war.

The same oppressive August heat of 1943 that invited Julius Walker to sleep, hastened Heinz's escape from his grandparents' apartment each morning. "Good-bye, Oma," yelled Heinz. Eagerly he ran down the stairs with a paper bag that held his glass water bottle and sandwich. For most of those early summer mornings Heinz and Erich Sprauer met with a large group of classmates from Schiller School. Afterward Heinz began his insufferable job as an apprentice mechanic in a paper factory. Heinz and Erich, always the first to arrive at the Hitler-Platz, paced while they waited for the others to arrive for a swim at Rappenwört, the public pool in nearby Daxlanden. Ringed by an immaculate beach house, massive umbrellalike trees, manicured green lawns, and rows of colorful flowers, the pool, fed by the locks of the adjacent Rhine River, was a well-attended escape for both children and adults.

On August 16, 1943, Erich pointed to the ring of limp Swastikas flags that surrounded them. The lack of any breeze meant an even more uncomfortable day than usual for the long walk to the pool. Heinz looked at the massive clock that struck the half hour. "Thirty minutes more," grunted Heinz. The boys passed the time throwing stones at the unreachable birds resting near the golden boy weather vane until Erich tried to run to the top of the pyramid. Heinz joined Erich in an unsuccessful challenge until the clock bells began to ring. Heinz's sweaty face erupted with a huge smile. He wiped away his matted hair, grabbed his paper bag, and yelled, "Eight o'clock, Erich! Let's go!"

The sprinting boys picked up their pace as the faint cries of "wait! wait!" from the snakelike procession of thirty boys grew more distant. Erich and Heinz slowed to allow the others, including the plump, red-faced sixteen-year-old Wilhelm, to catch up. Quickly they engaged in impromptu games of tag and war, where sticks and pebbles replaced knives and bullets.

After Wilhelm made his way to the head of the line, he called upon the others to join him in song. When the last chorus came to an end, Heinz's voice roared above the others. He shouted with a sense of urgency, "Hurry! If we run, we can watch them open up the locks!"

"Why do you care about the pool, Heinz? All you do is swim laps. We all know you are afraid to dive," spit out Wilhelm to Heinz.

"I wasn't talking to you, Wilhelm. I was talking to everyone but you," barked back Heinz.

"Well, I was talking to you, Heinz," said Wilhelm, who threw some pebbles at Heinz's tanned face. "Every day you say you will jump, but you never do it. Everyone but you," jabbed Wilhelm. The few stragglers in the rear could hear the yelling in the front of the line and ran in hopes of seeing a good fight, but Heinz was not stupid. He dropped his pebbles and unclenched his fists.

"What sport is there in jumping thirty-five feet into water? None of you, including you, Wilhelm, have raced me more than once. There are no gold medals for jumping feet first into water, but then again maybe you are right. When the war is over and the Olympics start again, Karlsruhe will be so proud of you when you return with a gold medal for the smallest splash from the biggest ass." The boys laughed with approval as they entered through the open gate to the pool. Heinz jogged confidently to the lock. "Wilhelm, let's race. I'll give you and your fat ass a ten-second lead, and I'll still beat you."

"Heinz," yelled the wounded boy. "The difference is we all raced you and lost. But you are a coward, because you are afraid to even try to jump."

Heinz heard the allegation, but hoped the others had not before he flew into a complete sprint. Heinz stood alone and watched the lock open and the fresh, cool water from the Rhine River raise the water level before he swam to the opposite end of the pool. After an hour, Heinz pulled himself out of the water and onto the cool grass protected by the shade of one of the immense sculpted trees. He closed his eyes to block out the few rays of sun that poked through the branches until the sound of crunching leaves caused him to nervously sit up with fists clenched.

"It's only me," called Erich, waving his lunch bag. "Heinz, he will keep bothering you. Even some of the boys have said things to me. Why don't you just do it? The platform is not that high." Heinz ripped open the paper bag that served as a plate and took a bite out of his sandwich. Erich tried again. "You know how they make a game out of it. They just like to gang up on the weak ones."

Heinz shot back, "I am not weak. I am a better athlete than any of them, swimming, running, soccer, and you know..."

"That's not the point. You know how they think. You act weak, you are weak. That's the way they are. We all do it. Besides, the truth is they all like you."

"I could care less if they like me or not," growled Heinz.

"Why are you looking for a fight, especially with me? Let's just get it over with. We can climb up together. Wilhelm and the others will see it and then it will be over." Erich threw a stick at Heinz. "If you do it now, it's because you want to do it, not because they want you to do it." Heinz's smiling friend pulled him to his feet.

"Wilhelm is watching, Heinz," said Erich between strokes. "Remember you first and then me." It was ten in the morning. The sun was still low on the horizon when Wilhelm's shrieks alerted the others. With each step up the ladder Heinz looked directly into the blinding sun that thankfully forced him to close his eyes. His toes and fingertips that tightly gripped the rope ladder became a brilliant white. While Heinz climbed higher he could not escape Wilhelm's nonstop taunts that urged the boys to become even more abusive.

"Don't stop, Heinz. A few more seconds and we are at the top," yelled Erich.

Heinz pressed his body against the swaying prickly rope ladder that left his chest raw. He looked at the immense single pole beneath the center of the platform and the six cables that were supposed to stabilize it, until three slaps at his ankle shot him onto the platform. Seconds later, when Heinz reached the platform, jeers from thirty-five feet below were replaced by cheers. He steadied himself on the platform. Erich shouted, "Remember, fifteen minutes up and one second down!"

Heinz walked to the end of the cross-shaped platform and put his arms out to his sides. Before his head broke the surface of the water, Heinz heard the boys singing the song they had sung earlier that morning. It was the same song he had heard in the streets of Karlsruhe since he was a little boy. The boys lined up along the edge of the pool and greeted Heinz with back slaps and warm embraces of friendship. Wilhelm encouraged the boys to continue to sing in honor of Heinz:

> "Youth knows no danger.
> Germany, you will stand bright
> May we also perish.
> Forward! Forward!
> Bright blaring fanfares
> Forward! Forward!
> Youth knows no danger.
> If the target is still so high
> Youth forcing it anyway.

Shortness flag flies before us.
In the future we take each man
We march for Hitler
And the flag will lead us into eternity!
Yes, the flag is more than death!"

When the song ended, Wilhelm shook Heinz's hand. "Now everyone in the Hitlerjugend has made the jump. You see, Heinz— we are all the same. We are all brothers!"

Hours earlier, Julius Walker had been served breakfast by his second wife, Luise, in their apartment in Stuttgart. Before Luise left the apartment, she placed some dark bread, coffee with rationed sugar, and a treat, some recently purchased jelly made from seaweed, on the table. When she returned thirty minutes later, she could not stop screaming. When the doctor arrived and pushed opened the unlocked front door, he found the right side of Julius Walker's face lying in his breakfast. The doctor reached for the right arm that dangled a few inches above the floor and placed his fingers on the wrist. The death certificate read that Alfred Julius Walker, who was three months past his thirty-sixth birthday, had on "...August 16, 1943 at 8:00 a.m.... died of a heart attack."

"Summary to 7-21-43

...Religious Interest: Kurt has continued attending Hebrew school, and seems very interested in this activity. He was given the Jewish name of Isaac at Hebrew school, and was rather pleased about this. The foster mother reports that he is less concerned about the observance of orthodox rituals than he was before. He still

wears his hat at meals, but now is willing to
tear paper on Saturday and goes to the movies
on that day, as long as someone else carries the
money.

Relationship to Own Family: Kurt has had no word
from his mother during this period. He does not
talk about her, and seems to have forgotten his
own family background, as he has identified
more completely with the foster family group.

Eleanor Frank."

THE FUNERAL

Heinz and his eight-year-old cousin, Gerhardt, hid behind the pillar while their grandmother and Gerhardt's mother, Martha, cried softly. Christian Walker slammed his documents on the counter at the railway station. "You can see that I work for the railways. My family and I are on our way to Stuttgart for my son's funeral. I need five tickets, and I remind you there is no fee for the fares."

When the door to the Stuttgart chapel opened after the fifty-six-mile trip, Heinz's eyes were drawn to the open casket and then to the woman who sat alone in front of the unadorned pine casket. She immediately turned toward the low groaning sounds from the door that announced the only other people to arrive that day. Heinz stared at the woman's distracting fist- size bun of brown hair that sat just off center on her head. He has never seen her before, but correctly assumed that she was Elisabeth Emma Walker, his father's wife. The fact that her maiden name was Ankener, she was born in Stuttgart, and lived at Ihmlinstrasse 17 was all Heinz knew about her.

Heinz remained at the rear of the chapel with Gerhardt while the others walked toward her. "My friends call me Luise," said the new widow. She did her best to force a smile while she nervously pressed the wrinkles out of her black dress with her sweaty hands. The greeting between the women was formal and unemotional. They exchanged whispered words that presumably offered words of condolence as a disinterested Christian stood solemnly before the body of his dead son. Martha and Luise politely excused themselves and approached the open casket. They kissed their fingertips before placing them on the face of Julius. When Christian looked to the rear of the chapel, Gerhardt acknowledged his grandfather's commanding wave and pulled his cousin past the distraught women.

"Here is Heinz, Opa," said Gerhardt.

Christian put his arm around Heinz. "Heinz, no matter what—he is still your father."

Heinz looked at the clownlike face of his father, whose formerly ruddy complexion had been restored by the artistry of a local mortician. He wanted to feel sad, to feel angry, or to feel something, but inexplicably he felt nothing while the tears and cries of the women filled the chapel. The cries ended abruptly when a man in a sun-faded dark suit asked everyone to sit and pray in silence for the loss of "Alfred Julius Walker, dear husband, father, son, brother, and uncle." While the others remained lost in prayer, Heinz was consumed with a seemingly insignificant fact. "I didn't even know his first name was Alfred," mumbled Heinz.

When the brief service was completed, the six mourners followed two workers who wheeled the casket out of the chapel and into a small building. The workers removed Julius Walker's body from the coffin and placed it into a cardboard box that was immediately slid past a small opening. Heinz pushed past the women just as a thick and grimy navy-blue curtain was rolled in front of him. He stood with his silent family until the unseen but unmistakable sounds of a closing metal door and whirling flames filled the crematorium.

After a few minutes the man in the faded suit appeared from behind the curtain and ushered everyone back into the chapel, where he whispered to Heinz's grandfather. Christian grunted as he took out the agreed upon sum of money and gave it to the funeral director, who walked out onto the street and pointed. "Just make a right, and you will come to Mittnacht-Bau. It is a very nice restaurant. You will enjoy a nice lunch there before the train leaves for Karlsruhe."

Innocent conversations between the self-absorbed adults continued as Heinz and Gerhardt nervously grabbed at the sides of the tiny lift that brought them to the rooftop restaurant on the eighth floor. After Heinz finished his meal of white bean soup and bread, he walked past laughing friends, soldiers on leave, and families until he reached a half wall where he looked out onto the city of Stuttgart. His few moments alone ended when Luise called out his name.

"Heinz, may I talk to you? I want to…I mean…I need to tell you that you should know that your father loved you," said Luise. She looked at her watch and then back at Christian, who stood at the lift. She waited for a response that acknowledged her warm words, but there was no response from Heinz, who wanted to run away from the unwanted messenger and her confusing words.

"So then," began the last words she would ever say to Heinz, "this is for you. Your father wanted you to have this. He made a point of telling me this when I married him." Heinz took the envelope as Luise bent forward to kiss him. She tearfully begged, "Will you please, dear Heinz, call me Mutti?" There was no kiss or answer from Heinz, who fled to his family.

When Heinz finally sat down on the train he could barely contain his rage. He repeatedly mumbled the last words of Julius Walker's wife before he threw the wrinkly brown eight-by-ten-inch envelope to the ground. When he awoke two hours later to the snores of the passengers on the crowded train, the discarded envelope lay in his lap.

"What's this?" asked Heinz. He tipped over the envelope and slapped at it until the contents spilled out onto his lap. "I remember..." said Heinz as he looked at the eight-by-ten photograph of the woman. "She came up to me and my friends at a carnival in Karlsruhe when I was nine or ten. We made fun of her when she said I was out too late and should be home. I told her to mind her own business, since she wasn't my mother. My friends kept laughing at her even when the crazy woman came up to me and whispered, 'Yes I am.'"

Heinz recalled how annoyed he had been with the woman before he looked back at the pictures of the same woman sitting alone with a baby and standing with a young boy. Heinz grabbed the envelope again and reached inside it and pulled out the short note. "Ilse, Ilse and Kurt, pregnant Ilse with Heinz." Heinz closed his eyes, and tears fell onto the image of Ilse Walker's face. He stared at the woman's eyes, her hair, her lips, and the single strand of pearls around her neck. When he turned over the photograph, the same photograph his father had given his mother years earlier, he read the words that were in the unmistakable handwriting of his father. They were words that made no sense: `"Christmas 1930. You can't always be with the one you love."`

THE MEETING

It took Eleanor Frank only minutes to fall asleep after she got on the Division Street trolley car. Unfortunately, it took only twenty minutes more to travel the two and a half miles to the final stop at California and Division in Humboldt Park. It was September 3, 1943, and it had been many weeks since she had seen Kurt, who had just returned from two months of vacation in the lakeside town of Union Pier, Michigan.

"Momma, I will get it," screamed Jolene. The door repeatedly opened and closed.

"Jolene, I said Momma will open the door! Now let go of the door!"

Irene threw her hands in the air and apologized by simply saying "Jolene" just as her inconsolable daughter ran to her room in tears.

"Congratulations," said Eleanor to an obviously pregnant Irene Kastel. "Why didn't you tell me about the good news yesterday?"

Irene led her to the living room. "The truth of the matter is," whispered Irene, "my husband and I were talking last weekend when he visited me and the kids in Union Pier. My husband left Herbert with a neighbor because of his summer job. I know we didn't contact you first, but it was only for a couple of days. I hope that's not a problem?"

"Irene, it's fine, it's fine. Herbert is almost a man. You didn't do anything wrong."

Irene got up from the couch and looked again for Jolene. "My Albert, he is such a good husband. He reminded me, not that he had to, that when I was pregnant with Jolene I had gotten very ill. I was constantly nauseous and lost weight." Irene twisted her fingers. "It was easier then because it was just me and Albert. Even so, I still had to stop working at my mother's fish market. I was so sick that I ended up in bed during the last part of my pregnancy. Well, in the last couple of weeks I have been starting to have the same problems. I probably should have come home earlier from Michigan, but the children were having such a wonderful time."

"I don't understand, Irene. What are you saying?"

"The truth is my husband and I don't see how we can continue as foster parents for the kids."

Eleanor's initial reaction was selfish given the limited resources of the bureau and the increasing demands upon her own time. Her directness confirmed her concerns.

"When, Irene?"

"Now." Irene's voice sped up. "I apologize. I know this is short notice, but I couldn't take care of myself when I didn't have Jolene, and now I have Jolene, Edith, Herbert, and Kurt."

When Irene caught Jolene spying from around a corner she ushered the worker outside for some privacy. Moments later, when Kurt arrived home from school through the back door of the apartment, Jolene made sure that Kurt saw her pouting. Kurt gave Jolene his daily comforting kiss that seemed to satisfy her. And with his responsibilities completed, he threw himself onto the couch under the open window in the living room and grabbed at a stack of old *Reader's Digests.*

"Eleanor, to be honest with you, Kurt is not the same boy. He is very independent now. He doesn't have any fear, and everyone that met him over the summer loved him. Even some of his strict observances are fading. The other day he drank milk with beef stew, and even though he still wears his hat during meals, I think this is more habit now as opposed to some religious conviction. I think he got all of this from his grandfather, but it's clearly not as important as it once was. I bet he would tell you that." Kurt was crushed upon hearing the truth about his nonobservant behavior. "I don't think it will be hard to find a new home for Kurt, and I have no doubt that he will adjust in another home."

Kurt ran to Herbert's bedroom. He buried his face in a pillow and prayed for forgiveness from his grandfather for violating his trust and the promises made so long ago on the Moche. Also he prayed not to be punished for these violations by being removed from the Kastels' home. Jolene pounded away at the door. "Kurt, are you all right?" Kurt threw a pillow at the closed door and screamed back in German, "Jolene, leave me alone."

While Jolene ran crying down the hallway, Eleanor Frank's head spun with Irene's news. The upcoming Thursday and Friday she was to take off to be with her family would now be spent in the office trying to find a new home for Kurt, Herbert, and Edith. "Irene, please don't say anything to the children. I need time."

"Eleanor, this is not in my control. Please don't think poorly of me, but the children have to go. It's just not fair to my family."

A queasy Irene excused herself briefly. When Irene returned, she said, "Jolene told me that Kurt ran out the back door, so why don't you talk to Herbert and Edith. They're in the kitchen."

When the conversations with Herbert and Edith were completed, Eleanor began her walk back to the trolley car until she saw Kurt sitting behind a large oak tree across the street.

"Kurt, we were looking for you," said the startled worker.

"I'm sorry. I've been outside playing," said Kurt. He beat a stick against the tree.

"Do you know Gene Krupa? He plays drums on 'Sing, Sing, Sing' with Benny Goodman."

"Sure. Everybody knows him."

"You sound just like him," smiled Eleanor to an unresponsive Kurt.

"You look so tan and healthy. Did you enjoy the summer?"

"It was very fun. I hope to go there again."

Eleanor did not have to be a social worker to appreciate that something was wrong given the flat responses to her superficial questions. "I understand you were attacked by a dog in Michigan. That must have been painful."

Kurt pointed to the faint white mark on his leg. The worker responded with mock horror. "It was not that bad," answered Kurt between taps of the stick.

"I'm so glad to hear that," said Eleanor before she sat next to Kurt.

When she returned to the Kastels a couple of weeks later, Eleanor was still seething over the September 10, 1943, phone call with Irene. Irene advised her that she had told Kurt, "That he was going to have to leave and go into a new foster home because she was ill." Eleanor held her tongue over the violation of their private agreement when she asked, "What did Kurt say after you talked to him about leaving?"

"He just asked if he could still see Herbert and Edith. I told him that was up to you. You know how he is. Nothing bothers him."

"... Worker talked with Kurt alone for a few minutes on this visit. He was quite off hand in manner, told worker he was satisfied to go to another home....He did not...ask about the kind of family worker planned for him..."

Eleanor J. Frank, September 15, 1943

BELLE AND WAG

The emotional roller coaster ride that defined a more than two-decade-old journey brought Isadore J. "Wag" Wagner and Belle Wagner to the offices of the Jewish Children's Bureau in 1942. Married at the age of twenty on June 29, 1920, Belle's twenties and thirties flew by with a positive attitude that she would have a child. However, by her fortieth birthday, her new reality found her avoiding baby showers, the birth of a niece or nephew, and a Bar Mitzvah, where proud parents joined their son at the bimah. Nonetheless, her brave face acknowledged to no one that those momentous and happy occasions that elevated the spirits of those around her left Belle slipping into a depression. For her friends and family who witnessed her obvious pain, she was not the actress she thought she was. And however well-intentioned the members of her inner circle may have been, their comments of "you are so lucky, you can travel, eat out when you want, go to shows and movies" cut her like a knife.

By the time Belle and Wag first contacted the JCB about adopting, they acknowledged that their age was a hindrance in securing a more desired infant. Eventually Belle rationalized to her friends and family with each passing day that she wanted to adopt a three- to five-year-old child because "babies cry a lot and I would not want my dearie's sleep disturbed."

Over the next months, Belle and Wag's conversations invariably turned to toys, clothing, parks, school, and pediatricians. Happily, they buried the bitter and debilitating memories of the past in favor of a happy future for two people who desperately wanted to be parents. But after six months, the Wagners tearfully acknowledged the truth: their journey to become parents had come to an end. There had been contacts with the bureau in the intervening months, but as Belle told her caring friends and family, "We never got past the phone call."

When Belle answered the phone call from a JCB caseworker in late September 1943, it had been almost a year since she and Wag had first contacted the bureau. Wag was concerned as he watched his wife sob silently during the brief conversation. He tried to get her attention to determine who had died or who was ill. He mouthed, "Is everything all right? What's the matter?" But Belle just turned away.

When she hung up the phone, Belle draped her arms around her husband. "Wag, it was the JCB. They want us to come in tomorrow—to talk about some good news. Wag, it's over. It's finally over." To most, Belle and Wag had enjoyed a long, successful marriage. It was the kind of marriage others envied. He was a successful advertising executive earning $8,000 a year in the middle of a war. They had a beautiful apartment in a hotel at 505 W. Belmont, located steps away from Lake Michigan and just a few miles from Chicago's downtown loop. They appreciated all of the material things that hard work and sacrifice had afforded them, but the gift of good news was worth millions. They were going to be a real family.

The next day Belle Wagner nervously pushed though the revolving glass door at 130 N. Wells. She took elevator number two to the eighth floor's marble hallway that led her to the pristine reception area of the Jewish Children's Bureau. After the initial introduction was made, Belle apologized profusely for her husband's tardiness. "It's a meeting. He couldn't get out of it." She shook under her tailored dress while she looked for a wince, a half smile, or anything else that might suggest disappointment with Wag's tardiness. Of course, there was none from the worker, who was more nervous than Belle.

"We try to be professional," said Eleanor Frank upon entering the conference room where two employees were eating their lunch. Her apologies were dismissed by Belle while the other social workers gathered their food on the way out the door. "Miss Frank, there is a war going on. I think I could have suffered the indignities of having people eat in the same room where we meet."

The worker thanked Belle for her graciousness. "We already have your answers to the questionnaire and documents you sent us last year, so if you don't mind, let's just talk while we wait for your husband." Belle took advantage of the opportunity to deliver her rehearsed speech that devolved into a long and sometimes disjointed narrative.

"My parents, three brothers, and three sisters were born in Austria. I'm not sure of the year, but they all came to America in the late 1890s, before I was born. We were like most immigrants, poor. One day Momma told my brother Abe to get the midwife. By the time he got home, I was born. That was February 27, 1900. Abe likes to say he was like Paul Revere yelling and screaming as he ran down the street, 'I have a baby sister. I have a baby sister.'

"I will tell you that the greatest thing that happened to my family was the Northwestern University settlement. If it wasn't for them, I don't know what would have happened to us. They helped poor people with basic things like shelter and food. They

provided kindergarten classes for one penny a session and summer camp in Rockford for twenty-five cents a week. We had
bonfires, singing, and storytelling." Belle apologized for her ramblings, but Miss Frank urged her to continue.

"When I was six we moved to a third-floor flat. Three floors
up and three floors down, then outside to the basement where
the toilet was. It wasn't long before we moved to 2150 Division.
We lived above the Boys Club printing house. It was a beautiful
apartment with a big back porch and a separate living room.
The toilet was outside the front door. Now that was real luxury,"
chuckled Belle.

"I don't know how they did it, but my parents bought a piano.
I had lessons for twenty-five cents a week. My husband and I still
play. In fact, my husband is in advertising and writes music for
radio jingles."

Miss Frank interjected, "I think I read about your husband in
Kup's Column in the *Sun-Times*. Something about him being the
inventor of radio jingles and that everyone hates him for that."

"Yes," laughed Belle. "That would be my husband, the man
everyone hates. They hate those jingles. 'Mommy—what is it
dear?—I want a Salerno butter cookie.'"

"Your husband wrote that?"

"Yes and a lot more."

"I'm sorry, Mrs. Wagner, I didn't mean to interrupt you.
Please go ahead."

And without missing a beat, Belle did just that. "We lived
across from the synagogue when we lived on Division. Mother

was very religious. She would have to sit in the balcony of the synagogue with all the other women. That's the way they did it back then, women in the balcony and men on the main floor. I must tell you, I did not like that. I think that's one of the reasons I don't belong to a synagogue anymore. Truth be told, most of the Jews back then, especially the children like myself, just wanted to fit in. Unlike the Eastern European Jews, we wanted to be Americans. We did not want any problems." Belle sighed after a long pause. "I hope I didn't offend you."

"Don't apologize," floated the life preserver from a much younger Eleanor, who was genuinely happy to listen to the way it used to be.

"On the high holidays, while Mother was at the synagogue fasting, I would bring a lemon pierced with cloves of garlic to keep her from fainting. I always brought her flowers too. She would tell my father how all the other women were jealous because their daughters didn't bring them flowers. She was so sweet. I always wanted to be just like her." Belle nervously looked at her watch and thought of Wag. "Should I just keep talking?"

"This is terrific. Please, where did you go to school?"

"Graduated from Tuley High School on Claremont Street near Division. I wanted to be a teacher or a nurse, but when the first war started, my brother Abe went to fight in France. I worked to bring in money for the family. Got seven dollars a week until I moved onto my millionaire job where I earned twelve dollars a week. This ended when Mother got sick during the first flu epidemic."

Belle twirled her wedding ring. "It was a Saturday morning. She died in my arms while I was combing her hair." Belle reverted to her upbeat voice. "Moved into my sister Lill's house and got married to—"

"I'm so sorry," stuttered Isadore J. Wagner. Belle saved the usually unflappable Wag by taking over the introductions so that her husband could collect himself.

"I was just getting ready to tell Miss Frank that we met at Tuley."

Wag pulled out a wedding photo from his wallet and placed it on the conference table. He pointed back and forth between himself and the photograph of Belle dressed in a long white layered gown and equally long sheer headdress that cascaded to the ground. He asked jokingly, "Can you guess which one is me?"

"Miss Frank, I know I shouldn't say this, especially now, but my family didn't think much of him," followed Belle.

Wag doubled over laughing. He always loved it when his wife told someone how little he was thought of by Belle's family when they first married. He would then become uncomfortable and embarrassed when she went on to say how her family came to love and appreciate him, "… this guy who did not drink, swear or smoke."

Belle and Wag had agreed that they would not bring up Wag's poor health and his 1938 heart attack that brought their extended family to his hospital bed to say a final good-bye. In that moment of imminent death, a previously unconscious Wag opened his eyes and reverted to one of his many admirable qualities, his humor. Upon seeing the doctors, nurses, and crying members of his family, Wag, ashen-faced, turned tears into laughter when he spoke to his premature mourners. "We have enough in this room for a good game of poker! Which is good, but if this is supposed to be my shiva, where are the lox and bagels?"

Belle and Wag became silent with their knowing look of that memory five years earlier before they answered the expected question, "Yes, we are both in good health."

Miss Frank seized upon the resulting quiet. "Let me tell you why we called you here today. We have some children that need help."

The Wagners' spirits soared upon hearing the obvious invitation to adopt. "Whatever you want," sang Belle.

"Yes, whatever we can do. That's why we came here a year ago," joined in Wag.

"That's terrific. We have a boy, Kurt Walker. He has been in a foster home in Humboldt Park since August of '42. The foster mother is pregnant. She is concerned about her ability to care for him since her last pregnancy was so difficult."

Belle and Wag caught each other's eye and smiled.

"I know you contacted the bureau about adopting, but because of your age we don't see you as candidates to adopt." Belle could not breathe. Wag grabbed her hand under the table. "But we would like to know if you would be interested in acting as foster parents?"

Belle tightened her grip on her husband's hand while the worker quickly tried to tell Kurt's story before the Wagners escaped. "This young man was born on May 17, 1931, in Germany. As with many of these refugee children, our facts can be a little iffy, but we feel generally confident about this one. He speaks

German, French, and Hebrew." Miss Frank looked up at the Wagners, but she read nothing from their blank faces before she returned to the thin file. "His English is getting better. Mother is Jewish and the father, a Protestant, divorced her in 1934. Kurt, his maternal grandparents, and mother were deported in October 1940 to camps in France. He ended up in an orphanage in France and came here in August of '42."

The worker nervously sipped from her empty cup of coffee before she continued. "I want to be candid with you: he might be 'slightly retarded.' It appears that the mother married the father just before the birth of an older brother. The best we can tell is that the father was not around by the time Kurt was born. He did not help financially. Also," the worker paused, "the father beat Kurt's mother."

Wag cleared his throat after the candid and abbreviated assessment of Kurt's life ended. "Well, where has the boy been since he came here?"

"New York State for a very short time before the foster home in Humboldt Park."

"This certainly is a lot of information to take in and—"

"I'm sorry, Mr. Wagner," interrupted the worker, who wanted to be anywhere else but in that room. "I want to go over one last thing that is very important. The interview of Kurt's mother taken in France confirms that Kurt's father is a Nazi and a Brownshirt. You must have seen the articles and pictures in *Life* magazine about what happened in Germany in 1938 with the temples being destroyed." Then she provided one last and false caveat. "Kurt does not know anything about this."

"My God," uttered Belle as she looked at Wag.

Miss Frank felt ill before the stunned Wagners. She knew she had taken advantage of a desperate family with a dishonest phone call.

"Worker visited the K. home and took Kurt to visit the Wagner home, a prospective free home. On the way to the home in worker's car, worker described the home as a childless couple who were anxious to have a little boy. Kurt was interested and asked whether the home was near a park, near the lake, and about the school he would go to. He also told worker about a trip he made to the south side to visit his relatives. When worker questioned him further about this, he told worker that Mr. Heinrich Weil was a brother to his grandmother on his mother's side. He first heard about these relatives from his cousin in New York...they took him to the Rosenwald Museum. He did not seem too interested in them..."

September 27, 1943 JCB entry by Eleanor Frank

KURT, BELLE, AND WAG

We're here," said Miss Frank as she pulled up to the hotel at 505 W. Belmont. Kurt jumped out of the slow-moving car while the tires scraped against the curb. He turned to see Miss Frank frantically running toward him. "My Lord, Kurt, you don't even know which building you are going to! Please don't do that again." Kurt shrugged his shoulders while he listened to the first of many instructions that began and ended with "Remember to smile."

She's so little, thought Kurt, smiling when the opened door revealed the five-foot-tall Belle. She wore a stylish charcoal-gray dress that tried to hide her slightly pudgy figure. He barely noticed her long brown hair, brown eyes, and inviting round face that seemed to disappear with her broad smile. Belle wrung her hands while the worker began the introductions. An equally plump Wag put his arm around his wife and whispered to her to be calm. He looked like a professor in his sweater vest and tie. Kurt liked the way his shiny hair reflected the hall light and how his deep blue eyes appeared more intense through his thick glasses.

Kurt shot his right hand out before he delivered the simple rehearsed greeting of, "Good evening, my name is Kurt Walker." He prayed that the time spent practicing with Herbert was successful in hiding his German accent. After Miss Frank reminded the Wagners that she would return at 9:00 p.m., an impishly grinning Kurt closed the door on the worker.

"How about a look-see, Kurt?" asked Wag. They began the brief tour of the three-and-a-half room apartment. "This is Mrs. Wagner's and my bedroom, and that's our bathroom. The living room couch has a sleeper bed, which is great for guests. Oh, and behind that door is another bathroom."

"You have two bathrooms for only two people? The Kastels had one for seven people. Wow!"

"And this is the kitchenette," said Belle, leading Kurt into the small dining room.

Kurt's eyes bulged. "Are you hungry?" asked an amused Wag. Kurt stared at the roast beef, mashed potatoes, soup, cooked vegetables, bread, milk, and a cooling apple pie. Wag put his arm around Kurt. "And since you are the guest, you get to sit at the head of the table."

Kurt had been so intent on pleasing the Wagners that it had never crossed his mind that these strangers would go to the trouble of making such a simple but dramatic gesture. Belle piled Kurt's plate so high that the bottom of the good china could not be seen. After the wall of serving plates and bowls encircled Kurt, his eyes squinted in disbelief as he watched Wag begin to pretend to eat from his empty plate.

```
"August 8, 1941 Gurs Censor No. 5

My dear little Kurt!

...What are you doing now in the school holi-
days? If it were only possible I would arrange
for you to come here. But unfortunately it is
impossible here, I cannot offer you anything,
```

although my longing for you is great, dear little Kurt. I hope that things will change for
us one day and that we may be together again.
From Uncle Heinrich we have not yet received
anything....We shall wait in vain I hope you are
spending your holidays happily.

Mutti"

"Do you see what's happened, Kurt? You're here only fifteen minutes and she has already forgotten me!" cried Wag, who sipped some invisible soup from his empty bowl. Kurt howled as Belle slapped Wag playfully on the shoulder and pushed the plates even closer to Kurt. While the last bits of food were eaten, Wag snuck over to the piano, where he serenaded Kurt with a song that he had made up on the spot.

"Wow, Mr. Wagner, you are good," said Kurt in his thick German accent.

"I played with my brother, Sol, in a band," said Wag. His hands flew over the keys. "In fact, have you ever heard of Al Capone?" Kurt pulled the trigger on his imaginary machine gun and nodded yes. "Well, Sol was Capone's piano player for a while."

"That makes you famous, Mr. Wagner," exclaimed Kurt while he stared at the piano player's fancy ring. Belle poked her head out from the kitchen and watched Kurt slide on the piano bench next to her husband. Wag moved Kurt's fingers over the black keys until he mastered his part of "Yankee Doodle Dandy." Wag and Kurt smiled as they played their parts, harmonizing over the quickly learned lyrics. Suddenly Kurt stopped and whispered to Wag.

"That's a great idea, Kurt," answered Wag. He spun around on the bench and called to a spying Belle, "C'mon, honey, join us." Belle placed her hands on Kurt's shoulders while they laughed more than sang. When the introduction to the song began again, Belle excused herself. She hid behind the protective wall of the kitchenette where she wiped at her eyes and called out, "Who wants apple pie and ice cream?"

A spontaneous wrestling match to get to the table first left Wag conceding. He wailed, "Get off my chest! Uncle! Uncle! You win, Kurt."

While Wag panted, Belle watched Kurt inhale his dessert. She also watched her anxious husband begin a conversation with Kurt. She shook her head, but Wag gestured with his eyes.

"So how has the last year been for you, Kurt?" asked Wag. Kurt swallowed the last of his third glass of milk.

```
"August 18, 1941 Gurs Censor No. 4

My Dear Little Kurt,

...At the moment we seem to have little but
potatoes. Do you also get potatoes? Quite a lot
of people have carrots"
```

He never batted an eye as he wiped his face with his sleeve. "Good. Let's play some more piano, Mr. Wagner."

"Let's chat a little," replied Wag. "How much school did you have in Germany?"

Kurt took a drink from his empty glass. "Three years in Germany. But no real school after they burned down the synagogues. Then another few months in France."

"The synagogues—that was November of '38?"

"Yes, sir."

Wag turned away from his wife. "Did you actually see it happening?"

Kurt bit his lips and wiped his hands back and forth on his thighs. "Yes, sir."

"And this camp in France…"

"I was only in Gurs for a few months. It was not that bad. And then I went to the Maison des Pupilles. I made a lot of friends there, especially Hugo and the Weilheimers."

"But about Gurs. I wanted to ask…"

Belle's frustrated "dear" in front of an obviously uncomfortable Kurt did not stop Wag. "If you had no school in Germany, what did you do with your free time? I mean for fun."

"I went to the castle, the zoo, and played with all my friends. I had a lot of friends. Probably more friends than anyone else I knew," bluffed Kurt. "So my family let me stay out until dinner. And I studied the Torah with my grandfather Isack."

Belle shook her head again at Wag. "I understand you lived with your grandparents and mother back home?" asked Belle's persistent husband.

"Yes, and sometimes my uncle Julius."

"And your father…"

"He divorced my mother and took my brother, but I don't know them," answered Kurt.

"How about another song, Wag?" interrupted Belle. Her angry glare found him literally dancing back to the piano. Minutes later Kurt was pulling his arm up and down with the end of Wag's version of the Dorsey Band's "Chattanooga Choo Choo." When the song came to an end, he pulled out the stuffed wallet his mother had given him the day he left Gurs.

Kurt searched through his papers. "This boy on my street invited me to go with him to a Junior Victory meeting in the Hearst Building. I memorized the address in case we got lost, 326 West Madison, Chicago, Illinois, United States of America." Kurt threw himself on the plush living room couch and motioned the Wagners to join him. "Now you probably won't believe me..." began Kurt. He anxiously tore through his filing cabinet until he began to grin from ear to ear.

Kurt pushed himself between the Wagners and pointed to the article from the *Chicago-Herald American* dated June 6, 1943. He did his best to mimic the picture of the boy standing at the microphone before he read the bold print, `"'Kurt WelKer, refugee from Germany and France, tells experiences to Capt. Jack Little at recruiting rally in Hearst Building.'` I know they spelled my name wrong, but that's me." He read the article for the thousandth time and then editorialized, "You see that shows that I am a good American. You have nothing to worry about with me!"

The Wagners began to congratulate Kurt, who nervously folded and unfolded the article. He looked at the clock that said 8:45 p.m. "Then after the newspaper reporter interviewed me, he called the Kastels, and Auntie gave permission. She even helped me."

"Helped you with what?" asked Belle, who fed into Kurt's energy.

"The people at WGN radio asked me to give a speech about coming to America. You know, to tell people about how good of an American I had become. I think you have to agree that I am a good American. It's not every day that you get to be in the news-paper and on the radio."

Belle caught Wag's eye. "Kurt, honey, you don't have to prove anything to us."

Kurt looked at the clock again and spoke faster. "When I came here, they put me in Lafayette School with the second graders, with little kids, babies. I was eleven years old, but I couldn't speak any English. But I knew what the kids were thinking when I went there that first day. I hadn't even walked into the school and this boy came up to me and asked me my name. When I told him, he called me a dirty Nazi. Edith—I live with her and her brother, Herbert—was standing next to me. So Edith said yes. So I did it. One punch and he was down. That proves I am a good American too. Oh, I forgot, but by the end of the year they put me in fifth grade. I was very proud of that."

Belle thought she was going to cry, but happily Wag jumped up and began shaking Kurt's hand. "Well, you should be proud. That's a rare accomplishment."

Kurt looked one last time at the clock that said the evening was coming to an end. "I know they write things about me and they talk about me. I guess they talked about me with you too. When I came back from vacation in the summer, Miss Frank came to see Auntie, and I snuck a look at my file, and it's not true. But please don't tell them I did that."

"Kurt, what are you talking about?" questioned Wag.

"Well, I just want you to know that you don't have to worry about me. I'm American through and through." Kurt paused. "I saw what Miss Frank wrote—you know, about what my teacher said about me."

"What did she write?" asked Belle.

`"...the boy still had some loyalty to Germany."`

Kurt tried to iron out the lines of the newspaper article with his hands. He looked down at the warm oak floors. "When I first came here, Herbert told me all about the stars on the windows on Thomas Street. I hate Germany, and you need to know that."

Belle and Wag said nothing as they helped Kurt gather his papers from his wallet, until Belle asked, "Who are these people?"

"This picture is of my grandfather in his uniform, and this one is my mother and me in the gardens back in Karlsruhe."

Wag put his hand out, and Kurt gently placed the fragile pictures in his hands. "Thanks for letting us look at them, Kurt. I bet you can't wait to see them again." This time it was Wag who paused. "You must be sure to never forget them."

"I'll get the door, Wag. It must be Miss Frank," said Belle.

When Kurt arrived at the Kastels', he ran to the pay phone in the apartment and picked up the precious slug. He looked up the Wagners' telephone number in the phone book and dropped in the slug. "Mr. Wagner. This is Kurt Walker. What is our address?" But all Kurt heard was, "Do you know what time it is?" before the phone went dead.

Devastated, he looked around the room to confirm that no one was present as tears welled up in his eyes. Mistakenly, Kurt, who had never stopped looking at the unique Chinese ring on Wag's finger, misread the etched single initial I as a T, which resulted in an unintended phone call to a Mr. T. Wagner.

"October 5, 1943
Miss Lotte Marcuse,
Director
European Jewish Children Aid
139 Centre

New York City, New York   Re: Kurt Walker

My Dear Miss Marcuse:

...I was able to work out a very nice <u>free home</u> plan for Kurt. In view of his mother's disappearance 'sans address' I felt we should try to give him a more permanent type home where he could get both emotional and material security. He's a darling, outgoing, well Americanized youngster and easy to "sell." Mr. and Mrs. Wagner are an American-born childless couple, aged 44 and 43. They applied to our agency last year for a child in adoption but because of their age, they were very ready to consider this type of situation...

I took Kurt to visit the Wagners last week. They were delighted with him and the placement took place on Friday. Kurt is very happy in his new home and I think this is going to be a very nice long-term plan. At the same time they know he has a mother and will help to keep alive Kurt's memory of her.

> Yours Sincerely,
>
> Eleanor J. Frank
>
> Director of Refugee Placements"

Report from Eleanor Frank

"<u>Relationship to Own Family</u>: Immediately after Kurt's placement in the W. Home, he wrote his relatives in New York about his new home and also telephoned his relative on the south side. He explained to the W's that this was a brother of his grandfather. Mr. Weil came to visit one Sunday. He seemed very nice. He told the W's about his 22 year old son at the University of Chicago. He had become a citizen and his son had been deferred from the army because of an eye condition. Mr. Weil brought some candy bars for Kurt. He was rather embarrassed when he saw that Kurt was in the home of a fairly well to do people..." EJF 6-21-44

FRANCIS W. PARKER SCHOOL

" **E**very night we would hear him scream from his room that the Nazis were behind his bed or under his bed. And we had quite a difficult time with that. That was our big problem. But after that blood curdling experience with him, it seemed after one nightmare, he forgot about them completely. This pleased us completely."

Belle Wagner, May 27, 1993

On October 4, 1943, Kurt and Belle arrived at the prestigious Francis W. Parker School in Lincoln Park to meet with the principal, Herbert Smith. Named for Civil War veteran Lieutenant Colonel Francis Parker, this father of progressive education had traveled to Humboldt University in Berlin in 1872 to study and develop a new way of teaching. His new method underscored his school's motto, "Everything to help and nothing to hinder." Opened in 1901, the school had by World War I begun to educate affluent children from preschool through high school.

Bursting with pride, Kurt threw his shoulders back and walked confidently around the principal's office, preening and pointing out each new article of clothing that the Wagners had purchased for him. The good-natured principal waited until the show was over before he addressed Kurt. "In all my years at Parker, I have never seen a better dressed student. But I have something very important for you to do. Mariann Marshall has agreed to show you around the school since my old legs are just saying no today."

"That's fine, Mr. Smith, but you don't look that old to me."

"I'll take that as compliment, young man," chuckled the principal.

Kurt started to follow Miss Marshall out of the room, but he stopped. "Aren't you coming, Mrs. Wagner? You aren't as old as Mr. Smith."

Belle stood up and hugged Kurt. "Mr. Smith has some questions for me, Kurt," said Belle reassuringly.

Kurt looked at Miss Marshall, raised her hand, and pledged, "Scout's honor. No more than fifteen minutes." Belle looked at Kurt's nervous eyes and crossed her heart. Kurt returned both her smile and the crossing of his heart before he puffed his chest out and walked out of the room.

```
"August 18, 1941 Gurs Censor No. 5

I am happy to know that you are well and
that you have settled and I thank you very much
for the greetings you sent us. Have you got the
same terrific heat that we have? Thank God it
is raining now and cooling off a little. When
we have some more stamps, I shall give them to
your dear mother. Stay well and work hard at
your lessons. Knowledge is the greatest wealth.

Sincerest greetings

From your Aunt Johanna"
```

The principal was direct. "Mrs. Wagner, we have no experience with refugees. We do the best we can for our students, but under these circumstances it will be difficult for Kurt to make the transition to Parker."

Belle and Wag had anticipated a negative response from the school. "My husband and I are prepared to do whatever is necessary to help Kurt. You can see he filled out the questionnaire, and he did it by himself, all twenty-three questions. He answered the questions about his interests and hobbies. Look at the one that asks about the things he likes best in school." The principal put on his glasses. "You can see he checked every box." Belle walked around the desk and pointed to the paper. "Right there—you see he checked all twelve: reading, math, dramatics, science. I assure you that neither I nor my husband told him to do that." Belle returned to her seat, feeling like a little child waiting to be scolded. She apologized for being "…a little too aggressive." But no sooner had she sat down than she popped up again. "We don't think he can make it in the public school system. We just want him to have a chance. Please help us."

Mr. Smith bit the end of his already chewed pencil. He put the form back into Kurt's file that contained three pieces of paper. "I am going to be honest with you, Mrs. Wagner. I called the JCB myself, because we had no information about Kurt. I also asked Miss Marshall from our psych department to get more information about Kurt after I talked to you. The bottom line is Kurt will have to stay in the fifth grade. You know he is already more than a year older than most of the other fifth graders, but he is just not ready."

"Although his I.Q is very low, 91 he might be able to do the work of the fifth grade…"

Mariann Marshall, examiner, Psychological Department, Francis
W. Parker School

Belle let out a laugh that brought about a strange look from
the principal. "I'm so sorry, Mr. Smith. It's just that I thought you
were going to say no to Kurt, that he could not come here because his father...My husband and I are committed to help Kurt
and to see that he takes advantage of everything that Parker has
to offer. This is where he needs to be."

Kurt's soon-to-be classmates were part of the upper echelon
academic cream of Chicago in 1943. Of the other thirty-five children who made up the high school graduating class of 1949–1950,
an unprecedented 100 percent would go on to prestigious colleg-
es such as Harvard, MIT, University of Chicago, Northwestern,
Amherst, Radcliffe, and Swarthmore. Immediately after Kurt's
acceptance into Parker, the Wagners honored their commitment.
They hired tutors and made frequent trips to museums and plays
to ensure that by the next school year, Kurt could make the double promotion into the seventh grade that was so important to
him. No stone was left unturned by the Wagners, including test-
ing by the University of Chicago Vocational Guidance Clinic.

The psychological part of the first of many exams stated in
part:

"The striking discrepancy between the two performances (Revised Stanford-Binet and Kuhlman
Test of Mental Development) might be an indica-
tion of emotional difficulties interfering with
efficient functioning.

...While it was felt that this boy is probably
not college material and that he would not be

interested in work along academic lines, it was suggested that he return to the clinic...to obtain a continuous picture of the development of his interests since it seems possible that he might not be functioning to full capacity at the present moment due to emotional difficulties."

RABBI SOLOMON GOLDMAN

During the early afternoon cab ride on October 5, 1943, to Anshe Emet Synagogue, Wag could not keep his eyes off the intriguing boy he barely knew. Kurt gave his best unaccented thanks to the cabbie, who wished Kurt and his "father" a pleasant day. While Wag paid the fare, Kurt scrambled out of the car onto the middle of a tree-lined street surrounded by newer apartment buildings in the Lakeview area of Chicago. He immediately felt the stares of the small group of boys who had stopped their bikes to look at the stranger. Instinctively Kurt looked to the ground and pretended to kick at the same imaginary pebble he had seen in Germany.

"Ready, my friend?" asked Wag as he playfully slapped Kurt on his shoulder.

"Sure, Mr. Wagner," answered Kurt. Wag looked over at the group of boys who immediately took off on their bikes.

The tense moment left Wag playing to his audience. Using his over-the-top Chicago accent, he said, "Dat way is Lake Michigan, 'bout a quarter of a mile. Dat way is Wrigley Field." Wag hiked his pants well above his socks. "And no more den five minutes from here—dat's where da Cubs play ball. Remember, kid—next season, youse and me are going there every game—got it!" Wag put his arm around Kurt. "Seriously, Kurt, I promise I will take you there. You can meet the players and the announcer, Bert Wilson. I hired Bert. He's a great guy. Next summer, every day it will be the Cubs and the beach for you. You can't beat it, my friend! In fact, after we meet the rabbi, let's go past the ballpark so you can take a look-see."

Wag gently pushed Kurt toward the massive entryway to the synagogue at the southwest corner of Grace and Pine Grove. He could feel Kurt's muscles stiffen as his foster child read the carved words high above the four huge columns of the building that greeted each congregant:

"MINE HOUSE SHALL BE CALLED AN HOUSE OF PRAYER FOR ALL PEOPLE."

"I can't hear you, Kurt. What did you say?"

"Nothing—just, it looks like the church in the Platz back home in Karlsruhe," answered Kurt in his guarded English.

Wag rubbed Kurt's back. "Well, Kurt, you are home. This is your home now."

After they walked past the main doors and into the sanctuary, Kurt ran past the rows of cranberry-colored movie theaterlike seats until he reached the huge bimah. Wag could not take his eyes off Kurt, who walked back and forth on the bimah like a caged animal. His pacing stopped, but only momentarily, until he saw the communal box containing hundreds of yarmulkes. Kurt jumped from the stage and picked at the box until he pulled out two black silky caps. He replaced his Cub's cap with one while he ran to Wag with the other one. Then he was off again, running back to the bimah where he pulled back the curtain that hid the ornate Torah. Kurt ran his fingers over the sculpted protective metal screen. Seconds later he jumped from the bimah. He stood inches from the first row of seats. The design of the synagogue that easily allowed for the rabbi's voice to be heard during services also allowed Wag to clearly hear Kurt say "A" as he looked at the metal plate on the aisle seat. Kurt paused for only a second more before he walked down the main aisle of the sanctuary where the Torah would be carried during services and touched each plate before he said, "D...J...M."

Other than being at a synagogue for Bar Mitzvahs or weddings, neither Wag nor Belle attended any synagogue with regularity. In that moment, Wag could not help but get caught up in Kurt's enthusiasm. "This is a big synagogue, Mr. Wagner! They must be able to have a million people here! And hey, look at that, Mr. Wagner!" rang Kurt's voice. He pointed to the six huge stained glass scenes. "What do they mean?"

But before Wag could say he had no idea, Kurt was pointing at the domed ceiling some one hundred feet above them. "What about that one, Mr. Wagner? And that one?" asked Kurt as he pointed to the second floor where the choir sat. "I mean it's huge—the Statue of Liberty, Abraham Lincoln, and George Washington. What are they doing here?"

Wag followed Kurt back toward the ark. "What are you doing," whispered Wag, watching Kurt pull back the ornate curtain and gate that protected the Torah. Kurt picked up a prayer book, kissed it, and then touched the Torah with it. "Mr. Wagner. Thank you, I am so happy," said Kurt.

"So am I, Kurt," said Wag before he guided Kurt into the main building, past the boys and girls carrying their Hebrew school books. After Wag thanked the receptionist for directions to the rabbi's office, both he and the startled receptionist turned to see Kurt bend at the knees and daven while he prayed. "I don't know why," answered Wag to the young woman before he put his arm around Kurt and walked him down the hallway.

"Kurt, sit here for a moment while I talk to the rabbi." The three knocks on the door followed by the Russian-accented, "Please come in" left Kurt curious about who was behind the quickly closing door. His unfocused curiosity ended when the door closed and Kurt began his examination of the community bulletin board. He flipped through the thumbtacked Anshe Emet newspaper, the *Bulletin*, which was hidden by the notices about Hebrew school and upcoming lectures. Reading in English was still difficult for Kurt. He pushed himself every day to hear the *po* sound in "potato" and the *gr* sound in "grow" in order to purge the German accent that brought stares of hatred. So when he pushed aside the *Bulletin* that covered the November 19, 1941, letter, he made sure to whisper as the children passed:

```
"Honorable Frank Knox,
Secretary of the Navy,
Washington, D.C.

My Dear Secretary Knox:

As a patriotic citizen, which I hope I am, I
should refrain from writing you. Your time and
energy are too valuable to be diverted even for
a fleeting second from the task that is yours.
And yet I take liberty of turning to you be-
cause in a certain sense this matter I desire
to bring to your attention is indirectly a part
of America's defense effort.

Our Synagogue, I believe, is more or less known
to you. We had the great privilege of seeing and
```

hearing you in our pulpit. Well, last August, some Nazi vandals smashed some of our precious stained glass windows, depicting scenes from Jewish history. The Board of the Congregation met and resolved that there was no better way of replying to the Nazi terrorists in our midst than by installing an American Window. This we have done and a beautiful window it is indeed. It portrays Washington and Lincoln, the New York Harbor, the Statute of Liberty and the approach of immigrants, Independence Hall and appropriate quotations from the Declaration of Independence and Lincoln's Gettysburg Address. The cost of the window, by the way, was defrayed by popular subscription.

The window is to be dedicated, and we are...

Respectfully and cordially,

Rabbi Solomon Goldman"

He angrily alternated between German and English, "The Nazis are not supposed to be here. This is America." When he felt a hand on his head, he jumped and closed his hands into fists.

"I see you are reading the letter. Unfortunately the secretary never came here. He had more important things to deal with after the Japanese attacked Pearl Harbor," stated Rabbi Solomon Goldman. "You must be Kurt Walker. This gentleman has been telling me some wonderful things about you."

Kurt saw the rabbi's lips moving, but he never heard a word as he gawked at his bouncing bright blue eyes and shock of wild white hair. The rabbi smiled as he waved his hand in front of Kurt. "Young man, my name is Rabbi Solomon Goldman, and I must advise you that you can only stare for five more seconds before I charge a fee." The rabbi made light of the moment while he ushered Kurt into his office. "Every day no matter where I go, the cabbies yell, 'Hey, Einstein.' Now you should know, Kurt, that Albert Einstein is a friend of mine," said the rabbi. He pointed to the framed picture of the famous scientist. "I wrote him that this happens all the time, but I always tell him that I am better looking. At least that's what my wife, Alice, says."

There was no response from Kurt as the rabbi's best effort to be engaging fell on deaf ears. "So, my young friend," tried the rabbi again. "Mr. Wagner tells me that you are living with him and his wife. Also, he tells me you have been all over the world at the age of what?"

"I'm twelve years old, Rabbi," replied Kurt, mesmerized.

"Mr. Wagner has also told me about some of your many experiences, both in this country and in Europe. We are so lucky to have you here in Chicago. He told me about your strong desire to complete your Jewish education."

"Yes, Rabbi," said Kurt confidently. "I need to be a good Jew. My thirteenth birthday will be in May, and I am afraid there is not enough time. That's why I am here. I need to join the synagogue to complete my responsibilities."

The rabbi looked at Wag. "I have spent so much time talking with Mr. Wagner about you, Kurt, that I feel like I already know you. But I was wondering if you would mind talking with me in private? How would you like that?" asked the rabbi as Wag exited the room.

"I would enjoy that, Rabbi."

Rabbi Goldman, a true renaissance man who could read thir-teen languages, attained national prominence as the first rabbi to be sued in an American court for heresy. In 1929, he was wooed away from Cleveland by three wealthy congregants. Promised a staggering yearly salary of $18,000, he was responsible for rein-vigorating the ninety members of Anshe Emet Synagogue. The ensuing stock market crash that made payment of his salary an occasional event did not stop him from increasing the member-ship of the former orthodox synagogue to 2,500 people. Vested in faith and his community, Rabbi Goldman lived on three hours of sleep a night and worked seven days a week, until his death at the age of fifty-nine in 1953. The rabbi's single-minded efforts resulted in transforming Anshe Emet into the largest conserva-tive synagogue in America. Those unknown accomplishments were irrelevant to Kurt, who instinctively knew that he had found his rabbi.

"I talked to your foster father. He told me a little about the exploits of a young Kurt Walker," continued the rabbi. "Also, I understand that the Wagners are not observant and that they do not belong to a synagogue. They don't even go to synagogue on the high holidays. But Mr. Wagner told me because of you, Kurt, and you should be very proud of this, because of you, they would like to join Anshe Emet."

"Yes, Rabbi, they promised me that they would join. I think this a good thing for them."

Rabbi Goldman clapped his hands. "And now for you, Kurt, how much formal Jewish education have you had? Studying Hebrew? Studying the Torah?"

"To be honest with you, Rabbi—I have tried to go to the synagogue near where I used to stay in Humboldt Park, but they do not take my studies seriously. But my Opa—Rabbi, would you mind if we talk in English? My English is not very good and I need to improve."

The rabbi smiled, "Of course not."

"My grandfather tried to help me, especially after the Nazis burned the synagogues. We enjoyed studying together, but it became difficult to find the time, and I apologize for that. But I promise you that I will be very serious about my studies."

"There is no reason to apologize, Kurt. I can tell you are very serious, and before you leave today, I would like to introduce you to Ben Aronin. The children call him Uncle Ben. He prepares everyone for their Bar and Bat Mitzvahs. He is a wonderful, interesting young man, only thirty-eight years of age. When he was in the Illinois National Guard he rode horses and won the boxing championship of the 122nd Field Artillery. I hold him in high esteem even though he is a lawyer by education," said the rabbi with a chuckle. "He tells me the word 'law' is so grim that he calls his children's spouses sons- and daughters-in-love." The rabbi waited for the laugh that always followed the anecdote about beloved Uncle Ben, but there was none from a somber Kurt. "You should also know that he teaches our 'bad class' here at Anshe Emet—for those who do not take their studies seriously."

"I want—I will do whatever you tell me to do. I just want to be a good Jew," promised Kurt. "This synagogue is so beautiful. I want everyone to be proud of me and to fulfill my responsibilities. Rabbi, I need you to help me do this."

The rabbi paused briefly. "On my mother's side there were ten generations of rabbis, Kurt. My father had hopes that I would become a lawyer. I think maybe my choices disappointed a few family members. So here today I ask you, what is it you want?"

Kurt looked confused. "But Rabbi, I told you what I want. I want to—I need to be a good Jew." Kurt returned to German. "Rabbi, I need to accomplish this. Please, Rabbi—can you help me?"

The next day and every day over the succeeding months after school, Kurt took the four-cent cable car ride from Francis W. Parker School to Anshe Emet and then the five-cent bus ride back home. On the first day at Anshe Emet, Kurt smiled and happily waved at the group of Jewish boys who stood at the massive front entry doors to the Anshe Emet.

"What's your name? You are new here," said one of the six boys who blocked the door. Slow and clear, thought Kurt. "Kurt Walker."

The sounds of Kurt's thick German accent brought a collective sneer to the crowd of twelve-year-old boys. The boy approached Kurt and put his finger on Kurt's chest. He snarled, "Fucking Nazi." Following the single punch, Kurt walked over the unconscious boy. He would not let the others see his tears as he entered the synagogue to begin his first Bar Mitzvah lesson with Uncle Ben.

"Mrs. W reported that Kurt came home quite upset one day and asked her if he had been 'adopted.' Mrs. W explained to him she and her husband were not able to adopt him but that they loved him just as much as if they had...Mrs. W explained that it was because of the fact that he had his own mother in Europe. Mrs. W subsequently learned that Kurt was upset because some other children had teased him and called him a German. Mrs. W made plans for Kurt to attend camp but changed those plans when she learned that the boys who had been teasing Kurt were going to attend the same camp." Eleanor J. Frank, JCB

Years late Belle wrote, "...after a talk with the principal at Parker school, we decided that I would take Kurt away for the summer and I would tutor him. We went to Browns Lake (Wisconsin), where, after breakfast each day we would sit under a tree and study reading writing and arithmetic. At the end of the summer he was tested at Parker and skipped a grade."

Belle Wagner, May 27, 1993

THE BAR MITZVAH

The newsletter from Anshe Emet Synagogue dated May 19, 1944, was similar to the prior issues. The front page, with the simple hand drawn images of Hanukkah menorahs, was the first thing a congregant saw each week upon receiving the *Bulletin*. For the cost of one dollar per year, the *Bulletin* published news in the same basic format. There was the Yahrzeit Record identifying the departed, along with a reminder that `"Their names will be read at the Friday evening Service,"` the names of the boys `"Now serving our country,"` a list of war service activities, a roll call of contributors, and general announcements of upcoming events. This particular issue contained an unprecedented article entitled, `"A Yarn of a Coy."` The exciting exposé written by British Jewish Lieutenant Rosser told of the Eighth Army Order of Gallantry he received in leading six Jewish soldiers within his company. The pride-filled congregants would discuss the bravery of these men for many weeks.

However, when Wag opened the mail at his apartment and pulled out volume fifteen, number twenty-eight of the *Bulletin*, he never read about Lieutenant Rosser's exciting escapades, the names of the contributors, or the Yahrzeit Record. His eyes were drawn to the first column on the first page. When he finished reading, he returned to the piano and retrieved the pen he had been using to write the music for a new radio commercial. He circled the small blurb on the first page and placed two small x's next to the circle before calling out to his wife. Belle slid the noodles for the kugel into the boiling water before she approached

424

Wag. He patted the well-worn mahogany piano bench and pointed to the circle. Belle held his hand and started to read:

"Bar Mitzvah

The Bar Mitzvah this Shabbat will be Kurt Wagner, son of Mr. and Mrs. I.J. Wagner."

After the religious service for Kurt's Bar Mitzvah was completed, there was a celebratory meal that included cakes and candies with Kurt's name printed on them. Before the reception began, Cookie, a family friend, rushed to be the first of many to embrace Wag and Belle. They reflected on the joyous and emotional day that left them all crying and laughing.

"...As long as I have started on the subject, I may as well tell you that something happened Saturday at Kurt's Bar Mitzvah that left one with a very exalted and wonderful feeling. It wasn't the dinner with its fine food and exquisite good taste, which was the last word in elegance, that really touched our hearts, but the closing words of Kurt's beautifully delivered speech where his voice choked with emotion because his little heart was so overflowing with love and gratitude for his parents."

Letter from Ruthie, "Cookie," to Wag dated May 22, 1944

"July 16, 1941 letter from Ilse, Censor No. 9

Dear little Kurt, we think of you so often. Don't overdo your football playing. I don't want you to have an accident! We had a photo of you once with your class teacher in Karlsruhe, it

```
was a good photo, but unfortunately we had to
leave it at home.... We hope that we shall soon
be back in Karlsruhe.

Mutti"
```

In the months leading up to Kurt's Bar Mitzvah, there was little time for frivolous activities. His regular studies at Francis W. Parker were followed every day by Hebrew School at Anshe Emet and then choir practice before he returned home to complete his studies. Kurt's unique and passionate drive in preparing for his Bar Mitzvah was acknowledged by everyone at Anshe Emet. This was true of Rabbi Goldman who met with Kurt before his Bar Mitzvah for his standard talk that seemed to intimidate the children.

The rabbi went through a speech he had given many times before as he looked at his watch that told him he was once again late for another meeting during his customary twenty-five-hour day. "You should know," explained the rabbi "that we call upon the children to talk to their friends and family from the bimah after they have made their Bar Mitzvah. I would like you to think about what it is you would want to say."

"Yes, Rabbi."

"Maybe in a couple of days we will talk again, and you can share with me and Uncle Ben what it is you would like to say."

"But I already know what I want to say, Rabbi."

"So what is it you want to talk about, Kurt?"

He slowed his speech to ensure an American *po* and *gr* sound. "I would like to say thank you, Rabbi."

"Well, that's a wonderful idea, Kurt. To say thank you from some-one who truly means it is a gift. Especially from someone who is no longer a boy, but a man." The rabbi smiled at Kurt, who looked tiny sitting in the massive, thickly upholstered chair. His legs extended straight out so that the soles of his shoes looked directly at the rabbi.

"Are you nervous?"

"Very."

"Good," laughed the rabbi. "That means you care." He dragged his chair in front of Kurt. "You know that with your approaching Bar Mitzvah everything changes for you. This entire process you have been going through is about becoming a complete member of the Jewish community. It's your statement to the world about moral responsibility, about connecting to the Torah, to God, and your family. With your Bar Mitzvah the world sees and hears what you have accomplished and what you intend to do. The commitments you make to these same things after your Bar Mitzvah are not always obvious, but they will always be known by you and God."

Kurt appeared confused. "Do you find that strange? Do you find it strange what I said, Kurt?"

"Rabbi, I'm sorry I don't think I understand what you are saying."

"Kurt, did you know this synagogue was the first synagogue in this country to allow girls to go through the same religious education that you have gone through?" Kurt did not answer. "We have always wanted to bring people in, not exclude them. Of course I would like everyone to come here every day for prayers. But I'm not stupid. I know some members of our synagogue who call themselves Jews don't even come here for the high holidays. All they do is pay their dues. Does that make them less of a Jew? Becoming a Bar Mitzvah gives you the right to wear a tallit and tefillin, lead the congregation in prayer, and be accorded the honor of being called up to the Torah, but it does not make you a good Jew." Kurt wanted to ask a question, but he still had no idea what the rabbi was saying.

"I see how studious you are. Uncle Ben tells me about your efforts. I can see this for myself. Also, I hear you don't tear paper or carry money on the Sabbath and that you wear your hat at meals. What I want to tell you, Kurt, is that all of the things that we do as Jews to honor our commitment to faith, community, God, and our family are what make us Jews. Some people who come to this house of God thinking they follow the rules of the Torah one hundred percent of the time believe that is what makes a Jew.

"I'm sure that some of those same people think they are a better Jew than the person who sits next to them for that reason alone. I have no doubt that some think they are a better Jew because they donate more money than their neighbors. In the *Bulletin*, we make a point of not mentioning the amount of a donation by a member.

Did you know before modern times we did not have a ceremony for a Bar Mitzvah? Back then, the Bar Mitzvah occurred just by virtue of your thirteenth birthday. Today we proudly show our friends, family, and community the commitment of our children in the synagogue with this beautiful ceremony."

The rabbi put Kurt's hands in his own. "I guess what I am telling you, Kurt, is that people have different reasons why they have a Bar Mitzvah, join a synagogue, or want to become a good Jew.

I know if it wasn't for you, the Wagners would not be a member of any synagogue. You have a level of desire to be a good Jew that I have rarely seen in people of any age. I want you to know that you are already a good Jew and you will always be a good Jew. And it will not be because you come to synagogue every day or you donate more money than your neighbor or you make this Bar Mitzvah. I know why your commitment is so strong and I am grateful for it, but I also want you to know that everything will be fine."

Kurt started to speak, but Rabbi Goldman uncharacteristically cut him off. "You have already fulfilled your promises to God. You have fulfilled your promises to everyone. Do you understand me?"

"August 17, 1942

I wanted to say that the degree of his orthodoxy, or his religious observance, seems quite confused as with several of the boys of his age groupwe have a distinct feeling that they aped and copied the children who really were orthodoxKurt wanted to wear his cap and pray although the counselors who understood Hebrew said they weren't even using Hebrew words but just something that sounded like it.

I imagine Kurt would be very happy if he were placed in an orthodox home at this moment but we question whether it has any meaning beyond the initial period."

Letter from Lotte Marcus of the German Jewish Children's Bureau to Eleanor Schwartz of the Jewish Children's Bureau while Kurt Walker was in Pleasantville

As the services for Kurt's Bar Mitzvah came to an end with Cantor Silverman's melodic chant, the Torah, which was almost as big as Kurt, was placed in his arms. Followed by Wag, Belle, Rabbi Goldman, and Uncle Ben, Kurt, smiling, walked down the aisles of the sanctuary as the congregants touched the Torah with their prayer books. When Kurt returned to the bimah, Wag's brother, Sol, was given the honor of completing the service by returning the Torah to the ark. Kurt acknowledged Uncle Ben's nod and walked to the lectern. It was a walk that began years earlier. It was a walk that ended when he stepped onto a stool and looked out into the sanctuary.

Rabbi Goldman and Cantor Silverman stood at the rear of the bimah and prayed. Kurt, dressed in his new brown tweed suit, straightened his blue-and-white prayer shawl and matching yarmulke. He cleared his throat. He prayed for the final wave of nervousness to pass while he recalled what Belle and Wag had said that morning. "If you get nervous, don't look at anyone else but us. You have no reason to be afraid of anything when you are with us. Just pretend we are talking in the living room."

Kurt pulled out six stiff typed three-by-five note cards from the inside breast pocket of his suit and stacked them neatly in front him. He would never look at them. From the moment he started to speak he made sure to never take his eyes off of the smiling faces of Belle and Wag.

"-1-

This synagogue is so beautiful. Every Sabbath morning I come to pray here with my classmates, to sing the songs, the Hebrew songs which I love, and to listen to Rabbi Goldman explain the reading from the Torah. When Cantor Silverman carries the Torah past me, I reach out to kiss it, for I know what a wonderful Book the Torah is, and I love it. The Torah teaches freedom. Freedom for everyone!

-2-

I know that there are countries where people bow before wicked men and it is good to live in America where we bow only to God and where all men are equal. In lands across the sea how different it is! There a Jew cannot walk proudly to his synagogue; there he must hide; there his life is in danger; there even the beautiful Sabbath day, the day of joy can bring him no happiness for there are ruins and death everywhere.

-3-

There little children do not laugh and play, they are too frightened. The only music they hear is bombs and guns and curses. The only uniforms that they see are the uniforms of the Nazis. But here we are so far away from all that misery and sorrow. Here we walk thru the streets and thru the park in the sunlight; we do not hide. Here we can laugh and sing and pray and study.

-4-

Here children are not torn away from the arms of their parents. Here children are happy. If it

were not for the radio and the newspapers, we
would never know the great sorrow in the world.
But we DO know, and since we know, we should be
grateful to God that the whole world is not covered with darkness, that there is still America,
the land of freedom for all men.

-5-

And so on this morning of my Bar Mitzvah, I am
glad that I am an American and a Jew. It is good
to live in a country which says to the world:
'Why can't you learn to live in freedom as we
do? Can't you see that all men are the children
of God?' Someday the world will learn that it
doesn't matter what color a man's skin is or
what language he speaks.

-6-

Someday the world will learn the lesson of the
Torah. There it is, up there on that window:
'All men are created equal.' America has learned
it and someday all the countries of the world
will learn it too. As a Bar Mitzvah I must try
to teach that lesson all my life. May God bless
my dear Mother and Dad for bringing me here to
study, to pray and to enjoy the companionship
of the fine Jewish boys and girls. May I make
my parents as happy as they have made me. That
is my hope; that is my prayer."

Tears easily flowed from the family and friends sitting in
the sanctuary. They watched Rabbi Goldman and Uncle Ben

embrace and kiss Kurt before they too shed their own tears of joy.

When Kurt woke up the next morning, he found notes from Belle and Wag sitting on top of the radio next to his bed.

"Darling Kurt: Mommy is very very proud of you today and all days. And I'll be proud of you always. All my love darling, Mommy.

Dear Son: I am one of the proudest parents there ever was. I am sure you will be a MAN who will be a credit to yourself, to Mommy and Daddy and to your faith and your country. Your Loving Daddy."

The following week a new entry was made in Kurt's file by Eleanor Frank. She skimmed past her first entry made some seven months earlier when she first made contact with the Wagners and noted, "Mrs. W assured the worker that they would see that he would not forget his mother."

Her newest entry was to the point:

"At Kurt's Bar Mitzvah worker observed that both Mr. and Mrs. W were very much moved. Kurt gave a speech in which he referred to the W's as his "parents" and about the same time learned through other contacts in the community that some people in the community thought that Kurt had been adopted by the W's. Worker sensed that Mr. and Mrs. W were encouraging Kurt's identification with them and that Kurt might be having a little conflict on this score."

On the same date, Eleanor Frank received a beautiful thank you card from Kurt for the tie clasp she had given him in honor of his Bar Mitzvah. She stamped the date of May 29, 1944, on the card and underlined the embossed words "**Kurt Wagner**" that had been printed on the exterior of the formal thank you card. Pursuant to instructions from the Jewish Children's Bureau, she made a home visit to discuss the status of Kurt's placement.

THE MEETING

"Feb. 14, 1944

Dear Kurt:

October First was OUR Valentine's Day For it
brought us a sweetheart from far away,
A perfect sweetheart OF A BOY,
To fill our home and hearts with joy.
Yes, Kurt, it's YOUand we'll feel fine.
If we may be YOUR Valentine.
Mommy and Daddy
WLYAYLUAAW!"

Valentine card from the Wagners to Kurt

On June 2, 1944, when Kurt opened the door and greeted Miss Frank, she was happy to learn that her intentional early arrival meant that Kurt was alone.

"Kurt, I wanted to thank you for the lovely card you sent me. You should be impressed that I still remember what you wrote. 'Dear Miss Frank: Thank you for the beautiful tie clasp. I expect to wear it often and I will think of you often too. Gratefully, Kurt.'"

"Wow," said Kurt. "I can't believe you remember that."

"I noticed that the card had the name Kurt Wagner on it," commented the worker.

"Yeah, I've been using Wagner for about three months. It's just easier, at least that's what the Wagners say," said Kurt matter-of-factly.

"Well, Kurt, I think that's great, because you are so lucky to have two mommies that love you. You know your mommy in Europe has not forgotten you. And I know that you haven't forgotten her. You haven't forgotten your mommy, have you?"

Kurt looked at the ground and shook his head.

"Well, that's great. I know she would be so happy to know that you have people in America who care so much about you."

When Kurt heard Belle call out from the opening door, "Kurt, are you here?" he jumped up and politely excused himself. "I have to help with the groceries."

Miss Frank grabbed Kurt's hand and told him how much she enjoyed their "private" conversation before he hurried out of the room. While the worker sat in the living room she could hear Kurt whispering and then Belle answer, "That's fine, Kurt. I hope you entertained her and didn't let her sit alone."

Kurt brought the last groceries into the kitchen before he ran out of the building. When Belle walked into the living room she immediately apologized. "I thought we weren't meeting until later, Eleanor, and…"

"Truth be told, my prior appointment cancelled. So since I was already in the area, I took a chance that you might be here. Kurt has been a great host in your absence."

"Later worker told Mrs. W that worker thought that the W's should not possess any hopes of the possibility of adopting Kurt because of the committee's commitment to the government rather than because of the existence of the mother in Europe. Worker suggested that it would be better for Kurt to feel that the W's loved him very much without having to adopt. Mrs. W indicated that she understood this and recognized that Kurt could be just as much their own child but said that her husband had hoped that it might be possible to adopt Kurt. She thought that it might make Kurt feel more secure to use their name and be adopted. Worker suggested that, since adoption was impossible, Kurt must understand that his use of W did not change his identity as Kurt Walker...worker indicated...that Mrs. W explain to Kurt that the matter of legal adoption did not in any way affect the amount of love which they gave him." Eleanor J. Frank, JCB

Days later, on August 22, 1944, Eleanor Frank made her last entry in Kurt's file. "On worker's last visit to the home worker explained that she was leaving the agency and that someone else would be responsible for the supervision of Kurt."

On October 22, 1944, the first entries were made by Kurt's new worker, Dorothy Alter. "...the family is moving to 3720 North Lake Shore Drive apt. 8B, telephone number Buck 6505" and "...the mother was last heard from about Nov '41 when she was interned in a camp in France and Heinz was with the grandmother in Germany."

OCTOBER 1, 1944

"Dear Kurt,

Today our son you are one year oldand all
the world, with all its gold could never bring,
oh nowhere near the joy you've brought in just
one year. We hope we've made you happy too,
that you love us as we love you. Like every
boy you're sometimes bad. But even then we love
you, lad. Mostly, though, you're so darn sweet.
You're really good enough to eat. So be a good
boy and then a good man, and we will always
work and plan to be the best parents a boy ever
hadGod bless you and love, Your Mommy and Daddy
WLYAYLUAAW!"

First birthday card from the Wagners to Kurt, dated October 1,
1944

"Gurs May 1, 1941

My Dear little Kurt!

...be good and study well so that I am very
pleased with you...Sincerest congratulations on
your upcoming birthday, dear Kurtle, wishing
you the best of luck and everything good from
us all. We hope that we will be able to spend
the next birthday together again. Now, dear
Kurtle, I am very sorry that I can't send you

anything, that I no longer have any money and can't get any from anyone...."

D ays before Kurt received his birthday card from the Wagners and moved to his new exclusive apartment overlooking Lake Michigan, the bombings in Karlsruhe started again. The resulting destruction left Kurt's unknown cousin, Gerhardt, and hysterical aunt Martha fleeing past the dead bodies and rubble to a vacant apartment in the same building where Heinz and his grandparents lived. Gerhardt, who had reached his tenth birthday on September 1, 1944, accepted the destruction of his home, just as he learned to accept the fact that his Wehrmacht soldier father was a prisoner of war. The loss of his home happily afforded him the opportunity to join Heinz's gang of neighborhood boys, who with sticks and stones stood in defense of their apartment building and nearby streets.

Gerhardt's serious face hid the thrill he felt as he met with the gang in the small building that housed the communal handcranked washing machines. Not a single boy said a word while they waited for the disinterested woman to close the door that ensured the gang's privacy. Heinz took one last look out a window before he pulled out the hidden signs that he and the other older boys had prepared. He whispered to the younger boys, "Nail them on the doors and then run."

It was another four days before a tip led the SS to arrest Heinz, Gerhardt, and the rest of the gang on suspicion of being spies. For the bored boys whose work and schooling had been disrupted by the bombings, their actions of placing signs that read "Death Will Destroy You!" was meant as a joke. But that was not the interpretation by the SS, who after many hours of intimidation and whippings released the weeping boys to their parents.

When the children, under the watchful eyes of the SS, were released from the police station, the parents yelled at their gang member child for dishonoring the führer, Germany, and family. Heinz remained mute as he limped behind his younger cousin. He had been afraid, but he made sure to hold back his tears. Gerhardt ran into his mother's arms while Christian screamed at Heinz. Christian maintained his angry appearance until they were out of sight of the SS. It was only then that he allowed himself the luxury of a tearful embrace with Heinz.

When Heinz reached the bottom step outside the station, the plump, red-faced Wilhelm and a small group of boys were staring at him. Their minimal efforts to hide around the corner were infuriating. Heinz was barely able to take an angry step toward them before he felt the viselike grip of his grandfather. Christian looked at the uniformed leader. "Who cares if he was the one, Heinz—it's over!"

"That's wrong, Heinz. It's not over," shouted Wilhelm. Heinz chewed away at the inside of his bleeding mouth.

"<u>The Home:</u> The Wagners now have a very beautiful and adequate home...at the present time they have five large rooms in one of the Lake Shore Drive skyscrapers (8th floor). Kurt has a room that might be described as being every boy's dream. It has something of a ranch atmosphere and has every little detail that is close to every boy's heart, a large desk, beautiful red leather furniture, a Hollywood bed, bookcases half way around the room filled with books, all sorts of knick-knacks including a good sized covered wagon with a team of horses, etc. Kurt told Mrs. Wagner that if he should die he hopes he will have as nice a room in heaven...."

JCB entry by Dorothy Alter

THEY ARE ALL DEAD

During the fourteen months after Kurt's Bar Mitzvah, the Wagners maintained regular contact with Kurt's legal guardian, the Jewish Children's Bureau of Chicago. Even though the bureau was making fewer demands upon the Wagners, Belle made sure that Dorothy Alter knew that the Wagners were providing for all of Kurt's needs. Belle took great pride in presenting glowing reports about Kurt's health, active social life, and educational accomplishments.

On August 4, 1946, almost three years since Kurt's placement with the Wagners, Dorothy Alter waved Belle into her office. Dorothy received her usual hug from Belle instead of the formal handshake from many of her other foster parents. Without asking, Dorothy left her office to complete the ritual of providing cups of coffee. The women gossiped and laughed so hard that Dorothy had to close her office door. In reality, there had not been enough telephone calls or face-to-face contacts between the two women to establish a true friendship, but for some reason they had clicked from their first meeting.

"I was at Marshall Field's and I thought I would drop by and say hello, Dorothy."

"Mary Lawrence told me that you were just here," responded Dorothy as she blew on the hot cup of coffee. There was no reaction from Belle, who felt she had been caught even as Dorothy went on, none the wiser, "Mary told me you've been here a number of times recently, but I'm in the field so much. Just give me a little notice and I will do my best to rearrange my schedule to see you."

Belle jabbed at the melting cubes of sugar with a pencil while she looked for the right moment. "So would you like to hear about my Kurt?" The resulting pause brought about another round of laughter that ended when Belle started listing things that had happened to Kurt since they last talked. Dorothy enjoyed Belle's enthusiastic and heartfelt stories.

"He's going to be a freshman at Francis. I'm sure he is going to do very well. And what a summer Kurt had!" Belle name-dropped JCB board member Nicholas Pritzker. "Mr. Pritzker's grandson, Donny, has been best friends with Kurt since he started at Parker. In fact, Kurt spent a month with Donny and his family in Eagle River, Michigan. Wag and I sure missed him, though. Just like last year, they swam, fished, and rode on horses. Then they took him to a ranch in Wyoming. Of course Wag and I were sad, but it was good for Kurt. At least that's what my Wag said to me every day while I had a sick puppy dog look on my face.

"When he came home, we went to New York and saw the sights, Radio City Music Hall, Statute of Liberty, and musicals. He loved *Annie Get your Gun* and *Show Boat*. We did all the touristy things. He had so much fun. That Kurt, he's doing it all. Wag and I are so lucky. He's such a nice boy. But then you already know that."

"Belle, you've given Kurt a great life. You make a wonderful family."

"Dorothy, I guess that's the problem," said Belle. She walked to the open window and looked at the train screeching on the elevated tracks that circled downtown Chicago. The noise was so loud that Belle had to stop talking. Her mind raced through her mental outline that she had prepared during the prior sleepless nights. She continued to look out the window even after the train passed. "Over the weekend Kurt had been playing outside, and some of the boys were giving him a hard time. You know how we have discussed this before. Anyway, I was making lunch for Wag, and Kurt came into the house crying like a baby. Wag started pulling up Kurt's sleeves and then his shorts to see where he is bleeding, and of course there is nothing there." Belle sighed. "And then he runs up to me and puts his arms around me and he is crying so hard that my new blouse got all wet. Can you imagine that someone could cry so much…"

Belle returned to her chair. "Wag said something like, 'Kurt, what's the matter?' But Kurt didn't say a word. He just stood there crying. So I took Kurt's hand and we walked over to the kitchen table and sat down next to Wag. We are just staring at each other and finally, out of nowhere, Kurt says, 'What's a blood relative?' Wag and I didn't know what to say. We must have looked like a couple of goofs with our mouths open. Then Kurt asks, 'Why can't I be a blood relative with you and Daddy?' To be honest with you, I was so taken back by how upset he was, and then he asks a question like that…" Belle tried to read Dorothy's thoughts.

Dorothy looked at Belle's face as the lines in her forehead became more pronounced and her eyes reddened. "When we calmed Kurt down, I took his hand and we all went into his bed-room. I mustered up the biggest smile I could and told him to wait. I'm sure I confused him when I ran out of the room. When I returned, we all sat on the floor in a circle holding hands telling each other how much we loved each other. While Wag was talking I pulled out a pin from my sewing kit and pricked my finger, then Wag's, and finally Kurt's. Then without missing a beat

Wag took our fingers and rubbed them together. He said, 'Now we are blood relatives. We are a family, and no one can ever take that from us." I looked at Kurt and he is nodding his head and smiling. Pretty childish, I guess, but little things like that seem to help Kurt. I think it makes him feel like no one is going to take him and that he's loved. At least that's what I think."

"Is that how Kurt feels or you and your husband?"

Belle looked at Dorothy but said nothing.

"Belle, are you afraid Kurt is going to be taken from you?" Belle looked back at the window and answered with a non sequitur. "I saw the report on Mary Lawrence's desk the last time I was here. The file was on her desk and I just started to read it. When Mary stepped out of her office…I did not want to forget, so I wrote it down on a scrap of paper. I wanted to show it to Wag."

"Belle, what you are talking about?"

"Dorothy, Mary called me on the phone because she had some questions about Kurt, and I told her that I would see her the next day. You know I am always happy to do what the JCB wants. I just came in because I thought it would be better." Dorothy was lost trying to understand Belle, who pulled out the scrap of paper and read,

"The record indicates little possibility of Kurt's finding natural ties or any cause for leaving this family."

"I wrote it down because I thought Wag would want to know that we don't have to worry anymore, that they won't take Kurt from us. I also saw the letter that Kurt sent to his mother from New York when he first came here. I saw it was returned. It had the word 'Infirmary' on the envelope, and it left no forwarding address. After I saw that, I left a note on Mary's desk that said I wasn't feeling well."

Belle's hands started to tremble. "I know this sounds terrible, but Ilse is dead. She has to be. And I don't wish it upon her or Kurt, but that is the truth."

Dorothy stopped looking at Belle and returned to Kurt's file. She pulled out a letter dated June 7, 1946, from Mary Lawrence to Deborah S. Portnoy of the European Jewish Children's Aid Inc. and read it out loud,

```
"Dear Miss Portnoy:

Mrs. Wagner, foster mother of Kurt, tells us
that they are in touch with the Weils here and
that neither they nor anyone else has had any
word from Kurt's people.

                    Sincerely yours,

                    (Mrs.) Mary Lawrence
                    Associate Executive
                    Director"
```

"Belle, is that true? Have you been in touch with the Weils? Did they tell you anything about Kurt's family? It's important that you tell us the truth."

There was no response. Dorothy skimmed through the thick file that she admittedly had not reviewed in some time. "Belle, did you ever talk to Jacob Kepecs? He's the executive director for the bureau."

"I've never met him."

"Have you been in contact with the Children's Aid in New York?"

Dorothy didn't let Belle answer. "Are you telling me the truth? You have not looked at Kurt's file other than what you just told me?"

"On the life of Kurt I have not."

"Then let me read this to you. It's from the field representative of the European Jewish Children's Aid Inc., dated May 6, 1946:

"I am writing to ask if you or Kurt's foster parents have received any message from Kurt's cousin, Heinrich Weil in Chicago, about Kurt's mother, grandfather or older brother.

Mr. Kepecs asked Miss Marcuse to make a special request of the Location Service for information about Mrs. Walker. The latest information in our file was a notation that mail addressed to her at Camp de Gurs in November 1942 was returned. The location agency's special efforts in such situations would be to obtain testimony from people who were deported with her or had heard from her later than the relatives here. If the relatives here are able to give us such clues, if they have had any communications about or from Mrs. Walker other than those you and we know about, tracing

these are our only hope of obtaining more
definite information.

> We are writing to the relatives in
> Brooklyn...
>
> Sincerely yours,
>
> Deborah S. Portnoy
>
> Field Representative"

"Belle, that was why Mary contacted you. She wanted to know the whereabouts of Kurt's family." Dorothy was angry at herself for her laziness. She quickly reviewed more documents and placed them in front of Belle. "I am going to get some coffee, Belle, and I will be back in fifteen minutes."

Belle looked back at the closed door before she grabbed a document with the heading of "Roos-message-War-information. May 2, 1946."

"This is a letter from Deborah Portnoy to Mr. Roos in New York about Kurt's family. Why are they writing to them?" whispered Belle. She looked over her shoulder.

"Since the war in Europe has ended, we know
that there have been messages from some survivors. If you have no recent message would you
know of any other relative, either in the United
States or in Europe, with whom we might communicate with for further information."

Belle picked up another document.

"Memo from Portnoy to Sadina Jacobson, Location Unit, dated May 8, 1946. Re: Walker, Ilse (nee Ettlinger) last known address on July 1945 camp de Gurs Ilot J. Infirmary, NRS file #S8185."

"I don't understand," commented Belle. "The camp was liberated by August 1944, and after that they used it to house Nazi prisoners. How could her last known address in July 1945 be the camp? This is insane. I mean, Kurt's letter to his mother came back stating that she was gone."

Belle massaged the sides of her temples. "This is a request for a special search, which we understand the Central Location Index is willing to undertake in certain particular situations.

The situation of Kurt Walker, son of the above mentioned Ilse Walker, we believe merits this special consideration, since the local agency and EJCA feel that a permanent plan with a view to adoption should be made for him, if his mother is no longer alive."

"My God," muttered Belle.

"At the time of Kurt's departure from Europe, in July 1942, his mother was in Camp de Gurs, where she, Kurt, and her father, Isaak Loeb Ettlinger, had been interned in October 1940. There has been no communication from Kurt's mother since he came to the United States. A

```
letter sent to notify her of his safe arrival
was returned with a notation 'Parti san Laiser
Addresse.' We are writing to the local agency to
ask if Mrs. Walker's distant relatives living in
the United States have received any subsequent
information. In 1944, we filed a location appli-
cation for Kurt's family. We had no more recent
information about them, but if we obtain any,
we will forward it to you."
```

She grabbed the letter from Selma Roos. "Thank God, she knows nothing about Ilse. I need to call Wag and tell him they want to help us. My God, my God, my God, they want us to adopt Kurt," cried Belle with happiness as she picked up the May 28, 1946, letter from Portnoy to a Dr. Senator in Forest Hills, New York.

```
"I am writing to ask your help in locating
information about one Ilse Walker nee Ettlinger
who was born in 1905 in Rastatt Germany."
```

"That's not true," thought Belle. "Ilse was born in 1906, and that other memo spelled Kurt's grandfather's name wrong."

```
"We have learned from the Central Location
Index that someone by the name Walker co Joint
Distribution Committee Berlin Zehlendorf,
Germany as trying to locate you. If you have
contacted this person in Berlin was the first
name Ilse or do you think there's some chance
that they might be related?"
```

Belle sat in the chair like a punch-drunk fighter who had nothing left. "Now she is alive. What are we going to do, Wag?"

asked Belle. She wiped her tears off the paper and read the last sentence on the short note from Dr. Senator.

```
"Referring to your inquiry about one Ilse
Walker nee Ettlinger who is supposed to try to
locate us, I am sorry to advise you that we have
not the slightest idea who this person could
be."
```

"This is too much, just too much," cried Belle.

By the time Dorothy returned, Belle had composed herself from the newest roller coaster ride that confirmed, at least in her mind, that Ilse was dead and the JCB and the European Jewish Children's Aid wanted Kurt to be adopted. After Belle hugged Dorothy good-bye, the worker completed her summary for the quarterly report that was sent to the EJCA:

```
"Mrs. Wagner is apparently anxious about go-
ing through formal adoption of Kurt and hopes
nothing will interfere with his permanent stay
with them. When she was in to see me I gave her
some support and assurances for which she seems
to be thankful. The record indicates little
possibility of Kurt's finding natural ties or
any cause for leaving this family."
```

THE SECOND KNOCK
ON THE DOOR

On January 10, 1945, neither the heavy flak from antiaircraft guns nor the freezing rain could prevent the four planes from dropping their bombs on the Karlsruhe railway yards near the Bahnhofplatz—the same Bahnhofplatz Isack Ettlinger returned to after World War I, and that Kurt and his family were taken to before they were taken to Camp de Gurs. For Heinz, the prior 135 emotionally devastating air raid warnings and resulting bombings terrorized him. The worst period, April through December 1944, saw thirteen separate incendiary bomb attacks, including the September 27, 1944, bombing of the Adolph-Hitler-Platz. The Schloss was no more, and its grounds were reduced to vegetable gardens in a sad attempt to supplement the meager food rations for Karlsruhe's citizens. The administration building and the golden boy that sat at its top, along with the Protestant church, were reduced to mountains of rubble. Amazingly, the pyramid, the final resting place for Margrave Karl Wilhelm von Baden-Durlach, who had fallen asleep in the woods and dreamed of a new city, remained undamaged.

Hitler's suicide on April 30, 1945, was followed quickly by Germany's unconditional surrender on May 7, 1945. For Heinz and most of the other Germans, the war had been over for a long time. The cost to Germany was seven million lives, almost 9.5 percent of the German prewar population. On April 5, 1945, a month before Germany's surrender, the city of Karlsruhe, the former "... gloomy forest that stretched from Durlach, the seat of the Margraves of Baden, to the impenetrable swamps and unchartered backwaters of the Rhine..." surrendered to the French First Army. Days before France's invasion, Christian Walker received ominous news, a more personal assault that had begun when Heinz had been attacked by fellow uniformed boys. They had tried to pull his pants down to confirm if the Jewish rumors were true. The unsuccessful attack left the Walkers with no options other than to secret Heinz away in order to avoid the certain death of the last Jew in Karlsruhe.

By the end of the war, ten thousand tons of bombs that were dropped on Karlsruhe resulted in the total destruction of 34 percent of all of its structures and the partial destruction of the vast majority of the remaining buildings. One thousand seven hundred and forty-five people died and three thousand five hundred and eight people were injured, and Heinz witnessed it all. His city was gone. What remained were painful memories that he tried to sweep away.

The lazy knock on the door to the Walker apartment on July 30, 1946, conveyed no sense of urgency for Heinz's grandmother. She had just completed drying the last breakfast dish and was getting ready to leave the apartment on one of her many daily trips to the food ration lines. When she opened the door, she was greeted by an American representative from the Red Cross and a bored American soldier whose M-1 rifle rested in his lap.

"Are you Frau Walker?" asked the Red Cross worker.

"Yes," followed the instant reply.

"I am looking for a Heinz Walker."

"Interpretation for Kurt Walker:

...The contrast between verbal and performance scores agrees with the findings of a year ago.... In both instances the inconsistencies can be interpreted as to due to neurotic inhibitions of intellectual functioning.

There are a great many references to food in the record probably indicating an unsatisfied need for basic satisfactions during the early years of his life. Definite neurotic shock is indicated on the Rorschach. The TAT...did suggest recurring themes. There is the feeling that the woman betrays the man and that the man is ashamed and hurt (possibly his own reaction to his early experience of being deserted by his mother, i.e. his interpretation of the physical separation). He is desirous of the approval of the father and is successful in attaining it at least in fantasy.

Conclusion:

Kurt is a boy with...possible superior intelligence (on the basis of the W-B and Rorschach)... Psychotherapy would be helpful in releasing him from handicapping constrictions and enable him to utilize his endowment more adequately.

University of Chicago Guidance Clinic"

THE HEART ATTACK

Wag's heart attack was followed by two months in bed before he returned to a work schedule of four days a week. He understood that this was necessary to take "...every precaution to prolong his life." His larger-than-life personality remained a constant. So did his comforting refrain as the year 1946 came to an end. "The only reason I want to take care of myself is to make sure that I made it to another Pritzker holiday party."

When Wag walked into Kurt's room in his bathrobe on a lazy winter Saturday afternoon, Kurt jumped with the mere mention of his name. "What have you got there, partner?" asked Wag of Kurt, who slammed shut his desk drawer.

"Nothing, Da-Da."

"Mr. Wagner told me of how Kurt can get anything he wants out of him when he calls him 'Da-Da.'"

Wag suppressed his smile in order to appear to be the disciplinarian he never was. "Kurt, I either caught you in something you should not have been doing or you want something."

"Aw, Pops, come on—that's not true. Well, not always true. So how you feeling, Pops?" asked Kurt. He pressed the closed desk drawer one more time.

Wags pushed Kurt's hand aside. He opened the drawer.

"I haven't seen this wallet in years. Isn't that the photograph of your mother? And that one is of your grandfather?" A broad smile filled Wag's face. "And Kurt, is that you? You were so little."

Kurt could barely look at Wag. "Kurt, you never talk about your family," began Wag as he confronted the unspoken past that lived with Kurt, Wag, and Belle.

"Mr. Wagner did tell me that this grandfather is the only person about whom Kurt ever spoke. He never mentions his parents nor his brother and it was the impression of the Wagners that the children were separated when they were very young, at the time of the divorce"

"Pops, do you remember when I started Hebrew school at Anshe Emet and I got into a fight that first day? It kept happening even after you wrote to Rabbi Goldman. Mommy got so upset that she would not let me go to summer camp because so many of those boys were going to be at the same camp. Every day they said I would stink up the place because I was German and because of my German accent."

"Sure, I remember."

"This was of course during the war when youngsters showed marked hostility toward anything German."

Kurt put the wallet back in the drawer. He looked out his bedroom window hoping that Wag would leave, but he knew better.

"Sit with me, son?" asked Wag.

"When I was in Germany," said Kurt flatly, "I was a dirty Jew, and when I came to America I was a dirty German." He was still small at four feet nine inches and just ninety pounds. Next to a sick Wag, he looked like a fragile doll. He whimpered, "I just don't want to leave here." It was all Wag could do to stop himself from crying as he watched the first of many tears from Kurt.

"Considering Kurt's background from the little information we have, the Wagners seem to have done a remarkable job with the boy. They tell me when Kurt first came to their home his feelings of inferiority and insecurity were marked."

Kurt buried his face in Wag's chest. "Mommy and I love you, Kurt. We love everything about you, including your German accent."

"The Wagners tell me that from the start Kurt found it easier to relate to Mr. Wagner. They seem to think that it was because he feared for an attachment for a woman having his own mother. I would interpret it rather to the contrary, namely that because he had a poor relationship with his mother he found it more difficult to relate to a woman..."

"I don't want you to think I don't love you. I don't want you to get rid of me like the Kastels did."

"Kurt, what are you talking about? This is crazy talk."

"I know what Mommy's sister said when we lived on Belmont. I always pretended like I was asleep when Aunt Sadie came down from her apartment for a visit. I heard her each time, because she wanted me to hear her."

"What did she say?" asked a disheartened Wag.

"It wasn't just what she said—it was what all of them said," answered Kurt. "Pop, promise me that you won't say anything to Mommy. I don't want her to get upset."

Wag crossed his heart. "Never, pal."

"I know Aunt Sadie and Mommy were so close. It was easy for Aunt Sadie to just come down one flight of stairs every day for a visit."

Wag tried to diffuse the situation. He joked, "And most nights for dinner."

"Well, that's part of it, Pops. I know why Aunt Sadie stopped coming to the apartment and why she doesn't come here. It's because of me."

"What are you talking about, Kurt?" followed Wag.

"She used to tell Mommy it was a mistake to take me, because I was a Kraut—you know with my accent and everything. That all Germans are arrogant and that I would leave my shoes outside my door of the apartment to be cleaned. She would get so mad because she could not spend time with Mommy like she used to, and the only reason she couldn't was because of me."

"Now you listen to me, Kurt," answered Wag, whose voice rose for one of the few times that Kurt had ever heard. "When you came here, my life and Mommy's changed for sure. Remember how physical you used to be? Mommy even had to cut her hair very short because of the way you wrestled with her. That first year you wore me out with the wrestling, the ball games, skating, swimming, bowling, and tennis."

"Now, since Mr. Wagner is no longer able to engage in such activities, he feels satisfied that he has given Kurt all he could and Kurt needed..."

"Every night Mommy and I helped you with your homework and we worked with you on your accent. You were so upset when you went to the museum with Mommy and you talked into the phone of the future and it played back your voice. I kept telling you we just need to work on your v's and w's."

"He would take two words like 'Very Well,' particularly difficult for Kurt to pronounce, and would drill him for days and weeks. One morning Kurt dashed into Mr. Wagner's room and asked him to inquire about how he felt, and Kurt replied in a perfect accent 'very well.' Mr. Wagner told of Kurt's discouragement, how he would cry and worry as to whether he would ever be able to get the correct accent. Mr. Wagner compared him to a fighter, asked him whether he couldn't do the same and put a punch into every word. On this particular morning Kurt came into the bedroom with his boxing gloves and punched out his words, 'very well' much to the delight of the Wagners."

Wag punched the air with his fists. "And remember you kept bothering us for a dog, and I said no every day until I came home to see that Mommy bought you Kibby?" Wag dropped his fists and shook his head. "I hate dogs, and now Mommy has me walking a toy collie around the neighborhood for exercise. Do you know how silly I look? Me, a grown man walking a tiny dog."

"Her name is Kibby, the first three letters taken from the name of Kurt and the Wagners." JCB entry by Dorothy Alter dated January 13, 1947

Suddenly Wag felt dizzy. He sucked in some air with his open mouth and produced an unintentional whistling sound. "A perfect C," sang Wag's failed attempt at humor before the room fell quiet again.

"Mrs. Wagner told me that in the early days when the previous worker would visit, he felt decidedly threatened, would ask Mrs. Wagner why anybody had to visit since she was not getting paid for his care."

"Kurt, I love you, and Mommy loves you, and if you don't know that then somehow we have failed you."

"The Wagners tell me that Kurt still enjoys reading fairy tales, wants his kiss at bed time and indications are all around that he is still is somewhat emotionally retarded."

"You have no idea what you have given us. When you get older and you have your own family, you will understand. You gave us a life. You gave us a family."

"I was told that when Mr. Wagner...had a serious heart attack, Kurt was quite upset and when Mr. Wagner returned home, Kurt with his own savings purchased a bowl of goldfish for him. He reasoned that during the long hours Mr. Wagner would be bedridden at home, that it might be distracting for him to watch the goldfish from

time to time. Mr. Wagner has never forgotten
this..."

JCB entries by Dorothy Alter dated January 13, 1947

"Each day helping you with your homework, going to the ball
game...I mean I got to see the Cubs in the World Series with my
son. That was not a chore but a joy. I have been blessed with a
wonderful life, and that is because you are my son."

"The Wagners are very warm people and I observed that they melt away at the sight of Kurt."

"We will always be a part of you and you will always be a part
of us. You are our son and nothing will ever change that. Do you
understand? I want to hear you say that. I want you to say that out
loud. Not just for you, but for me?"

"Where are my boys?" yelled Belle. "Kibby needs to go out."

"Always and always," answered Kurt.

"Me too," mouthed Wag. "Say," whispered Wag, "how about
I get dressed and we sneak out of here and get a hot dog with
all the trimmings? Make sure you don't say anything to Mom.
Oh, and one more thing. No more vacations out west with the
Pritzkers. I don't think my lonely heart can take you being away
so long. My letters to you are not enough for me, pal."

"They showed me several of Kurt's letters at
the time he was away...one of which he says 'I
almost kissed the mailman when he brought your
letter."

"You got it, Pops. I'll take Kibby out for a walk first," said
Kurt, looping his thumb into his pocket.

"Recently they were kidding Kurt about wanting to adopt a girl to which Kurt replied 'I think everyone should be satisfied with what they got' showing a rather negative reaction toward the presence of any other child in the house."

After Kurt returned to the apartment, Wag slowly closed the door on a barking Kibby. Kurt and Wag quietly tiptoed down the hallway until Wag screamed, "Now, partner!" Seconds later, they ran arm in arm past their startled neighbors to the elevator.

"...In a very pathetic tone, Mr. Wagner told me he only wants to live long enough to see Kurt on his own, much as any father would say about his natural son."

JCB entries by Dorothy Alter dated January 13, 1947

THE LETTER

On December 17, 1946, Belle received a phone call from the JCB. On the following Friday, the twentieth, Belle glided through the snow to the JCB with bags of Hanukkah and Christmas gifts. She pushed through the frosted revolving door at 130 North Wells and into the lobby where she greeted every person. In all the years she had been coming to the bureau she had become a creature of habit in which she always took elevator number two. She liked the way the elderly Irish operator always wished everyone a "good day." Belle kicked off the snow from her boots before she entered the crowded elevator and beat the smiling operator with a "good day and merry Christmas."

When Belle entered Dorothy's office, she reminded herself to not talk so much since she promised Wag and Kurt that she would be on time for the Pritzkers' Hanukkah party. The ritual hugs were quickly exchanged before Dorothy presented her with the waiting coffee with three bobbing cubes of sugar. "Happy Hanukkah, Dorothy," sang Belle. She presented her with a small wrapped gift. Dorothy's tearful thank you was never completed. "Dorothy, it's just a box of candy. Besides, you're too skinny."

When Mary Lawrence walked into the office, she greeted Belle with her own warm embrace. She stared at Dorothy with a look that screamed, "Knock it off!" Belle, uncertain, asked, "What's happening with my Kurt? Wag and I have not said a word to Kurt. We want to surprise him just before we go to court for the adoption." The bizarre silence found Belle answering her own question. "The meeting is about the adoption, isn't it?"

Mary Lawrence quickly responded. "There is a problem, Belle."

"What kind of problem? I thought everyone wanted the adoption to proceed."

"Belle, they found Heinz and Isack," said Mary. She produced the paper clipped group of documents from Kurt's inches-thick file. "We just received a report from a location service, the United Service for New Americans dated December 2, 1946, and a letter from Deborah S. Portnoy to me dated December 10, 1946."

Belle's lips moved quickly as she inhaled the information.

```
"December 2, 1946
```

```
According to the report just received from our
representatives in Germany, Heinz WALKER, born
in 1929, is presently living Buntestrasse 3,
Karlsruhe (Germany). He is in good health and
resides with his grandfather. His mother was
deported.
```

```
P.S. Please convey the above report to your ap-
plicant in the event he is not already aware of
this information."
```

```
"December 10, 1946
```

```
...that Kurt's brother, Heinz born in 1929 is
living with his grandfather, Isaac Ettlinger....
This information came through the American
Joint Distribution Committee, Paris....We shall
```

be interested in knowing how you and the foster
family decide to use this information."

"This is impossible," said Belle. She flung the papers on
Dorothy's desk. "I don't believe it. First of all, Heinz was not born
in 1929, he was born in 1930. And what do they mean Heinz is
living with Isack? That's not even how you spell his name. He
was an old man when all of this started. He could not have lived
through all of this. And didn't his wife die in the camp? We all
know that's true." The women did not try to stop Belle. "What
does is mean that the mother was deported? It does not say anything else. Are they trying to say she is alive? This is silly, just silly.
Why are they even doing this? And why do they even care?"

"Mr. Kepecs is the executive director of the bureau. He had
no choice. The problem is…" said Mary, just as the petite Belle
shot up from her chair and banged the desk yelling, "There is no
problem."

Dorothy gently guided Belle to her seat. "The predicament
is that New York wants to know what the bureau, you, and your
husband want to do with this information."

Belle felt empowered by Dorothy's last words. "I will contact
Ilse's uncle Heinrich. I'm sure they will not say anything to Kurt,
especially since he has not talked to him in years, but I will ask
them to try to contact Heinz and the grandfather right away.
When they get back to me I will contact you."

Belle felt like a general making clear and decisive decisions.
"To answer Mr. Kepecs's question, we do nothing. We do absolutely nothing, and the reason we do nothing is because this information is not true. It is not true. It is not true. It is not true."
Belle reached out to the women. "Wag and I have always tried

to do whatever was asked of us. I am so appreciative of not only the both of you but everyone in the bureau and everyone in New York. You have allowed Wag, Kurt, and I to have a family, and I can never repay you. I also understand you have a job and you have to answer this letter, but this…"

Belle stopped in midsentence. "My husband is not a well man, and any time an issue is raised regarding Kurt he gets terribly upset. He becomes physically ill. Now, even if you accept that Isack is alive and living with Heinz, how will that information help anyone? I'm sure Kurt believes that Isack is dead and has come to terms with this. He has barely mentioned Isack, let alone Ilse. And as to Heinz," Belle chose her words carefully. "Kurt does not look at him as a brother. I can assure you of this."

Mary and Dorothy refused to interrupt. "When Kurt's parents were divorced he was three. I'll bet you anything that Heinz went to live with the father who had remarried and lived in Stuttgart with his gentile wife. What do you think happened? We all know they raised Heinz to be a full-blooded gentile and Nazi like his father. Kurt's family—they were murdered by the Nazis. Do we want Kurt to make contact with the Nazi son of the Nazi father?"

Belle picked up a handful of the papers from Kurt's file and waved it in the air. "Now if Heinz is living with his grandfather that could only happen because his father and stepmother were killed. I know Kurt loved Isack. I know that he was the one who raised him while Ilse was out trying to earn money to keep the family afloat. It makes no sense that Isack would take on the responsibilities of taking care of the Nazi's son. I want to be clear. You asked me what we should do, and here again is my answer, nothing. And I do not want Kurt or Wag to know anything about Isack or Heinz or any of this."

After Belle left the bureau, Dorothy Alter dictated a letter to Lotte Marcuse, director of placements at the European Jewish Children's Aid Inc. that was signed off by Mary Lawrence. The closing paragraph of the letter stated:

```
"Since as you are aware, Kurt has an un-
usually fine home, we feel that the matter of
this information should depend entirely upon
the wishes of the foster parents and have told
them so. We therefore hope that there will be
no direct communication with Kurt between his
grandfather, brother and him."
```

On Tuesday afternoon, New Year's Eve, 1947, Dorothy placed a telephone call to Belle and read a letter from Lotte Marcuse dated December 26, 1946:

```
"We have your letter indicating Mrs. Wagner's
attitude about the correspondence from Kurt's
brother. We assume that you agree with her
decision not to reveal to Kurt that he has a
brother living. Does this mean that you and the
Wagners have thought of their home as a possi-
ble adoptive one, and if so, would you be ready
at this time to proceed with whatever action is
necessary to complete the adoption?

It would be important it seems to us for Mr.
and Mrs. Wagner to realize if they decide not
to tell Kurt that his brother is living, that
```

they must be prepared someday to tell him and to explain why they made this decision.

Since Kurt's relatives, the Weils, know about Heinz, is there not a chance too that Kurt will find out from them?

If the Judge of our Court which has jurisdiction over adoptions is willing to accept a petition with what little we know about the probable death of Kurt's parents, would you ask for guardianship, so that the agency can later consent to the adoption? This would be the procedure as clarified in our conference of agency executives in Chicago in April 1945."

"Belle, they are saying you can adopt Kurt," reassured Mary. "We need to talk. Can I stop by and see you and Wag?"

THE NEW YEAR–1947

```
"When Kurt came into this home at age 12
12, he started we might say at 'scratch' as
far as his emotional background was concerned.
According to the Wagners he was at first some-
what overwhelmed over the amount of affection
he received, told them that the only kiss he
recalls was one from his maternal grandfather
at a time he was taking a trip..."
```

JCB entry by Dorothy Alter dated January 13, 1947

When the doorbell rang on the evening of January 9, 1947, Kurt ran to the door yelling, "I got it."

"Kurt—look at you! You look like a man, not like a little boy," remarked Dorothy.

Kurt led Dorothy to the living room where she was embraced by Belle and kissed on the cheek by Wag. "Please give me your coat. How have your holidays been?" beamed Wag. She had no chance to respond as Kurt excitedly talked about their post-New Year's party where eventual household names such as Irv Kupcinet, Paul Harvey, and Studs Terkel attended.

When Kurt spoke, his speech was instinctive, no longer guard-ed, and totally absent of any German accent. "Did you know that Daddy hired Mr. Terkel for his radio show? Have you ever lis-tened to it? Mommy loves the show."

"Well, Kurt…"

"In fact, when Mr. Terkel came to our house, he brought me some records. And Mr. Kupcinet and Mr. Harvey…"

"Enough, Kurt," said Wag. He playfully grabbed Kurt from behind and placed his hand over his mouth. By the time Belle returned to the living room with coffee and cookies, Kurt had broken free from Wag. He peppered Dorothy with questions, punching out each word with his fists into Wag's palms.

"How"—boom—"are"—smack—"you"—smash—"Mrs."—pow—"Alter?"

"This is the way it is every night, Dorothy," laughed Wag.

Dorothy punched the air. "I enjoyed the boxing match."

Wag, out of breath, joined Dorothy and Belle on the couch. "Kurt, I saw Studs today, and he wanted me to give you some new records. They are on my bed." Kurt ran off as Wag yelled, "There are two Burl Ives and one Al Jolson. You can listen to them now, but excuse yourself first."

Seconds later Kurt was sliding on the wooden floors with the records. "I hope you had a happy Hanukkah and a great New Year," said Kurt. He kissed Wag. "Thanks for the records, Pop. So do we all want to listen?"

"I have an idea, Kurt," said Wag. "Since Mrs. Alter is only going to be here for a quick visit, why don't you listen to the records a few times and pick out the one you think we might all want to hear."

"You got it, Pop!" said Kurt before he ran into his bedroom where his Hanukkah present, a new phonograph player, was proudly displayed.

"September 16, 1941 Censor No. 3

...Dear little Kurt!

I too want to add my best wishes for the New Year and hope that I shall still get to know you. I am looking forward to the day when this might happen. Your dear mother tells me that you are well and so are we. It is a pity that none of us knows when we shall meet again. Then we shall have a lot to tell one another. For to- day only another greeting and a kiss from your loving Aunt Jenny"

Wag picked up a pot of coffee and filled the empty cups. "Belle told me some good news about Kurt. We have been tested like many other people in our situation. We wanted a family so badly, and for whatever reason it didn't happen. There was so much emptiness for the both of us and then to have Kurt come into our lives..."

"My God, Kurt," laughed Belle as Burl Ives's "Blue Tail Fly" interrupted the candid moment.

"Ai, ai, ai," protested Wag, smiling. He placed his hands over his ears and mouthed, "I will be right back."

When Wag returned, he wasted no time in picking up where he left off. However, this time he was more direct.

"Dorothy, Belle tells me so many good things are happening. We are so excited, and we look forward to making everything legal and doing whatever is expected of us. So where do we go from here?"

"You know I have always tried to be honest with you, but we have a new problem."

The color in Belle's face drained. "What do you mean a new problem?" Belle muttered. "I'm so tired of seeing papers." Dorothy placed a document on the glass coffee table while the booming sounds of Burl Ives's "Poor Wayfaring Stranger" carried throughout the apartment. Wag placed the single sheet of paper between himself and Belle:

```
"Letter from Lotte Marcuse to Mary Lawrence
dated December 17, 1946. I do not know who
opened the letter which was forwarded to us by
the American Joint Distribution Committee. I
thought I should know of its contents before
sending it on, and I must confess that few let-
ters from survivors have disturbed me quite as
much as this one: The brother writes that the
father died in 1943 of a heart attack. He hopes
that the mother, grandparents and Uncle Julius
are with Kurt! He assumes that Kurt suffered
greatly through the war, etc.

I wonder whether you would want us to write to
Heinz and describe the situation?"
```

Dorothy placed the referenced letter on the table. "Apparently it was the Red Cross who made contact with Heinz."

"July 30, 1946

Dear Brother Kurt:

It was with great rejoicing that I learned today
on the 39th of July, through a committee, that
you are alive and that you are happy and well
in New York City. However, with all this great
joy, I feel very sad. Where is our mother, our
grandparents and our Uncle Julius?

I wish with all my heart that they too are still
alive. I can hardly believe after such a long time
I finally heard from you. The horrible war and the
Nazism are finally over. Unfortunately, our dear
father did not live to see the end. He died already
on August 16, 1943 of a heart attack. I myself am
still with the grandparents in Bunte Street.

Karlsruhe is a city almost completely destroyed.
We too are partially bombed out. My Aunt Martha
lost everything, but we are still alive, and
lived through these terrible times. But you
dear brother have probably suffered a great
deal. However, how happy can you be dear Kurt
that you survived the horrors of the Nazi hell.
None of us will ever forget these horrors. In
spite of that we want to be grateful for our
faith and hope for a better future.

Of all the other things, I shall write to you after
I hear from you. Until then, my best and hearti-
est regards, and many kisses from your brother,

```
                         Heinz
```

P.S. Hoping that our dear Mother, our grandparents, and our uncle Julius are with you, I send them my best regards too.

```
                         Heinz
```

P.S. Many warm greetings and best wishes from my grandparents, Aunt Martha, Uncle Rudi and Gerhardt. Write soon."

"So what does this mean?" asked Wag. He looked at Kurt's closed door.

"This means we have a problem," whispered Dorothy.

Belle answered assertively, "We do not have a problem. Nothing has changed. We proceed with the adoption. Everything you have showed us is full of speculation and errors."

"Dear, please keep your voice down—remember Kurt," said Wag. He pushed the documents back to Dorothy and pulled Belle back onto the couch.

"Dorothy, are you telling us we have gone from adopting Kurt to losing him?" Belle rose to her feet again and repeated her version of the truth. "This is what I know. Ilse is dead, the Nazi father is dead, Isack is dead. They are all dead."

"September 16, 1941 Censor No. 3

My Dear Little Kurt!

I have received your letter with the little heart enclosed, it gave us all great joy. Aunt Johanna died last week from dysentery..."

"What about Heinz, Belle? What about Heinz!" pressed Dorothy.

"Listen to me, Dorothy! Heinz is dead, and if he isn't, what does a Nazi teenager have to do with Kurt's adoption? I'll answer the question. Nothing!"

"Your voice, Belle," begged Wag again. Burl Ives's voice became louder with the opening of the bedroom door. "Belle, please bring Kurt some cookies and milk," said an unflappable Wag.

"So how do you feel? Your wife has demonstrated, to say the least, a strong position."

Wag chuckled. "When it comes to Kurt, I would agree."

"But what do you think? But before you answer, I want to go over the documents that I showed Belle." Dorothy handed Wag the December 2 memo and December 10 letter from Mary Lawrence. "I wasn't aware of this," said Wag.

"Dorothy, my sense is that Belle is correct. Isack is dead, Ilse is dead, Julius is dead. I don't know after hearing all of this if Heinz is alive. I mean, the letter is five months old. Is it possible Heinz is living with Isack or the father's parents or even the father? There seems to be so many documents that say conflicting things or things that are just wrong."

Wag moved closer to Dorothy while Belle and Kurt sang together with Al Jolson. "Dorothy," whispered Wag, "I think Kurt should know everything and be involved in this. He should not be on the platform watching the train go by. In fact, he should be the engineer of the train. In a few months he will be sixteen years old. There were American kids not much older than Kurt fighting and dying in Europe and Germany a short time ago. We have no right to keep this from Kurt."

Later that evening when Wag was alone with Kurt he asked, "If we could find Heinz, would you want Mommy and me to bring him to America?"

There was no hesitation. Kurt answered, "No."

When Dorothy met with Mary Lawrence the next morning the discussion was brief. "Mary, it's clear that there is a problem, and the problem is not with Mr. Wagner, but with Mrs. Wagner."

"...when I met with Mr. Wagner, I was inclined to feel that it was not Mr. Wagner but his wife who really felt threatened by this information. In fact, Mr. Wagner, as I discussed casually the possibility of locating relatives, stated emphatically that he thought Kurt ought to know at any time that any information will be revealed about his brother or grandparents...they would be perfectly willing to take a chance of going through with adoption papers provided our agency and the Court would see fit to issue an adoption decree...I told them...we were planning to take this situation up with our Board, after which they would be told the decision."

Dorothy Alter, JCB entry, January 17, 1947

THE JEWISH CHILDREN'S BUREAU
AND THE SPECIAL MEETING

On Friday, February 28, 1947, five of the eleven members of the JCB Committee on Children in Foster Homes met with Mary Lawrence and two staffers. Judge Brandi called the meeting to order in the cramped conference room and immediately deferred to Mary Lawrence. She spoke without any notes as staffer Bertha Elman took notes that contained numerous errors.

"This meeting of the Committee on Foster Homes has been called to discuss the status of one of its children. The minutes of this meeting will be forwarded to New York so they can make the final decision," began Mary Lawrence. The board members ate their cold sandwiches and drank from their warm bottles of Coca-Cola. "The matter for review and consideration today is the adoption of a refugee child, Kurt Walker, who was born on May 17, 1931, in Karlsruhe, Germany."

Board members Julius Weiss and Lazarus Krinsley waved off the offer of another Coca-Cola as Mary Lawrence continued amid the usual sounds of laughing and screaming children running past the closed conference room door. "The father is Protestant and apparently worked in some capacity for the railroads. The mother is Jewish and is a dressmaker. If these parents are alive today, they would be about forty-three years of age. The young man arrived in Chicago on a corporate affidavit in August of 1942. The background information for Kurt admittedly has a number of holes, but the best that we have been able to determine is that the parents apparently divorced, and I remember the quote, 'under pressures of political developments in 1934.' Apparently during this process the maternal grandfather, Isaac (sic), was given guardianship of Kurt by the courts in Germany.

"When Kurt was nine, he, along with his mother and grandfather, was sent on a forced transport to a Camp de Gurs in France. Kurt has a brother, Heinz, who was twelve at the time. He remained in Karlsruhe with his father and paternal grandparents. We do not know what happened to the maternal grandmother.

"After about a year Kurt was released and sent to Maison des Pupilles de La Nation. It was run by the French. His mother stayed behind. When Kurt came here he was described as a bright, attractive boy who spoke both French and German. He refused to talk or answer questions about his father or brother. Kurt was emphatic that he wanted to be raised as an Orthodox Jew like his maternal grandfather and not like his mother, who was not religious. Before his arrival in the States, his total schooling was three years in Germany and three months in France.

There are some family members known to us, including a Mr. Roos in New York, who showed very little interest in the boy. When Kurt came here, he stayed with the Kastels, an Orthodox Jewish family who kept kosher. He was there for one year. There were a number of observations during that one-year period. I would like to refer to the worker's notes." She put on her glasses and read:

"Kurt is a very likable boy, but he had brought with him many fears. He was afraid to sleep alone, and became hysterical at the sight of a clown on the street.

He wanted, very much, to belong to the family, and talked about marrying, ultimately, the foster parents' child of 3, so that the foster parents would also be his.

He was fanatically religious, attended Services on Friday and Saturday. Ate with his hat on, would partake only of Kosher foods, etc...

...shortly after he came here he wrote a letter to his mother, which was returned marked 'Address Unknown.' That letter was sent by Kurt on August 6, 1942. This was the last word regarding Mrs. Walker. There has been absolutely no communication from the mother or the maternal grandfather since that date, and according to the European-Jewish Children's Aid Society, it can be construed that the mother was probably killed. Kurt has a distant relative in Chicago, an older man by the name of Mr. Weil, who supports himself by selling Fuller brushes. This old man has occasionally visited Kurt, but his visits seem to have little meaning. When Kurt was asked about his father he said his father was dead, and later he elaborated that he hated his father because the latter divorced his mother and because he had been abusive to her, therefore, Kurt thought, 'he might as well be dead.'"

The board members impatiently looked at their watches. Mary Lawrence was well acquainted with the significance of the wandering eyes and squirming in the uncomfortable wooden chairs. She quickly recited the remaining information.

"On October 1, 1943, Kurt moved in with the Wagners because the prior foster mother became ill. The Wagners have been married twenty-three years. He is forty-three and she is forty-two. They came to us initially in early 1943 about adopting since they were childless. They are both educated. He is a college graduate and holds an executive position with an advertising agency. The wife, Belle, is a high school graduate and was a stenographer before she married. When they first approached us, they stated their income was eight thousand dollars a year. They made a point of telling us they wanted no financial assistance. Mr. Wagner is the vice president of Olian Advertisement Company. He is presently earning twenty-five thousand.

"They enrolled Kurt in Francis Parker along with giving him private tutoring. Also, they became members of Anshe Emet, where Kurt attended Hebrew school. In October 1944, the family moved to a very comfortable apartment, 3270 North Lake Shore Drive, where he had his own room. Kurt has spent the last few summers at Eagle River with a classmate from Parker, who is the son of board member Jack Pritzker and grandson of Nicholas Pritzker, a former board member."

Upon hearing Jack Pritzker's name, the board members applauded. "Mary, make sure that Jack knows we all applauded at the mere mention of his name. Better yet, tell his father. We don't want to offend the son of the most powerful man in Chicago."

After the laughter died down, Mary continued. "The Wagners brought Kurt to New York and sent him to a ranch for summer vacation. All costs for Kurt's medical care have been paid by the Wagners. Most importantly, the Wagners look upon Kurt as their own child. They feel the adoption will give him added security.

"There is one family complication. Mr. Wagner had a second heart attack in 1945, but has made a good recovery. He still has some limitations on his activities. For example, he only goes to the office four days a week. He recently purchased a thirty-six-thousand-dollar life insurance policy."

Mary Lawrence looked at the members. "So it's up to you. I need to contact New York."

"October 21, 1941

My Dear little Kurt!

I have had your dear little letter and am glad to know that you are well I am so homesick for you. I am not at my best right now. I would be so happy if I could only see you. My dear Kurt, I should have liked to have sent you a little parcel by now but have not received anything myself. From your letter I understand you are well and I thank God for that.

Life at home was better than here. You know that I wanted to do everything possible for you as far as I was able. I like making your favorite dishes. Here it is always the same people who receive parcels and more dissatisfied than we, the poor ones. The poor are having a bad time..."

THE JUDGES

By 1924, the twenty-five-year-old Cook County Juvenile Court system had become bureaucratic, unresponsive, and over-burdened. Also, it had become a dumping ground for political patronage. This was epitomized when the Chicago Democratic machine assigned Judge Frank H. Bicek as its presiding judge. His abuse of staff, children, and parents became legendary in adoption cases. His long tenure made him feel invincible even under the constant criticisms of hearing private cases in his chambers instead of in open court and further allegations of misusing the court's funds as his own.

By 1946, friction between child welfare agencies and the juvenile court came to a head. Marie Schwartz, placement supervisor at the Jewish Vocation Service, wrote to Emily Dean, president of a citizen's committee that had been formed in 1939 to monitor the juvenile Court system. Her letter stated in part, "In my opinion Judge Bicek has demonstrated his incompetence throughout the years he has been on the bench. I earnestly believe that it is time your committee took some definite steps toward removing Judge Bicek from the bench of the Juvenile Court."

In 1948, the Honorable Judge Frank H. Bicek was, without any explanation, transferred out of the juvenile courts. Although he remained a judge until his eightieth birthday in 1970, he never again heard a case involving a minor.

Edmund Kasper Jarecki was born in Posen, Poland, in 1879 and immigrated with his parents to Chicago at the age of five. He trained and worked as a draftsman until he graduated from Northwestern Law School in 1908. In 1914 he accepted an appointment to fill a vacancy for municipal judge, a position he successfully ran for in the next election. In 1922, at the age of forty-three, he ran for the powerful position of Cook County judge against the Republican machine candidate of Mayor "Big Bill" Thompson. Jarecki's campaign stressed the purity of the election process at a time when voting scandals inundated elections in Chicago. The victory left him dissatisfied because he could not shake the stinging criticism in the press that he was a puppet of the Democratic machine, even though his singular autonomy brought him enemies from within his own party.

In the early morning of April 1, 1924, Judge Jarecki's character was tested when he was informally petitioned for help by a group of concerned citizens from the adjacent mob-infested town of Cicero. On the evening before Cicero's local election, Al Capone initiated a plan to hijack the election by using fists, guns, kidnapping, and even the killing of one official. After Judge Jarecki received this plea for help, he immediately hand delivered a letter to the mayor of Chicago, William E. Dever, requesting, "...at least 70 men to be detailed to my charge in the Election Commissioners Office...to protect these polling places, in order to prevent fraud."

Judge Jarecki's action in deputizing seventy Chicago police officers as deputy sheriffs was described as an act of bravery. At twelve noon, Al Capone's brother, Frank, came face to face with the squad of newly deputized sheriffs outside a polling place near the Western Electric plant at Twenty-Second Street and Cicero

Avenue. Hours later, Al Capone became enraged when he saw his brother's body, riddled with bullets. Judge Jarecki told the press that he refused to accept any blame. `Practically all the dirty work was done by Chicago gangsters hired to go there and swing the election.`

Days later, Capone still seethed when he thought of Judge Jarecki on his way to bury his brother at Mount Olivet Cemetery. It took the efforts of another mobster, Johnny Torrio, to ensure that Judge Jarecki did not suffer the same fate as Frank Capone. Judge Jarecki would later lament that his efforts to preserve the election process was for nothing since the Capone-backed officials prevailed in the election. The judge's actions epitomized a lifelong struggle to fight the system, ignore the Democratic bosses with impunity, and win election after election, until his retirement at the age of seventy-five in 1954.

On October 16, 1966, when the life of Edmund K. Jarecki was celebrated in a *New York Times* obituary, it acknowledged that at the time of his retirement, his span of office was the longest in Cook County's history. Few readers of his obituary appreciated that this simple man, who died of a heart attack while napping at the age of eighty-six, epitomized the best of the judiciary.

It would be Judge Edmund Kasper Jarecki's name that Kurt heard on September 18, 1947, when the bailiff announced to the almost empty courtroom, "All rise. The Honorable Judge Edmund Kasper Jarecki presiding." Just like the many thousands of times before, the door at the back of the courtroom swung open to reveal the black-robed sixty-eight-year-old judge's flapping arms that implored all to be seated. Although this plain-speaking man tried to dismiss it, his profile, framed by a forty-eight-star American flag that hung on the wall behind him, pince-nez glasses dangling from a herringbone chain, bow tie, and morning coat, gave those who appeared before Judge Jarecki the impression that a member of some aristocracy was in their presence.

"Wow," said Kurt as he pulled on Wag's shoulder. "He should be on a postage stamp, Daddy."

The judge looked over the top of his glasses and held back his smile so as to not embarrass the young man. He viewed the adoption call as different. In most cases there were two sides fighting to persuade Judge Jarecki about the correctness of their position. He enjoyed the sparring, the intellectual challenge, and the judicial process that ended with a proper ruling that satisfied not a party but the search for truth. After thirty-one years on the bench he had seen it all. He admitted to those close to him how he looked forward to those days off when the next legal case was not infected with rancor and fighting. This was especially true in family court, where the usual formalities were dispensed with.

Billy, his clerk of twenty years, handed the file to the judge. He whispered, "Ed, only one case today. Walker, Kurt." The judge placed his pince-nez glasses comfortably into the indentation marks on his nose. "Thanks, Billy," said the judge. He dumped the contents of the file into a neat pile on the court's bench while Billy announced, `"IN THE MATTER OF THE PETITION OF Isadore J. Wagner and Belle Wagner To Adopt Kurt R. Walker Case No. 117488."`

The judge placed his thumb and first finger on his glasses and placed them back in his breast pocket as he called out Kurt's name. Kurt raised his hand, but the seemingly blind judge stood up and looked past the Wagners, their counsel, and Kurt and into the empty back rows of dark stained oak benches reserved for the public. Kurt repeatedly turned until he saw the smiling faces of the Wagners, the judge, and Billy. "Jeeze," muttered Kurt, who buried his face in his hands until the last of the courtroom's chuckles faded away.

If it pleases the court," stated the attorney. "My name is Nicholas Jay Pritzker. I am the attorney for the Wagners in case number one one seven four eight eight. If I may approach and…"

Judge Jarecki's birdlike arms waved again as he implored the Wagner's attorney, "Enough, enough. I know who you are. You're the big shot lawyer who only handles really important cases, and this has to be one of those or you would not be here." He winked at the Wagners, who responded with a nervous smile.

Nicholas Jay Pritzker was, in 1947, well on his way to establishing himself as the patriarch of a family whose fortune would one day be worth billions of dollars. Like Judge Jarecki, he was an immigrant. He arrived in Chicago at the age of ten in November 1881 from the Jewish ghettos in the Ukraine. His own immigrant story began by selling the *Chicago Tribune* newspaper, shining shoes, and working as a tailor's assistant before becoming a licensed pharmacist. He attended evening classes at DePaul law school so he could continue to work during the day. At the age of thirty he graduated from law school, and shortly thereafter, on June 5, 1902, he opened his law practice on the prestigious LaSalle Street corridor in Chicago. His three sons eventually formed with their father the law firm of Pritzker and Pritzker. By the 1930s the firm represented only one client, the Pritzkers.

The Pritzker family had always been extremely philanthropic, giving both their money and time to many causes. Jack

Pritzker, like his father, was an unpaid board member of the Jewish Children's Bureau of Chicago. His son Donny's friendship with Kurt sparked an equally close relationship between Donny's parents and the Wagners. It was that fortuitous relationship that brought Nicholas Pritzker's talent, prestige, and influence to the courtroom.

Satisfied that any obvious anxiety on the part of the Wagners was not present, Judge Jarecki gave another wink of his eye, which was easily interpreted by the attorney. "If it pleases the court, I am very happy to be here today in my capacity as the attorney for the Wagners regarding the adoption of their foster son, Kurt Walker." The lawyer pulled from his tan leather briefcase the thick stack of indexed documents that had been prepared in the same professional manner as if he was making a presentation regarding some big deal.

And as they had been coached, the Wagners and Kurt approached the judge. The lawyer continued his brief introductions. "Before Your Honor are Belle Wagner and Isador J. Wagner, foster parents of Kurt Walker, who stands to my left."

Although there may have been an appearance of informality in the courtroom, the judge was more than familiar with Kurt's file. It included a letter he had just read in chambers from Kurt's principal that had left him laughing out loud.

"Dear Mr. Wagner:

Kurt is suspended for two days—next Monday and Tuesday—for gambling. He and three other boys were playing cards for money here in school. I am of course concerned for the breach of school discipline; but I am more concerned that the

boy realize the seriousness of the practice itself. Can you help me bring it home to him?"

In addition to the brief time he spent reading the letter, he
had spent parts of the last three days reviewing the file and the
new adoption laws for the state of Illinois. He had underlined
and circled certain sentences, placed exclamation points where
he deemed it appropriate, and wrote questions about points
that required clarification. While the judge looked at Nicholas
Pritzker and Kurt Walker, he momentarily reflected upon his
own immigrant background before he spoke. "First of all, I wish
to thank the Wagners for coming here today. I have read quite a
bit about you folks. Your efforts, care, obvious concern, and love
for Kurt are second to none."

Belle's body heaved forward. Wag responded confidently with
a courteous, "Thank you."

"How are you, young man?" asked the judge. He reached over
the bench to shake Kurt's hand. Kurt was startled by the unexpected and kind gesture. "Fine, Judge. Thanks for asking."

Jarecki sat back in his chair. "My general procedure is to
take the lawyer back in chambers before we proceed in open
court." This was of course a lie. It was rarely necessary to go back
in chambers on an adoption case. In a long career as a Cook
County, Illinois, jurist in which Judge Jarecki presided over sixty
thousand adoptions, he would, in 1946, be responsible for entering final decrees that gave 1,801children a family. However, on
the day Kurt appeared in his courtroom, the personal statistics
of Judge Jarecki would be irrelevant to the judge and the lawyer
who knew there was a problem regarding file no. 117488.

"Dear Mr. Smith

...From what I understand, Kurt's foster parents have been shopping around for vocational guidance for him the last year or two. At both the University of Chicago Clinics as well as Miss Miller's agency the parents were told that what Kurt needs is psychiatric help more than vocational guidance. Apparently the parents have not been able to accept this. In both places Kurt was given projective tests which showed that he is emotionally disturbed and needs help. ...The parents have never approached the school psychologist. Should we, as the school psychologists, do anything to help the parents and Kurt, or should we wait until they eventually come to us with their troubles?

Erika Fromm"

IN CHAMBERS

W hen the senior Pritzker walked into the chambers, the judge was in the process of removing his robe, completing a phone call, and taking notes on another file. It had been a couple years since the lawyer had entered these chambers, and the judge's multitasking gave him the opportunity to once again examine the walls covered in framed letters, photos, and plaques. When the phone call finally ended, the lawyer and judge smiled at each other.

Pritzker, as the judge called him, pointed his finger at a plaque that had honored the judge's twenty years of service. "It must be difficult to be placed in situations where you have the power to impact someone's life in extraordinary ways. I would always question myself. Did I do the right thing? I just could never be a good judge. That's why I have so much respect for the court."

A crooked smile appeared on Judge Jarecki's face while the lawyer continued to read out loud the most laudatory parts of one plaque after another. He paced back and forth as he delivered his impromptu speech about his love of the judiciary. When Pritzker finally paused, the judge pointed to the seat. "Please."

"Your Honor, who is the artist?" asked Pritzker as he bounced up from the plush leather chair. He pointed to the two-foot-by-two-foot crocheted writing that hung on the wall next to the stuffed owl. It was clear that the seventy-six-year-old iconic lawyer was looking for any opportunity to avoid discussing the law and facts of the case. Even a lay person could appreciate that any legal presentation that avoids both the facts and the law is fatally flawed, and the Wagners' counsel was far from a lay person.

"My wife," answered the judge, who removed his glasses.

The prescient Judge Jarecki never let anyone put him on the defensive. That included Nicholas Pritzker. "Are you familiar with the New Testament, Pritzker?" questioned the judge. The lawyer nodded yes as the judge pulled the crocheted writing from the wall. His baritone voice accentuated each word. "Suffer the little children to come unto me. Now let me answer the question you were in the process of tactfully trying to ask me. No, I am not God. I recognize that many of the children that have come before me have suffered and will continue to suffer. I pray to God every day that he helps me to do the right thing. No, Pritzker!" said the judge in an uncharacteristically harsh tone. "I am not God, and, I presume, neither are you." The lawyer surrendered with a simple bow.

The familiarity between the two men allowed the old warriors to talk candidly. "Let's not waste any more time on this, Nicholas. You and I don't know everything that happened to this young man. I dare say he does not even know some very important things about his own life, let alone his family back in Germany, France, Poland, Russia, or wherever they are. So I ask you, how can we have an adoption when you, the child, the foster parents, the Jewish Children's Bureau, the European Jewish Children's Aid, the Red Cross can't tell me with any certainty about the status of the mother, the father, brother, or the grandparents? I must tell you that a purported letter many months ago from Heinz is a double-edged sword. Is he the brother? If he is, is the father dead as he says? And if he is dead, I guess that is a good argument, at least in part, that this matter should continue.

But in that letter he asks about the mother. He never once suggests that she is dead. Should I dismiss that?"

The judge poured himself a glass of water and waved an empty glass at the lawyer who motioned no. "Now I have a letter that says Heinz is living with the paternal grandfather. I have another document, a letter from Deborah S. Portnoy to Mary Lawrence of the European Jewish Children's Aid that states he is living with the maternal grandfather. Who is he living with, Nicholas? The maternal or the paternal grandfather? And does it make any difference which one it is? Because the question, the legal question for me is don't the grandparents have a say in this proceeding?"

The judge interrupted Pritzker's attempt to answer. "I know you are a big man outside my courtroom. I'm not punishing you for that, but we changed the adoption code in '45 to stop questionable practices. I will not be a hypocrite. If I close my eyes and enter a decree for the adoption and Kurt's mother shows up or a grandparent shows up, there will be hell to pay. My God Almighty, this boy's records are so messed up. I shudder to think about what further damage is going to happen to this kid if we continue with this sham."

The judge brought his next victim into his crosshairs. "Now the bureau, in its infinite wisdom, continued the mismanagement of this case when they left it up to the foster parents to determine what information should be disclosed to this young man. That includes whether Ilse Walker is alive. And if that is not enough, I understand that the maternal grandfather was granted legal guardianship of Kurt by the German courts. It's clear that Kurt has a strong and loving relationship with this man."

The judge kicked the door to his chambers shut. "Kurt never saw that letter from Heinz. That's not the foster family's decision to make. I'm not blaming the Wagners. They should have never been put in that situation in the first place. No sir! I am also aware that you folks tried to accomplish this adoption by going through Bicek in the juvenile court division. Even that idiot's office asked for proof about the death of Kurt's family. What was the bureau's legal response? Their uncontroverted proof was an article from the *New York Times*. Just shocking! Just shocking!" yelled the judge as he waved the June 2, 1947, article, `"Surrogates Free Refugees' Funds."` "If you want a sham then go back to that Democratic machine flunky Bicek, but make sure you bring a couple of bucks with you."

Judge Jarecki rested hands on his desk and tapped his fingers. "Whether there is an adoption or not will not change a thing, Nicholas. They already are a family. I read that BS about Kurt's inheritance rights being vested if he is adopted. These people love him. I bet you that young man is the beneficiary of their estates."

He spun around in his chair under the watchful glass eyes of the stuffed owl and pulled out the new adoption code. "Pritzker, I told you I am not God, and you will have a chance to speak, but right now you listen."

"Ed," said Pritzker, "I've read the code."

"Indulge me. I'm not going to bother you with all the sections of the adoption code that you are apparently asking me to violate, but please, `'...Section 3-3, If upon the date of the entry of decree, the child sought to be adopted is of the age of fourteen years or upward, the` adoption shall not be made without the consent of such child. Such consent shall be in writing and shall be acknowledged by the child in open court.' This young man has not even executed the consent."

Pritzker interrupted sarcastically. "I admit it. We were trying to avoid certain things…If you want the consent signed, we will do it."

The judge slammed his fist on his desk. "Damn it, Pritzker, that's the point. It's not that I want it, that's what the law says! That's what the GD statute says, not what I say! Now you just sit there and listen. 'Chapter 4, section 2-1, whenever the consent of either or both of the parents of the child is not presented with the petition, the court—that's me, Nicholas. I'm the GD court—shall require proof, by documentary evidence or oral testimony of the reason for the failure to present such consent shall be given at the hearing.' Not only do you not have any proof to explain the failure of the parents to be present, but you have proof to the contrary."

The reluctant student sat with his arms gracefully folded in his lap as his professor continued with his tutorial on the Illinois adoption code. "You should know that more than a year ago, I had a meeting to discuss the new adoption laws with Jacob Kepecs of the bureau. We went over the issues raised by the new laws."

The judge was clearly on a roll, and Pritzker knew not to interrupt. "I am not even going to talk to you about whether or not this court has jurisdiction to hear this case other than to ask a rhetorical question. The boy is a citizen of Germany, his grandfather was granted guardianship in Germany, and we are attempting to proceed with an adoption in Illinois. How does that happen?"

The judge looked at what appeared to be a sleeping Nicholas Pritzker. "Nicholas, Nicholas, are you ill?"

"You know, Judge," responded the lawyer without missing a beat, "I remember one of the first times I came into your chambers. It must have been sometime in the early thirties. No, I will tell you exactly. It was when that nut tried to assassinate Roosevelt and killed Mayor Cermak by mistake. Anyway, I came in your chambers for a pretrial on some case. I saw that painting of that gentleman," said Pritzker, pointing. "How do you say his name? Thaddeus Kosciusko?"

The judge looked at the painting of the general in his ornate military uniform. "Yes. Your Polish is very good for a Russian."

"You were so passionate about his story. You said he came here at the age of thirty from Poland and joined Washington's army. He was appointed a general and was eventually given fifteen thousand dollars and five hundred acres of land in Ohio by the United States Congress in consideration of his service. By the war's end, Congress even made him an American citizen. What I've never forgotten was that Kosciusko was so inspired by Thomas Jefferson's authorship of the Declaration of Independence that he sought out the man to tell him just that."

Jarecki was moved by the recollections of the lawyer.

"I remember," said Pritzker as he sat forward in his chair and clasped both of his hands, "how you told me that the general was repulsed by the institution of slavery that he encountered when his military duties took him into the South.

You said, 'The general was conflicted by the sentiments of the Constitution and the repugnancy of slavery in action.'" Pritzker paused again before he tapped the judge's desk several times. "But he did not let the repugnancy of slavery affect his relationship with Jefferson. In fact, you told me that he made Jefferson the executor of his will. It provided for his Ohio land to be sold upon his death and the proceeds be used to purchase slaves, free them, and provide for their education. Each time I came to your chambers after you told me that story, I was drawn to that painting. When my grandson Donny was about ten or so, I told him about the general. He was so fascinated by your story that he wanted to know more, so I did some research on my own. He died in 1817, and apparently he did not do such a great job drafting his will. Did you know that, Judge? I apologize. I don't mean to be presumptuous."

The judge responded with a simple, "No."

"There was a major fight over the will. It went all the way up to the United States Supreme Court in 1851 or 1852. Anyway, the court said that the money, which had grown substantially over the years, should go to his relatives in Europe. I couldn't believe it. No slaves were freed, no slaves were educated. When I read the Supreme Court case it was pretty clear, at least to me, what the general wanted to do, but for some reason the court just couldn't get it right. A cynic might argue that the court was not going to let a bunch of negroes be freed and educated. I remember talking to Donny about it. He said, 'Grandpa, that just seems stupid. You're a lawyer, Dad's a lawyer, my uncles are lawyers. Aren't you supposed to make sure that the right thing happens?' Ed, I have to admit that the kid got me on that one."

The chambers became quiet again.

"There are no perfect results with this one, Ed. Bad facts and bad laws, even well-intentioned laws can sometimes make a competent lawyer, even a great lawyer, turn into a very bad lawyer. I get it. Today I have the potential of being worse than a bad lawyer. I have the potential of being a shitty lawyer. I am not trying to take the moral high ground at the expense of making this process a fraud or have you violate your oath. I get that there is a chance something bad, really bad could happen if this adoption goes ahead. But those same bad things will happen whether there is an adoption or not. All I can say is that at the end of the day you and I are on the same side of this one. We're both just trying to do the right thing."

When Judge Jarecki and Nicholas Pritzker reentered the empty courtroom, more than an hour had passed since they had sequestered themselves. "I'll get them, Judge. I told them it was all right to go in the hallway," said Billy. Moments later the Wagners and Kurt rushed into the courtroom. They pushed past the swinging gates as the formerly confident Wag nervously apologized for being late. The judge did not respond while he completed his final notes.

When he finished, he put on his pince-nez glasses. Looking out into the courtroom, he asked if there was a Kurt Walker in the room. Kurt, smiling, along with the Wagners, approached the bench and stood alongside their attorney. "Kurt, Mr. Pritzker is passing you a document that confirms that you want this decree of adoption to be entered. Is that correct?"

"Yes, sir," answered Kurt, whose nervousness caused just the hint of a German accent to reappear. Judge Jarecki acknowledged the receipt of the executed consent for the record and placed it in the court file. Kurt, unsure, looked at the lawyer and then back to the Wagners. Judge Jarecki waited patiently while the attorney retrieved from his briefcase a two-page document before tendering to the court.

Judge Jarecki quickly read over the preamble of the pleading that stated that the court had jurisdiction over the parties and the subject matter. His stony appearance was unreadable by Kurt. The wordy legalese, which was tantamount to a foreign language, left Wag, Belle, and Kurt in a fog until the judge got to the factual allegations in paragraphs eight and nine:

"8. That the Petitioners are reputable persons, of good character with sufficient ability and financial means to rear, nurture and educate the said child in a suitable and proper manner.

9. That the allegations of the petition are true as therein alleged, and it is fit and proper and for the best interest of the said child that the adoption be allowed herein.

IT IS THEREFORE ORDERED, ADJUDGED AND DECREED, that on this date, KURT WALKER, a minor, shall be to all legal intents and purposes, the child of the petitioners, ISADORE J. WAGNER AND BELLE WAGNER his wife; and for purposes of inheritances and all other legal incidents and consequences, shall be the same as if he had been born in lawful wedlock.

IT IS FURTHER ORDERED that the name of the said child be changed to KURT WAGNER."

"Billy, please enter the final decree of adoption." The judge removed his glasses and placed them into his breast pocket. "Mr. and Mrs. Wagner, congratulations and best wishes. And to you, Kurt Wagner, I wish you only the best and continued happiness with a mother and father who truly love you. These proceedings are concluded."

GERMAN PANCAKES

Immediately after court, the Wagners and Nicholas Pritzker went across the street for a celebratory lunch at the six-hundred-room Bismarck Hotel on Randolph Street. The temperature had already reached its high of a Lake Michigan-cooled ninety-two degrees. The group welcomed the opportunity to relax in the block-long air-conditioned art deco hotel. Kurt fell behind the hungry adults and lingered in the lobby, where he stared at the huge American flag that reflected the patriotism in the years following the end of World War II.

Moments later, he inched toward the Wagners, Nicholas Pritzker, and the long line of patrons at the Swiss Chalet Restaurant who were anticipating the best German fare in Chicago. However, as soon as Kurt started moving he stopped. He snuck a quick look at Wag before he moved to a mural-covered wall depicting a hunting scene with elk running in the Black Forest and the shelved collection of beer steins outside the magnificent Walnut Room.

Kurt looked at the entryway beer advertisement and called upon his forgotten German accent as he read each syllable for "Pschorr Brau Munich." Lost in private thoughts, Kurt ran his fingers over the raised lettering on the brass plaque that hung just beneath the sign. He read, "The Bismarck Hotel was built by the Eitel brothers who were born in Stuttgart, Germany." Kurt removed his fingers. "Oh, maybe they knew my dear father," spit out Kurt in a moment of anger that he thought had long ago left him.

Seconds later, his fists clenched when he felt an unexpected arm around his shoulder. "I guess you don't want to eat?" asked Wag. He placed both of his palms near his face.

Kurt, smiling, punched out each word of his answer, "Yes, I do! Yes, I do! Yes, I do!"

After the party of four was seated at the round table, they engaged in comfortable conversations about the weather, current events, everything and anything. Nicholas Pritzker, who had become tired of always being the center of false and even sincere attention, was grateful to sit back and enjoy the wonderful meal of German pancakes dusted with powdered sugar. Mostly he enjoyed watching the Wagners holding hands, kissing, and begging each other again and again to "Tell Mr. Pritzker about the time..."

Nicholas Pritzker refused to accept any money for his legal services that day. At that point in his life, he no longer got the feeling of accomplishment that he once did when he completed a big deal. For Nicholas Pritzker, sitting around the table with the Wagners on that hot day eating German pancakes was about as good as it got.

When everyone finished their meal, Nicholas Pritzker shook hands with the Wagners and nodded a good-bye to Kurt. He wished them the best as his finger bounced off the brim of his summer hat. Belle embraced the old man long enough to whisper three times through happy tears, "Thank you."

For a person whose weapon was words, all he could do was squeeze Belle's hand. But before he took his first steps back to his office on LaSalle Street, Kurt walked over to the lawyer with an outstretched hand. This "King of Chicago" was again thunderstruck as he enthusiastically shook Kurt's hand and struggled for something witty, profound, or insightful to say regarding Kurt's journey through life.

Their silence ended when Kurt said, "I just wanted to thank you. I want to thank you on behalf of my mother, my father—for my entire family." Kurt looked back at his parents. He spoke without any sense of nervousness and, more importantly to him, without any trace of an accent. "This has been very hard on them, and I understand why. My grandfather, my Opa, Isack Ettlinger, had an expression that he used to say when things might not be going well. He would look at me and say, 'Kurtela, ganna gut.' I want to thank you for everything you have done, and you should know that for me and my family everything will be ganna gut—no matter what happens."

The old man tugged on the crisply starched embroidered cuffs of his white shirt three times and straightened his tie. All the while, he never took his eyes off Kurt. He straightened his tie one last time before he approached Kurt and cupped his hands around Kurt's face. He whispered so that no one else could hear, "Kurt, you are right. Everything will be ganna gut."

AL JOLSON

After the Wagners arrived home, Kurt charged into his bedroom so he could catch the end of the Cubs game on WJJD radio. Belle and Wag could hear Kurt yell "aw jeez" as Bert Wilson proclaimed the Cubs had just lost their seventy-ninth game of a 154-game season.

"I can't believe it, Pop. The New York Giants are pretty good, but they lost nine to five to some guy named Sheldon Jones. I mean who's Sheldon Jones?" exclaimed Kurt. "Daddy," screamed Kurt again. "Mr. Wilson just said the Cubs just made this guy a five hundred pitcher. It's September. The season is almost over and this guy only had one win. Aw jeez!"

"Who was the losing pitcher?" yelled Wag from his room.

"That idiot, Ox Miller," wailed Kurt. "Why did they bring him up, Pops? I can't believe this. We were in the World Series two years ago." Kurt grabbed the pillow on his bed and wrapped it around his head as he heard Bert Wilson having to adjust his catch phrase to yet another Cubs loss. Kurt would mouth the words with a contorted face.

"I don't care who wins," sang the announcer, "as long as it's the Cubs! And today, I just don't care."

Wag yelled again as he changed out of his suit, "Did Bert say it yet? Did he say we'll sic 'em tomorrow?" A smiling Wag could not help himself. "Don't listen to Bert, partner. Turn off the radio and put on one of the records that Studs gave you. Forget about today, forget about tomorrow, we'll get 'em next year," said Wag, laughing.

Belle playfully slapped her husband on the shoulder. "Don't say things like that. You know how much he loves the Cubs."

Kurt happily turned off the radio. He sorted through his massive record collection until he announced, "That's the one." He cradled the record between the palms of his hands just as Studs Terkel had shown him. He delicately guided the heavy seventy-eight record onto the stem of the brown Bakelite RCA phonograph player. Then, with his fingers already snapping, the pops and crackles from the needle scarring the grooves of the record gave way to the music.

"Daddy, you will love this one. It's by Al Jolson. Studs Terkel plays it all the time." Belle and Wag hurried to Kurt's room where Kurt and Al Jolson were singing together. Mother and father stood at the open door and held hands while they watched their son, Kurt James Wagner, spinning and singing to "I'm Sitting on Top of the World."

"Don't want any millions,
I'm getting my share.
I've only got one suit,
That's all I can wear.
A bundle of money won't make you feel gay.
A sweet little honey is making me say:
I'm sitting on top of the world,
Just rolling along,
Just rolling along.
I'm quitting the blues of the world,
Just singing along,
Just singing along...."

EPILOGUE

"Dear Miss Marcuse,

...We wish to advise you that Kurt's adoption was
consummated....The decree was entered on 9-19-47.
Kurt, as you well know, has an excellent home
with the Wagners who have been quite successful
in business and can give Kurt the finest advan-
tages our country has to offer in every area.
We are closing this case."

Letter from Mary Lawrence of the Jewish Children's Bureau to
Lotte Marcuse of the European Jewish Children's Aid, October
2, 1947

After Kurt graduated from Francis Parker in the spring of
1950, he enrolled in Ripon College in Wisconsin. While
at Ripon, he received twenty letters from Wag. They all of began with "Dear Son-and-Partner" and ended with "Your
lonesome, loving Partner." When Kurt opened up Wag's
November 28, 1950, letter, it contained a single piece of candy.
He sucked on the cool treat as he slowly read,

"...I hope you like this stationery better than
the half-assed stuff I have been using recently.
Just get a good look at what it says up there:
BEVERLY HILLS HOTEL AND BUNGALOWS, some stuff,
eh? This is the swankiest hotel I have ever been
in. $15.00 a day...Good luck. Stay well, and now

we'll start counting again, counting the days
until Christmas. I used to think that counting
the days until Christmas was rather silly, but
there's a lot to it now..."

On Sunday, December 3, 1950, while Kurt was studying in
room 207 of Bartlett Hall, his roommate shouted from the dorm
phone, "Hey, Wagner, you gotta call."

"Hi, Uncle Sol. What's up?" said Kurt.

The obituary in the *Chicago Sun-Times* stated, "Irvin J.
Wagner, 51,...died yesterday in Los Angeles...he
was the originator of spot radio commercials.
He leaves his widow, Belle; a son Kurt..."

Tony Weitzel of the *Chicago Daily News* used his column, "The
Town Crier," to tell his readers that "Chicago's advertising row
is mourning the sudden death of I.J. Wagner...who...was one of
the kindest of men...with a great heart and a wonderfully warm
sense of humor..."

Paul Harvey wrote:

"You're going to die someday...just as sure as you
are born....But knowing it has to happen doesn't
make it easier to say good-bye to a friend.
There'll be a funeral tomorrow in Chicago for
I.J. Wagner. Advertising man. He died Sunday
night on the West Coast. It was the death of
an advertising man. His gentle heart stopped...
just a few hours after he signed a fruitful new
contract. I don't know what they will say about
him tomorrow. But I have an idea they'll say

the usual nice things about the departed. What a fine man he was. How dearly he loved his family and was loved by them. Only thing is, in Wag's case, all the things they usually say... will be true. Wag was one of the gentlest men I have ever known. No tears for Wag. The shadow is across our Christmas. Not his."

Studs Terkel eulogized his friend. However, the words from the future Pulitzer Prize winner are forever lost. Decades later when I interviewed ninety-five-year-old Studs for this book, I brought a copy of the last book he wrote, *Touch and Go*. Just before I left his home I asked for an autograph. While Studs sat in a massive chair that made him look like a tiny frail doll, he said yes in a strong voice before he wrote what was probably the essence of his eulogy. "Here's to a world of Peace, Grace and Beauty and remembering a wonderful man 'Wag.'"

Reflecting years after that terrible day in 1950, Belle wrote:

"In December of 1950, shortly after talking with Kurt's Dad in California, I received a call that my Sweetie had passed away. When I talked to him earlier he wanted me to take a plane that day to join him in California. I explained how ridiculous that would be since he was due home on Tuesday and this was already Sunday...within a couple of hours Kurt was home. He told me not to worry because he would take care of me, and take care of me he did."

Devastated by the irreplaceable loss of his father, Kurt never returned to Ripon College. Instead, with the Korean conflict calling in October 1951, this German refugee enlisted for a two-year tour of duty in the United States Army. Kurt wrote to his mother every day, and when Belle begged him to come home on leave Kurt refused. Kurt was sure if he did, he would go AWOL. On the advice of Belle's doctor, she sought out a job that would force her to leave her bed and free her from her debilitating depression. It took only a few weeks before Belle found employment with the Continental Assurance Company. She remained there until her forced retirement at the age of sixty-five.

Years later, Belle recalled how on her first day at work the receptionist commented how happy she looked and what a nice smile she had. "I was a darn good actress," observed Belle. After her retirement she became a full-time secretary to her rabbi for another twenty-one years. Belle's second retirement led her to volunteer at a senior citizen's home where she played the piano and took on secretarial duties.

After becoming a naturalized citizen of the United States of America in 1954, Kurt married Marilyn Fishman in 1955. Two years later, Belle moved in with Kurt and his bride. They would live together until her death on July 19, 1994. Her long life allowed her to be a significant part of the lives of Kurt's two sons, two brothers, Irvin and Stuart. Today they and their families live within minutes of each other.

At a seventy-fifth birthday party for Belle, Kurt spoke of Belle's devotion: "...I'd like to turn the clock back...specifically to the 1940s...a time of great discontent in the world...Although we caught up with Hitler and his mad men, the damage he did must never be forgotten...Unfortunately, I came out of this world of bitterness and cruelty...The love and tenderness given by this beautiful lady and, of course, my dad, was the cure needed. My faith in the Almighty has since been restored even though He works in strange and mysterious ways He somehow manages to balance the scale."

A few years before her death, Belle prepared a document titled "To Be Read at My Funeral." Her declaration of life closed as follows:

"...When my hubby passed away I thought I would be a forlorn old lady, but due to Kurt and a;11 that followed him I became the happiest woman in the world. Kurt married a lovely girl who has been the kindest daughter anyone would ever want to have. Marilyn has been a gem all these years. She has taken care of my every need...between Marilyn and Kurt, every convenience was given to me to make me feel safe and comfortable and loved....I only want you to know that in my heart I hope God will be good to you....It has been a proud life for me, it has been a joyous life for me because of my getting Kurt. Maybe God was good to me for the deed I did back in 1943. I thank God for giving me the opportunity to have Kurt....As he said on my 75th birthday, God works in mysterious ways. Indeed he does. So I say farewell with no tears in my eyes. I am a happy lady who appreciates everything that has been done for me and the life God has blessed me with. Thank you."

Years after Kurt's escape to America, Heinz, closely guarded, hid from his friends and family many of the events of his early life. This included the discovery by the Nazis of his Mischling

identity in 1945. Heinz remained forever thankful to the victorious French troops marching down the Kaiserstrasse, who unknowingly saved him from certain death. After February 1948,
when Heinz met his future wife, Irene, at a dance in the destroyed
city of Karlsruhe, Belle and Wag began to correspond with Heinz.
Over time, they eventually approached Heinz about coming to
America to be adopted. Cautiously, they also approached Kurt
about Heinz coming to America. Kurt's emotionless objections
were immediately given. But in the end, it made no difference
to Heinz, whose burgeoning relationship with Irene made his
acceptance impossible.

After Wag's death, Belle continued with letters and care packages of money and clothing to Heinz, while Kurt, burdened by
his assumptions of his Nazi brother, remained indifferent. In the
postwar years, it fell upon Irene, whom Heinz married on March
5, 1950, to become Heinz's lone confidant about the truth of
those early years and about the painful loss of his mother and
Kurt.

Like Heinz and Kurt, Heinz's only child, Ben, was born in
Karlsruhe. Upon Kurt's discharge from the army in 1953, he sent
one hundred dollars of his three hundred-dollar muster pay to
Heinz. "I hope this helps with the baby," said the short note. Six
months after Ben's birth, Heinz's family suffered a devastating
loss when his grandmother died. Heinz's ailing grandfather's
attempt to live independently came to an end in 1957 when
Heinz's family moved in with Christian. They lived together
until Christian's death in 1965. He died in the arms of Irene,
who selflessly took care of her demanding grandfather-in-law's
every need. Today Ben, the father of two daughters, resides in
Karlsruhe with his wife, Mariann.

Although the brothers' superficial contacts of birthday and holiday cards became more frequent, the brothers knew instinctively to never bring up the past. Then in 1978, Kurt received a different knock on his door. "I'm Willie—Heinz's father-in-law. I'm here in Chicago to visit my sister." Willie judged Kurt's stony face before he said, "Irene told me where you live." There were polite handshakes before the men walked to a local tavern on Lincoln Avenue in Chicago. "If Heinz could only see us," muttered Willie. Empty bottles that cluttered the table were pushed aside as the old German placed his hand on Kurt's shoulder. "It would be so nice if you could go to Germany to see Heinz." Kurt quietly seethed at the thought of a return to the land of the Nazis. "Just think about it," said Willie as he shook Kurt's hand good-bye.

Kurt did think about it. In 1979, Kurt and his sons went to Karlsruhe where Heinz and Kurt, two strangers, awkwardly embraced and spoke for the first time since they played together in their grandparents' home. When I asked Kurt how he felt before he met his brother, he answered he was afraid and unsure. In my later interviews with Irene, she too recalled how fearful Heinz was in anticipation of the brothers' meeting. Immediately after the reunion, the united brothers walked through the rebuilt Marktplatz, where a new golden boy spun with each subtle breeze, and past the undamaged pyramid, the still pristine train station, the rebuilt Schloss, and the fortresslike police station with a memorial plaque that acknowledged the first mass deportation of German Jews out of Germany. They also entered a newly constructed synagogue and prayed.

When the brothers found themselves alone on Heinz's apartment balcony, the painful silence was finally interrupted with Kurt's unforgiving declaration, "Your father was a son of a bitch."

"You don't know everything," answered Heinz.

"Well," shot back Kurt as the brothers stared at each other. "We can agree to disagree."

That was it. Decades after their separation ended, the night ended with the word "disagree." Never again would the brothers speak of the past. Nonetheless, they pushed ahead, and in 1979, 1980, and 2001, Heinz and Irene came to America. In honor of Heinz and Irene's 1979 trip, Kurt and Marilyn threw a party where friends and family warmly welcomed Heinz and Irene. In attendance was the president of Chicago's Roosevelt University, Rolf Weil; the same Rolf Weil who waved at Kurt when his father, Heinrich Weil, drove away in a beautiful blue car from the Ettlinger apartment in 1936.

Before Heinz was introduced to anyone, Kurt took Belle's hand while he beckoned Heinz with a wave. "Heinz, this is my mother." Belle, crying, embraced Heinz and then, without any hesitation, introduced him to every person in the crowded room. "This is my Kurt's brother, Heinz."

Later that evening Heinz whispered to Kurt, "You are so lucky. I never had a mother and you had two."

After Heinz returned to Germany, Kurt opened the small leather wallet his mother had given him just before he left Camp de Gurs. He stared at the photos and letters from his mother that had remained hidden over the prior decades. Later that day he placed a phone call to his rabbi, Jay Karzan. He asked the rabbi for a favor that was almost forty years in the making. "Please, when you go to Israel—can you go to Yad Vashem (the worldwide center for Holocaust research)? I would like you to find out anything you can about Ilse Walker, Isack Ettlinger, and Julius Ettlinger."

When the rabbi returned from his trip, he met with Kurt. "Pitchipoi, Kurt. They are all gone, Kurt."

A decade later when Kurt opened a letter dated December 14, 1989, he immediately flashed back to the summer of 1942. It began, "My dear brother of Aspet, I hope you still understand enough German so that you can read my letter. It is a miracle that I received your address." It ended with "Your sister of Aspet, Hanna." Hanna, one of the forty-eight children from Aspet, had for decades been searching for Kurt, but because of his adoption and a changed last name, he had remained lost, but never forgotten.

Hanna explained that she had been in Karlsruhe for a memorial dedicated to the October 22, 1940, deportation of German Jews. While there, she struck up a conversation with a stranger. "Why, I know this man," answered the man when he learned that Hanna was trying to obtain information about Kurt. "But his name is not Walker anymore. His name is Kurt Wagner. He is my brother." It was then that Hanna learned of the story of the two brothers. When she wrote to Kurt, the lost child of Aspet, Hanna made sure to place at the top of the letter the address and phone number for an old friend, Hugo Schiller.

Because of that letter, Hugo, the Weilheimers, and Hanna were reunited. Sadly, I remember the tearful phone call from Kurt on November 28, 2009, when Kurt told me that Richard had died the day before. I am thankful that Hugo and Kurt remain friends today. Over the succeeding years, there have been many opportunities for Kurt to meet the other children of Aspet in America, Israel, and Europe, but he has refused.

Hanna's letter also spoke of a living Alice Resch, the "Angel of Aspet." Although Alice never had any children of her own, her selfless acts were credited with saving the lives of 253 Jewish children. Over the years since Kurt received Hanna's letter, Hugo, Richard, and many of the other brothers and sisters of Aspet joyously reunited with the woman who saved their lives. Although Kurt refused to participate in these reunions, he maintained a longstanding relationship with Alice by letter and phone. On the eve of Alice Resch-Synnestvedt's one hundredth birthday, the Angel of Aspet died. In 1982, Alice Resch-Synnestvedt was awarded in Jerusalem the title of "Righteous Among the Nations" in honor "...of a small minority who mustered enough extraordinary courage to uphold human values."

Before I began this project, Kurt had reconnected with Edith (Mann) Cohn, the German foster child that had also lived with the Kastels. Unfortunately, by the time I spoke to Edith, her brother, Kurt's American mentor, Herbert, had passed away. On September 25, 2010, I was able to reunite little Jolene Kastel and Kurt for the first time in almost seventy years. Present at the emotional reunion was Jolene's younger brother, Ralph Kastel. We all laughed as Kurt thanked Ralph for making his mother so ill that Kurt was forced to move to the Wagners'.

I start this paragraph six and a half years after I first spoke to Kurt Wagner about the story of two brothers. Throughout the writing of this book I had always hoped that the book would end on a positive note with issues resolved and lessons learned. It always bothered me that Kurt and Heinz were never able to resolve the past before Heinz's death on March 20, 2007. When I approached Irene, Heinz's wife, about this in August 2008, there were only tears that recognized this painful truth. When I returned from Karlsruhe, I played the DVDs of my interview with Irene for Kurt. He listened as Irene, tearful, talked for the first time in front of her family about the early years of Heinz's life. When the DVD ended, an emotionally raw Kurt excused himself and left my home.

The summer after I went to Germany, Heinz's son, Ben, his wife, Mariann, and one of their two daughters, Jenny, came to America. One morning we met for breakfast in a restaurant crowded with families. It was Irene's birthday, and a phone was passed around the table so that best wishes could be given. All the while, I looked at Kurt and Ben. Kurt's German by this time was flawed, and Ben's English was equally poor. The seemingly innocuous moment left me transfixed, watching a laughing uncle and nephew enjoying their breakfast of German pancakes dusted with powdered sugar.

After Kurt's nephew and his family returned to Germany, I talked to Kurt about a conversation that we had the first time I interviewed him. It was a conversation about two little boys separated by religion, war, death, divorce, an ocean, and time; about two brothers "who could never get it right." I told him that I was wrong. Kurt looked confused until I reminded him of his breakfast of German pancakes with Heinz's son, Ben. "You know, Kurt, I think you and Heinz did get it right." For one of the few times, I saw Kurt cry as he nodded his head.

More than a decade after Paul Harvey wrote of his friend's death, he wrote one last time about Wag:

"...One of my best friends in Chicago was a Jewish gentleman named I.J. Wagner. Wag was infinitely kind, had a rare good humor, was deeply devoted to his fellow man. He lived the kind of goodness most men only preach. Wag, a Jew, was Christ like in nature as any man I ever knew. They adopted a war refugee from Nazi Germany. And Kurt Wagner grew up to be a fine young man..."

I agree.

14789218R00298

Made in the USA
Middletown, DE
11 October 2014